JOURNAL OF WILLIAM ELLIS

The William Alexander Smith, from his Family and Business Capacity.

Derby. del.

C. Taylor. sc.

The Author, Missionary from the Society and Sandwich Islands.

JOURNAL OF WILLIAM ELLIS

Narrative of a Tour of Hawaii, or Owhyhee;
with Remarks on the History, Traditions
Manners, Customs, and Language
of the Inhabitants of the
Sandwich Islands

by William Ellis

with an introduction
by Thurston Twigg-Smith

and an introduction to the new edition
by Terence Barrow, Ph.D

Charles E. Tuttle Company
Rutland, Vermont & Tokyo, Japan

Representatives
Continental Europe: BOXERBOOKS, INC., Zurich
British Isles: PRENTICE-HALL INTERNATIONAL, INC., London
Australasia: BOOK WISE (AUSTRALIA) PTY. LTD.
104–108 Sussex Street, Sydney 2000

Published by the Charles E. Tuttle Company, Inc.
of Rutland, Vermont & Tokyo, Japan
with editorial offices at
Suido 1-chome, 2–6, Bunkyo-ku, Tokyo, Japan

© 1979 by Charles E. Tuttle Co., Inc.

Library of Congress Catalog Card No. 78-54936

International Standard Book No. 0-8048-1298-5

First British and American edition, 1825
Revised edition, 1827
Honolulu Advertiser reprint edition, 1917, 1963 (reset)
First Tuttle edition, 1979

PRINTED IN JAPAN

CONTENTS

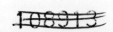

LIST OF ILLUSTRATIONS

INTRODUCTION TO THE NEW EDITION

THE *Journal of William Ellis* is a classic of Pacific literature, ranking with the journals of Captain Cook and his men as a record of life and customs of the traditional Hawaiians. No other book rivals it as an account of the life of the Hawaiians in the early 19th century.

The Reverend William Ellis was a remarkable man. Today we wonder why there were not more missionaries like him. His close observation of native life and his sympathy with a people struggling to readjust to changing times mark him as a man apart in the Hawai'i of his time. Our knowledge of 18th and 19th century Polynesians is to a large extent based on written records. Of all resident foreigners, missionaries had the best opportunity to record the traditional customs of the Hawaiians. However, of the twelve "companies" of American missionaries who arrived in the islands from 1820 onwards, the majority wrote about Hawaiians primarily as heathens in need of salvation, not as members of a different culture.

The Reverend Hiram Bingham's *A Residence of Twenty-One Years in the Sandwich Islands* (first published in 1847 and reissued by the Charles E. Tuttle Company in 1979) is also a classic of Hawaiian history. Yet it is unlike the *Journal of William Ellis.* Ellis was open-minded to Hawaiian customs while Bingham was unsympathetic. Bingham's book is concerned with the history of missionary enterprise in Hawai'i and the principal characters of the time. William Ellis is the ethnologist. One does not, for example, expect that a missionary would be interested in the place of the dog in daily life, but Ellis is interested in such details. He tells us how Hawaiian dogs were used as food, as pets, as objects of sacrifice, as tribute, in trade, and that there were wild dogs. The book is packed with information that is of great interest to students of traditional Hawai'i.

William Ellis was born in London, England, in 1794. As a young man he entered the London Missionary Society Training School then served in the Pacific from 1816 to 1824. Years later, from 1862 until 1865, he served in missionary work in Madagascar, after which he returned to England, where he died in 1872.

His first visit to Hawai'i was in 1822, when he traveled with a missionary deputation that had arrived from Tahiti via the Marquesas Islands on the cutter *Mermaid*. While the vessel was detained in Honolulu, it became evident that Ellis and the two Tahitians with him were able to use the native tongue readily because of the close relationship of the Tahitian and Hawaiian languages.

In the preface to the American edition of the *Journal,* there is this interesting comment: "The natives became so much interested in them [Ellis and the Tahitians] as to invite them to remain permanently at the Sandwich Islands. This invitation being strongly seconded by the American Missionaries, was accepted. At the close of the year, Mr. Ellis went to Huahine for his family, and returned in the February following." The same preface goes on to say that recent arrivals of missionary reinforcements from America called for "an enlargement of operations" that involved a survey of the island of Hawai'i ". . . with a view to the judicious occupation of that large and populous island."

This book is the story of that survey. The party included Mr. Ellis; the pioneer missionary, Reverend Asa Thurston; the Reverend Artemas Bishop; a licensed preacher, Joseph Goodrich; and a nonmissionary named Harwood. The party was a relatively youthful one; Ellis was 28 years of age and the Reverend Thurston, the oldest member, was 35 years.

Such a journey was no picnic. Had the high chief Kuakini of Hawai'i not provided a guide (a man named Makoa) and canoes to help convey the party along particular stretches of coast and transport the luggage, it is doubtful that the missionaries would have finished an encirclement of the island. Although they were hospitably received by the Hawaiians, some of whom had never met a foreigner before and spoke no English, the trials of thirst, diarrhea, sunburn, and fleas were intense. After two months and some days, and over one hundred sermons later, the party returned to Kailua, Kona, from the north.

An especially remarkable stage of the journey was a detour up the mountain Mauna Loa to visit the volcanic region of Kilauea, the place which is now the Hawaii Volcanoes National Park. The party was the first non-Hawaiian group to enter this sacred realm of Pele, the goddess of fire, and her sister Hi'iaka, the goddess of hula and the ohi'a lehua groves.

In the succeeding century profound changes were to take place on the island of Hawai'i. The Hawaiian language and the customs witnessed by Ellis and the others were to virtually disappear. The population of native Hawaiians was to dwindle to a few thousands. Such a record of the island at that early time is of course invaluable. Without it we would be so much the poorer in our understanding of Hawaiian culture.

The story of this journey with its many observations makes a fascinating and full book. If Ellis had not been obliged to leave the Pacific due to the failing health of his wife, he might never have written this or his other books. In fact, Ellis's journal was written en route to England from Hawai'i. The London edition, published in 1827, was proclaimed a remarkable book. Within three years it went through five editions. Samuel Taylor Coleridge, the friend of William Wordsworth and one of the most distinguished literary men of his time, said that the work was the most interesting account of a journey he had ever read. In an age when travel books were in vogue, this was a compliment indeed.

In the summer of 1973 a party of men retraced the 1823 journey. This group called itself the William Ellis II Expedition, and left Kailua, Kona, to follow the original itinerary as closely as possible. The members were delighted that so much of what they saw and experienced fitted with Ellis's descriptions. The modern Hawaiians were no less hospitable than those of the early 19th century although they were a greatly changed people.

The idea of such a reenactment came from Bob Krauss, author, veteran writer of the *Honolulu Advertiser*, and Ellis enthusiast. He proposed that such a venture would be a fitting observation of the 150th anniversary of the event. Thurston Twigg-Smith, president and publisher of the *Honolulu Advertiser* and great-great grandson of the Reverend Asa Thurston of the original party, was sympathetic. He gave the idea his full backing and personally joined this hardy band. The venture resulted in a good book (*The Island Way* by Bob Krauss, Island Heritage, Honolulu 1975), and a group called Friends of the William Ellis Trail. The latter organization proposes that the state of Hawaii establish a hiking trail following, as far as is feasible, the Ellis trail, which is, apart from the one inland venture to Kilauea, always within several feet to a few hundred yards from the sea coast. The Ellis II party, following the original route, used canoe travel along the precipitous and deep-ravined Hamakua coast.

All things considered, the trail proved remarkably intact. Agricultural and other developments have obstructed parts of the original trail, yet much of the country along the way is still as it was in the early 19th century. It is certainly one of the most fantastic walks in the world, and what other trails have such a guidebook as the *Journal of William Ellis?*

The Charles E. Tuttle Company published the *Journal of William Ellis* in its original small format as part of the four-volume set entitled *Polynesian Researches*. (*Polynesian Researches: Hawaii*, which contains the Ellis journal and a new foreword by Col. Edouard Doty, appeared in 1969 in hard cover and was separately reissued as a soft cover Tut Book in 1974; at the time of this writing it is still in print.) However, this present edition is a considerably different book. Its evolution is explained in the introduction by Mr. Thurston Twigg-Smith, which is here reprinted by his kind permission.

The Charles E. Tuttle Company also wishes to thank Mr. Twigg-Smith for permission granted by the Honolulu Advertiser, Inc., for the use of the Honolulu edition of 1963 with its several prefaces and valuable subject headings within the text. The index, based on the 1963 edition and never before published, appears here through the courtesy of Mr. Ray Lanterman of Honolulu, who compiled it in the first instance as a private reference to aid his own art work and interest in Hawaiian history.

Mr. Robert E. Van Dyke of Honolulu generously made available the original engravings, as those in the reprint were insufficient clear for adequate reproduction.

TERENCE BARROW, PH.D.

Honolulu, Hawai'i

MANY ACCOUNTS of physical and social conditions in Hawaii have been written but few, if any, surpass in clearness, accuracy and detail the account written by the Reverend William Ellis in 1824 and 1825.

Mr. Ellis was an English missionary to the South Pacific islands who visited Hawaii in 1822 and 1823 and in all lived here about two years.

The Advertiser reprinted his journal in 1917 in response to a demand then for material of historical significance. This current reprinting is the result of the interest of Meiric K. Dutton, late manager of The Advertiser Commercial Printing Division, who was a student of Hawaiiana and president of the Hawaiian Historical Society. He believed this journal to be of such significance that he had the 1917 edition re-set over a period of several years in this larger, more readable type.

The type had been available for several years prior to his death in March, 1961. When the Commercial Printing Division moved in August, 1962 to its new building on Pohukaina Street, the type was converted into plate for the possible later printing of the book. The interest of Hawaiian Historical Society members helped bring about the present decision to go ahead with publication.

The 1917 reprinting included a foreword by my grandfather, the late Lorrin A. Thurston, then publisher of The Honolulu Advertiser. His comments on the background of Mr. Ellis and the various editions of his journal are of interest and are reprinted below as he dictated them in Honolulu in November, 1916:

"The following is a resume of the facts incident to the visit of Mr. Ellis to Hawaii, and of the publication of the 'Journal' and the several editions of the 'Tour.'

"The extension of missionary effort to Hawaii, by the American Board of Foreign Missions, in 1820, was preceded, in the South Pacific, by the London Mission Society, who, in 1796 dispatched an expedition to, and early in 1797 established mission settlements at, the Marquesas, Friendly and Society Islands.

"These missionaries suffered great hardship, assaults upon them being numerous and some were murdered. Owing to the frequent inter-tribal wars, some of the stations were abandoned, and it was not until the discouraging struggle had been carried on for fifteen years that a change for the better took place; after which progress at some of the stations was rapid.

"In 1822, a deputation from the home society visited the English Missions, and, in company with Rev. William Ellis, who had for six years been a missionary at the Society Islands, and two natives, extended their observations to Hawaii, where they intended to spend a few weeks. Owing to the exigencies of transportation, their stay was extended for four months. The American missionaries at Hawaii and the Hawaiian chiefs were so much pleased with Mr. Ellis and his native assistants, that they were invited to remain permanently, which invitation was accepted. Mr. Ellis returned to Huahine for his family, arriving back in Hawaii in February, 1823.

"The American Mission had, at that time, established permanent stations on Oahu and Kauai only. It was thereupon decided that an exploration of the Island of Hawaii should be made, for the purpose of learning more of the country and people, with a view to establishing mission stations there. Mr. Ellis and three of the American missionaries, Asa Thurston, Artemas Bishop and Joseph Goodrich, were dispatched for the purpose, in June, 1823, landing at Kailua and spending two months in making the circuit of the island. So far as the records show, they were the first white men to accomplish this, being also the first white men to visit the volcano of Kilauea.

"Upon the return of the party to Honolulu, a joint journal of their journey and observations was prepared. A copy of this, together with a report by the American missionaries, was printed in Boston in 1825.

"Mr. Ellis returned to England in 1824 and after rewriting the journal in the form of a personal narrative, and adding thereto a large number of his own observations, together with comparisons of life and customs in Hawaii with those in the Society Islands, published five editions in London between 1825 and 1828. Later, in 1842, the same material, as a whole, was published by him, in connection with other material concerning the South Sea Islands, under the title of "Polynesian Researches." This also went through several editions.

"A number of these many editions differ more or less from each other.

"For the purposes of this publication, one of the English editions of 1827 has been followed, there being added thereto the preface and report of the American missionaries, from the American edition, and illustrations from all of them.

"The combination constitutes the clearest, most accurate and detailed account extant, of the physical and social conditions existing in Hawaii in 1823.

"The information secured by Mr. Ellis from the natives concerning a great number of subjects, and here recorded, also constitutes a mine of information concerning Polynesian lore, which, but for him, would have been lost or known in much less detail.

"The poet, Coleridge, is reported to have stated that he considered Ellis' 'Tour Through Hawaii' to be the most interesting and instructive book of travel that he had ever read.

"All of the many editions of this book have been out of print for many years, and are only to be found in a few libraries, or at rare intervals second-hand and at prohibitory prices in a few book stores.

"The sub-headings throughout the book are inserted by myself as a convenience in referring to the contents. Some of the longer paragraphs have been broken into shorter ones, but no change has otherwise been made. I have also added an index."

THURSTON TWIGG-SMITH

Honolulu, Hawaii
February 19, 1963

xvi

IN THE YEAR 1819, Tamehameha, king of the Sandwich Islands, died, and his son Rihoriho succeeded to his dominions; and immediately afterwards, the system of idolatry, so far as it was connected with the government, was abolished. This measure seems to have been owing to three causes: First, a desire on the part of the king to improve the condition of his wives, who, in common with all the other females of the islands, were subject to many painful inconveniences from the operation of the tabu; secondly, the advice of foreigners, and of some of the more intelligent chiefs; and thirdly, and principally, the reports of what had been done by Pomare, in the Society Islands. A war, which this act occasioned, was suppressed by a decisive battle described in this volume. At this time, and before intelligence of the death of Tamehameha reached the United States, missionaries, sent forth by the American Board of Commissioners for Foreign Missions, were on their way to the islands, where they arrived, a few months afterwards, with the Gospel of Jesus Christ.

SETTLEMENT OF MISSIONARIES IN HAWAII

After some hesitation on the part of the rulers of the islands, the missionaries, so opportunely arrived, were allowed to remain and commence their work. Some took up their abode on Hawaii, where the king then resided; others went to Tauai, under the patronage of Taumuarii, king of that island; but the main body settled at Honoruru, on the island of Oahu, where is the principal harbour for shipping. This was in April, 1820. At the close of the year, the king and the missionaries removed from Hawaii, and the latter joined their brethren at Honoruru.

During the following year, some progress was made in settling the orthography of the language, a task, which the great prevalence of liquid sounds rendered extremely difficult. The alphabet adopted, was that proposed by the Hon. John Pickering, of Salem, Mass., in his "Essay on a Uniform Orthography for the Indian languages of North America," published in the Memoirs of the American Academy of Arts and Sciences; excepting that the Hawaiian language requires a less number of letters than that alphabet contains. Every sound has its appropriate sign; every word is spelled exactly as it is pronounced; and thus the art of reading and writing the language, is rendered to the natives simple and easy. A press being at the command of the missionaries, the first sheet of a Hawaiian spelling-book was printed in the beginning of 1822. This work was soon in great demand. Other works in the native language have since been published.

ARRIVAL OF REV. WILLIAM ELLIS

In the spring of this year, the Rev. William Ellis, an English Missionary, who had resided several years at the Society Islands, came to the Sandwich Islands, on his way to the Marquesas. He was accompanied by the Rev. Daniel Tyerman and George Bennet, Esq., two gentlemen who had been sent by the London Missionary Society as deputies to their missions in the South Seas; and, also, by two Tahitian chiefs, who were sent, with their wives, by the church of Huahine, as missionaries to the Marquesas.

This company having been detained at the Sandwich Islands for a considerable period, and Mr. Ellis and the two Tahitians being almost immediately able to use the Hawaiian language with facility, the natives became so much interested in them, as to invite them to remain permanently at the Sandwich Islands. This invitation being strongly seconded by the American Missionaries, was accepted. At the close of the year, Mr. Ellis went to Huahine for his family, and returned in the February following.

ORGANIZATION OF THE EXPEDITION

In April, the mission received a further accession of strength by the arrival of new labourers from the United States. This called for an enlargement of operations. Two missionaries were sent to Maui, and, as soon as circumstances would permit, arrangements were made for surveying Hawaii, with a view to the judicious occupation of that large and populous island. Mr. Ellis, the English missionary, the Rev. Asa Thurston, the Rev. Charles S. Stewart, the Rev. Artemas Bishop, and Mr. Joseph Goodrich, (a licensed preacher,) American missionaries, were selected for this purpose.

Mr. Stewart was detained from the service by ill health. The rest commenced the tour of the island early in the summer of 1823, and completed it in a little more than two months. The results of the tour form the subject matter of this volume.

DEPARTURE OF KING TO ENGLAND

A short time after the return of the Deputation from Hawaii, the king, Rihoriho, embarked in a whaling ship for England. His object seems to have been chiefly to increase his knowledge of the world. Accompanied by his favourite queen, a chief, and some other native attendants, he arrived in London early in the following summer; but, in the course of a few weeks, both he and his wife sickened and died. The remains of these two personages were sent back to the islands in the Blonde, an English Frigate, commanded by Lord Byron, brother [cousin—L. A. T.] to the poet; and upon their arrival, the funeral rites were performed, in a Christian manner, by their affectionate and sorrowing people. A younger brother succeeds to the government, which seems to rest upon a solid basis.

The progress of the missionaries in attracting the attention of the natives to religious instruction, and in teaching them to read and write their own language, especially of late, has been truly surprising. Schools, managed by natives themselves, have become quite numerous, and are constantly increasing in number, popularity, and effect.

AUTHORSHIP OF JOURNAL

The following Journal was drawn up by Mr. Ellis, from minutes kept by himself, and by his associates on the tour, who subsequently gave it their approbation. The Report of the Deputation, which forms a

xviii

convenient introduction to the main work, was written by another hand.

The Appendix was prepared by the Assistant Serretary of the Board of Foreign Missions, who performed the duties of an editor, while the work was passing through the press : but, as those duties were performed amidst numerous cares and frequent interruptions, it will not be surprising if inaccuracies should exist.

REPORT OF THE DEPUTATION

To The Members and Patrons of the Sandwich Island Mission.

Brethren and Friends:—Having, by favour of Providence, performed, in the period of ten weeks, the interesting service, for which we were lately appointed, it is with no small satisfaction, that we lay before you a brief outline of our proceedings.

AN APPRECIATION OF KUAKINI

By sea and by land we have enjoyed the protection of God, and the countenance and patronage of the king and chiefs. Especially would we notice the kindness of Kuakini, the Governor of Hawaii, more known in this country by the name of John Adams, who received us with great hospitality, and freely lent his influence and authority to aid us in the attainment of our immediate objects; and with a view to the permanent establishment of a missionary station there, has promptly commenced the erection of a chapel at Kairua for the worship of Jehovah, whose rightful and supreme authority he has publicly acknowledged.

We would early and devoutly acknowledge our obligations of gratitude to the Great Lord of the harvest, who has enabled us, without opposition or material disaster, so fully to investigate the moral state, and comparative claims, of that portion of our field of labour, and so freely and frequently to proclaim to its perishing thousands the unsearchable riches of Jesus Christ. While we have endeavored steadily to pursue these grand objects of our enterprise with reference to a permanent maintenance of the Gospel on that island, we have been enabled to collect considerable information on a variety of subjects, which, though of secondary moment in the missionary's account, are, nevertheless, interesting and important; such as the natural scenery, productions, geology, and curiosities; the traditionary legends, superstitions, manners, customs, &c.

In the prosecution of our design to explore and enlighten the long benighted Hawaii, we have ascended its lofty and majestic mountains, entered its dark caverns, crossed its deep ravines, and traversed its immense flelds of rugged lava. We have stood with wonder on the edge of its ancient craters, walked tremblingly along the brink of its smoking chasms, gazed with admiration on its raging fires, and witnessed, with no ordinary feelings of awe, the varied and sublime phenomena of volcanic action, in all its imposing magnificence and terrific grandeur.

We have witnessed, too, with sorrow, the appalling darkness, which has hitherto over-spread the land; have wept over the miseries of its untutored inhabitants; have sighed for their speedy emancipation from the bondage of iniquity; and through their fertile vales, barren wastes, and clustering villages, have proclaimed the Lord Jesus Christ, as the Hope and Deliverer of man.

Commencing our tour at Kairua, on the western shore of Hawaii, we travelled to the south, the east, and the north; twice crossed the interior in different parts; remained a night and a day at the great volcano of Kirauea; visited all the principal settlements, both on the coast, and in the interiour; spent a Sabbath in each of the five large divisions of the island; and have endeavored to convince the inhabitants, that the objects of the mission are benevolent and disinterested, intended to lead them to the enjoyment of the lights of science, and the blessings of Christianity.

We have not forgotten the command of our Saviour, "As ye go, preach;" and it has been our comfort, in obedience to that command, to hold the cup of his salvation to the parched lips of those, who had never tasted the heavenly draught, and whom we found most emphatically without hope and without God in the world. Strengthened by the divine promise, "Lo, I am with you alway," we have on our tour preached in more than sixty different places, to collections of people of from fifty to one thousand in number, and in most cases have been heard with attention.

CENSUS AND CAUSES OF DECREASE OF POPULATION

We have also carefully numbered the habitations of the natives, and have estimated the inhabitants of Hawaii to be 85,000; a number much greater than the population of all the other islands of the group; but far less than the estimate of its celebrated discoverer, and of reputable subsequent voyagers. To contemplate the waste of population here indicated,—whether we attribute it to the ravages of war, whose restless spear is scarcely restrained by the approach of the cross; to the desolating pestilence, which has more than once swept through these isles; to the cruel superstition, which has but recently abolished her immolating rights; to that most unnatural of all crimes, that gain admittance to "the habitations of cruelty," infanticide; or to the prevalence of vice, rendered doubly destructive by foreign causes,—cannot but be deeply affecting to the feelings of philanthropy.

The light of the Gospel has broken the gloom, which, like a long and cheerless night, has, from time immemorial, rested on the hills and vallies of Hawaii; and a jubilee has, we trust, dawned upon its miserable inhabitants.

IDOLATRY RENOUNCED BUT SUPERSTITION REMAINS

But though the chiefs have renounced their ancient idolatry, and the priests no longer perform the mystic and bloody rites of the heiau, (Temple), and though on the ruins of their temples, altars are now erecting for the worship of the living God, yet the deep impressions made in childhood, by the songs, legends, and horrid rites connected with their long established superstitions, and the feelings and habits cherished by them in subsequent life, are not, by the simple proclamation of a king, or the resignation of a priest, to be removed at once from the mind of the unenlightened Hawaiian, who, in the sighing of the breeze, the gloom of night, the boding eclipse, the meteor's glance, the lightning's flash, the thunder's roar, the earthquake's shock, is accustomed to recognize the dreaded presence of some unpropitious deity. Nor must we be surprised, if the former views which the Hawaiian has been accustomed to entertain respecting Pele, the goddess he supposes to preside over volcanoes, should not at once be eradicated; as he is continually reminded of her power, by almost every object that meets his eye, from the rude cliffs of lava, against which the billows of the ocean dash, even to the lofty craters, her ancient seat amid perpetual snows. Nor is it to be expected, that those who feel themselves to have been released from the oppressive demands of their former religion, will, until they are more enlightened, be in haste to adopt a substitute, which presents imperious claims in direct opposition to all their unhallowed affections; especially since, while thus ignorant of the nature of Christianity, their recollections of the past must awaken fears of evil, perhaps not less dreadful than those from which they have just escaped.

PEOPLE OF A RECEPTIVE DISPOSITION

But though we found the people generally ignorant of Jehovah and indifferent to his worship, and many of them retaining their household gods, and cherishing a sort of veneration for the bones of their chiefs, and relatives, yet not a few, when they heard of the love of God in the gift of his Son, desired to be more fully instructed, and "intreated that the word might be spoken to them again."

"The harvest is plenteous, but the labourers are few." Nine preachers only are employed in the Sandwich Islands; and such is the importance of the stations occupied in Oahu, Maui and Tauai, (heretofore written Woahoo, Mowee and Atooi.—Ed.), that but four at most can be spared for Hawaii, or one to every 21,000 inhabitants, a number more than equal to the whole population of the Society Islands, where twelve missionaries are advantageously employed. But to furnish Hawaii even with one missionary to every 4,200 souls, sixteen more than the mission can now assign to it, would be required.

LOCATION OF MISSION STATIONS RECOMMENDED

We are happy to state, that, on different parts of the island, there are eight eligible stations, Kairua, Kearakekua, Honaunau, Honuapo, Kaimu, Waiakea, Waipio, and Towaihae. These we earnestly recommend for early and permanent occupation, as affording to the missionary encouraging prospects, not of freedom from privation, but of extensive usefulness.

Kairua, on the west, claims, doubtless, our earliest attention. Not less than 60 of its 3,000 inhabitants, including the governor, have been taught to read and write their own language, and have been made acquainted with the first principles of Christianity. (Kairua, Kearakekua, and Waiakea, have since been occupied.—Ed.)

Near Kearakekua, memorable for the lamented fall of Captain Cook, we were surprised and delighted to find a friendly chief, Kamakau, who espouses with lively interest, the cause of the Gospel, and earnestly desires to be taught himself, and to teach his people, the word of God. The expected residence here of Naihe and Kapiolani, interesting chiefs, renders it still more desirable that missionaries should reside here.

Honaunau, the frequent residence of former kings, where a depository of their bones, and many images of their gods, still remain, has a dense population waiting for Christian instruction.

Including these three places, the coast, for twenty miles, embraces more than forty villages, containing a population of perhaps 20,000 souls, to whom missionaries, stationed at these posts, might convey instruction.

Honuapo, on the southern shore, is an extensive village, with a considerable population in its vicinity.

Kaimu is a pleasant village on the southeast shore, with 700 inhabitants, and with twice that number of people in its vicinity.

At most of the above places, unless wells can be obtained, the missionaries will often experience the want of good water.

Waiakea, on the east, well watered, fertile and beautiful, having a commodious harbour, with an extensive population, demands, next to Kairua, our earliest arrangements for permanent missionary operations.

DETAILS IN JOINT JOURNAL

Waipio, little less fertile and beautiful, having in its immediate neighbourhood Waimanu, a valley of similar beauty and importance, is waiting to receive the precious seed.

Towaihae on the north-west, a considerable village, presents nearly equal claims.

Several other places, which have not been named, are scarcely less inviting.

The whole field is open to spiritual cultivation, "and he that goeth forth and weepeth, bearing precious seed, shall doubtless come again with rejoicing, bringing his sheaves with him."

Such is the general view, which we proposed to lay before you. But for more particular information on the various subjects of our inquiry; for detailed descriptions of the places eligible for missionary operations, and of the recently established and flourishing station visited by one of us at Maui; and for minute and copious accounts of Hawaii, and of the sentiments, characters, and employments, of its ingenious inhabitants; we beg leave respectfully to refer you to our joint journal of the tour. Believing that you will rejoice with us in the cheering prospect of the early and ultimate success of missionary operations there, and encouraged as we are with the assured hope of the complete and glorious triumph of the Gospel in every island, permit us affectionately to invite you to unite with us, "even as also ye do," in humble and earnest prayer for this interesting portion of our race; that the seed already sown among them may be as "the handful of corn upon the tops of the mountains, the fruit whereof shall shake like Lebanon;" that the promise to the Redeemer of the nations may be remembered for their good; and that divine mercies may descend from heaven upon them in rich and joyful profusion, "as the dew of Hermon, and as the dew that descended upon the mountains of Zion, for there the Lord commanded the blessing, even life forever more."

THE GREATER PART of the following Narrative was written in the Sandwich Islands, from notes taken by my fellow-travellers and myself, while
engaged in the Tour it describes. At my request, a member of the
American Mission was associated in preparing it; but circumstances
requiring his presence in another island, the task devolved on myself
alone.

The journal, when prepared, was submitted to most of the missionaries, and approved. As the chief object of the Tour,—a survey of the
religious state of the inhabitants of the island,—was one in which the
American Society had an equal interest with the London Missionary
Society, with which I am connected, a copy of the journal approved in
the islands, was, according to previous agreement between the American
missionaries and myself, left by me in America, and I believe will be
published there.

ADDITIONS TO JOURNAL

The continued narrative form, as more agreeable than that of a daily
journal, has been adopted in the present publication; and the writer
appears in the first person, instead of the third. I have not felt it incum-
bent on me to confine myself to the mere contents of the document left
in America; but have, in various parts, made large additions from my
own private observations.

The biographical accounts of various important persons, many descriptions of the superstitions, manners, customs, and traditions of the
people, the nature of their government, and the remarks on their language, are taken from my own memoranda, which a knowledge of their
language enabled me to make, during my daily intercourse with the
natives for the space of two years.

I have occasionally illustrated my remarks by allusions to the Society
Islands, where I spent six years in missionary occupations. I have invariably represented the natives as we found them, exhibiting freely the
lights and shades of their character, without exaggeration; and can assure my readers, that it has been my constant aim to offer nothing, the
accuracy of which may not be relied upon; and, in many descriptions,
have rather diminished than enlarged the objects described.

PICTURES AND MAPS

The drawings were sketched on the spot. The outline of the map is
from Vancouver's survey, unaltered, except slightly in two places, viz.
Kairua and Waiakea. The geographical division, &c. were inserted during the Tour; and specimens brought to this country, of the lava, &c.
described in the narrative, have been inspected by individuals of eminence in the study of mineralogy.

It is hoped, that in various points of view, the following narrative
will be found interesting. It will introduce to the more accurate knowledge of our country a portion of the human race, with which they have
been hitherto very imperfectly acquainted; and tend to remove some

prejudices which may have existed respecting the supposed invincible ferocity of the Sandwich Islanders. It will prove that they are rapidly emerging from their former condition, and preparing to maintain a higher rank in the scale of nations. Above all, it will furnish a decisive and triumphant illustration of the direct tendency of Christian principles, and Christian institutions, to promote the true amelioration of mankind in all the relations of social life.

POWER OF CHRISTIANITY

Without depreciating the value of those efforts, which mere political philanthropists may employ for the interests of humanity; such facts as those presented to the world, in the recent history of the Society and Sandwich Islands, prove, that CHRISTIANITY ALONE supplies the most powerful motives, and the most effective machinery, for originating and accomplishing the processes of civilization. While the spiritual welfare and the eternal destinies of men are the primary objects of its solicitude, it provides for all their subordinate interests on true and permanent principles, and thus lays a solid foundation for personal happiness, domestic comfort, and national prosperity. These are the legitimate triumphs of the gospel; these are moral demonstrations of its efficiency and its origin; these are proofs, in perfect harmony with other illustrations of the fact, that "the foolishness of God is wiser than men, and the weakness of God is stronger than men;" and that "godliness hath the promise of the life that now is, and of the life which is to come."

The candid reader will pass over all the defects in the execution of the work, when assured, that every pretension, except to a simple narrative of facts, is disclaimed; that it was prepared amidst a variety of engagements, and under the pressure of severe domestic affliction, and that the last ten years of my life have been so much devoted to the study of the uncultivated languages of the Pacific, that when most of it was written, they were more familiar than my native tongue.

London, February 23, 1826.

JOURNAL OF WILLIAM ELLIS

*Narrative of a Tour of Hawaii, or Owhyhee; with Remarks
on the History, Traditions, Manners, Customs
and Language of the Inhabitants of the
Sandwich Islands*

CHAPTER I

IT IS NEARLY HALF A CENTURY since Captain Cook, in search of a
northern passage from the Pacific to the Atlantic, discovered a group
of islands, which, in honour of his patron the Earl of Sandwich, first
lord of the Admiralty, he called the SANDWICH ISLANDS. The importance he attached to this discovery may be gathered from his own
words; for, when speaking of the circumstances under which the vessels
anchored for the first time in Kearake'kua bay, the appearance of the
natives, &c. he remarks, "We could not but be struck with the singularity
of this scene; and, perhaps, there were few on board who now lamented
our having failed in our endeavours to find a northern passage homeward
last summer. To this disappointment we owed our having it in our
power to revisit the Sandwich Islands, and to enrich our voyage with a
discovery, which, though last, seemed, in many respects, to be the most
important that had hitherto been made by Europeans throughout the
extent of the Pacific ocean."

These are the last words recorded in the journal of that enterprising
and intelligent navigator ; a melancholy event shortly afterwards occurred
on the shores of this very bay, which arrested his career of discovery,
and terminated his existence.

On the return of the survivors, a detailed account of the islands and
their inhabitants was given to the world, and excited no small degree of
interest, not only in England, but throughout the continent of Europe.

CHARACTER OF COOK'S REPORTS

The descriptions which Captain Cook's Voyages contained, of the
almost primitive simplicity, natural vivacity, and fascinating manners,
of a people who had existed for ages, isolated, and unknown to the rest
of the world, were so entirely new, and the accounts given of the mild-

1

ness and salubrity of the climate, the spontaneous abundance of delicious fruits, and the varied and delightful appearance of the natural scenery in the Sandwich and other islands of the Pacific, were so enchanting, that many individuals were led to imagine they were a sort of elysium, where the highly favoured inhabitants, free from the toil and care, the want and disappointment, which mar the happiness of civilized communities, dwelt in what they called a state of nature, and spent their lives in unrestrained gratification and enjoyment.

These descriptions, were, I am convinced, faithful transcripts of the first impressions made on the minds of Captain Cook and his companions, and in every respect correct, so far as their partial observation extended.

A residence of eight years in the Society and Sandwich islands, has afforded me an opportunity of becoming familiar with many of the scenes and usages described in their voyages, and I have often been struck with the fidelity with which they are uniformly portrayed. In the inferences they draw, and the reasons they assign, they are sometimes mistaken; but in the description of what they saw and heard, there is throughout a degree of accuracy, seldom if ever exceeded in accounts equally minute and extended. Still their acquaintance with the islands and the people was superficial, and the state of society which they witnessed was different from what generally existed.

EFFECT ON NATIVES OF COOK'S ARRIVAL

An event so important and surprising as their arrival,—the ships and the foreigners,—the colour, dress, arms, language, manners, &c. of the latter, whom they regarded at first as superior beings, so powerfully affected the minds of the natives, that the ordinary avocations of life were for a time suspended. The news of such an event rapidly spread through the island and multitudes flocked from every quarter to see the return of Orono, or the motus, (islands) as they called their ships.

The whole island was laid under requisition, to supply their wants, or contribute to their satisfaction. Hence the immense quantity of provisions presented by Taraiopu; the dances, &c. with which they were entertained. The effect also produced on the minds of those early visitors, by what they saw during their transient stay among the islands, was heightened by all the attractions of novelty, and all the complacency which such discoveries naturally inspire.

IMPRESSION OF MISSIONARIES DIFFERENT FROM COOK'S

Far different are the impressions produced on the minds of the missionaries who have resided for some years in the islands. Having acquired their language, observed their domestic economy, and become

2

acquainted with the nature of their government, the sanguinary character of their frequent wars, their absurd and oppressive system of idolatry, and the prevalence of human sacrifice, they are led, from the indubitable facts which have come under their notice, to more just and accurate conclusions in awful accordance with the faithful testimony of divine revelation.

DESCRIPTION OF ISLANDS

Although ten in number, only eight of the Sandwich Islands are inhabited, the other two being barren rocks, principally resorted to by fishermen. They lie within the tropic of Cancer, between 18° 50′ and 22° 20′ north latitude, and between 154° 53′ and 160° 15′ west longitude from Greenwich, about one-third of the distance from the western coast of Mexico, towards the eastern shores of China. The Sandwich Islands are larger than the Society Islands, or any of the neighbouring clusters.

HAWAII, the principal island of the group, resembles in shape an equilateral triangle, and is somewhat less than three hundred miles in circumference, being about ninety-seventy miles in length, seventy-eight in breadth, two hundred and eighty miles in circumference, and covering a surface of 4000 square miles. It is the most southern of the whole, and, on account of its great elevation, is usually the first land seen from vessels approaching the Sandwich Islands. Its broad base and regular form renders its outline different from that of any other island in the Pacific with which we are acquainted.

The mountains of Hawaii, unlike the peak of Teneriffe in the Atlantic, the mountains of Eimeo, and some other islands of the Pacific, do not pierce the clouds like obelisks or spires, but in most parts, and from the southern shore in particular, the ascent is gradual, and comparatively unbroken, from the sea beach to the lofty summit of Mouna Roa.

HAWAII COMPARED WITH TAHITI

The whole appearance of Hawaii is less romantic and picturesque than that of Tahiti, the principal of the Society Islands, but more grand and sublime, filling the mind of the beholder with wonder and delight.

On approaching the islands, I have more than once observed the mountains of the interior long before the coast was visible, or any of the usual indications of land had been seen. On these occasions, the elevated summit of Mouna Kea, or Mouna Roa, has appeared above the mass of clouds that usually skirt the horizon, like a stately pyramid, or the silvered dome of a magnificent temple, distinguished from the clouds beneath, only by its well-defined outline, unchanging position, and intensity of brilliancy occasioned by the reflection of the sun's rays from the surface of the snow.

3

The height of these mountains has been computed by some navigators who have visited the Sandwich Islands, at 12,000, and by others at 18,000 feet. The estimate of Captain King,* we think, exceeds their actual elevation, and the peaks of Mouna Kea, in the opinion of those of our number who have ascended its summit, are not more than 1000 feet high. But admitting the snow to remain permanent on the mountains of the torrid zone at the height of 14,600 feet, the altitude of Mouna Kea and Mouna Roa is probably not less than 15,000 feet.

The base of these mountains, is, at the distance of a few miles from the sea shore, covered with trees; higher up, their sides are clothed with bushes, ferns, and alpine plants; but their summits are formed of lava, partly decomposed, yet destitute of every kind of verdure.

FEW INLAND SETTLEMENTS

There are a few inland settlements on the east and north-west parts of the island, but, in general, the interior is an uninhabited wilderness.

The heart of Hawaii, forming a vast central valley between Mouna Roa, Mouna Kea, and Mouna Huararai, is almost unknown, no road leads across it from the east to the western shore, but it is reported, by the natives who have entered it, to be "bristled with forests of ohia," or to exhibit vast tracts of sterile and indurated lava.

The circumstance of large flocks of wild geese being frequently seen in the mountains, would lead to the supposition that there must be large ponds or lakes to which they resort; but if any exist, they have hitherto remained undiscovered.

The greatest part of the land capable of cultivation, is found near the sea shore; along which, the towns and villages of the natives are thickly scattered. The population at present is about 85,000, and will most probably be greatly increased by the establishment of Christianity, whose mild influence, it may reasonably be expected, will effect a cessation of war, an abolition of infanticide, and a diminution of those vices, principally of foreign origin, which have hitherto so materially contributed to the depopulation of the islands.

* In Cook's Voyages, Captain King, speaking of Mouna-Kaah, (Kea,) remarks that it "may be clearly seen at fourteen leagues' distance." Describing Mouna-Roa, and estimating it according to the tropical line of snow, he observes, "This mountain must be at least 16,020 feet high, which exceeds the height of the Pico de Teyde, or Peak of Teneriffe, by 724 feet, according to Dr. Heberden's computation, or 3680 according to that of Chevalier de Borda. The peaks of Mouna-Kaah appeared to be about half a mile high; and as they are entirely covered with snow, the altitude of their summits cannot be less than 18,400 feet. But it is probable that both these mountains may be considerably higher; for in insular situations, the effects of the warm sea air must necessarily remove the line of snow, in equal latitudes, to a greater height, than where the atmosphere is chilled on all sides by an immense tract of perpetual snow."

4

Hawaii is by far the largest, most populous, and important island of the group, and, until within a few years, was the usual residence of the king, and the frequent resort of every chief of importance in the other islands. Foreigners, however, having of late found the harbours of some of the leeward islands more secure and convenient than those of Hawaii, have been induced more frequently to visit them; and this has led the king and principal chiefs to forsake, in a great degree, the favourite residence of their ancestors, and excepting the governor, and the chiefs of Kaavaroa, to spend the greater part of their time in some of the other islands.

MAUI DESCRIBED

Separated from the northern shore of Hawaii by a strait, about twenty-four miles across, the island of MAUI is situated in lat. 20° N. and lon. 157° W. This island is forty-eight miles in length, in the widest part twenty-nine miles across, about one hundred and forty miles in circumference, and covers about 600 square miles. At a distance it appears like two distinct islands, but on nearer approach a low isthmus, about nine miles across, is seen uniting the two peninsulas. The whole island is entirely volcanic, and was probably produced by the action of two adjacent volcanoes, which have ejected the immense masses of matter of which it is composed. The appearance of Maui resembles Tahiti more than the neighbouring island of Hawaii. The southern peninsula, which is the largest of the two, is lofty; but though its summits are often seen above the clouds, they are never covered with snow. The high land is steep and rugged; and frequently marked with extinct craters, or indurated streams of lava; yet whenever the volcanic matters have undergone any degree of decomposition, the sides of the mountains, as well as the ravines by which they are intersected, are covered with shrubs and trees.

In the northern peninsula there are several extensive tracts of level and well-watered land, in a high state of cultivation; and although this part of the island is evidently of volcanic formation, the marks of recent eruption, so frequent in the southern peninsula, are seldom seen here. The population of Maui has been estimated at 18,000 or 20,000, and the number of inhabitants do not probably fall short of that number.

MISSION ESTABLISHED AT LAHAINA

In the month of May, 1823, a Christian Mission was commenced at Lahaina, the most important and populous district in the island, and the endeavors of Messrs. Stewart and Richards and the native teachers by whom they were accompanied, have been attended with the most decisive and extensive success. Public preaching on the Sabbath is regularly attended by numerous audiences, and thousands of the people are daily receiving instruction in useful knowledge, and the principles of Christianity, in the various native schools, which are patronized by the young Prince Kauikeouli, younger brother and successor to the late king,—by his sister Nahienaena,—and by all the principal chiefs of Maui. The most lasting benefits may be expected to result, not only to the present race, but to every future generation of the inhabitants.

KAHOOLAWE AND MOLOKINI DESCRIBED

To the south of Maui, and only a few miles distant from its southern peninsula, is situated the small island of TAHAURAWE, about eleven miles in length, and eight across. It is low, and almost destitute of every kind of shrub or verdure, excepting a species of coarse grass. The rocks of which it is formed are volcanic, but we are not aware of the existence of any active or extinct craters on the island; and from its shape and appearance, it is not improbable that it once formed a part of Maui, from which it may have been detached by some violent convulsion connected with the action of the adjacent volcanoes of Maui or Hawaii. There are but few settled residents on the island, and these are considered as under the authority of the governor of Maui.

MOROKINI, a barren rock, lies between these two islands, and would render the navigation of the strait exceedingly dangerous, were it not so much elevated above the sea as to be at all times visible from vessels passing between the islands. Morokini is only visited by fishermen, who on its barren surface spread their nets to dry, and for this purpose it may be considered a convenient appendage to the adjacent islands.

LANAI DESCRIBED

RANAI, a compact island, seventeen miles in length and nine in breadth, lies north-west of Tahaurawe, and west of Lahaina, in Maui, from which it is separated by a channel, not more than nine or ten miles across. Though the centre of the island is much more elevated than Tahaurawe, it is neither so high nor broken as any of the other islands: great part of it is barren, and the island in general suffers much from the long droughts which frequently prevail; the ravines and glens, notwithstanding, are filled with thickets of small trees, and to these many of the inhabitants of Maui repair for the purpose of cutting posts and rafters for their small houses. The island is volcanic; the soil shallow, and by no means fertile; the shores, however, abound with shell-fish, and some species of *medusae* and cuttle-fish. The inhabitants are but few, probably not exceeding two thousand. Native teachers are endeavouring to instruct them in useful knowledge and religious truth, but no foreign

6

missionary has yet laboured on this or the neighboring island of Morokai, which is separated from the northern side of Ranai, and the eastern end of Maui, by a channel, which, though narrow, is sufficiently wide for the purposes of navigation.

MOLOKAI DESCRIBED

MOROKAI is a long irregular island, apparently formed by a chain of volcanic mountains, forty miles in length, and not more than seven miles broad; the mountains are nearly equal in elevation to those of Maui, and are broken by numerous deep ravines and watercourses, the sides of which are frequently clothed with verdure, and ornamented with shrubs and trees. There is but little level land in Morokai, and consequently but few plantations; several spots, however, are fertile and repay the toils of their cultivators. The population is greater than that of Ranai, though it does not probably exceed three thousand persons. Native teachers are engaged in the instruction of the people; many of the natives also occasionally visit the missionary stations in the adjacent islands of Oahu and Maui, and participate in the advantages connected with these institutions.

OAHU DESCRIBED

OAHU, the most romantic and fertile of the Sandwich Islands, re-sembling in the varied features of its natural scenery, several of the Society Islands,—lies nearly west-northwest of Morokai, from which it is between twenty and thirty miles distant. This beautiful island is about forty-six miles long, and twenty-three wide; its appearance from the roads off Honoruru, or Waititi is remarkably picturesque: a chain of lofty mountains rises near the centre of the eastern part of the island, and, extending perhaps twenty miles, reaches the plain of Eva, which divides it from the distant and elevated mountains that rise in a line parallel with the north-west shore. The plain of Eva is nearly twenty miles in length, from the Pearl River to Waiarua, and in some parts nine or ten miles across: the soil is fertile, and watered by a number of rivulets, which wind their way along the deep water-courses that in-tersect its surface, and empty themselves into the sea. Though capable of a high state of improvement, a very small portion of it is enclosed, or under any kind of culture; and in travelling across it, scarce a habi-tation is to be seen. The whole island is volcanic, and, in many parts, extinguished craters of large dimensions may be seen; but, from the depth of mould with which they are covered, and the trees and shrubs with which they are clothed it may be presumed that many ages have elapsed since any eruption took place.

7

The plain of Honoruru exhibits in a singular manner the extent and effects of volcanic agency; it is not less than nine or ten miles in length, and, in some parts, two miles from the sea to the foot of the mountains; the whole plain is covered with a rich alluvial soil, frequently two or three feet deep; beneath this, a layer of fine volcanic ashes and cinders extends to the depth of fourteen or sixteen feet; these ashes lie upon a stratum of solid rock by no means volcanic, but evidently calcareous, and apparently a kind of sediment deposited by the sea, in which branches of white coral, bones of fish and animals, and several varieties of marine shells, are often found. A number of wells have been recently dug in different parts of the plain, in which, after penetrating through the calcareous rock, sometimes twelve or thirteen feet, good clear water has been always found: the water in all these wells is perfectly free from any salt or brackish taste, though it invariably rises and falls with the tide, which would lead to the supposition that it is connected with the waters of the adjacent ocean, from which the wells are from 100 yards to three quarters of a mile distant. The rock is always hard and compact near the surface, but becomes soft and porous as the depth increases; and it is possible that the water in these wells may have percolated through the cells of the rock, and by this process of filtration have lost its saline qualities. The base of the mountains which bound the plain in the interior appears to have formed the original line of coast on this side of the island, but probably in some remote period an eruption took place from two broad-based truncated mountains, called by foreigners Diamond Hill and Punchbowl Hill, evidently extinguished craters; the ashes and cinders then thrown out were wafted by the trade-winds in a westerly direction, filled up the sea, and formed the present extensive plain; the soil of its surface having been subsequently produced either by the decomposition of lava, or the mould and decayed vegetable matter washed down from the mountains during the rainy season of the year.

NUUANU VALLEY

Across this plain, immediately opposite the harbour of Honoruru, lies the valley of Anuanu, leading to a pass in the mountains, called by the natives Ka Pari, the precipice, which is well worth the attention of every intelligent foreigner visiting Oahu. The mouth of the valley, which opens immediately behind the town of Honoruru, is a complete garden, carefully kept by its respective proprietors in a state of high cultivation; and the ground being irrigated by the water from a river that winds rapidly down the valley, is remarkably productive. The valley rises with a gradual ascent from the shore to the precipice, which is seven or eight miles from the town. After walking about three miles through one unbroken

8

series of plantations, the valley becomes gradually narrower, and the mountains rise more steep on either side. The scenery is romantic and delightful: the bottom of the valley is gently undulated; a rapid stream takes its serpentine way from one side of the valley to the other, sometimes meandering along with an unruffled surface, at other times rushing down a fall several feet, or dashing and foaming among the rocks that interrupt its progress.

The sides of the hills are clothed with verdure; even the barren rocks that project from among the bushes are ornamented with pendulous or creeping plants of various kinds; and in several places, beautiful cascades roll their silvery streams down the steep mountain's side into flowing rivulets beneath.

NUUANU PALI

The beauty of the scenery around increases, until at length, after walking some time on a rising ground rather more steep than usual, and through a thicket of hibiscus and other trees, the traveller suddenly emerges into an open space, and, turning round a small pile of volcanic rocks, the Pari all at once bursts upon him with an almost overwhelming effect.

Immense masses of black and ferruginous volcanic rock, many hundred feet in nearly perpendicular height, present themselves on both sides to his astonished view; while immediately before him, he looks down the fearful steep several hundred feet, and beholds hills and valleys, trees and cottages, meandering streams and winding paths, cultivated plantations and untrodden thickets, and a varied landscape many miles in extent, bounded by lofty mountains on the one side, and the white-crested waves of the ocean on the other—spread out before him as if by the hand of enchantment.

I have several times visited this romantic spot, and once climbed the rocky precipice from the district of Kolau, on the northern side: the ascent is at first gradual and easy, but in two places, towards the highest edge, the volcanic rocks appear to rise perpendicularly, presenting an even, and apparently projecting front, which it seems impossible to ascend; but though the passage is thus difficult, and the elevation of the upper ridge, over which the path leads, is from four to five hundred feet above the level land below, yet the natives not only pass and repass without much difficulty, but often carry heavy burdens from one side to the other.

TALES OF THE PALI

It is reported that a native female, on one occasion, carried her husband, who was in a state of intoxication, down the precipice in safety. This appears hardly possible, and the story is probably one of those

9

fabulous wonders, with which inquiring foreigners are often entertained during their stay among the islands.

On one of my visits, however, I saw a party, heavily laden with provisions for the king's household, ascend the Pari, and one of them had a pig of no very small size fastened on his back, with which he climbed the steep, but not without difficulty.

THE GODS OF THE PALI

Within a few yards of the upper edge of the pass, under the shade of surrounding bushes and trees, two rude and shapeless stone idols are fixed, one on each side of the path, which the native call "Akua no ka Pari," gods of the precipice; they are usually covered with pieces of white tapa, native cloth; and every native who passes by to the precipice, if he intends to descend, lays a green bough before these idols, encircles them with a garland of flowers, or wraps a piece of tapa round them, to render them propitious to his descent. All who ascend from the opposite side make a similar acknowledgment for the supposed protection of the deities, whom they imagine to preside over the fearful pass. This practice appears universal, for in our travels among the islands, we have seldom passed any steep or dangerous paths, at the commencement or termination of which we have not seen these images, with heaps of offerings lying before them.

SURVIVAL OF SUPERSTITION

Until very recently, it is evident the influence of superstition was very strong in the minds of the great mass of the people, for although the natives who accompanied us in our excursions, either from a conviction of the absurdity of the notions of their countrymen, or from mere wantonness, usually overturned the idols, battered them with stones, or rolled them down the precipice or passage which they were supposed to defend; yet on passing the same path only a very short time afterwards, we have invariably found them replaced; or, if broken, their places supplied by fresh ones. This conduct of our native companions was never the consequence of our directions, and seldom received our approbation, for we were not ambitious to become Iconoclasts; our object was rather to enlighten the minds of the people, and convince them of the absurdity and evil of idolatry, to present before them the true God as the only legitimate object of rational homage, lead them to the exercise of a better faith, and the adoption of a purer worship; well assured that, if under the blessing of God we succeeded in this, they themselves would, with the adoption of the Christian system, not only renounce idolatry, but abolish the appendages by which it was upheld.

10

The Pari of Anuanu was an important position in times of war, and the parties in possession of it were usually masters of the island. In its vicinity many sanguinary battles have been fought, and near it the independence of Oahu was lost in or about the year 1790. Tamehameha invaded Oahu; the king of the island assembled his forces to defend his country, between Honoruru and the Pearl river; an engagement took place, in which his army was defeated, and his ally, Taeo, king of Tauai and Nihau, was slain. The king of Oahu retreated to the valley of Anuanu, where he was joined by Taiana, an ambitious and warlike chief of Hawaii. Hither Tamehameha and his victorious warriors pursued them, and, about two miles from the Pari, the last battle in Oahu was fought. Here the king of Oahu was slain, his army fled towards the precipice, chased by the warriors of Tamehameha; at the edge of the Pari, Taiana made a stand, and defended it till he fell: the troops of the fallen chiefs still continued the conflict, till being completely routed, a number of them, it is said four hundred, were driven headlong over the precipice, dashed to pieces among the fragments of rock that lie at its base, and Tamehameha remained master of the field, and sovereign of the island.

The natives still point out the spot where the king of the island stood, when he hurled his last spear at the advancing foe, and received the fatal wound; and many as they pass by, turn aside from the path, place their feet on the identical spot where he is said to have stood, assume the attitude in which he is supposed to have received his mortal wound, and, poising their staff or their spear, tell their children or companions that there the last King of Oahu died defending his country from its invading enemies.

THE CITY OF HONOLULU

Immediately south of the valley of Anuanu is situated the town and harbour of Honoruru; the harbour is the best, and indeed the only secure one at all seasons, in the Sandwich Islands, and is more frequented by foreign vessels than any other; seldom having within it less than three or four, and sometimes upward of thirty, lying at anchor at the same time.

The town has also, since the number of shipping has increased, become populous, and is one of the largest in the islands, usually containing 6000 or 7000 inhabitants. It is the frequent residence of the king and principal chiefs, who are much engaged in traffic with foreigners visiting the islands, or residing on shore, for purposes of trade.

There are twelve or fourteen merchants, principally Americans, who have established warehouses on shore for foreign goods, principally

11

piece goods, hardware, crockery, hats and shoes, naval stores, &c., which they retail to the natives for Spanish dollars or sandal wood.

On the eastern side of the basin is a strong fort, one hundred yards square, mounting sixty guns. It was begun by the Russians, who were expelled but finished by the natives, from an apprehension that these foreigners, in connexion with the Russian settlements on the north-west coast of America, were about to take possession of the island.

FOUNDING OF THE AMERICAN MISSION

Here also, in the month of April, 1820, an American mission was commenced, which, under God, has been the means of producing a most happy moral and domestic change in the character of many of the people, whose advancement in the arts of civilized life, as well as Christian knowledge, is truly gratifying. Several thousands are under religious instruction, and numbers regularly attend the preaching of the gospel, which we earnestly hope will result in the conversion of many. Several have forsaken their grass huts, and erected comfortable stone or wooden houses, among which, one built by Karaimoku, the prime minister, is highly creditable to his perseverance and his taste.

THE MOANALUA SALT LAKE

About six miles to the west of Honoruru, and nearly as far from the village of Eva, on the Pearl river, there is a singular natural curiosity, a small circular lake, situated at a short distance from the sea shore, so impregnated with salt, that twice in the year the natives take out between two and three hundred barrels of fine, clear, hard, crystallized salt: this lake is not only an interesting natural curiosity, but an important appendage to the island. It belongs to the king, and is not only useful in curing large quantities of fish, but furnishes a valuable article of commerce; quantities of it having been sent for sale to Kamtschatka, and used in curing seal skins at the different islands to which the natives have sent their vessels for that purpose, or sold in the islands to Russian vessels, from the settlements on the north-west coast of America. The population of Oahu is estimated at about 20,000.

THE ISLAND OF KAUAI

North-west of Oahu, and distant from it about seventy-five miles, is situated the island of TAUAI, which is a mountainous island, exceedingly romantic in its appearance, but not so fertile as Oahu, or the greater part of Maui. It is forty-six miles in length, and twenty-three in breadth, and covers a surface of 520 square miles. The population probably amounts to nearly 10,000. The principal settlements are in the neighbourhood of Waimea river, the roads at the entrance of which are the usual resort of vessels touching at Tauai. Near the mouth of the river is a strong fort, in excellent repair, mounting twenty-two guns. It was erected several years since, and is well adapted for defence.

CESSION OF KAUAI AND NIIHAU AND A REBELLION

This, and the neighbouring island of Nihau, were not invaded and conquered by Tamehameha, by whom all the other islands of the group were subdued. Taumuarii, the king, rendered a tacit acknowledgment of dependence on that ambitious prince, and paid annually a nominal tribute both to him, and his son, the late Rihoriho, and, shortly before his death, which took place in 1824, he formally ceded the islands which he had governed to Karaimoku, the present regent of the Sandwich Islands, for the King, who was then absent on a visit to Great Britain.

The son of the late king, and several old warriors, dissatisfied with the conduct of their sovereign, took up arms to rescue the islands from the dominion of the chiefs of the windward island, but being defeated in a battle fought in a valley near Waimea, the island is now under the authority of the young prince Kauikeouli, the successor to Rihoriho, and the present sovereign of the whole of the Sandwich Islands.

ESTABLISHMENT OF THE MISSION ON KAUAI

Soon after the commencement of the Mission in Oahu, a similar institution was commenced in Tauai, under the friendly auspices of the late king, and continued to prosper until the civil war, which followed his death, obliged the Missionaries to remove from the island, and suspend their endeavours for the instruction of the natives. Since the restoration of peace, however, their labours have been resumed with more extensive and encouraging prospects of success than had been previously enjoyed. The inhabitants are in general a hardy and industrious race; but it is remarkable that in their language they employ the *t* in all those words in which the *k* would be used by the natives of the other islands.

THE ISLAND OF NIIHAU

NIHAU, a small island, twenty miles in length, and seven miles wide, politically connected with Tauai, lies in a westerly direction, about fifteen miles distant. The inhabitants are not numerous, and, in the general features of their character, resemble the people of Tauai.

These islands are celebrated throughout the whole group for the manufacture of the fine painted or variegated mats, so much admired by foreigners, and which, for the purpose of sleeping on, the chiefs in all the islands prefer to any others.

These mats are sometimes very large, measuring eighteen or twenty

13

WEATHER RECORD FOR HONOLULU
1821-22

MONTHS	Greatest heat	Least heat	Range	General Range		Mean Temperature	General course of wind	General State of the Weather
1821								
August	88°	74°	14°	75° to	85°	79°	N.E.	Clear; rain but once.
September	87	74	13	76 —	84	78	N.E.	Rained on five days.
October	86	73	13	76 —	83	78	N.E.	Clear; rain but once.
November	82	71	11	75 —	80	76	N.E.	Clear; rain but once.
December	80	62	18	70 —	78	72	N. & N.E.	Clear; rain twice.
1822								
January	80	59	21	68 —	76	70	Variable	Rain 1 day; 7 others cloudy.
February	77	61	16	68 —	75	71	N.E.	Rain 4 days; 10 others cloudy.
March	78	66	12	71 —	75	72	N.E.	Rain 5 days; 8 others cloudy.
April	81	62	19	72 —	78	73	Variable	Rain 5 days; 12 others cloudy.
May	81	72	9	75 —	80	76	N.E.	Rain 4 days; 3 others cloudy.
June	84	71	13	76 —	81	78	N.E.	Cloudy 6 days.
July	84	74	10	76 —	83	78	N.E.	Rain 5 days; 7 others cloudy.
Result for the year...	80°	61°	27°	70° —	83°	75°	N.E.	Rain on 40 days; generally clear at other times.

yards in length, and three or four yards in breadth, yet they are woven by the hand, without any loom or frame, with surprising regularity and exactness.

They are made with a fine kind of rush, part of which they stain of a red colour with vegetable dyes, and form their beautiful patterns by weaving them into the mat at its first fabrication, or weaving them in after it is finished.

The natives of these islands are also distinguished for the cultivation of the yam, which grows very large, both at Tauai and Nihau, and contributes essentially to the support of the inhabitants. As they are not cultivated to any extent in the other islands, many ships are induced to visit there, principally for the purpose of procuring a supply; they are not only an excellent root, but will keep a long time at sea without deterioration.

THE ISLAND OF KAULA

TAURA, is another small island belonging to the group, lying in a south-western direction from Tauai; but it is only a barren rock, the resort of vast numbers of aquatic birds, for the purpose of procuring which, it is occasionally visited by the natives of the windward islands.

Adjacent to the shores of most of the islands, small reefs of white coral, common throughout the Pacific, are occasionally found; but they are not so varied in their kind, so frequently met with, nor so extensive, as in all the southern islands.

The climate is not insalubrious, though warm, and debilitating to an European constitution. There is nothing like winter; and the only variation in the uniformity of the seasons, is occasioned by the frequent and heavy rains, which usually fall between December and March, and the prevalence of southerly and variable winds during the same season.

The accompanying tabular view of a meteorological journal *(see page 16),* kept by the American missionaries, will show more fully the state of the weather for a year, from August, 1821, to July, 1822; the thermometer was noted at 8 a.m., 3 p.m. and 8 p.m.

Rain falls but seldom on the western shores of any of the islands, excepting in the season above mentioned, though showers are frequent on the eastern or windward side, and in the mountains occur almost daily.

The soil is rich in those parts which have long been free from volcanic eruptions; but the general appearance of the country is hardly so inviting as when first discovered; many parts, then under cultivation, are now lying waste.

PHYSICAL CHARACTERISTICS OF NATIVES

The natives are in general rather above the middle stature, well formed, with fine muscular limbs, open countenances, and features frequently resembling those of Europeans. Their gait is graceful, and sometimes stately.

The chiefs in particular are tall and stout, and their personal appearance is so much superior to that of the common people, that some have imagined them a distinct race. This, however, is not the fact; the great care taken of them in childhood, and their better living, have probably occasioned the difference. Their hair is black or brown, strong, and frequently curly; their complexion is neither yellow like the Malays, nor red like the American Indians, but a kind of olive, and sometimes reddish-brown. Their arms, and other parts of the body, are tatau'd; but, except in one of the islands, this is by no means so common as in many parts of the Southern sea.

POPULATION—CAUSES OF DEPOPULATION

Compared with the inhabitants of other islands, they may be termed numerous. They were estimated by their discoverers at 400,000. There is reason to believe this was somewhat above the actual population at that time, though traces of deserted villages, and numerous enclosures formerly cultivated, but now abandoned, are every where to be met with.

At present it does not exceed 130,000 or 150,000, of which 85,000 inhabit the island of Hawaii.

The rapid depopulation which has most certainly taken place within the last fifty years, is to be attributed to the frequent and desolating wars which marked the early part of Tamehameha's reign; the ravages of a pestilence brought in the first instance by foreign vessels, which has twice, during the above period, swept through the islands; the awful prevalence of infanticide; and the melancholy increase and destructive consequences of depravity and vice.

ANIMALS OF HAWAII

The natural history of the islands, as it regards the animal kingdom, is exceedingly circumscribed. The only quadrupeds originally found inhabiting them, were a small species of hogs, with long heads and small erect ears; dogs, lizards, and an animal larger than a mouse, but smaller than a rat. There were no beasts of prey, nor any ferocious animals, except the hogs, which were sometimes found wild in the mountains.

There are now large herds of cattle in Hawaii, and some tame ones in most of the islands, together with flocks of goats, and a few horses and sheep, which have been taken there at different times, principally from the adjacent continent of America.

Horses, cattle, and goats, thrive well, but the climate appears too

16

warm for sheep, unless they are kept on the mountains, which, in consequence of the keenness of the air, are seldom inhabited by the natives.

Birds, excepting those which are aquatic, and a species of owl that preys upon mice, are seldom seen near the shores. In the mountains they are numerous; and the notes of one kind, whose colour is brown and yellow speckled, are exceedingly sweet, resembling those of the English thrush. Several are remarkably beautiful, among which may be reckoned a small kind of paroquet of a glossy purple, and a species of red, yellow, and green woodpecker, with whose feathers the gods were dressed, and the helmets and handsome cloaks of the chiefs are ornamented. But the feathered tribes of Hawaii are not in general distinguished by variety of plumage, or melody in their notes.

There are wild geese in the mountains, and ducks near the lagoons or ponds in the vicinity of the sea shore; the domestic fowl was found there by their first discoverer, and though now seldom used as an article of food, is raised for the supply of shipping.

In common with the other islands of the Pacific, they are entirely free from every noxious and poisonous reptile, excepting centipedes, which are neither large nor numerous.

Fish are not so abundant on their shores as around many of the other islands; they have, however, several varieties, and the inhabitants procure a tolerable supply.

PRODUCTS OF THE SOIL

The vegetable productions, though less valuable and abundant than on some of the islands both to the west and the south, are found in no small variety, and the most serviceable are cultivated with facility.

The natives subsist principaly on the roots of the *arum esculentum,* which they call taro, on the *convulvulus batatas,* or sweet potato, called by them uara, and uhi, or yam.

The principal indigenous fruits are the uru, or bread-fruit; the niu, or cocoa-nut; the maia, or plantain; the ohia, a species of eugenia; and the strawberry and raspberry.

Oranges, limes, citrons, grapes, pine-apples, papaw-apples, cucumbers, and water melons, have been introduced, and, excepting the pineapples thrive well. French beans, onions, pumpkins, and cabbages, have also been added to their vegetables, and, though not esteemed by the natives, are cultivated, to some extent, for the purpose of supplying the shipping.

Sugar-cane is indigenous, and grows to a large size, though it is not much cultivated.

17

Large tracts of fertile land lie waste in most of the islands; and sugar-cane, together with cotton, coffee, and other valuable inter-tropical productions, might be easily raised in considerable quantities, which will, probably, be the case when the natives become more industrious and civilized.

COMMERCIAL ADVANTAGES OF HAWAII

The local situation of the Sandwich Islands is important, and highly advantageous for purposes of commerce, &c. On the north are the Russian settlements in Kamtschatka, and the neighbouring coast; to the north-west the islands of Japan; due west the Marian islands, Manila in the Philippines, and Canton in China; and on the east the coast of California and Mexico. Hence they are so frequently resorted to by vessels navigating the northern Pacific.

The establishment of the independent states of South America has greatly increased their importance, as they lie in the track of vessels passing from thence to China, or Calcutta and other parts of India, and are not only visited by these, but by those who trade for skins, &c. with the natives of the north-west coast of America.

VISITS TO HAWAII AFTER DISCOVERY

From the time of their discovery, the Sandwich Islands were unvisited until 1786, when Captains Dixon and Portlock, in a trading voyage to the north-west coast for furs and sea-otter skins, anchored, and procured refreshments in the island of Oahu. The island of Maui was visited about the same time by the unfortunate La Perouse.

After this period the islands were frequently visited by vessels engaged in the fur trade. Captain Douglas, of the *Iphigenia,* and Captain Metcalf, of the *Eleanor,* an American boat, were nearly cut off by the turbulent chiefs, who were desirous to procure the guns and ammunition belonging to their vessels, to aid them in carrying their purposes of conquest into effect.

DESTRUCTION OF "FAIR AMERICAN"—CAPTURE OF DAVIS AND YOUNG

The son of the latter, a youth of sixteen, who commanded a schooner, called the *Fair American,* which accompanied the *Eleanor* from Canton, when close in with the land off Mouna Huararai, was becalmed; the natives thronged on board, threw young Metcalf overboard, seized and plundered the vessel, and murdered all the crew, excepting the mate, whose name was Isaac Davis. He resided many years with Tamehameha, who very severely censured the chief under whose direction this outrage had been committed.

A seaman whose name is Young, belonging to the *Eleanor,* who was

18

on shore at the time, was prevented from gaining his vessel, but was kindly treated by the king, and is still living at Towaihae.

VISIT OF VANCOUVER AND CESSION OF ISLAND TO BRITISH

In the years 1792 and 1793, Captain Vancouver, while engaged in a voyage of discovery in the North Pacific, spent several months at the Sandwich Islands; and notwithstanding the melancholy catastrophe which had terminated the life of Captain Cook, whom he had accompanied, and the treacherous designs of the warlike and ambitious chiefs towards several of his predecessors, he met with the most friendly treatment from all parties, and received the strongest expressions of confidence from Tamehameha, sovereign of the whole group, who had been wounded in the skirmish that followed the death of their discoverer, but who had ever lamented with deepest regret that melancholy event.

He alone had prevented the murderous intentions of his chieftains towards former vessels from being carried into effect; and it was his uniform endeavour to shew every mark of friendship to those who visited his dominions. His attachment to the English induced him, during the stay of Captain Vancouver, to cede the island of Hawaii to the British crown, and to place himself and his dominions under British protection; an act which was repeated by his son, the late king, on his accession to the sovereignty of all the islands.

The natives received many advantages from the visit of Captain Vancouver; a breed of cattle, and a variety of useful seeds, had been given. Generous and disinterested in his whole behaviour, he secured their friendship and attachment, and many still retain grateful recollections of his visit.

THE SANDAL-WOOD AND WHALING INDUSTRIES

After his departure, the islands were seldom resorted to, except by traders from the United States of America, who, having discovered among them the sandal-wood, conveyed large quantities of it to Canton, where it is readily purchased by the Chinese, manufactured into incense, and burnt in their idol temples.

Subsequently, the South Sea whalers began to fish in the North Pacific, when the Sandwich Islands afforded a convenient rendezvous for refitting and procuring refreshments during their protracted voyages, particularly since they have found the sperm whale on the coast of Japan, where of late years the greater parts of their cargoes have been procured.

ENGLISH MISSION IN THE SOUTH SEAS

So early as the year 1796, the London Missionary Society despatched the ship *Duff* to the South Sea islands; and early in 1797, missionary

19

settlements were established in the Marquesan, Friendly, and Society islands.

The missionary left at the Marquesas, after spending about a year among the people, returned.

The establishment in the Friendly Islands was relinquished, though not till some of the individuals of which it was composed had fallen a sacrifice to the fury of the islanders in their civil wars.

The missionaries in the Society Islands have been enabled to maintain their ground, though exposed to many dangers and privations, and some ill usage. The greater part of them were at one time obliged to leave the islands, in consequence of violent assaults, and the civil wars among the natives. Several of those who left, returned after a very short absence, and rejoined their companions who had remained, and the labours of the missionaries were continued with patience and industry for fifteen years, from the time of their first establishment, without any apparent effect.

FINAL SUCCESS OF MISSION

After this protracted period of discouragement, God has granted them the most astonishing success; and the happy change in the outward circumstances of the people, and the great moral renovation which the reception of the gospel has effected, have more than realized the ardent desires of the missionaries themselves, and the most sanguine anticipations of the friends of the mission.

But though the effects of the London Missionary Society were continued under appearances so inauspicious, with a degree of perseverance which has since been most amply compensated, various causes prevented their making any efforts towards communicating the knowledge of Christ to the Sandwich islanders. While their southern neighbours were enjoying all the advantages of Christianity, they remained under the thick darkness, and moral wretchedness, of one of the most cruel systems of idolatry that ever enslaved any portion of the human species.

ESTABLISHMENT OF AMERICAN MISSION IN HAWAII

The attention of the American churches was at length directed to the Sandwich Islands. Their sympathies were awakened, and resulted in a generous effort to meliorate the wretchedness of their inhabitants. A society already existed, under the name of the American Board of Commissioners for Foreign Missions, the chief seat of whose operations was in the city of Boston, Massachusetts, though including among its members many distinguished individuals in different states of the Union.

In the autumn of 1819, a select and efficient band of missionaries was appointed by this society to establish a mission in the Sandwich

Islands. They landed at Kairua, in Hawaii, on the 4th of February, 1820, and had the satisfaction to find the way in a measure prepared for them, by one of those remarkable events which distinguish the eras in the history of nations, whether barbarous or civilized. This was no other than the abolition of the national idolatry, which, though it was closely interwoven with all the domestic and civil institutions of every class of the inhabitants, upheld by the combined influence of a numerous body of priests, the arbitrary power of warlike chiefs, and the sanction of venerable antiquity, had been publicly and authoritatively prohibited by the king only a few months before their arrival.

THE KING AND THE MISSIONARIES

The motives which influenced the monarch of Hawaii in this decisive measure, the war it occasioned, and the consequences which ensued, are detailed in the following narrative. The missionaries could not but view it as a remarkable interposition of divine Providence in their favour, and a happy prelude to the introduction of that gospel which they had conveyed to these shores.

They had naturally expected that their landing would be opposed by the institutions of a system, which, however degrading and oppressive in its influence, had presented more than human claims to the support of its adherents,—and to be withstood by a numerous and influential class of priests, whose craft would be endangered so soon as they should present the paramount claims of the true God to the homage of the heart and uniform obedience of the life.

A NATION WITHOUT A RELIGION

Instead of this, they found the laws of the Tabu entirely abrogated, and priests no longer existing as a distinct body, but merged in the other classes of the community.

The whole nation was without any religion, and in this respect at least prepared to receive the dispensation of the gospel, recommended as it was, by an exemption from all the miseries of their former system, and the animating prospects of life and immortality.

Notwithstanding this, the missionaries, in the commencement of their efforts to instruct the natives, met with some opposition from misinformed and jealous individuals, who entertained groundless suspicions as to the ultimate object of their mission. This, however, was overruled by Karaimoku, Keopuolani, and other leading chiefs, and the king willingly allowed them to remain at least for a year.

They were accompanied by several native youths, whom a roving disposition had induced to visit America, where they had been educated in a school for instructing the aborigines of various heathen nations,

21

designated the Foreign Mission School, and who, having given pleasing evidence of piety, and understanding English, were qualified to act as interpreters, and assist the missionaries in the acquisition of the language.

The difficult task of settling the orthography of an unwritten language, required all their energies; but by diligent application, and the help of the elementary books in the dialects of the Society Islands and New Zealand, they were enabled, in the beginning of 1822, to put to press the first sheet of a Hawaiian spelling-book, and to present the natives with the elements of the vernacular tongue in a printed form.

Schools were established on a scale less extended than the missionaries desired, but not without advantage, as many of their early scholars made encouraging proficiency, and have since become useful teachers. The more public instructions were generally well received by the people.

Tamehameha, who had governed the islands thirty years, and whose decease took place not twelve months before their arrival, had invariably rendered the most prompt and acceptable aid to those English vessels which had touched at the islands. In return for the friendship so uniformly manifested, the British government instructed the governor of New South Wales to order a schooner to be built at Port Jackson, and sent as a present to the king of the Sandwich Islands. In the month of February, 1822, his majesty's colonial cutter, *Mermaid,* having in charge the vessel designed for the king of Hawaii, put into the harbour of Huahine for refreshments. The captain of the *Mermaid* politely offered a passage either to the deputation from the London Missionary Society, then at Huahine, or any of the missionaries who might wish to visit the Sandwich Islands.

We had long been anxious to establish a mission among the Marquesas; and as he intended touching at those islands on his return, it appeared a very favourable opportunity for accomplishing it, and at the same time visiting the American missionaries, the intelligence of whose embarkation for Hawaii had been previously received.

MISSIONARY DELEGATION VISITS HAWAII

Two pious natives, members of the church, and one of them a chief of some rank in the islands, were selected for the Marquesas; and I accompanied the deputation on their visit to Hawaii, for the purpose of aiding in the establishment of the native teachers in the former islands, observing how the people were disposed to receive instructors, and obtaining such other information as might be serviceable in directing our future endeavours to maintain permanent missionary stations among them.

In the month of March we reached the Sandwich Islands, and received a cordial welcome, not only from the American missionaries, but from the king and chiefs, to whom the generous present of the British government was peculiarly acceptable.

Shortly after our arrival, a public council of the king and chiefs of Hawaii was held at Oahu. Auna and his companion, from Huahine, were invited to attend, and had an opportunity of answering the inquiries of the king and chiefs relative to the events which had transpired in the Society Islands, and of testifying to the feelings of friendship and esteem entertained by Pomare, and the rulers of those islands, much to the satisfaction of the latter; who were convinced that the reports which had been circulated among them respecting the hostile intentions of the southern islanders, and the dangerous influence of Christian missions there, were totally groundless.

ELLIS REMAINS IN HAWAII

We did not expect, when we first arrived, to spend more than a fortnight or three weeks in the Sandwich Islands; but circumstances unforeseen, and entirely beyond our control, detained us four months in Oahu.

In two months I was enabled to converse with facility, and preach to the people in their own language, which I soon perceived was only a dialect of that spoken by the natives of Tahiti, and the neighbouring islands.

Auna and his companion were at the same time diligently and acceptably employed in teaching some chiefs of distinction in Hawaii, who requested that he would relinquish his voyage to the Marquesas, and fix his residence among them; to which he cheerfully consented.

Several of the principal chiefs also expressed a wish that I should associate with the teachers already engaged in their instruction. The American missionaries at the same time affectionately inviting me to join them, and the measure meeting the approbation of the deputation, it appeared my duty to comply with their request.

Early in February, 1823, I returned to Oahu with my family, experienced a kind reception from the king and chiefs, and was privileged to commence my missionary pursuits in harmonious coöperation with my predecessors, the American missionaries, who were diligently employed in their benevolent exertions for the spiritual well-being of the nation; AVOIDING, AS THEY HAVE UNIFORMLY DONE EVER SINCE, ALL INTERFERENCE WITH THE ÇIVIL, COMMERCIAL, AND POLITICAL CONCERNS OF THE PEOPLE, AND ATTENDING SOLELY TO THEIR INSTRUCTION IN USEFUL KNOWLEDGE AND RELIGIOUS TRUTH.

The difficulties attending the acquisition of the language, and other circumstances, had hitherto confined the labours of the missionaries

23

almost entirely to the islands of Oahu and Tauai; but in April, 1823, a reinforcement arriving from America, enabled them to extend their efforts, particularly towards Maui and Hawaii.

EXPLORING EXPEDITION TO HAWAII

In order that arrangements for the establishment and permanent maintenance of missionary stations in the latter, the largest, most important, and most populous island of the group, might be made with all the advantages of local knowledge, it was agreed that three of the American missionaries and myself should visit and explore that interesting island, to investigate the religious and moral condition of the people, communicate to them the knowledge of Christ, unfold the benevolent objects of the mission, inquire whether they were willing to receive Christian teachers, and select the most eligible places for missionary stations.

These, though the principal, were not the only objects that occupied our attention during the tour. We availed ourselves of the opportunities it afforded to make observations on the structure of the island, its geographical character, natural scenery, productions, and objects of curiosity; and to become more fully acquainted with the peculiar features of the system of idolatry, the traditions, manners, and customs of the inhabitants,—a detailed account of which is given in the following narrative.

HAWAIIAN ORTHOGRAPHY EXPLAINED

Before entering upon the tour, a few remarks on the orthography of the Hawaiian names which are occasionally introduced, explaining the reasons for its adoption, and assisting in the pronunciation of native words, will probably be acceptable to most of our readers.

The visits which most foreigners have paid to the Sandwich and other islands of the Pacific, have been too transient to allow them, however well qualified they may have been, to become acquainted with the nice distinction of vowel sounds, and peculiar structure, of the aboriginal languages of the islands; and those individuals whom purposes of commerce have induced to remain a longer period among them, whatever facility they may have acquired in speaking it, have not attended to its orthographical construction, but have adopted that method of spelling names of persons and places which happen to have been used by those of their predecessors, with whose printed accounts they were most familiar.

The want of a standard orthography cannot be better illustrated, than by noticing the great variety of methods adopted by different voyagers to represent the same word.

24

We have seen the name of Tamehameha, the late king, spelt in various publications twelve or fourteen different ways; and the same variety has also prevailed in other popular names, though perhaps not to an equal extent. The above word is a reduplication of the simple word meha, (lonely, or solitary,) with the definite article Ta prefixed, which is a part of the name; though rejected in Cook's Voyages, where he is called Maihamaiha. Captain Vancouver calls him Tamaahmaah, which is somewhat nearer.

This disagreement in different writers arises, in the first place, from the deficiency in the vowel characters as used in the English language, for expressing the native vowel sounds.

The English language has but one sign, or letter, for the vowel sound in the first syllable of father and fable, or the words tart and tale; but in Hawaiian the sense of these sounds, which frequently occur unconnected with any other, is so different, that a distinct character is essential.

The first sound is often a distinct word, and frequently marks the future tense of the verb, while the second sound distinguishes the past, and is also a distinct word. These two sounds often occur together, forming two distinct syllables, as in the interrogation e-a? what? and the word he-a, to call.

In the English language, two letters, called double vowels, are used to lengthen the same sound, as ee in thee, or to express one totally different, as oo in pool; but in Hawaiian there is often a repetition of the vowel sound, without any intervening consonant, or other vowel sound, as in a-a, a bag or pocket, e-e, to embark, i-i, a name of a bird, o-o, an agricultural instrument; which must be sounded as two distinct syllables.

Hence when the ee is employed to express a lengthened sound of e, as in Owhyhee, and oo to signify the sound of *u* in rule, as in Karakakooa, which is generally done by European visitors; it is not possible to express by any signs those native words in which the double vowels occur, which are invariably two distinct syllables.

IGNORANCE OF CONSTRUCTION OF LANGUAGE

Another cause of the incorrectness of the orthography of early voyagers to these islands, has been a want of better acquaintance with the structure of the language, which would have prevented their substituting a compound for a single word.

This is the case in the words Otaheiti, Otaha, and Owhyhee, which ought to be Tahiti, Tahaa, and Hawaii.

The O is no part of these words, but is the sign of the case, denoting it to be the nominative answering to the question who or what, which would be O wai?

The sign of the case being prefixed to the interrogation, the answer uniformly corresponds, as,

Nom.   O wai ia aina?—What that land,
       Ans. O Hawaii:—Hawaii.
Pos.   No Hea oe?—Of whence you?
       Ans. No Hawaii:—Of or belonging to Hawaii.
Obj.   Hoe oe i hea?—Sailing you to where?
       Ans. I Hawaii:—To Hawaii.

       Mai hea mai oe?—From whence you?
       Ans. Mai Hawaii mai:—From Hawaii.

In pronouncing the word Ha-wai-i, the Ha is sounded short as in Hah, the wai as wye, and the final i as e in me.

COOK'S AND VANCOUVER'S SPELLING

Atooi in Cook's voyages, Atowai in Vancouver's, and Atoui in one of his contemporaries, is also a compound of two words, a Tauai, literally, and Tauai.

The meaning of the word tauai is to light upon, or to dry in the sun; and the name, according to the account of the late king, was derived from the long droughts which sometimes prevailed, or the large pieces of timber which have been occasionally washed upon its shores.

Being the most leeward island of importance, it was probably the last inquired of, or the last name repeated by the people to the first visitors. For should the natives be pointed to the group, and asked the names of the different islands, beginning with that farthest to windward, and proceeding west, they would say, O Hawaii, Maui, Ranai, Morotai, Oahu a (and) Tauai: the copulative conjunction preceding the last member of the sentence, would be placed immediately before Tauai; and hence, in all probability, it has been attached to the name of that island, which has usually been written, after Cook's orthography, Atooi; or Atowai, after Vancouver.

The more intelligent among the natives, particularly the chiefs, frequently smile at the manner of spelling the names of places and persons, in published accounts of the islands, which they occasionally see, and doubtless wonder how we can employ two letters of the same kind to express two distinct sounds, as aa, for the sound of a in mark, and a in make; or oo for a sound so distinct as us.

PRONUNCIATION OF HAWAIIAN NAMES

The orthography employed in the native names which occur in the succeeding narrative, is in accordance with the power or sound of the

26

letters composing the Hawaiian alphabet, and the words are represented as nearly as possible to the manner in which they are pronounced. by the natives.

A is always as a in father, or shorter as a in the first syllable of aha, e as a in hate, i as i in machine, ee in thee, o as o in note, u as oo in food, or short as in bull, and the diphthong ai as i in wine or mine. The consonants are sounded as in English.

The native words may be correctly pronounced by attending to the above sounds of the vowels.

The following list of the principal names will likewise assist in the proper pronunciation of Hawaiian words. The h is inserted after the a, only to secure that vowel's being sounded as in the exclamation ah!

PLACES

Ha-wai-i, *pronounced as*	Ha-wye-e
O-a-hu	O-ah-hoo
Tau-ai	Tow-i, or Tow-eye
Mau-i	Mow-e
Kai-ru-a	Ky-roo-ah
Ke-a-ra-ke-ku-a	Kay-a-ra-kay-koo-ah
Wai-a-ke-a	Wye-ah-kay-ah
Wai-pi-o	Wye-pe-o
Ki-rau-ea	Ke-row-ay-ah
Pu-ho-nu-a	Poo-ho-noo-ah
Mou-na-hu-a-ra-rai ...	Mow-nah-hoo-ah-ra-rye
Mouna Ro-a	Mow-nah Ro-ah
Mou-na Ke-a	Mow-nah Kay-ah
K-a-a-va-ro-a	Kah-ah-vah-ro-ah

PERSONS

Ta-mé-ha-mé-ha	Ta-mé-hah-mé-hah
Ri-ho-ri-ho	Ree-ho-ree-ho
Ta-u-mu-a-ri-i	Ta-oo-moo-ah-re-e
Ka-a-hu-ma-nu	Ka-ah-hoo-ma-noo
Ke-o-pu-o-la-ni	Kay-o-poo-o-lah-ne
Ku-a-ki-ni	Koo-ah-ke-ne
Ka-rai-mo-ku	Ka-rye-mo-koo
Bo-ki	Bo-ke
Li-li-ha	Le-le-hah
Mau-ae	Mow-aye
Ma-ko-a	Ma-ko-ah

27

CHAPTER II

TAUMUARII, the friendly king of Tauai, having generously offered the missionaries chosen to make the tour of Hawaii, (Owhyhee), a passage in one of his vessels bound from Oahu to Kairua; Messrs. Thurston, Bishop, and Goodrich, repaired on board in the afternoon of June 24, 1823. They were accompanied by Mr. Harwood, an ingenious mechanic, whom curiosity, and a desire to assist them, had induced to join their party. The indisposition of Mrs. Ellis prevented my proceeding in the same vessel, but I hoped to follow in a few days.

At 4 p.m. the brig was under weigh, standing to the S. E. Having cleared the bar, and the reefs at the entrance of the harbour, the trade-wind blowing fresh from the N. E. they were soon out of sight of Honoruru. They passed the islands of Morokai, Ranai, and the principal part of Maui (Mowee) during the night, and at daybreak on the 25th were off Tahaurawe, a small island on the south side of Maui.

The *Haaheo Hawaii,* (Pride of Hawaii) another native vessel, formerly the *Cleopatra's Barge,* soon after hove in sight; she did not, however, come up with them, but tacked, and stood for Lahaina. In the evening, the wind, usually fresh in the channel between Maui and Hawaii, blew so strong, that they were obliged to lay-to for about three hours; when it abated, and allowed them to proceed.

A QUICK TRIP TO KAILUA

On the 26th, at 4 p.m., the vessel came to anchor in Kairua bay. The missionaries soon after went on shore, grateful for the speedy and comfortable passage with which they had been favoured, having been only forty-nine hours from Oahu, which is about 150 miles to the leeward of Kairua. They were heartily welcomed by the governor, Kuakini, usually called by the foreigners, John Adams, from his having adopted the name of a former president of the United States of America. They took tea with him; and after expressing their gratitude to God in the native language with the governor and his family, retired to rest in an apartment kindly furnished for them in his own house.

The next morning their baggage was removed from the vessel, and deposited in a small comfortable house, formerly belonging to Tamehameha, but which the governor directed them to occupy so long as they should remain at Kairua. He also politely invited them to his table, during their stay; in consequence of which, without forgetting their character, they sat down to their morning repast.

Their breakfast room presented a singular scene. They were seated around a small table with the governor and one or two of his friends, who, in addition to the coffee, fish, vegetables, &c., with which it was furnished, had a large wooden bowl of poë, a sort of thin paste made of baked taro, beat up and diluted with water, placed by the side of their plates, from which they frequently took very hearty draughts.

Two favourite lap-dogs sat on the same sofa with the governor, one on his right hand and the other on his left, and occasionally received a bit from his hand, or the fragments on the plate from which he had eaten.

A number of his punahele, (favourite chiefs), and some occasional visitors, sat in circles on the floor, around large dishes of raw fish, baked hog, or dog, or goat, from which each helped himself without ceremony, while a huge calabash of poë passed rapidly round among them. They became exceedingly loquacious and cheerful during their meal; and several who had been silent before, now laughed loud, and joined with spirit in the mirth of their companions.

Neat wooden dishes of water were handed to the governor and his friends, both before and after eating, in which they washed their hands.

Uncivilized nations are seldom distinguished by habits of cleanliness; but this practice, we believe, is an ancient custom, generally observed by the chiefs, and all the higher orders of the people, throughout the islands.

SCARCITY OF WATER AT KAILUA

Kairua, though healthy and populous, is destitute of fresh water, except what is found in pools, or small streams, in the mountains, four or five miles from the shore. An article so essential to the maintenance of a missionary station, it was desirable to procure, if possible, nearer at hand. The late king Tamehameha used frequently to beg a cask of water from the captains of vessels touching at Kairua; and it is one of the most acceptable presents a captain going to this station could make, either to the chiefs or missionaries. As soon therefore as breakfast was ended, the party walked through the district in a south-east direction, to examine the ground, with a view to discover the most eligible place for digging a well.

The whole face of the country marked decisively its volcanic origin; and in the course of their excursion they entered several hollows in the lava, formed by its having cooled and hardened on the surface, while, in a liquid state underneath, it had continued to flow towards the sea, leaving a crust in the shape of a tunnel, or arched vault, of varied thickness and extent.

Before they returned, they also explored a celebrated cavern in the vicinity, called Raniakea. After entering it by a small aperture, they passed on in a direction nearly parallel with the surface; sometimes along a spacious arched way, not less than twenty-five feet high and twenty wide; at other times, by a passage so narrow, that they could with difficulty press through, till they had proceedel about 1200 feet; here their progress was arrested by a pool of water, wide, deep, and as salt as that found in the hollows of the lava within a few yards of the sea. This latter circumstance, in a great degree, damped their hopes of finding fresh water by digging through the lava.

More than thirty natives, most of them carrying torches, accompanied them in their descent; and on arriving at the water, simultaneously plunged in, extending their torches with one hand, and swimming about with the other.

The partially illuminated heads of the natives, splashing about in this subterranean lake; the reflection of the torch-light on its agitated surface; the frowning sides and lofty arch of the black vault, hung with lava, that had cooled in every imaginable shape; the deep gloom of the cavern beyond the water; the hollow sound of their footsteps; and the varied reverberations of their voices, produced a singular effect; and it would have required but little aid from the fancy, to have imagined a resemblance between this scene and the fabled Stygian lake of the poets.

The mouth of the cave is about half a mile from the sea, and the perpendicular depth to the water probably not less than fifty or sixty feet. The pool is occasionally visited by the natives, for the purpose of bathing, as its water is cool and refreshing. From its ebbing and flowing with the tide, it has probably a direct communication with the sea.

HUALALAI IN ERUPTION

In the afternoon, Messrs. Thurston and Bishop walked out in a N.W. direction, till they reached the point that forms the northern boundary of the bay, on the eastern side of which Kairua is situated. It runs three or four miles into the sea; is composed entirely of lava; and was formed by an eruption from one of the large craters on the top of Mouna Huararai, (Mount Huararai), which, about twenty-three years ago, inundated several villages, destroyed a number of plantations and extensive fish-ponds, filled up a deep bay twenty miles in length, and formed the present coast.

An Englishman, who has resided thirty-eight years in the islands, and who witnessed the above eruption, has frequently told us he was astonished at the irresistible impetuosity of the torrent.

Stone walls, trees, and houses, all gave way before it; even large masses or rocks of hard ancient lava, when surrounded by the fiery stream, soon split into small fragments, and falling into the burning mass, appeared to melt again, as borne by it down the mountain's side.

Numerous offerings were presented, and many hogs thrown alive into the stream, to appease the anger of the gods, by whom they supposed it was directed, and to stay its devastating course.

All seemed unavailing, until one day the king Tamehameha went, attended by a large retinue of chiefs and priests, and, as the most valuable offering he could make, cut off part of his own hair, which was always considered sacred, and threw it into the torrent.

A day or two after, the lava ceased to flow. The gods, it was thought, were satisfied; and the king acquired no small degree of influence over the minds of the people, who, from this circumstance, attributed their escape from threatened destruction to his supposed interest with the deities of the volcanoes.

In several places they observed that the sea rushes with violence twenty or thirty yards along the cavities beneath the lava, and then, forcing its waters through the apertures in the surface, forms a number of beautiful *jets d'eau,* which falling again on the rocks, roll rapidly back to the ocean.

SUBURBS OF KAILUA DESCRIBED

They enjoyed a fine view of the town and adjacent country. The houses, which are neat, are generally built on the sea-shore, shaded with cocoa-nut and kou trees, which greatly enliven the scene.

The environs were cultivated to a considerable extent; small gardens were seen among the barren rocks on which the houses are built, wherever soil could be found sufficient to nourish the sweet potato, the water-melon, or even a few plants of tobacco, and in many places these seemed to be growing literally in the fragments of lava, collected in small heaps around their roots.

The next morning, Messrs. Thurston, Goodrich, and Harwood, walked towards the mountains, to visit the high and cultivated parts of the district. After travelling over the lava for about a mile, the hollows in the rocks began to be filled with a light brown soil; and about half a mile further, the surface was entirely covered with a rich mould, formed by decayed vegetable matter and decomposed lava.

Here they enjoyed the agreeable shade of bread-fruit and ohia trees; the latter is a deciduous plant, a variety of eugenia, resembling the *eugenia malaccensis,* bearing a beautifully red pulpy fruit, of the size and consistence of an apple, juicy, but rather insipid to the taste. The trees are elegant in form, and grow to the height of twenty or thirty feet; the leaf is oblong and pointed, and the flowers are attached to the branches by a short stem. The fruit is abundant, and is generally ripe, either on different places in the same island, or on different islands, during all the summer months.

INLAND CULTIVATION

The path now lay through a beautiful part of the country, quite a garden compared with that through which they had passed on first leaving the town. It was generally divided into small fields, about fifteen rods square, fenced with low stone walls, built with fragments of lava gathered from the surface of the enclosures. These fields were planted with bananas, sweet potatoes, mountain taro, paper mulberry plants, melons, and sugar-cane, which flourished luxuriantly in every direction.

Having travelled about three or four miles through this delightful region, and passed several valuable pools of fresh water, they arrived at the thick woods, which extend several miles up the sides of the lofty mountain that rises immediately behind Kairua.

Among the various plants and trees that now presented themselves, they were much pleased with a species of tree ferns, whose stipes were about five feet long, and the stem about fourteen feet high, and one foot in diameter.

A smart shower of rain (a frequent occurrence in the mountains) arrested their further progress, and obliged them to return to their lodgings, where they arrived about five in the afternoon, gratified, though fatigued, by their excursion.

Mr. Bishop called on Thomas Hopu, the native teacher, who has for some time resided at Kairua, and was pleased to find him patient under the inconveniences to which his situation necessarily subjects him, and anxious to promote the best interests of his countrymen.

29th. The Sabbath morning dawned upon the missionaries at Kairua under circumstances unusually animating, and they prepared to spend this holy day in extending, as widely as possible, their labours among the benighted people around them.

Mr. Thurston preached in the native language twice at the governor's house, to attentive audiences. Mr. Bishop and Thomas Hopu proceeded early in the morning to Kaavaroa, a village about fourteen miles distant, on the north side of Kearake'kua, (Karakakooa), where they arrived at 11 a.m.

KAMAKAU, A BENEFICENT CHIEF

Kamakau, chief of the place, received them with many expressions of gladness, led them to his house, and provided some refreshments; after which, they walked together to a ranai, (house of cocoa-nut leaves), which he had some time ago erected for the public worship of Jehovah. Here they found about a hundred of his people assembled, and waiting their arrival.

Mr. Bishop, with the aid of Thomas, preached to them from John iii :16, and endeavoured in the most familiar manner to set before them the great love of God in sending his Son to die for sinners, and the necessity of forsaking sin, and believing in him, in order to attain eternal life.

Towards the latter part of the discourse, the preacher was interrupted by Kamakau, who, anxious that his people might receive the greatest possible benefit by the word spoken, began earnestly to exhort them to listen and regard, telling them, their salvation depended on their attention to the truths which they heard. After the service was concluded, he again addressed them, affectionately recommending them to consider these things.

Kamakau wished them to meet with the people again, but as the day was far spent, they thought it best to return. He then told them, that after their departure he should assemble his people, and repeat to them what they had heard. He asked many questions on religious subjects, several respecting the heavenly state; and appeared interested in the answers that were given; especially when informed that heaven was a holy place, into which nothing sinful could enter.

A DISCARDED IDOL

As they went from his house to the beach, they passed by a large idol, that Kamakau had formerly worshipped, lying prostrate and mutilated on the rocks, and washed by the waves of the sea as they rolled on the shore. It was a huge log of wood, rudely carved, presenting a hideous form, well adapted to infuse terror into an ignorant and superstitious mind.

On his being asked why he had worshipped that log of wood? he answered,—because he was afraid he would destroy his cocoa-nuts. But were you not afraid to destroy it? "No, I found he did me neither good nor harm. I thought he was no god, and threw him away." Bidding him farewell, they stepped into their canoe, and returned to Kairua, where they arrived in the evening, encouraged by the incidents of the day.

Kamakau is a chief of considerable rank and influence in Hawaii, though not immediately connected with any of the reigning family. He is cousin to Naihe, the friend and companion of Tamehameha, and the principal national orator of the Sandwich Islands. His person, like that of the chiefs in general, is noble and engaging. He is about six feet high, stout, well-proportioned, and more intelligent and enterprising than the people around him. For some time past he has established family worship

33

in his house, and the observance of the Sabbath throughout his district; having erected a place for the public worship of the true God, in which, every Lord's day, he assembles his people for the purpose of exhortation and prayer, which he conducts himself.

He is able to read, writes an easy and legible hand, has a general knowledge of the first principles of Christianity, and, what is infinitely better, appears to feel their power on his heart, and evince their purity in his general conduct. His attainments are truly surprising, manifesting a degree of industry and perseverance rarely displayed under similar circumstances.

His sources of information have been very limited. An occasional residence of a few weeks at Honoruru, one or two visits of the missionaries and of some of the native teachers to his house, and letters from Naihe, are the chief advantages he has enjoyed.

He appears, indeed, a modern Cornelius, and is a striking manifestation of the sovereignty of that grace of which we trust he has been made a partaker; and we rejoice in the pleasing hope that He who has "begun a good work, will perform it until the day of Christ."

INCIDENTS OF LIFE AT KAILUA

In the forenoon of the first of July, two posts of observation were fixed, and a base line of 200 feet was measured, in order to ascertain the height of Mouna Huararai; but the summit being covered with clouds, they were obliged to defer their observation.

In the afternoon they walked through the S. E. part of the town to select a spot in which to dig for fresh water. After an accurate investigation of the places adjacent, in which they thought it might be found, they chose a valley, about half a mile from the residence of the governor, and near the entrance of Raniakea, as the spot where they were most likely to meet with success.

The 4th of July being the anniversary of the American independence, guns were fired at the fort, the colours hoisted, and a hospitable entertainment given at the governor's table. The missionaries employed the greater part of the day at the well, which early in the morning they had commenced.

In the evening, while at tea, considerable attention was attracted by a slender man, with a downcast look, in conversation with the governor.

It afterwards appeared, that this was a stranger, from Maui, who wished to be thought a prophet, affirming that he was inspired by a shark, that enabled him to tell future events. The governor said, many of the people believed in him, and from them he obtained a living.

The excavations of the well proceeded but slowly during the next day. Hard and closely imbedded lava rendered the work difficult. But as the governor promises assistance, they are encouraged to proceed.

RELIGIOUS INSTRUCTION IMPARTED

The next day being the Sabbath, Mr. Bishop preached twice at the governor's house, Thomas Hopu acting as interpreter. The congregation consisted principally of Kuakini's attendants and domestics, the greater part of the population conceiving themselves under no obligation to hear preaching, as they do not know how to read; pretending, that ignorance exempts them from all obligation to attend religious exercises.

Leaving Kairua early, in a canoe with four men, provided by the governor, Messrs. Thurston and Goodrich reached Kaavaroa about nine o'clock in the morning. Kamakau was waiting for them, and seemed to rejoice at their arrival. He led them to his house, and provided them with a frugal breakfast, after which they repaired in company to the ranai for public worship. On reaching it, they found about one hundred of the people already there. Before the service commenced, the chief arose, directed them to remain quiet, and pay the greatest attention to the word of life, which they were about to hear.

Shortly after the conclusion of the service, the missionaries passed over Kearake'kua bay, in a canoe, landed on the opposite side, and walked along the shore about a mile, to Karama. Here, in a large house, they collected about three hundred people; to whom Mr. Thurston preached, and was pleased with the interest they manifested. Some who stood near the speaker, repeated the whole discourse, sentence by sentence, in a voice too low to create disturbance, yet loud enough to be distinctly heard.

There were seven or eight American and English seamen present, who requested that they might be addressed in their own language. Mr. Goodrich accordingly preached to them from Rev. iii. 20.

REMINISCENCES OF CAPTAIN COOK

Returning from Karama to the southern side of Kearake'kua bay, where they had left their canoe, they passed the ruins of an old heiau, the morai mentioned in Captain Cook's voyage, where the observatory was erected.

The remaining walls were one hundred feet long and fifteen high, and the space within was strewed with animal and human bones, the relics of the sacrifices once offered there; a scene truly affecting to a Christian mind.

Leaving this melancholy spot, they returned in their canoe to Kaavaroa: and when the people had assembled in the ranai, Mr. Thurston preached to them from Psalm cxviii. 24: "This is the day the Lord hath made: we will rejoice and be glad in it."

About sun-set, Mr. Goodrich ascended a neighbouring height, and visited the spot where the body of the unfortunate Captain Cook was cut to pieces, and the flesh, after being separated from the bones, was burnt. It is a small enclosure, about fifteen feet square, surrounded by a wall five feet high; within is a kind of hearth, raised about eighteen inches from the ground, and encircled by a curb of rude stones. Here the fire was kindled on the above occasion; and the place is still strewed with charcoal. The natives mention the interment of another foreigner on this spot; but could not tell to what country he belonged, or the name of the vessel in which he was brought.

MISSION ASSISTED BY KAMAKAU

Kamakau and his people had interested his visitors so much, that they determined to spend the night at his house. After supper, the members of the family, with the domestics and one or two strangers, met for evening worship: a hymn was sung in the native language, and Kamakau himself engaged in prayer with great fervour and propriety. He prayed particularly for the king, chiefs, and people, of Hawaii, and the neighbouring islands; and for the missionaries, who had brought the good word of salvation to them.

The brethren were surprised to hear him use so much evangelical language in prayer. During the conversation of the evening, he expressed a desire, which has since been gratified, that a missionary might reside in his neighbourhood, that he and his people might be instructed in the word of God; might learn to read and write, and become acquainted with what the missionaries were teaching at the stations where they dwelt. He is about fifty years of age, and regretted exceedingly, as many others have also done, that he was so far advanced in life before the missionaries arrived at the islands.

The Sabbath passed away pleasantly, and, it is to be hoped, profitably, both to the interesting inhabitants of the place, and their guests; and the latter retired to rest, animated and encouraged by what they had that day witnessed. Early next morning they set out for Kairua, where they arrived about nine o'clock in the forenoon.

Unable to proceed with the well for want of proper instruments with which to drill the rocks, the greater part of this day was spent in ascertaining the population of Kairua.

Numbering the houses for one mile along the coast, they found them to be 529; and allowing an average of five persons to each house, the inhabitants in Kairua will amount to 2645 persons. This certainly does not exceed the actual population, as few of the houses are small, and many of them large, containing two or three families each.

The varied and strongly marked volcanic surface of the higher parts of the mountain called Mouna Huararai, in the immediate neighbourhood of Kairua; the traditional accounts given by the natives of the eruptions, which, from craters on its summit, had in different ages deluged the low land along the coast; the thick woods that skirt its base, and the numerous feathered tribes inhabiting them, rendered it an interesting object, and induced the travellers to commence its ascent.

About eight o'clock in the morning of the 9th, they left Kairua, accompanied by three men, whom they had engaged to conduct them to the summit. Having travelled about twelve miles in a northerly direction, they arrived at the last house on the western side of the mountain. Here their guides wished to remain for the night; and on being urged to proceed, as it was not more than three o'clock in the afternoon, declared they did not know the way, and had never been beyond the spot where they then were. Notwithstanding this disappointment, it was determined to proceed. Leaving the path, the party began to ascend in a S.E. direction, and travelled about six miles, over a rough and difficult road, sometimes across streams of hard lava, full of fissures and chasms, at other times through thick brushwood, or high ferns, so closely interwoven as almost to arrest their progress.

CAMPING ON HUALALAI

Arriving at a convenient place, and finding themselves fatigued, drenched also with the frequent showers, and the wet grass through which they had walked, they proposed to pitch their tent for the night. A temporary hut was erected with branches of the neighbouring trees, and covered with the leaves of the tall ferns that grew around them. At one end of it they lighted a large fire, and, after the rains had abated, dried their clothes, partook of the refreshments they had brought with them, and, having commended themselves to the kind protection of their heavenly Guardian, spread fern leaves and grass upon the lava, and lay down to repose. The thermometer which is usually about 84° on the shore, stood at 60° in the hut where they slept.

The singing of the birds in the surrounding woods ushering in the early dawn, and the cool temperature of the pure mountain air, excited a variety of pleasing sensations in the minds of all the party, when they awoke in the morning, after a comfortable night's rest. The thermometer, when placed outside of the hut, stood at 46°.

Having united in their morning sacrifice of thanksgiving to God, and taken a light breakfast, they resumed their laborious journey. The road, lying through thick underwood and fern, was wet and fatiguing for about two miles, when they arrived at an ancient stream of lava, about twenty rods wide, running in a direction nearly west. Ascending the hardened surface of this stream of lava, over deep chasms, or large

37

volcanic stones imbedded in it, for a distance of three or four miles, they reachèd the top of one of the ridges on the western side of the mountain.

As they travelled along, they met with tufts of strawberries, and clusters of raspberry bushes, loaded with fruit, which, as they were both hungry and thirsty, were very acceptable. The strawberries had rather an insipid taste; the raspberries were white and large, frequently an inch in diameter, but not so sweet or well-flavoured as those cultivated in Europe and America.

Between nine and ten in the forenoon they arrived at a large extinguished crater, about a mile in circumference, and apparently 400 feet deep, probably the same that was visited by some of Vancouver's people, in 1792. The sides sloped regularly, and at the bottom was a small mound, with an aperture in its centre. By the side of this large crater, divided from it by a narrow ridge of volcanic rocks, was another, fifty-six feet in circumference, from which volumes of sulphureous smoke and vapour continually ascended. No bottom could be seen; and on throwing stones into it, they were heard to strike against its sides for eight seconds, but not to reach the bottom. There were two other apertures near this, nine feet in diameter, and apparently about 200 feet deep.

As the party walked along the giddy verge of the large crater, they could distinguish the course of two principal streams, that had issued from it in the great eruption, about the year 1800. One had taken a direction nearly north-east; the other had flowed to the north-west, in broad irresistible torrents, for a distance of twelve or fifteen miles to the sea, where, driving back the waters, it had extended the boundaries of the island. They attempted to descend this crater, but the steepness of its sides prevented their examining it so fully as they desired.

After spending some time there, they walked along the ridge between three and four miles, and examined sixteen different craters, similar in construction to the first they had met with, though generally of smaller dimensions.

The whole ridge, along which they walked, appeared little else than a continued line of craters, which, in different ages, had deluged the valleys below with floods of lava, or showers of burning cinders. Some of these craters appeared to have reposed for ages, as trees of considerable size were growing on their sides, and many of them were covered with earth, and clothed with verdure.

In the vicinity of the craters they found a number of small bushes, bearing red berries in crowded clusters, which, in size and shape, much resembled whortleberries; though insipid, they were juicy, and supplied the place of fresh water, a comfort they had been destitute of since the preceding evening.

RETURN TRIP FROM HUALALAI

They continued ascending till three p.m. when, having suffered much from thirst, and finding they should not be able to reach the highest peak before dark, the sky also being overcast, and the rain beginning to fall, they judged it best to return to Kairua, without having reached the summit of Mouna Huararai; particularly as they were somewhat scattered, and found difficulty in pursuing the most direct way, on account of the thick fog which surrounded the mountain.

On their return they found the aid of their pocket compass necessary to enable them to regain the path by which they had ascended in the morning.

After travelling some time, they beheld with gladness the sun breaking through the fog in which they had been so long enveloped, and, looking over the clouds that rolled at their feet, saw him gradually sink behind the western wave of the wide extended ocean.

The appearance of the sky, at the setting of the sun, in a tropical climate, is usually beautiful and splendid; it was so this evening; and from their great elevation, the party viewed with delight the magnificent yet transient glories of the closing day.

They travelled about three miles further, when, being wet with the fog, and weary with travelling, they erected a hut on the lava, and encamped for the night. They succeeded in making a good fire, dried their clothes, and then sat down to partake of the little refreshment that was left. It consisted of a small quantity of hard taro paste, called by the natives ai paa. A little water would have been agreeable, but of this they were destitute. Having gathered some fern leaves, they strewed them on the lava, and laid down to repose.

On the morning of the 11th, the party still felt unwilling to return without reaching the top of the mountain, and hesitated before they began again to descend; but having been a day and two nights without water, and seeing no prospect of procuring any there, they were obliged to direct their steps towards Kairua.

They walked several miles along the rough stream of lava by which they had ascended, till they arrived at the woody part of the mountain. Two of them, in searching for a more direct road to Kairua, discovered an excellent spring of water. They soon communicated the agreeable intelligence to their companions, who hastened to the spot, and, with copious draughts, quenched their thirst. Having filled their canteens, they, with renewed strength and grateful hearts, kept on their way to the town.

39

Owing to the roughness of the paths, and the circuitous route by which they travelled, they did not arrive at Kairua until after sunset, much fatigued, and almost barefoot, their shoes having been destroyed by the sharp projections in the lava.

They refreshed themselves at the governor's, and after uniting with him and his family in an evening tribute of praise to God, they repaired to their lodgings, somewhat disappointed, yet well repaid for the toil of their journey.

CHAPTER III

EIGHT DAYS after the departure of Mr. Thurston and his companions, I followed in a small schooner belonging to Keopuolani, bound first to Lahaina, and then to Hawaii for sandal wood.

Kalakua, one of the queens of the late Tamehameha, and Kekauruohe her daughter, were proceeding in the same vessel to join the king and other chiefs at Maui. The trade wind blew fresh from the northeast, and the sea was unusually rough in the channel between Oahu and Morokai. The schooner appeared to be a good sea-boat, but proved a very uncomfortable one; the deck, from stem to stern, being continually overflowed, all who could not get below were constantly drenched with the spray.

The cabin was low, and so filled with the chief women and their companions, that, where space could be found sufficient to stand or sit, it was hardly possible to endure the heat. The evening, however, was fine, and the night free from rain.

At daylight next morning, being close in with the west point of Morokai, we tacked, and stood to the southward till noon, when we again steered to the northward, and at four o'clock in the afternoon were within half a mile of the high bluff rocks which form the southern point of Ranai.

STOPPING THE SHIP TO FISH

A light air then came off the land, and carried us slowly along the shore, till about an hour before sun-set, when Kekauruohe said she wished for some fish, and requested the master to stop the vessel while she went to procure them among the adjacent rocks. Her wishes were gratified, and the boat was hoisted out.

Kekauruohe and three of her female attendants proceeded towards the rocks that lie along the base of the precipice, about half a mile distant. The detention thus occasioned afforded time to observe more particularly the neighbouring coast.

The face of the high and perpendicular rocks in this part of the island indicate that Ranai is either of volcanic origin, or, at some remote period, has undergone the action of fire. Different strata of lava, of varied colour and thickness, are distinctly marked from the water's edge to the

41

highest point. These strata, lying almost horizontally, are in some places from twelve to twenty feet thick, in others not more than a foot or eighteen inches.

After fishing about an hour, Kekauruohe and her companions returned with a quantity of limpets, peri-winkles, &c., of which they made a hearty supper. The wind died away with the setting of the sun, until about 9 p.m. when a light breeze came from the land, and wafted us slowly on our passage.

The southern shore of Ranai is usually avoided by masters of vessels acquainted with the navigation among the islands, on account of the light and variable winds or calms generally experienced there; the course of the trade-winds being intercepted by the high lands of Maui and Ranai.

It is not unusual for vessels, passing that way, to be becalmed there for six, eight, or even ten days. The natives, with the small craft belonging to the islands, usually keep close in shore, avail themselves of the gentle land-breeze to pass the point in the evening, and run into Lahaina with the sea-breeze in the morning; but this is attended with danger, as there is usually a heavy swell rolling in towards the land. One or two vessels have escaped being drifted on the rocks, only by the prompt assistance of their boats.

DESCRIPTION OF LAHAINA

At day-break, on the 4th, we found ourselves within about four miles of Lahaina, which is the principal district in Maui, on account of its being the general residence of the chiefs, and the common resort of ships that touch at the island for refreshments. A dead calm prevailed, but by means of two large sweeps or oars, each worked by four men, we reached the roads, and anchored at 6 a.m.

The appearance of Lahaina from the anchorage is singularly romantic and beautiful. A fine sandy beach stretches along the margin of the sea, lined for a considerable distance with houses, and adorned with shady clumps of kou trees, or waving groves of cocoa-nuts. The former is a species of cordia; the *cordia sebastina* in Cook's voyages.

The level land of the whole district, for about three miles, is one continued garden, laid out in beds of taro, potatoes, yams, sugar-cane, or cloth plants. The lowly cottage of the farmer is seen peeping through the leaves of the luxuriant plantain and banana tree, and in every direction white columns of smoke ascend, curling up among the wide-spreading branches of the bread-fruit tree.

The sloping hills immediately behind, and the lofty mountains in the interior, clothed with verdure to their very summits, intersected by deep and dark ravines, frequently enlivened by glittering waterfalls, or divided by winding valleys, terminate the delightful prospect.

Shortly after coming to anchor, a boat came from the barge, for the chiefs on board, and I accompanied them to the shore.

On landing, I was kindly greeted by Keoua, governor of the place; and shortly afterwards met and welcomed by Mr. Stewart, who was just returning from morning worship with Keopuolani and her husband.

We waited on Rihoriho, the late king, in his tent. He was, as usual, neatly and respectably dressed, having on a suit of superfine blue, made after the European fashion.

We were courteously received, and after spending a few minutes in conversation respecting my journey to Hawaii, and answering his inquiries relative to Oahu, we walked together about half a mile, through groves of plantain and sugar cane, over a well-cultivated tract of land, to Mr. Butler's establishment, in one of whose houses the missionaries were comfortably accommodated, until their own could be erected, and where I was kindly received by all the members of the mission family.

After breakfast I walked down to the beach, and there learned that the king had sailed for Morokai, and that Kalakua intended to follow in the schooner in which she had come from Oahu. This obliged me to wait for the *Ainoa,* another native vessel, hourly expected at Lahaina, on her way to Hawaii.

ATTITUDE OF QUEEN KEOPUOLANI

The forenoon was spent in conversation with Keopuolani, queen of Maui, and mother of Rihoriho, king of all the islands. She, as well as the other chiefs present, appeared gratified with an account of the attention given to the means of instruction at Oahu, and desirous that the people of Lahaina might enjoy all the advantages of Christian education. Taua, the native teacher from Huahine, appeared diligently employed among Keopuolani's people, many of whom were his scholars; and I was happy to learn from Messrs. Stewart and Richards, that he was vigilant and faithful in his work.

At sun-rise next morning, Mr. Stewart and I walked down to Keopuolani's, to attend the usual morning exercises, in the large house near the sea. About fifty persons were present. In the afternoon I accompanied the missionaries to their schools on the beach. The proficiency of many of the pupils in reading, spelling, and writing on slates, was pleasing.

A HULA DESCRIBED

Just as they had finished their afternoon instruction, a party of musicians and dancers arrived before the house of Keopuolani, and commenced a hura ka raau, (dance to the beating of a stick). Five

43

musicians advanced first, each with a staff in his left hand, five or six feet long, about three or four inches in diameter at one end, and tapering off to a point at the other.

In his right hand he held a small stick of hard wood, six or nine inches long, with which he commenced his music, by striking the small stick on the larger one, beating time all the while with his right foot on a stone, placed on the ground beside him for that purpose.

Six women, fantastically dressed in yellow tapas, crowned with garlands of flowers, having also wreaths of the sweet-scented flowers of the gardenia on their necks, and branches of the fragrant mairi, (another native plant), bound round their ankles, now made their way by couples through the crowd, and, arriving at the area, on one side of which the musicians stood, began their dance.

Their movements were slow, and though not always graceful, exhibited nothing offensive to modest propriety.

Both musicians and dancers alternately chanted songs in honour of former gods and chiefs of the islands, apparently much to the gratification of the numerous spectators.

FROM HULA TO PRAYERS

After they had continued their hura, (song and dance), for about half an hour, the queen, Keopuolani, requested them to leave off, as the time had arrived for evening worship. The music ceased; the dancers sat down; and, after the missionaries and some of the people had sung one of the songs of Zion, I preached to the surrounding multitude with special reference to their former idolatrous dances, and the vicious customs connected therewith, from Acts xvii. 30. "The times of this ignorance God winked at, but now commandeth all men every where to repent."

The audience was attentive; and when the service was finished, the people dispersed, and the dancers returned to their houses.

On our way home, the voice of lamentation arrested our attention. Listening a few moments, we found it proceeded from a lowly cottage, nearly concealed by close rows of sugar-cane. When we reached the spot, we beheld a middle-aged woman, and two elderly men, weeping around the mat of a sick man, apparently near his end. Finding him entirely ignorant of God, and of a future state, we spoke to him of Jehovah, of the fallen condition of man, of the amazing love of Christ in suffering death for the redemption of the world, and recommended to him that he pray to the Son of God, who was able to save to the uttermost.

He said that until now he knew nothing of these things, and was glad he had lived to hear of them. We requested one of his friends to

44

come to our house for some medicine; and having endeavoured to comfort the mourners, bade them farewell.

The *Ainoa* was seen approaching from the southward, on the morning of the 6th. About two p.m. she came to anchor, having been becalmed off Ranai four days.

A SUNDAY'S WORK AT LAHAINA

This day being the Sabbath, at half-past ten the mission family walked down to the beach to public worship. Most of the chiefs, and about three hundred people, assembled under the pleasant shade of a beautiful clump of kou trees, in front of Keopuolani's house. After singing and prayer, I preached from Luke x. 23, 24. "Blessed are the eyes which see the things which ye see: for I tell you, that many prophets and kings have desired to see those things which ye see, and have not seen them; and to hear those things which ye hear, and have not heard them."

After service, when we went to present our salutations to Keopuolani, we found her, Kaikioewa, and several chiefs, conversing about Tamehameha, and others of their ancestors, who had died idolaters, and expressing their regret that the gospel had not been brought to the Sandwich Islands in their day. "But perhaps," said Keopuolani, "they will have less punishment in the other world for worshipping idols, than those, who, though they do not worship wooden gods, yet see these days, and hear these good things, and still disregard them."

As we returned, I visited the sick man; found him rather better than on the preceding evening, and again recommended the Son of God as all-sufficient to save.

GAME OF PUHENEHENE DESCRIBED

I afterwards saw a party at buhénehéne. This is one of the most popular games in the Sandwich Islands, and the favourite amusement of the king, and higher order of chiefs, frequently occupying them whole days together. It principally consists in hiding a small stone under one of five pieces of native tapa, so as to prevent the spectators from discovering under which piece it is hid.

The parties at play sit cross-legged, on mats spread on the ground, each one holding in his right hand a small elastic rod, about three feet long, and highly polished.

At the small end of this stick there is a narrow slit or hole, through which a piece of dog's skin, with a tuft of shaggy hair òn it, or a piece of ti leaf, is usually drawn.

Five pieces of tapa, of different colours, each loosely folded up like a bundle, are then placed between the two parties, which generally consists of five persons each.

One person is then selected on each side to hide the stone. He who is first to hide it, takes it in his right hand, lifts up the cloth at one end, puts his arm under as far as his elbow, and, passing it along several times, underneath the five pieces of cloth, which lie in a line contiguous to each other, he finally leaves it under one of them.

The other party sit opposite, watching closely the action in the muscles of the upper part of his arm; and, it is said, that adepts can discover the place where the stone is deposited, by observing the change that takes place in those muscles, when the hand ceases to grasp it.

Having deposited the stone, the hider withdraws his arm; and, with many gestures, separates the contiguous pieces of cloth into five distinct heaps, leaving a narrow space between each.

The opposite party, having keenly observed this process, now point with their wands or sticks to the different heaps under which they suppose the stone lies, looking significantly, at the same time, full in the face of the man who had hid it. He sits all the while, holding his fingers before his eyes, to prevent their noticing any change in his countenance, should one of them point to the heap under which it is hid.

Having previously agreed who shall strike first, that individual, looking earnestly at the hider, lifts his rod, and strikes a smart blow across the heap he had selected. The cloth is instantly lifted up; and should the stone appear under it, his party have won that hiding, with one stroke; if it is not there, the others strike, till the stone is found.

The same party hide the stone five or ten times successively, according to their agreement at the commencement of the play; and whichever party discovers it the given number of times, with fewest strokes, wins the game.

Sometimes they reverse it; and those win, who, in a given number of times, strike most heaps without uncovering the stone.

GAMBLING FREQUENT

Occasionally they play for amusement only; but more frequently for money, or other articles of value, which they stake on the game.

I went to the party, whom I found thus engaged; and after a few minutes' conversation, told them, that it was the sacred day of God, and induced them to put aside their play, and promise to attend public worship in the afternoon.

Leaving them, I passed through a garden, where a man was at work weeding and watering a bed of cloth plants. I asked him if he did not know it was the sacred day, and improper for him to work?

The man answered, yes, he knew it was the la tabu, (sacred day,) and that Karaimoku had given orders for the people of Lahaina not to work on that day; but said, he was hana maru no, (just working

46

secretly) ; that was some distance from the beach, and the chiefs would not see him.

I then told him he might do it without the chiefs seeing him, but it was prohibited by a higher power than the chiefs, even by the God of heaven and earth, who could see him alike in every place, by night and by day.

He said he did not know that before, and would leave off when he had finished the row of cloth plants he was then weeding!

Mr. Stewart conducted an English service in the afternoon. The sound of the hura in a remote part of the district was occasionally heard through the after-part of the day, but whether countenanced by any of the chiefs, or only exhibited for the amusement of the common people, we did not learn.

At four o'clock we again walked down to the beach, and found about two hundred people collected under the kou trees; many more afterwards came, and after the introductory exercises, I preached to them upon the doctrine of the resurrection and a future state, from John xi. 25.

The congregation seemed much interested. Probably it was the first time many had ever heard of the awful hour, when the trumpet shall sound, and the dead shall be raised, and stand before God. At the conclusion of the service, notice was given of the monthly missionary prayer-meeting on the morrow evening, and the people were invited to attend.

SINCERITY OF KEOPUOLANI

Taua, the native teacher of Keopuolani, visited the family in the evening, and gave a very pleasing account of Keopuolani's frequent conversations with him, on the love of God in sending his Son, on the death of Christ, and on her great desire to have a new heart, and become a true follower of the Redeemer. He informed us, that after most of the attendants had retired, she had several times sent for him, at nine or ten o'clock in the evening, to engage in prayer with her and her husband, before they retired to rest.

This account was truly gratifying, and tended much to strengthen the pleasing hope, which, from her uniform, humble, and Christian conduct, had for some time been indulged, that a saving change had taken place in her heart.

In the afternoon of the 7th I walked to the sea side with Mr. Richards, and waited on the queen Keopuolani, to converse with her respecting the houses and fences which she had kindly engaged to erect for the missionaries.

The interview was satisfactory. Keopuolani seemed anxious to make them comfortable, and assured Mr. Richards that the houses would soon be ready for them.

47

We then visited Maaro, the chief of Waiakea, a large district on the eastern side of Hawaii. He had been on a short visit to the king, at Oahu, and was returning to his land in the *Ainoa*.

He received us kindly, and, when informed that I wished to proceed in the vessel to Hawaii, said, "It is good that you should go; we shall sail tomorrow."

The eastern part of Lahaina, in which he had his encampment, was highly cultivated, and adorned with some beautiful groves of kou trees and cocoa-nuts. There were also several large ponds, well stocked with excellent fish.

On returning from our visit to Maaro, we found the people collecting under the cool shade of their favourite trees, in front of Keopuolani's house, for the purpose of attending the monthly missionary prayer meeting. About five o'clock the service commenced. I gave an address from the Saviour's commission to the first missionaries to the heathen. Matt. xxviii. 19. "Go ye, therefore, and teach all nations."

The audience appeared gratified with the brief account given of the missionary operations of the present day, especially those among the various clustering islands of the Pacific, with whose inhabitants they feel themselves more particularly identified, than with the native tribes of Africa or Asia.

It was a circumstance truly animating to see so many of those who, wrapt in the thick darkness of paganism, had till lately worshipped the work of their own hands, and "sacrificed" their fellow-creatures "to devils," now joining in concert with Christians of every nation, in praying for the spread of the gospel of Jesus throughout the world.

A CONVERSATION WITH THE KING'S SERVANTS

After breakfast on the 8th, I visited a neat strong brick house, which stands on the beach, about the middle of the district. It was erected for Tamehameha; appears well built, is forty feet by twenty, has two stories, and is divided into four rooms by strong boarded partitions. It was the occasional residence of the late king, but by the present is used only as a warehouse.

Several persons who appeared to have the charge of it, were living in one of the apartments, and having looked over the house, and made some inquiries about the native timber employed for the floor, beams, &c. I sat down on one of the bales of cloth lying in the room where the natives were sitting, and asked them if they knew how to read, or if any of them attended the school, and the religious services on the Sabbath? On their answering in the negative, I advised them not to neglect these advantages, assuring them that it was a good thing to be instructed, and to know the true God, and his son Jesus Christ, the only Saviour.

48

They said, "Perhaps it is a good thing for some to attend to the palapala and the pule (to reading and prayers,) but we are the king's servants, and must attend to his concerns. If we (meaning all those that had the care of the king's lands) were to spend our time at our books, there would be nobody to cultivate the ground, to provide food, or cut sandal wood for the king."

I asked them what proportion of their time was taken up in attending to these things? They said they worked in the plantations three or four days in a week, sometimes from daylight till nine or ten o'clock in the forenoon; that preparing an oven of food took an hour; and that when they went for sandal wood, which was not very often, they were gone three or four days, and sometimes as many weeks.

They were the king's servants, and generally work much less than the people who occupy the lands, or cultivate them.

I asked them what they did in the remaining part of those days in which they worked at their plantations in the morning; and also on those days when they did not work at all?

They said they ate poë, laid down to sleep, or kamailio no (just talked for amusement).

They were then asked, which they thought would be most advantageous to them, to spend that time in learning to read, and seeking the favour of Jehovah and Jesus Christ, that they might live for ever, or wasting it in eating, sleeping, or foolish talking, and remaining ignorant in this world, and liable to wretchedness in that which was to come?

They immediately endeavoured to give a different turn to the conversation, by saying, "What a fine country yours must be, compared with this!

"What large bales of cloth come from thence, while the clothing of Hawaii is small in quantity, and very bad."

"The soil there must be very prolific, and property easily obtained, or so much of it would not have been brought here."

I informed them, that the difference was not so great between the countries as between the people.

That, many ages back, the ancestors of the present inhabitants of England and America possessed fewer comforts than the Sandwich islanders now enjoy; wore skins of beasts for clothing; painted their bodies with various colours; and worshipped with inhuman rites their cruel gods: but since they had become enlightened and industrious, and had embraced Christianity, they had been wise and rich; and many, there was reason to hope, had, after death, gone to a state of happiness in another world; that they owed all their present wealth and enjoyment to their intelligence and industry; and that, if the people of either country were to neglect education and religion, and spend as much of their time in eating, sleeping, and jesting, they would soon become as poor and as ignorant as the Sandwich islanders.

They said, perhaps it was so; perhaps industry and instruction would make them happier and better, and, if the chiefs wished it, by and by they would attend to both.

After again exhorting them to improve the means now placed within their reach by the residence of the missionaries among them, I took leave of them.

During the forenoon, I went into several other houses, and conversed with the people on subjects relating to the mission, recommending their attention to the advantages it was designed to confer. Some approved, but many seemed very well satisfied with their present state of ignorance and irreligion, and rather unwilling to be disturbed.

After having united with the family in their evening devotions, on the 9th I took my leave, grateful for the hospitable entertainment and kind attention I had experienced, during my unexpected stay at their interesting station. I regretted that the illness of Mr. Stewart, which had been increasing for several days, prevented his accompanying me on my projected tour.

DIFFICULTIES OF INTER-ISLAND TRAVEL

At nine o'clock I walked down to the beach, but waited till midnight before an opportunity offered for getting on board. On reaching the brig, I learned that they did not intend to sail till daylight.

There were such multitudes of natives on board, and every place was so crowded, that it was impossible to pass from the gangway to the companion without treading on them; and it was difficult any where, either below or upon deck, to find room sufficient to lie down.

Early in the morning of the 10th the vessel was under way, but the light winds, and strong westerly current, soon rendered it necessary to anchor. Between eight and nine I went on shore, and after break-fasting with the Mission family, returned to the beach, that I might be ready to embark whenever the wind should become favourable. I sat down in Keopuolani's house, and entered into an interesting conversation with her, Hoapiri, and several other chiefs, respecting their ancient traditions and mythology.

KEOLOEVA—A MAUI GOD

One of the ancient gods of Maui, prior to its subjugation by Tame-hameha, they said, was Keoroeva. The body of the image was of wood, and was arrayed in garments of native tapa. The head and neck were formed of a kind of fine basket or wicker work, covered over with red feathers, so curiously wrought in as to resemble the skin of a beautiful

50

bird. A native helmet was placed on the idol's head, from the crown of which long tresses of human hair hung down over its shoulders. Its mouth, like the greater number of the Hawaiian idols, was large and distended.

In all the temples dedicated to its worship, the image was placed within the inner apartment, on the left hand side of the door, and immediately before it stood the altar, on which the offerings of every kind were usually placed.

They did not say whether human victims were ever sacrificed to appease its imagined wrath, but large offerings, of every thing valuable, were frequent.

Sometimes hogs were taken alive, as presents. The large ones were led, and the smaller ones carried in the arms of the priest, into the presence of the idols. The priest then pinched the ears or the tail of the pig till it made a squeaking noise, when he addressed the god, saying, "Here is the offering of such a one of your kahu," (devotees).

WHEN A PIG WAS SUPERIOR TO A MAN

A hole was then made in the pig's ear, a piece of cinet, made of the fibres of the cocoa-nut husk, was fastened in it, and the pig was set at liberty until the priest had occasion for him. In consequence of this mark, which distinguished the sacred hog, he was allowed to range the district at pleasure; and whatever depredations he might commit, driving him away from the enclosures into which he had broken, was the only punishment allowed to be inflicted.

Keoroeva's hogs were not the only ones thus privileged. The same lenient conduct was observed towards all the sacred pigs, to whatever idol they had been offered.

Tiha, a female idol, they said was also held in great veneration by the people of Maui, and received nearly the same homage and offerings as Keoroeva.

THE GODS OF LANAI AND MOLOKAI

The people of Ranai, an adjacent island, had a number of idols, but those best known by the chiefs with whom I was conversing, were Raeapua and Kaneapua, two large carved stone images, representing the deities supposed to preside over the sea, and worshipped chiefly by fishermen.

Mooarii, (king of lizards or alligators), a shark, was also a celebrated marine god, worshipped by the inhabitants of Morokai, another island in the neighbourhood. The chiefs informed me, that on almost every point of land projecting any distance into the sea, a temple was formerly erected for his worship.

Several kinds of fish arrive in shoals on their coast, every year, in

51

their respective seasons. The first fish of each kind, taken by the fishermen, were always carried to the heiau, and offered to their god, whose influence they imagined had driven them to their shores.

In some remote period, perhaps, they had observed the sharks chasing or devouring these fish, as they passed along among their islands, and from this circumstance had been led to deify the monster, supposing themselves indebted to him for the bountiful supplies thus furnished by a gracious Providence.

MANY SEA GODS

They had a number of sea gods, besides those whom they imagined directed the shoals of fishes to their shores. They had also gods who controlled the winds and changed the weather.

During a storm, or other season of danger at sea, they offered up their paro, or pule kurana, a particular kind of prayer; but it is not known to what idol they addressed it. On these occasions, their dread of perishing at sea frequently led them to make vows to some favourite deity; and if they ever reached the land, it was their first business to repair to the temple, and fulfil their vows. These vows were generally considered most sacred engagements; and it was expected that, sooner or later, some judgment would overtake those who failed to perform them.

It is not improbable, that the priests of those idols, in order to maintain their influence over the people, either poisoned the delinquents, or caused them to sustain some other injury.

KALAIPAHOA, THE GREAT POISON GOD

Karaipahoa was also a famous idol, originally belonging to Morokai. It was a middling-sized wooden image, curiously carved; the arms were extended, the fingers spread out, the head was ornamented with human hair, and the widely distended mouth was armed with rows of shark's teeth.

The wood of which the image was made was so poisonous, that if a small piece of it was chipped into a dish of poë, or steeped in water, whoever ate the poë or drank the water, the natives reported, would certainly die in less than twenty-four hours afterwards.

We were never able to procure a sight of this image, though we have been repeatedly informed that it still exists, not indeed in one compact image, as it was divided in several parts on the death of Tamehameha, and distributed among the principal chiefs.

It is a known fact, that the natives use several kinds of vegetable poison; and probably the wood of which the idol was made is poisonous. But the report of the virulence of the poison is most likely one of the many stratagems so frequently employed by the chiefs and priests, to maintain their influence over the minds of the people.

A smaller image of the same god was formed of nioi, a hard yellow wood, of which idols were usually made. This was left at Morokai, the original being always carried about by Tamehameha, and, it is said, placed under his pillow whenever he slept.

THE TRADITION OF THE ORIGIN OF KALAIPAHOA

The following is the tradition given by the natives of the original idol.

In the reign of Kumaraua, an ancient king of Morokai, lived Kaneakama, a great gambler. Playing one day at maita, (a Hawaiian game), he lost all that he possessed, except one pig, which, having dedicated to his god, he durst not stake on his game.

In the evening he returned home, laid down on his mat, and fell asleep. His god appeared to him in a dream, and directed him to go and play again, on the following day, and stake this pig on his success in a particular part of the play. He awoke in the morning, did as the god had directed, and was remarkably successful through the day. Before he returned home in the evening, he went to the temple of his idol, and there dedicated the greater part of his gain.

During his sleep that night the god appeared to him again, and requested him to go to the king, and tell him, that a clump of trees would be seen growing in a certain place in the morning; and that if he would have a god made out of one of them, he would reside in the image, and impart to it his power, signifying also, that Kaneakama should be his priest.

A MIRACULOUS POISON TREE

Early the next morning, the man who had received the communication from his god went and delivered it to the king, by whom he was directed to take a number of men, and cut down one of the trees, and carve it into an image.

As they approached Karuakoi, a small valley on the side of one of the mountains in Morokai, they were surprised at beholding a clump of trees, where there had been none before, the gods having caused them to grow up in the course of the preceding night. Into these trees, Tane, and some other gods, are reported to have entered.

When they arrived at the spot, the gods, by some sign, directed Kaneakama which tree to cut down. They began to work with their short-handled stone hatchets; but the chips flying on the bodies of one or two of them, they instantly expired.

Terrified at the dreadful power of the wood, the others threw down their hatchets, and refused to fell the tree; being urged by Kaneakama, they resumed their work; not, however, till they covered their bodies and faces with native cloth, and the leaves of the ti plant, leaving only a small aperture opposite one of their eyes. Instead of their hatchets,

53

they took their long daggers, or pahoas, with which they cut down the tree, and carved out the image. From this circumstance, the natives say, the idol derived its name, Karai-pahoa, which is literally, dagger cut or carved; from karai, to chip with an adze, or carve, and pahoa, a dagger.

Excepting the deities supposed to preside over volcanoes, no god was so much dreaded by the people as Karaipahoa. All who were thought to have died by poison, were said to have been slain by him.

IDENTITY OF TAHITIAN AND HAWAIIAN TRADITIONS

Before I left the party, I could not help stating to them the striking identity between some of their traditions and those of the Tahitians; and expressed my conviction that both nations had the same origin.

They said, tradition informed them that their progenitors were brought into existence on the islands which they now inhabit; that they knew nothing of the origin of the people of the Georgian and Society Islands, yet Tahiti, the name of the largest of the Georgian Islands, was found in many of their ancient songs, though not now applied exclusively to that island.

PROPOSED INTERMARRIAGE BETWEEN ROYAL FAMILIES OF TAHITI AND HAWAII

With the people of Borabora, (the name they gave to the Society Islands), they said they had no acquaintance before they were visited by Captain Cook, but that since that time, by means of ships passing from one group of islands to the other, several presents and messages of friendship had been interchanged between Tamehameha and Pomare I, and that, in order to cement their friendship more firmly, each had agreed to give one of his daughters in marriage to the son of the other.

In consequence of this amicable arrangement, a daughter of Pomare was expected from Tahiti, to be the wife of Rihoriho, late king of Hawaii; and Kekauruohe, one of the daughters of Tamehameha, was selected by her father to be the bride of Pomare, the late king of Tahiti.

Wanting a conveyance from Hawaii to Tahiti, Tamehameha was unable to send Kekauruohe; which, together with the death of Pomare before he had any opportunity of sending one of his relatives to Hawaii, prevented the intended intermarriages between the reigning families of Hawaii and Tahiti.

VOYAGING FROM LAHAINA TO KAWAIHAE

About two o'clock in the afternoon, the *Ainoa* hove up her anchor. I went on board in a canoe just as she was leaving the roads. The brig being about ninety tons burden, one of the largest the natives have, was, as has been already observed, much crowded, and, owing to the

54

difference between the motion of the vessel and that experienced in their small canoes, many of the natives soon became seasick.

It was calm through the night, but the wind blew fresh in the morning from N. N. E. and continued until noon, when, being under the lee of the high land of Kohala, one of the large divisions of Hawaii, we were becalmed.

At four o'clock p.m. a light air sprung up from the southward, and carried us slowly on towards Tawaihae, a district in the division of Kohala, about four miles long, containing a spacious bay, and good anchorage. The vessel stood in towards the north side of the bay, leaving a large heiau, (heathen temple), situated on the brow of a hill, to the southward, and heading directly for a deep gully, or water-course, called Honokoa, opposite the mouth of which, about 7 p.m. she came to anchor, in 10 fathoms, with a good bottom.

The north side of the bay affords much the best anchorage for shipping, especially for those that wish to lie near the shore. It is the best holding ground, and is also screened by the kuahive (high land) of Kohala from those sudden and violent gusts of wind, called by the natives mumuku, which come down between the mountains with almost irresistible fury, on the southern part of Towaihae, and the adjacent districts.

A MEETING WITH JOHN YOUNG

At six a.m. the next day, I went on shore, and walked along the beach about a mile to the house of Mr. J. Young, an aged Englishman, who has resided thirty-six years on the island, and rendered the most important services to the late king; not only in his various civil wars, but in all his intercourse with those foreigners who have visited the islands.

I found him recovering from a fit of illness, received from him a cordial welcome, and, as he was just sitting down to his morning repast, joined him, with pleasure, at his frugal board.

THE GREAT HEIAU AT KAWAIHAE

After breakfast, I visited the large heiau or temple called Bukohola. It stands on an eminence in the southern part of the district, and was built by Tamehameha about thirty years ago, when he was engaged in conquering Hawaii, and the rest of the Sandwich Islands.

He had subdued Maui, Ranai, and Morokai, and was preparing, from the latter, to invade Oahu, but in consequence of a rebellion in the south and east parts of Hawaii, was obliged to return thither.

When he had overcome those who had rebelled, he finished the heiau, dedicated it to Tairi, his god of war, and then proceeded to the conquest of Oahu. Its shape is an irregular parallelogram, 224 feet long, and 100

55

wide. The walls, though built of loose stones, were solid and compact. At both ends, and on the side next the mountains, they were twenty feet high, twelve feet thick at the bottom, but narrowed in gradually towards the top, where a course of smooth stones, six feet wide, formed a pleasant walk. The walls next the sea were not more than seven or eight feet high, and were proportionally wide. The entrance to the temple is by a narrow passage between two high walls.

HUMAN SACRIFICES

As I passed along this avenue, an involuntary shuddering seized me, on reflecting how often it had been trodden by the feet of those who relentlessly bore the murdered body of the human victim as an offering to their cruel idols.

The upper terrace within the area was spacious, and much better finished than the lower ones. It was paved with various flat smooth stones, brought from a considerable distance.

At the south end was a kind of inner court, which might be called the sanctum sanctorum of the temple, where the principal idol used to stand, surrounded by a number of images of inferior deities.

WHERE THE ORACLE WORKED

In the centre of this inner court was the place where the anu was erected, which was a lofty frame of wicker-work, in shape something like an obelisk, hollow, and four or five feet square at the bottom. Within this the priest stood, as the organ of communication from the god, whenever the king came to inquire his will; for his principal god was also his oracle, and when it was to be consulted, the king, accompanied by two or three attendants, proceeded to the door of the inner temple, and standing immediately before the obelisk, inquired respecting the declaration of war, the conclusion of peace, or any other affair of importance. The answer was given by the priest in a distinct and audible voice, though, like that of other oracles, it was frequently very ambiguous. On the return of the king, the answer he had received was publicly proclaimed, and generally acted upon.

I have frequently asked the people, whether, on these occasions, there was not some previous agreement between the king and the priest. They generally answered in the negative, or said they did not know.

On the outside, near the entrance to the inner court, was the place of the rere (altar), on which human and other sacrifices were offered. The remains of one of the pillars that supported it were pointed out by the natives, and the pavement around was strewed with bones of men and animals, the mouldering remains of those numerous offerings once presented there.

About the centre of the terrace was the spot where the king's sacred house stood, in which he resided during the season of strict tabu, and at the north end, the place occupied by the houses of priests, who, with the exception of the king, were the only persons permitted to dwell within the sacred enclosure.

Holes were seen on the walls, all around this, as well as the lower terraces, where wooden idols of varied size and shape formerly stood, casting their hideous stare in every direction. Tairi, or Kukairimoku, a large wooden idol, crowned with a helmet, and covered with red feathers, the favourite war-god of Tamehameha, was the principal idol. To him the heiau was dedicated, and for his occasional residence it was built.

HUMAN VICTIMS

On the day in which he was brought within its precincts, vast offerings of fruit, hogs, and dogs, were presented, and no less than eleven human victims immolated on its altars. And, although the huge pile now resembles a dismantled fortress, whose frown no longer strikes terror through the surrounding country, yet it is impossible to walk over such a golgotha, or contemplate a spot which must often have resembled a pandemonium more than any thing on earth, without a strong feeling of horror at the recollection of the bloody and infernal rites so frequently practised within its walls.

Thanks be to God, the idols are destroyed! Thanks to his name, the glorious gospel of his Son, who was manifested to destroy the works of the devil, has reached these heretofore desolate shores! May the Holy Spirit make it the "savour of life unto life" to the remnant of the people!

Leaving Bukohola, accompanied by some natives, I visited Mairikini, another heiau, a few hundred yards nearer the shore. It was nearly equal in its dimensions to that on the summit of the hill, but inferior in every other respect. It appeared to have been literally crowded with idols, but no human sacrifices were offered to any of its gods.

A TRIP FROM KAWAIHAE TO KAILUA

On returning to Mr. Young's house, I was informed that the vessel would sail that evening for Kairua, a circumstance I much regretted, as I hoped to spend the sabbath at Towaihae. Mr. Young, however, collected his family and neighbours together, to the number of sixty. A short exhortation was given, and followed by prayer; after which I took leave of my kind host, repaired on board, and the vessel soon after got under way.

It was daylight the next morning before we had left Towaihae bay, as the wind during the night had been very light. The sea breeze had, however, set in early, and carried us along a rugged and barren shore of lava towards Kairua, which is distant from Towaihae about thirty miles.

It being the sabbath, I preached on deck in the afternoon from Mark iv. 38, 39. to a congregation of about 150 natives, including the greater part of the crew. Many of the people were afterwards observed sitting together in small groups, and conversing about what they had heard, though some were inclined to make sport of it.

In the evening we were opposite Laemano (Shark's Point), but strong westerly currents prevented our making much progress.

On the morning of the 14th, we found ourselves becalmed to the southward of Kairua, several leagues from the shore. The snow-covered tops of the mountains were distinctly seen at sunrise, but they soon after became enveloped in clouds, and continued so through the day. A light breeze carried the vessel towards the land, and at nine a.m. the boat was lowered down, and I proceeded to the shore.

On my way I met the governor Kuakini, and Messrs. Goodrich and Harwood, who were coming off in the governor's boat. We returned together to the shore, where I was gladly received by Messrs. Thurston and Bishop, whom I found waiting to proceed on the tour of the island.

STROLLING MUSICIANS AND DANCERS DESCRIBED

In the afternoon, a party of strolling musicians and dancers arrived at Kairua. About four o'clock they came, followed by crowds of people, and arranged themselves on a fine sandy beach, in front of one of the governor's houses, where they exhibited a native dance, called hura araapapa.

The five musicians first seated themselves in a line on the ground, and spread a piece of folded cloth on the sand before them. Their instrument was a large calabash, or rather two, one of an oval shape about three feet high, the other perfectly round, very neatly fastened to it, having also an aperture about three inches in diameter at the top.

Each musician held his instrument before him with both hands, and produced his music by striking it on the ground, where he had laid the piece of cloth, and beating it with his fingers, or the palms of his hands. As soon as they began to sound their calabashes, the dancer, a young man, about the middle stature, advanced through the opening crowd. His jet-black hair hung in loose and flowing ringlets down his naked shoulders; his necklace was made of a vast number of strings of nicely braided human hair, tied together behind, while a paraoa (an ornament made of a whale's tooth) hung pendent from it on his breast; his wrists

58

W.Ellis del.

J. M. Gray sc.

A Hura, or Native Dance, performed in presence of the Governor at Kairua.

were ornamented with bracelets, formed of polished tusks of the hog, and his ankles with loose buskins, thickly set with dog's teeth, the rattle of which, during the dance, kept time with the music of the calabash drum. A beautiful yellow tapa was tastefully fastened round his loins, reaching to his knees. He began his dance in front of the musicians, and moved forwards and backwards, across the area, occasionally chanting the achievements of former kings of Hawaii. The governor sat at the end of the ring, opposite to the musicians, and appeared gratified with the performance, which continued until the evening.

CHAPTER IV

JULY 15TH. Our whole number being now together at the place where we had previously agreed to commence our tour, we no longer delayed to decide on the route we should take, and the manner in which we should endeavour to accomplish the objects of our visit.

Anxious to gain a thorough acquaintance with the circumstances of the people, and their disposition relative to missionary operations, we agreed to travel on foot from Kairua, through the villages on the southern shore, to pass round the south point, and continue along the southeast shore, till we should arrive at the path leading to the great volcano, situated at the foot of Mouna Roa, about 25 miles distant from the sea, which we thought it improper to pass unnoticed.

We proposed, after visiting the volcano, either to descend to the shore and travel along the coast through the division of Puna, or across the interior to the division of Hiro, as circumstances might then render most expedient.

From Waiakea in Hiro, we agreed to proceed along the eastern shore, till an opportunity should offer for part of our number to cross over the mountains of Kohala, while the rest should travel along the shore, round the north point of the island, and meet their companions at Towaihae, whence they could return direct to Oahu, if a means of conveyance should present itself, or to Kairua, and there wait for a vessel.

The plan of our tour being thus arranged, we were anxious to receive the aid of the governor in the execution of it. Mr. Thurston and myself were therefore chosen to wait upon him in the afternoon, to make him acquainted with our wishes, and solicit his assistance for their accomplishment.

A "PEOPLE'S FORT"

I afterwards accompanied Mr. Thurston to the well, where we found the natives boring the hard rocks of lava which they intended to blast. We encouraged them in their laborious work, and then visited the ruins of an old military fortification, formerly belonging to the makaainana, (common people, as distinguished from the aristocracy, or reigning chiefs).

In those periods of their history, during which the island of Hawaii was divided into a number of independent governments under different

61

chiefs, which were frequent prior to the reign of Taraiopu, who was king at the time of its discovery by Captain Cook; this had been a place of considerable importance.

All that at present remains is part of the wall, about eighteen or twenty feet high, and fourteen feet thick at the bottom, built of lava, and apparently entire. In the upper part of the wall are apertures resembling embrasures; but they could not have been designed for cannon, that being an engine of war with which the natives have but recently become acquainted.

The part of the wall now standing, is near the mouth of Raniakea, the spacious cavern already mentioned, which formed a valuable appendage to the fort. In this cavern, children and aged persons were placed for security during an assault or sally from the fort, and sometimes the wives of the warriors also, when they did not accompany their husbands to the battle.

The fortification was probably extensive, as traces of the ancient walls are discoverable in several places; but what were its original dimensions, the natives who were with us could not tell. They asserted, however, that the cavern, if not the fort also, was formerly surrounded by a strong palisade.

ASSISTANCE FROM THE GOVERNOR

In the afternoon we waited on the governor, according to appointment; made him acquainted with our arrangements, and solicited the accommodation of a boat, or canoe, to carry our baggage, and a man acquainted with the island, to act as a guide, and to procure provisions, offering him, at the same time, any remuneration he might require for such assistance. After inquiring what baggage we intended to take, and how long we expected to be absent from Kairua, he generously offered to send a canoe as far as it could go with safety, and also to furnish a guide for the whole tour without any recompense whatever. He recommended that we should take a few articles for barter, as, occasionally, we might perhaps be obliged to purchase our food, or hire men to carry our baggage. After thanking him for his kindness, we returned.

MORE MUSIC AND DANCING

About four o'clock in the afternoon, another party of musicians and dancers, followed by multitudes of people, took their station nearly on the spot occupied yesterday by those from Kau. The musicians, seven in number, seated themselves on the sand; a curiously carved drum, made by hollowing out a solid piece of wood, and covering the top with shark's skin, was placed before each, which they beat with the palm or fingers of their right hand. A neat little drum, made of the shell of a

62

W.Ellis del.

I.Dixon. sc.

Ruins of an ancient Fortification, near Kairua.

large cocoa-nut, was also fixed on the knee, by the side of the large drum, and beat with a small stick held in the left hand.

When the musicians had arranged themselves in a line, across the beach, and a bustling man, who appeared to be master of the ceremonies, had, with a large branch of a cocoa-nut tree, cleared a circle of con-

C.Taylor. sculp.

KUAKINI,.

Governor of Hawaii

siderable extent, two interesting little children, (a boy and a girl), apparently about nine years of age, came forward, habited in the dancing costume of the country, with garlands of flowers on their heads, wreaths around their necks, bracelets on their wrists, and buskins on their ankles.

When they had reached the centre of the ring, they commenced their dance to the music of the drums; cantilating, alternately with the musicians, a song in honour of some ancient of Hawaii.

The governor of the island was present, accompanied, as it is customary for every chieftain of distinction to be on public occasions, by a retinue of favourite chiefs and attendants.

64

Having almost entirely laid aside the native costume, and adopted that of the foreigners who visit the islands, he appeared on this occasion in a light European dress, and sat on a Canton-made arm chair, opposite the dancers, during the whole exhibition.

A servant, with a light kihei of painted native cloth thrown over his shoulder, stood behind his chair, holding a highly polished spittoon, made of the beautifully brown wood of the cordia in one hand, and in the other a handsome kahiri, an elastic rod, three or four feet long, having the shining feathers of the tropic-bird tastefully fastened round the upper end, with which he fanned away the flies from the person of his master.

The beach was crowded with spectators, and the exhibition kept up with great spirit, till the overspreading shades of evening put an end to their mirth, and afforded a respite to the poor children, whose little limbs must have been very much fatigued by two hours of constant exercise.

DANCING EXCLUDED RELIGION

We were anxious to address the multitude on the subject of religion before they should disperse; but so intent were they on their amusement, that they could not have been diverted from it. I succeeded, however, in taking a sketch of the novel assemblage, in which, a youth, who had climbed a high pole, (that, looking over the heads of the throng who surrounded the dancers, he might witness the scene), formed a conspicuous object.

A messenger now invited us to sup with the governor, and we soon after joined him and his friends around his hospitable board.

DIPPER ACCOMPANIED BY MINISTRELSY

Our repast was not accompanied by the gladsome sound of "harp in hall" or "aged minstrel's flowing lay," yet it was enlivened by an interesting youthful bard, twelve or fourteen years of age, who was seated on the ground in the large room in which we were assembled, and who, during the supper, sung, in a monotonous but pleasing strain, the deeds of former chiefs, ancestors of our host. His fingers swept no "classic lyre," but beat, in a manner responsive to his song, a rustic little drum, formed of a calabash, beautifully stained, and covered at the head with a piece of shark skin.

The governor and his friends were evidently pleased with his lay, and the youth seemed repaid by their approbation.

In the morning of the 16th, Messrs. Goodrich and Harwood endeavoured to ascertain the height of Mouna Huararai, by means of two observations at the extremity of a base line of 2230 feet. They made the height of the mountain to be 7822 feet; but their quadrant being an inferior one, we thought the height of the mountain greater than that given above, though it is never covered with snow.

The accounts the natives gave us of the roads we were to travel, and the effects the short journeys already made had produced on our shoes, convinced us that those we had brought with us would be worn out before we had proceeded even half way round the island. We therefore provided a substitute, by procuring a tough bull's hide from the governor's store-house, and making ourselves rude sandals; which we afterwards found very serviceable, as they enabled us to travel over large tracts of lava with much more expedition and comfort than we could possibly have done without them.

RELIGIOUS TRUTHS SUBSTITUTED FOR THE HULA

At four p.m. the musicians from Kau again collected on the beach, and the dancer commenced a hura, similar to that exhibited on Monday evening. We had previously appointed a religious meeting for this evening, and, about an hour before sun-set, proposed to the governor to hold it on the beach, where the people were already assembled. He approved, and followed us to the edge of the circle, where we took our station, opposite the musicians.

At the governor's request the music ceased, and the dancer came and sat down just in front of us. We sang a hymn; I then offered up a short prayer, and afterwards addressed the people from Acts xiv. 15; "And preach unto you, that ye should turn from these vanities unto the living God, which made heaven and earth, and the sea, and all things that are therein." The multitude collected was from different and distant parts of the island, and appeared to listen with attention to the word spoken. To many, it was doubtless the first time they had heard of the name of Jehovah, or of Jesus Christ his Son, and we afterwards heard them conversing among themselves about the truths they had heard.

DISCUSSIONS WITH THE GOVERNOR

After supper and family worship at the governor's, I spent the evening in conversation with him, partly on traditions respecting some remarkable places in the neighbourhood of Kairua, and partly on the subject of religion. I spoke on the desirableness of his building a place

66

for the public worship of the true God, and the advantages of keeping the Sabbath as a day of holy rest, recommending him to set the common people a good example, and use his influence to induce them to attend public service on the Lord's day.

He said it was his intention to build a church by and by, when the maka-ainana should become interested in these things, and when they should have a missionary to reside permanently with them; but that at present the people at Kairua were quite indifferent to all religion.

ROYAL WOMEN MAKING TAPA

For several days past we have observed many of the people bringing home from their plantations bundles of young wauti, (a variety of the *morus papyrifera),* from which we infer that this is the season for cloth-making in this part of the island.

This morning, the 17th, we perceived Keoua, the governor's wife, and her female attendants, with about forty other women, under the pleasant shade of a beautiful clump of *cordia* or kou trees, employed in stripping off the bark from bundles of wauti sticks, for the purpose of making it into cloth.

The sticks were generally from six to ten feet long, and about an inch in diameter at the thickest end. They first cut the bark, the whole length of the stick, with a sharp serrated shell, and having carefully peeled it off, rolled it into small coils, the inner bark being outside. In this state it is left some time, to make it flat and smooth.

Keoua not only worked herself, but appeared to take the superintendence of the whole party. Whenever a fine piece of bark was found, it was shewn to her, and put aside to be manufactured into wairiirii, or some other particular cloth. With lively chat and cheerful song, they appeared to beguile the hours of labour until noon, when having finished their work, they repaired to their dwellings.

CULTIVATION OF TAPA PLANTS

The wauti plant, of which the greater part of the cloth on this side of the island is made, is cultivated with much care in their gardens of sugar-cane, plantain, &c. and whole plantations are sometimes devoted exclusively to its growth. Slips about a foot long are planted nearly two feet apart, in long rows, four or six feet asunder. Two or three shoots rise from most of the slips, and grow till they are six or twelve feet high, according to the richness of the soil, or the kind of cloth for which they are intended. Any small branches that may sprout out from the side of the long shoot, are carefully plucked off, and sometimes the bud at the top of the plant is pulled out, to cause an increase in its size.

67

Occasionally they are two years growing, and seldom reach the size at which they are fit for use, in less than twelve or even eighteen months, when they are cut off near the ground, the old roots being left, to produce shoots another year.

The bark, when stripped off and rolled up, as described above, is left several days; when, on being unrolled, it appears quite flat. The outer bark is then taken off, generally by scraping it with a large shell, and the inner bark, of which the cloth is made, is occasionally laid in water, to extract the resinous substances it may contain. Each piece of bark is then taken singly, and laid across a piece of wood, twelve or eighteen feet long, six inches square, smooth on the top, but having a groove on the under side, and is beaten with a square mallet of hard heavy wood, about a foot in length, and two inches wide; three sides are carved in grooves or ribs, the other into squares, in order that one mallet may answer for the different kinds of cloth they are accustomed to make.

When they have beaten the bark till it is spread out nine inches or a foot wide, it is either dried and reserved for future use, or wrapped up in leaves, laid by for a day or two, and then beaten out afresh till the required extent and texture are produced.

DIFFERENT KINDS OF TAPA

Various sorts of cloth are made with this plant, some remarkably fine and even; that which has been beaten with a mallet, carved in different patterns, much resembles muslin at first sight, while that made with a grooved mallet appears, until closely examined, something like dimity. There are other kinds, very thick and tough, which look like wash-leather; but the most common sort is the pau, worn round the waists of the females. To make this, a piece of bark is beaten till it is four yards long, and more than a yard wide, and of an equal texture throughout.

Sometimes two or three pieces of bark are necessary to make one piece of cloth. Five of these pieces, when finished, are spread out one upon the other, and fastened together at one end. These five pieces make only one pau. The inside pieces are usually white, or yellow; but the outside piece is always stained, or painted, with vegetable dyes of various colours.

No gum is used in the manufacture of the pau, except that contained in the bark, yet the fibres adhere firmly together. Those painted red or yellow, &c. are sometimes rubbed over with a vegetable oil, in which chips of sandal wood, or the seeds of the pandanus odorotissima, have been steeped. This is designed to perfume the cloth, and render it impervious to wet; it is, however. less durable than the common pau.

There is another kind of cloth, called tapa moe, (sleeping cloth,) made principally for the chiefs, who use it to wrap themselves in at night, while they sleep. It is generally three or four yards square, very thick, being formed of several layers of common tapa, cemented with gum, and beaten with a grooved mallet till they are closely interwoven. The colour is various, either white, yellow, brown, or black, according to the fancy of its owner.

Nearly resembling the tapa moe is the kihei, only it is both thinner and smaller. It is made in the same manner, and is about the size of a large shawl, or counterpane. Sometimes it is brown, but more frequently white or yellow, intermixed with red and black. It is generally worn by the men, thrown loosely over one shoulder, passed under the opposite arm, and tied in front, or on the other shoulder.

TAPAS FOR PA-US AND MALOS

But the best kind of cloth made with the cultivated plant is the wairiirii, which is made into paus for the females, and maros for the men.

The paus are generally four yards long, and about one yard wide, very thick, beautifully painted with brilliant red, yellow, and black colours, and covered over with a fine gum and resinous varnish, which not only preserves the colours, but renders the cloth impervious and durable. The maros are about a foot wide, and three or four yards long.

The colours they employ are procured from the leaves, bark, berries, or roots of indigenous plants, and require much skill in their preparation.

One or two kinds of earth are also used in mixing the darker colours. Since foreigners have visited them, they have found, upon trial, that our colours are better than theirs, and the paint they purchase from ships has superseded in a great degree the native colours, in the painting of all the most valuable kinds of cloth.

MANNER OF PAINTING TAPAS

Their manner of painting is ingenious. They cut the pattern they intend to stamp on their cloth, on the inner side of a narrow piece of bamboo, spread their cloth before them on a board, and having their colours properly mixed, in a calabash by their side, dip the point of the bamboo, which they hold in their right hand, into the paint, strike it against the edge of the calabash, place it on the right or left side of the cloth, and press it down with the fingers of the left hand. The pattern is dipped in the paint after every impression, which is continued till the cloth is marked quite across, when it is moved on the board, and the same repeated till it is finished.

The tapa in general lasts but a little while, compared with any kind of wove cloth, yet if kept free from wet, which causes it to rend like paper, some kinds may be worn a considerable time. The fabrication of it shews both invention and industry; and whether we consider its different textures, its varied and regular patterns, its beautiful colours, so admirably preserved by means of the varnish, we are at once convinced that the people who manufacture it are neither deficient in taste, nor incapable of receiving the improvements of civilized society. Specimens of the principal kinds of native cloth, manufactured in the Sandwich Islands, may be seen in the Missionary Museum, Austin Friars.

During the forenoon, Mr. Harwood made an auger, to aid the welldiggers in boring the rocks. I walked with Mr. Thurston to see what progress they had made, and to encourage them to persevere. The rocks they said were hard, and their progress slow, yet they were not discouraged, but hoped to find the work easier as they descended.

RELIGIOUS DISCUSSION WITH GOVERNOR KUAKINI

After dinner, the governor entered freely into conversation on religious subjects, particularly respecting the resurrection of the body, the destruction of the heavens and the earth at the last day, and the final judgment.

After listening attentively to what was said upon these subjects, he inquired about the locality of heaven and hell.

He was told that we did not know where the one or the other was situated, as none had ever returned from either, to tell mankind about them; and we only know, that there is a place called heaven, where God makes glorious manifestations of his perfections, and where all good men are perfectly happy; and that there is a place where wicked men are shut up in darkness, and endure endless misery.

He then said, "How do you know these things?" I asked for his bible, and translated the passages which inculcate the doctrine of the resurrection, &c. and told him it was from that book we obtained all our knowledge of these things; and that it was the contents of that book which we had come to teach the people of Hawaii.

THE GOVERNOR ASKS EMBARRASSING QUESTIONS

He then asked if all the people in our native countries were acquainted with the bible.

I answered, that from the abundant means of instruction enjoyed there, the greater portion of the people had either read the book, or had in some other way become acquainted with its principal contents.

He then said, How is it that such numbers of them swear, get intoxicated, and do so many things prohibited in that book?

He was told, that there was a vast difference between knowing the word of God, and obeying it; and that it was most likely those persons knew their conduct was displeasing to God, yet persisted in it, because agreeable to their corrupt inclinations.

He asked if God would not be angry with us for troubling him so frequently with our prayers? If he was like man, he said, he was sure he would.

I replied, that God was always "waiting to be gracious," more ready to hear than we were to pray; that indeed he was not like man, or his patience would have been exhausted long ago by the wickedness of men; but that he continued exercising long-suffering and forbearance towards sinners, that they might turn from their wickedness and live.

THE TRIP BEGINS

We supped with the governor as usual, and, after family worship with his household, prepared our baggage for our journey, some of which we left to be forwarded by the Ainoa to Waiakea, a district on the eastern side of the island.

About eleven o'clock in the forenoon, on the 18th, we waited on the governor to express our grateful sense of the generous hospitality we had experienced from him, during our protracted stay at Kairua. We also thanked him for the friendly advice he had given, and the acceptable aid he had so kindly furnished for the prosecution of our journey, and informed him that we were ready to proceed. He had before given instructions to our guide. He now directed the man who was going in the canoe, to take care of our things, and told us he would send some men to carry our baggage by land, as far as Kearake'kua. We then took leave of him, and proceeded on our journey. Messrs. Bishop and Harwood went in the canoe, the rest of our number travelled on foot.

MAKOA, THE GUIDE, DESCRIBED

Our guide, Makoa, who had been the king's messenger many years, and was well acquainted with the island, led the way. He was rather a singular looking little man, between forty and fifty years of age. A thick tuft of jet black curling hair shaded his wrinkled forehead, and a long bunch of the same kind hung down behind each of his ears. The rest of his head was cropped as short as shears could make it. His small black eyes were ornamented with tataued vandyke semicircles.

Two goats, impressed in the same indelible manner, stood rampant

71

over each of his brows; one, like the supporter of a coat of arms, was fixed on each side of his nose, and two more guarded the corners of his mouth.

The upper part of his beard was shaven close; but that which grew under his chin, was drawn together, braided for an inch or two, and

MAKOA.

The Guide who Piloted the Party Around Hawaii.

then tied in a knot, while the extremities below the knot spread out in curls like a tassel.

A light kihei, (cloth worn like a shawl,) was carelessly thrown over one shoulder, and tied in a knot on the other; and a large fan, made of cocoa-nut leaf, in his hand, served to beat away the flies, or the boys, when either became too numerous or troublesome.

THE COUNTRY SOUTH OF KAILUA

Leaving Kairua, we passed through the villages thickly scattered along the shore to the southward. The country around looked unusually

72

green and cheerful, owing to the frequent rains, which for some months past have fallen on this side of the island. Even the barren lava, over which we travelled, seemed to veil its sterility beneath frequent tufts of tall waving grass, or spreading shrubs and flowers.

The sides of the hills, laid out for a considerable extent in gardens and fields, and generally cultivated with potatoes, and other vegetables, were beautiful.

The number of heiaus, and depositories of the dead, which we passed, convinced us that this part of the island must formerly have been populous. The latter were built with fragments of lava, laid up evenly on the outside, generally about eight feet long, from four to six broad, and about four feet high. Some appeared very ancient, others had evidently been standing but a few years.

HEIAU OF KAUAIKAHALOA DESCRIBED

At Ruapua we examined an interesting heiau, called Kauaikaharoa, built of immense blocks of lava, and found its dimensions to be 150 feet by 70. At the north end was a smaller enclosure, sixty feet long and ten wide, partitioned off by a high wall, with but one narrow entrance. The places where the idols formerly stood were apparent, though the idols had been removed.

The spot where the altar had been erected could be distinctly traced; it was a mound of earth, paved with smooth stones, and surrounded by a firm curb of lava. The adjacent ground was strewed with bones of the ancient offerings.

The natives informed us that four principal idols were formerly worshipped there, one of stone, two of wood, and one covered with red feathers.

One of them, they said, was brought from a foreign country. Their names were Kanenuiakea, (great and wide spreading Kane,) who was brought from Tauai, Kaneruruhonua, (earth-shaking Kane,) Rorama-kaeha, and Kekuaaimanu.

GODS OF THE FISHERMEN

Leaving the heiau, we passed by a number of smaller temples, principally on the sea shore, dedicated to Kuura, a male, and Hina, a female idol, worshipped by fishermen, as they were supposed to preside over the sea, and to conduct or impel to the shores of Hawaii, the various shoals of fish that visit them at different seasons of the year. The first of any kind of fish, taken in the season, was always presented to them, especially the operu, a kind of herring. This custom exactly accords with the former practice of the inhabitants of Maui and the adjacent islands, and of the Society islanders.

73

At two p.m. we reached Horuaroa, a large and populous district. Here we found Keoua, the governor's wife, and her attendants, who had come from Kairua for wauti, with which to make cloth.

Shortly after, we reached a village called Karuaokalani, (the second heaven,) where was a fine heiau, in good preservation. It is called Pakiha; its dimensions were 270 feet by 210.

We could not learn the idol to which it was dedicated, but were informed it was built in the time of Keakealani, who, according to tradition, was queen of Hawaii about eleven generations back.

The walls were solid, thick, and nearly entire; and the singular manner in which the stones were piled upon the top, like so many small spires, gave it an unusually interesting appearance.

A TALE OF A GIANT

Before we left Karuaokalani the inhabitants pointed out to us a spot called Maukareoreo, the place of a celebrated giant of that name, who was one of the attendants of Umi, king of Hawaii, about twelve generations since, and who, they told us, was so tall that he could pluck the cocoa-nuts from the trees as he walked along; and when the king was playing in the surf, where it was five or six fathoms deep, would walk out to him without being wet above his loins; and when he was in a canoe, if he saw any fish lying among the coral at the same depth, would just put his hand down and take them.

They also told us he was a great warrior, and that, to his prowess principally, Umi was indebted for many of his victories.

The Hawaiians are fond of the marvellous, as well as many people who are better informed; and probably this passion, together with the distance of time since Maukareoreo existed, has led them to magnify one of Umi's followers, of perhaps a little larger stature than his fellows, into a giant sixty feet high.

GROVES OF KOU TREES

Our road now lay through a pleasant part of the district, thickly inhabited, and ornamented occasionally with clumps of kou trees. Several spots were pointed out to us, where the remains of heiaus, belonging to the late king Tamehameha, were still visible.

After travelling some time, we came to Kanekaheilani, a large heiau more than 200 feet square. In the midst of it was a clear pool of brackish water, which the natives told us was the favorite bathing place of Tamehameha, and which he allowed no other person to use. A rude

74

figure, carved in stone, standing on one side of the gateway by which we entered, was the only image we saw here.

About fifty yards further on, was another heiau, called Hale o Tairi (house of Tairi). It was built by Tamehameha soon after he had assumed the government of the island. Only one mutilated image was now standing, though it is evident that, but a few years ago, there had been many.

TAIRI THE FLYING WAR GOD

The natives were very desirous to shew us the place where the image of Tairi the war-god stood, and told us that frequently in the evening he used to be seen flying about in the neighbourhood, in the form of a luminous substance like a flame, or like the tail of a comet.

We told them that the luminous appearance which they saw was an occurrence common to other countries, and produced by natural causes: that the natives of the Society Islands formerly, whenever they observed such a phenomenon, supposed it to be Tane, one of their gods, taking his flight from one marae to another, or passing through the district seeking whom he might destroy, and were consequently filled with terror; but now, they wondered how they could ever have given way to such fears, from so inoffensive a circumstance.

We asked them if they did not see the same appearances now, though the god had been destroyed, and his worship discontinued?

They said, "No; it has not been seen since the abolition of idolatry."

We assured them it did not proceed from the power of the god Tairi, but that it was a luminous vapour, under the control of Jehovah, the creator and governor of all things which they beheld.

CANOE MAKING—FUTURE STATE DISCUSSED

We walked on to Pahoehoe, where we entered a large house, in which many workmen were employed in making canoes. About fifty people soon after assembled around us. We asked them if they would like to hear about the true God, and the way of salvation? They answered, Yes. I then addressed them for about twenty minutes on the first principles of the gospel. As soon as I began to speak, they all sat down, and observed perfect silence.

Shortly after this service we took our leave, and proceeded along the shore to Kahaluu; where a smart shower of rain obliged us to take shelter in a house by the road side. While resting there, the voice of wailing reached our ears. We inquired whence it came? and were informed by the people of the house, that a sick person in the neighbourhood had just expired.

We asked where the soul was gone to?

They answered, they knew not whither, but that it would never return.

I spoke to them respecting the condition of departed souls; the resurrection of the body, and the general judgment which will follow; telling them afterwards of the love of Christ, who had brought life and immortality to light, and by his death secured eternal happiness to all that believe in him.

They listened attentively, and continued the conversation till the rain abated, when we pursued our journey.

APPROACHES TO AND ENVIRONS OF KEAUHOU

We passed another large heiau, and travelled about a mile across a rugged bed of lava, which had evidently been ejected from a volcano more recently than the vast tracts of the same substance by which it was surrounded. It also appeared to have been torn to pieces, and tossed up in the most confused manner, by some violent convulsion of the earth, at the time it was in a semifluid state.

There was a kind of path formed across the most level part of it, by large smooth round stones, brought from the sea-shore, and placed about three or four feet apart. By stepping from one to another of these, we passed over the roughest piece of lava we had yet seen; and soon after five p.m. we arrived at Keauhou, a pleasant village containing one hundred and thirty-five houses, and about eight miles from Kairua. Messrs. Bishop and Harwood reached the same place about an hour earlier, and here we proposed to spend the night.

We had not been long in the village, when about one hundred and fifty people collected round the house in which we stopped.

After singing and prayer, Mr. Thurston preached to them. They gave good attention; and though we conversed with them a considerable time after the service was ended, they still thronged our house, and seemed unwilling to disperse.

ESTIMATE OF POPULATION—TALKS WITH THE PEOPLE

During our walk from Kairua to this place we counted six hundred and ten houses, and allowed one hundred more for those who live among the plantations on the sides of the hills.

Reckoning five persons to each house, which we think not far from a correct calculation, the population of the tract through which we have travelled today will be about 3550 souls.

We also passed nineteen heiaus, of different dimensions, some of which we carefully examined.

Late in the evening we spread our mats on the loose pebbles of which the floor of the house was formed, and, thankful for the mercies we had received, laid ourselves down, and enjoyed a comfortable night's repose. Thermometer at sunset 71°.

Early the next morning numbers of the natives collected around our lodgings, and when informed that we intended to perform religious worship, sat down on the ground, and became quite silent. After singing a hymn in their language, I gave a short exhortation, followed by prayer.

They afterwards kept us in conversation till about half-past eight, when we set out from Keauhou, and pursued our journey. Mr. Harwood proceeded in the canoe; the rest of our number travelled on foot along the shore.

LAVA COUNTRY DESCRIBED

Our way lay across a rough tract of lava, resembling that which we passed over the preceding afternoon. In many places it seemed as if the surface of the lava had become hard, while a few inches underneath it had remained semifluid, and in that state had been broken up, and left in its present confused and irregular form. This rugged appearance of the external lava was probably produced by the expansive force of the heated air beneath the crust, but that could not have caused the deep chasms or fissures which we saw in several places.

We also observed many large spherical volcanic stones, the surface of which had been fused, and in some places had peeled off like a crust or shell, an inch or two in thickness. The centre of some of these stones, which we broke, was of a dark blue colour and compact texture, and did not appear to have been at all affected by the fire which had calcined the surface.

SCENE OF BATTLE WITH SUPPORTERS OF IDOLATRY

After travelling about two miles over this barren waste, we reached the place where, in the autumn of 1819, the decisive battle was fought between the forces of Rihoriho, the present king, and his cousin, Kekuaokalani, in which the latter was slain, his followers completely overthrown, and the cruel system of idolatry, which he took up arms to support, effectually destroyed.

The natives pointed out to us the place where the king's troops, led on by Karaimoku, were first attacked by the idolatrous party. We saw several small heaps of stones, which our guide informed us were the graves of those who, during the conflict, had fallen there.

We were then shewn the spot on which the king's troops formed a line from the sea-shore towards the mountains, and drove the opposing party before them to a rising ground, where a stone fence, about breast

77

high, enabled the enemy to defend themselves for some time, but from which they were at length driven by a party of Karaimoku's warriors.

The small tumuli increased in number as we passed along, until we came to a place called Tuamoo. Here Kekuaokalani made his last stand, rallied his flying forces, and seemed, for a moment, to turn the scale of victory; but being weak with the loss of blood, from a wound he had received in the early part of the engagement, he fainted and fell. However, he soon revived, and, though unable to stand, sat on a fragment of lava, and twice loaded and fired his musket on the advancing party. He now received a ball in his left breast, and immediately covering his face with his feather cloak, expired in the midst of his friends.

MANONA, THE FAITHFUL WIFE

His wife Manona during the whole of the day fought by his side with steady and dauntless courage.

A few moments after her husband's death, perceiving Karaimoku and his sister advancing, she called out for quarter; but the words had hardly escaped from her lips, when she received a ball in her left temple, fell upon the lifeless body of her husband, and instantly expired.

The idolaters having lost their chief, made but feeble resistance afterwards; yet the combat, which commenced in the forenoon, continued till near sunset, when the king's troops, finding their enemies had all either fled or surrendered, returned to Kairua.

Karaimoku grieved much at the death of Kekuaokalani, who was his own sister's son. He delayed the engagement as long as possible; and, the same morning that the battle took place, sent a messenger, addressing the young chief as his son, and requesting him to refrain from hostilities till they could have an interview, and, if possible, effect an accommodation. But the message was rejected, and the messenger obliged to jump into the sea, and swim to save his life. In the moment of victory, also, he acted with humanity; and, contrary to the usual custom, the vanquished were not pursued and murdered in their retreats.

A CAVE OF REFUGE—WOMEN IN BATTLE

A little way south of the spot where the chief fell, was a small cave, into which, in the confusion that followed the death of Kekuaokalani, a woman attached to his party crept, and, drawing a piece of lava over its mouth, remained until night, beneath whose friendly cover she fled to the mountains, not knowing that the victors had returned without pursuing their foes.

The wives of warriors often accompanied their husbands to battle, and were frequently slain. Their practice, in this respect, resembled that of the Society islanders on similar occasions. They generally followed in the rear, carrying calabashes of water, or of poë, a little dried fish, or other portable provision, with which to recruit their husband's strength when weary, or afford a draught of water when thirsty or faint; but they followed, more particularly, to be at hand if their husbands should be wounded.

Some women, more courageous than the rest, or urged on by affection, advanced side by side with their husbands to the front of the battle, bearing a small calabash of water in one hand, and a spear, a dart, or a stone, in the other; and in the event of the husband being killed, they seldom survived.

A MONUMENT TO KEKUAOKALANI AND MANONA

A pile of stones, somewhat larger than the rest, marked the spot where the rival chief and his affectionate and heroic wife expired. A few yards nearer the sea, an oblong pile of stones, in the form of a tomb, about ten feet long and six wide, was raised over the grave in which they were both interred. A number of lowly flowering bushes grew around, and a beautiful convulvulus in full bloom almost covered it with foliage and flowers.

We could not view this rudely constructed tomb without renewed lamentation over the miseries of war, and a strong feeling of regret for the untimely end of the youthful pair, especially for the affectionate Manona, whom even the horrors of savage fight, in which the demon of war wears his most terrific form, could not prevent from following the fortune, and sharing the dangers, that she might administer to the comfort, of her much-loved husband. This feeling was not a little increased by the recollection of the delusion of which they were the ill-fated victims, and in support of which they were prodigal of their blood. Alas! they knew not, till from the fatal field they entered the eternal world, the value of that life which they had lost, and the true nature of that cause in which they had sacrificed it.

The piles of stones rose thick around the spot where they lay; and we were informed that they were the graves of his kahu, (particular friends and companions,) who stood by him to the last, manifesting a steadfastness which even their enemies admired, and a degree of courage worthy of being exercised in a better cause.

THE ABOLITION OF IDOLATRY AND THE TABU

Kekuaokalani was first cousin to Rihoriho. He is represented by some as having been an enterprising and restless young man, aspiring to share the government with his cousin, if not to reign in his stead.

The late king Tamehameha, a short time before his death, left the government of the islands to his eldest son Rihoriho, and the care of the gods, their temples, and the support of their worship, to the king and Kekuaokalani, together with the rest of the chiefs.

Almost the first public act of the young king Rihoriho, was the abolition of the national idolatry, and all the restrictions of the tabu system by which it was upheld. This system, with all its superstitious cruelty, had existed, and had exerted its degrading yet almost super-natural influence over the people, from time immemorial; and it required no small degree of courage by one single act to abrogate its inflexible laws, and destroy its dreaded power. But several acts of Rihoriho's reign shew that he possessed a mind well adapted for such undertakings.

LIHOLIHO'S MOTIVES FOR ABOLISHING TABU

His motives for this decisive measure appear to have been, in the first place, a desire to ameliorate the condition of his wives, and the females in general, whom the tabu sunk into a state of extreme wretchedness and degradation, obliging them to subsist only on inferior kinds of food, and not allowing them to cook their provisions, such as they were, at the same fire, or even eat in the same place where the men took theirs.

And in the second place, he seems to have been influenced by a wish to diminish the power of the priests, and avoid that expenditure of labour and property which the support of idolatry required, and which he was anxious to employ for other purposes. He had also heard what Pomare and the Tahitian chiefs had done in the Society Islands.

THE HIGH PRIEST'S ADVICE

He consulted some of the principal chiefs, particularly Karaimoku, who declared his intention not to keep or observe any more tabus; and though several of the priests said the gods would recompense any neglect with vengeance, Hevaheva, the high priest of his father's war-god, said no evil consequences would follow the discontinuance of the worship of the gods.

Soon after this, the king made a feast, to which many chiefs of the different islands were invited. The guests assembled, as usual; the men in one place, the women in another. The food was cut up, and when all were about to begin their meal, the king ordered his attendants to carry some fowls, and such prohibited food, to the place where his wives and other females were assembled; he then went, and, sitting down with them, began to eat, and directed them to do the same.

A shout of surprise burst from the multitude around; several other chiefs followed his example.

The men and women sat promiscuously, and ate the same food,

80

which they called ai noa, general or common eating, in opposition to the former ai tabu, restricted or sacred eating.

The ai tabu was one of the perpetual restrictions imposed by their idolatry on all ranks of the people, from their birth until their death.

PRIESTHOOD ABOLISHED—IDOL WORSHIP ENDED

This public violation of it manifested the king's intention to destroy the whole system, which very shortly after was accomplished by the priest Hehaheva's resigning his office, and the king declaring that there should no longer be any priests, or any worship rendered to the gods.

Kekuaokalani, though he had no share in the government, yet had, in common with the other high chiefs, received a charge concerning the gods. Urged on by the priests, who promised him victory by a superstitious reverence for the idols of his ancestors, and perhaps also by a hope of defeating Rihoriho, and securing the government to himself, he took up arms.

EFFECT OF ABOLITION OF TABU

The abolition of idolatry by Rihoriho was thus the immediate occasion of the war, which terminating in his favour, left him sole monarch of the Sandwich Islands. This was the summit of his ambition, and the consummation of his wishes, though probably the least among the allwise and benevolent purposes of Him, who ruleth all things after the counsel of his own will, and causeth even the wrath of man to praise him.

Little did the pagan chief imagine, when he collected his forces, offered his sacrifices, and, preceded by his war-god, marched to the battle, that he was urging on his way to remove the most formidable barrier that existed to the introduction of a religion which should finally triumph over every system of idolatry in the world; and as little did the victorious chiefs, when they beheld themselves masters of the field, and returned in triumph to the king, think that success had only prepared the way for their own subjection to a peaceful Prince, whose heralds (then on their way) should soon proclaim his laws in their camp, and demand their allegiance to his crown;—whose divine power should erect among them a kingdom, of which they themselves should delight to become subjects, and commence a reign that should be everlasting.

AT HONUAINO AND HOKUKANO

Leaving Tuamoo, we passed on to Honuaino, where, being thirsty and weary, we sat down on the side of a canoe, under the shade of a fine-spreading hibiscus, and begged a little water of the villagers.

We had not remained many minutes before we were surrounded by about 150 people. After explaining to them in few words our feelings on

81

meeting them, we asked them if they would like to hear what we had to say to them. They replied, Ae (yes,) and sat down immediately.

We sung a hymn and prayed, and I addressed them for about half an hour on the first principles of Christianity. They all appeared gratified, said they were naau po, (dark hearted,) and should be glad to be instructed in all these things, if any body would teach them.

We now travelled on to Hokukano, where we passed a pahu tabu, (sacred enclosure,) which the natives told us was built by Taraiopu, (Terreoboo in Cook's Voyages,) king of the island at the time it was discovered by Captain Cook.

A BURIAL TOMB AND SHARK HEIAU

A little further on we examined a buoa (tomb) of a celebrated priest. It was composed of loose stones, neatly laid, about eight feet square and five high.

In the centre was a small mound of earth, higher than the walls; over this a house had formerly been erected, but it was now fallen to decay; around it were long poles, stuck in the earth, about three or four inches apart, and united together at the top.

We asked why the grave was enclosed with those tall sticks? Some said it was a custom so to inter persons of consequence; others said it was to prevent the spirit from coming out.

On the top of a high mountain, in the neighbourhood, stood the remains of an old heiau, dedicated to Ukanipo, a shark, to which, we were informed, all the people along the coast, for a considerable distance, used to repair, at stated times, with abundant offerings.

AT KAAWALOA

Passing on along a rugged road, we reached Kaavaroa soon after 2 p. m.

Kamakau received us kindly, spread out a mat for us to sit down on, handed us a calabash of good fresh water, (a great luxury on this side of the island,) and ordered a goat to be prepared for our refreshment. He appeared as zealous in his pursuit of truth, earnest in his desires after his own salvation, and concerned for that of his people, as when some of our party had formerly visited him.

One or two inferior chiefs, from a district belonging to him, in the south part of the island, were sitting in the house when we entered. He afterwards began to talk with them on matters of religion, with a seriousness and intelligence which surprised us.

In the afternoon Mr. Thurston and I climbed the rocks, which rise in a north-east direction from the village, and visited the cave in which the body of Captain Cook was deposited, on being first taken from the beach. These rocks, which are entirely composed of lava, are nearly two hundred feet high, and in some parts very steep. A winding path of rather difficult ascent leads to the cave, which is situated on the face of the rocks, about half-way to the top. In front of it is a kind of ledge three or four feet wide, and immediately over it the rocks rise perpendicularly for a yard or two, but afterwards the ascent is gradual to the summit.

The cave itself is of volcanic formation, and appears to have been one of those subterranean tunnels so numerous on the island, by which the volcanoes in the interior sometimes discharge their contents upon the shore. It is five feet high, and the entrance about eight or ten feet wide. The roof and sides within are of obsidian or hard vitreous lava; and along the floor it is evident that in some remote period a stream of the same kind of lava has also flowed.

INTERVIEWS WITH WITNESSES OF COOK'S DEATH

There are a number of persons at Kaavaroa, and other places in the islands, who either were present themselves at the unhappy dispute, which in this vicinity terminated the valuable life of the celebrated Captain Cook, or who, from their connexion with those who were on the spot, are well acquainted with the particulars of that melancholy event. With many of them we have frequently conversed, and though their narratives differ in a few smaller points, they all agree in the main facts with the account published by Captain King, his successor.

"The foreigner," they say, "was not to blame; for, in the first instance, our people stole his boat, and he, in order to recover it, designed to take our king on board his ship, and detain him there till it should be restored.

"Kapena Kuke (Captain Cook's name is thus pronounced by the natives) and Taraiopu our king were walking together towards the shore, when our people, conscious of what had been done, thronged around the king, and objected to his going any further. His wife also joined her entreaties that he would not go on board the ships.

"While he was hesitating, a man came running from the other side of the bay, entered the crowd almost breathless, and exclaimed, 'It is war!—the foreigners have commenced hostilities, have fired on a canoe from one of their boats, and killed a chief.'

CIRCUMSTANCES INCIDENT TO COOK'S DEATH

"This enraged some of our people, and alarmed the chiefs, as they feared Captain Cook would kill the king. The people armed themselves with stones, clubs, and spears. Kanona entreated her husband not to go. All the chiefs did the same. The king sat down.

"The captain seemed agitated, and was walking towards his boat, when one of our men attacked him with a spear: he turned, and with his double-barrelled gun shot the man who struck him. Some of our people then threw stones at him, which being seen by his men they fired on us.

"Captain Cook then endeavoured to stop his men from firing, but could not, on account of the noise. He was turning again to speak to us, when he was stabbed in the back with a pahoa; a spear was at the same time driven through his body; he fell into the water, and spoke no more. We have several times inquired, particularly of the natives acquainted with the circumstances, whether Captain Cook was facing them, or had his back towards them, when he received the fatal thrust; and their answer, in general, has been as here stated, which accords very nearly with Captain King's account, who say, 'Our unfortunate commander, the last time he was seen distinctly, was standing at the water's edge, and calling out to the boats to cease firing, and pull in.'

"If it be true, as some of those present have imagined, that the marines and boatmen fired without his orders, and that he was desirous of preventing any further bloodshed, it is not improbable, that his humanity, on this occasion, proved fatal to him: for it was remarked, that whilst he faced the natives, none of them had offered him any violence, but that having turned about, to give his orders to the boats, he was stabbed in the back, and fell with his face into the water." See Captain King's Continuation of Cook's Voyages, 4to. vol. iii. pages 45 and 46.

SOUVENIRS OF COOK

"After he was dead, we all wailed. His bones were separated—the flesh was scraped off and burnt, as was the practice in regard to our own chiefs when they died. We thought he was the god Rono, worshipped him as such, and after his death reverenced his bones."

Not only were his bones so treated, but almost every relic left with them.

Among other things, a sledge, which, from their description of it, must have come from the north-west coast of America, left at the islands by Captain Cook, or some of his companions, was afterwards worshipped by the people. They called it, probably from its singular shape, Opaitauarii, a crab or shrimp, for a chief to rest on; from opai, a crab or shrimp, tau, to rest or sit, and arii, a chief.

Many of the chiefs frequently express the sorrow they feel whenever they think of the Captain; and even the common people usually speak of these facts with apparent regret. Yet they exonerate the king Taraiopu from all blame, as nothing was done by his orders.

I was once in a house in Oahu with Karaimoku, and several other chiefs, looking over the plates in the folio edition of Cook's Voyages. They were greatly affected with the print which represented his death, and inquired if I knew the names of those who were slain on that occasion.

I perceived Karaimoku more than once wipe the tears from his eyes, while conversing about this melancholy event.

He said, he recollected Captain Cook's visit, if not also his person, though he was at Maui at the time of his death.

More than once, when conversing with us on the length of time the missionaries had been in the Society Islands, they have said, Why did you not come here sooner? Was it because we killed Captain Cook?

WHY COOK'S BOAT WAS STOLEN

We have sometimes asked them what inducement they had to steal the boat, when they possessed so many canoes of their own.

They have generally answered, that they did not take it to transport themselves from one island to another, for their own canoes were more convenient, and they knew better how to manage them; but because they saw it was not sewed together, but fastened with nails. These they wanted,—therefore stole the boat, and broke it to pieces the next day, in order to obtain the nails to make fish-hooks with.

We have every reason to believe that this was the principal, if not the only motive, by which they were actuated in committing the depredation which ultimately led to such unhappy consequences.

They prize nails very highly; and though we do not know that they ever went so far in their endeavours to obtain a more abundant supply, as the Society islanders did, who actually planted them in the ground, hoping they would grow like potatoes, or any other vegetable, yet such is the value they still set on them, that the fishermen would rather receive a wrought nail, to make of it a fish-hook according to their own taste, than the best English-made fish-hook we could give them.

COOK SUPPOSED TO BE A GOD

It has been supposed that the circumstance of Captain Cook's bones being separated, and the flesh taken from them, was evidence of a savage and unrelenting barbarity; but so far from this, it was the result of the highest respect they could shew him.

We may also mention here, the reason for which the remains of Captain Cook received, as was the case, the worship of a god.

Among the kings who governed Hawaii during what may in its

85

chronology be called the fabulous age, was Rono or Orono; who, on some account, became offended with his wife, and murdered her; but afterwards lamented the act so much, as to induce a state of mental derangement. In this state he travelled through all the islands, boxing and wrestling with every one he met.

He subsequently set sail in a singularly shaped canoe for Tahiti, or a foreign country. After his departure he was deified by his countrymen, and annual games of boxing and wrestling were instituted in his honor.

As soon as Captain Cook arrived, it was supposed, and reported, that the god Rono was returned; the priests clothed him with the sacred cloth worn only by the god, conducted him to their temples, sacrificed animals to propitiate his favour, and hence the people prostrated themselves before him as he walked through the villages.

WHAT UNDECEIVED THE NATIVES

But when, in the attack made upon him, they saw his blood running, and heard his groans, they said, "No, this is not Rono."

Some, however, after his death, still supposed him to be Rono, and expected he would appear again.

Some of his bones, his ribs, and breastbone, were considered sacred, as part of Rono, and deposited in a heiau (temple) dedicated to Rono, on the opposite side of the island. Captain King was led to presume that the bones of the trunk were burnt with the flesh. Part of them probably were so disposed of, but not the whole.

It appears that none of them were returned; for, describing those brought to Captain Clarke, which were all they received, he says, "When we arrived at the beach, Eappo came into the pinnace, and delivered to the captain the bones wrapped up in a large quantity of fine new cloth, and covered with a spotted cloak of black and white feathers.

PORTIONS OF COOK'S BODY RETURNED

We found in it both the hands of Captain Cook entire, which were well known, from a remarkable scar on one of them, that divided the thumb from the forefinger, the whole length of the metacarpal bone; the skull, but with the scalp separated from it, and the bones that form the face wanting; the scalp, with the hair upon it cut short, and the ears adhering to it; the bones of both arms, with the skin of the fore arms hanging to them. The thigh and leg bones joined together, but without the feet. The ligaments of the joints were entire; and the whole bore evident marks of having been in the fire, except the hands, which had the flesh left upon them, and were cut in several places, and crammed with salt, apparently with an intention of preserving them.

86

The lower jaw and feet, which were wanting, Eappo told us, had been seized by different chiefs, and that Terreeoboo was using every means to recover them.

Speaking of Eappo's first visit after the death of Captain Cook, he says, "We learned from this person, that the flesh of all the bodies of our people, together with the bones of the trunks, had been burnt." —Captain King's Continuation of Cook's Voyages, vol. iii. pages 78, 79, and 80.

There religious homage was paid to them, and from thence they were annually carried in procession to several other heiaus, or borne by the priests round the island, to collect the offerings of the people, for the support of the worship of the god Rono.

The bones were preserved in a small basket of wicker-work, completely covered over with red feathers; which in those days were considered to be the most valuable articles the natives possessed, as being sacred, and a necessary appendage to every idol, and almost every object of religious homage throughout the islands of the Pacific. They were supposed to add much to the power and influence of the idol, or relic, to which they were attached.

VAIN SEARCH FOR COOK'S BONES

The missionaries in the Society Islands had, by means of some Sandwich islanders, been long acquainted with the circumstance of some of Captain Cook's bones being preserved in one of their temples, and receiving religious worship; and since the time of my arrival in company with the deputation from the London Missionary Society, in 1822, every endeavour has been made to learn, though without success, whether they were still in existence, and where they were kept.

All those of whom inquiry has been made have uniformly asserted, that they were formerly kept by the priests of Rono, and worshipped, but have never given any satisfactory information as to where they are now.

Whenever we have asked the king, or Hevaheva the chief priest, or any of the chiefs, they have either told us they were under the care of those who had themselves said they knew nothing about them, or that they were now lost.

The best conclusion we may form is, that part of Captain Cook's bones were preserved by the priests, and were considered sacred by the people, probably till the abolition of idolatry in 1819: that, at that period they were committed to the secret care of some chief, or deposited by the priests who had charge of them, in a cave, unknown to all besides themselves. The manner in which they were then disposed of, will, it is presumed, remain a secret, till the knowledge of it is entirely lost.

87

The priests and chiefs always appear unwilling to enter into conversation on the subject, and desirous to avoid the recollection of the unhappy circumstance.

COOK'S DEATH UNPREMEDITATED

From the above account, as well as every other statement given by the natives, it is evident that the death of Captain Cook was unpremeditated, and resulted from their dread of his anger; a sense of danger, on the momentary impulse of passion, exciting them to revenge the death of the chief who had been shot.

Few intelligent visitors leave Hawaii without making a pilgrimage to the spot where he fell. We have often visited it, and, though several natives have been our guides on different occasions, they have invariably conducted us to the same place. A number of cocoa-nut trees grow near the shore, and there are perforations through two of them, which the natives say were produced by the balls fired from the boats on the occasion of his death.

We have never walked over these rocks without emotions of melancholy interest. The mind invariably reverts to the circumstances of their discovery; the satisfaction of the visitors; the surprise of the natives; the worship they paid to their discoverer; and the fatal catastrophe which here terminated his days; and, although in every event we acknowledge an overruling Providence, we cannot but lament the untimely end of a man whose discoveries contributed so much to the advancement of science, introduced us to an acquaintance with our antipodes, and led the way for the philosopher in his extended researches, the merchant in his distant commerce, and the missionary in his errand of mercy, to the unenlightened heathen at the ends of the earth.

CHURCH AND SCHOOL AT SITE OF COOK'S DEATH

It will be gratifying to the Christian reader to know, that, under the auspices of the governor of the island, and the friendly influence of the present chief of the place, Naihe, and his wife Kapiolani, who are steady, intelligent, discreet, and one, if not both, it is to be hoped, pious persons, a missionary station has since been formed in this village; and that on the shore of the same bay, and not far from the spot where this murderous affray took place, and where Captain Cook was killed, a school has been opened, and a house erected for Christian worship; and that the inhabitants of the neighbourhood are instructed in the elements of learning and the peaceful principles of the Christian religion.

INVESTIGATIONS AT KAAWALOA

Towards evening we examined another buoa, similar to the one we had passed at Hokukano. On entering it, we found part of a canoe, several calabashes, some mats, tapa, &c. and three small idols, about eighteen inches long, carefully wrapped in cloth.

The man who accompanied us said, "My father lies here,. don't disturb him; I have not yet done weeping for him, though he has been dead some years."

We assured him of our sympathy with him in the loss of his father; and having satisfied our curiosity, which he was willing to gratify by allowing us to enter the tomb, we returned to Kamakau's, in conversation with whom we passed the evening.

He made many inquiries; such as, if he should bathe on the Sabbath, or eat fish that was caught or brought to him on that day; whether the same body would rise again at the last day; and if the spirit proceeded into the presence of God immediately on quitting the body.

During our journey today, we have numbered 443 houses and eight heiaus. In the shade, the thermometer at sun-rise stood at 71°, at noon 76°, at sun-set 71°.

Much rain fell during the night, but the following morning was bright and serene. It was the Sabbath, and a wide field of usefulness presented its claim to our attention on this holy day, which we felt was to be specially employed in exhibiting to the heathen around the unsearchable riches of Christ.

RELIGIOUS INTEREST OF KAMAKAU

The village of Kaavaroa, where we lodged, stretched along the north shore of the bay. A number of villages with a considerable population were scattered on the southern shore, and it appeared our duty to go over and preach to them. Mr. Bishop and myself, having procured a canoe from Kamakau, passed over the bay about nine a. m. Messrs. Thurston, Goodrich, and Harwood, remained at Kaavaroa, where Mr. Thurston preached to attentive congregations, both in the morning and afternoon.

The good chief Kamakau was so anxious that his people might profit by the word spoken, that he could not forbear interrupting the preacher, to request them to be attentive. After the conclusion of the services, he also addressed them, and exhorted them to be in earnest in seeking salvation through Jesus Christ.

The missionaries observed, with great pleasure, that during the day he was frequently engaged in affectionate conversation on religious subjects, with some one or other of his people.

PREACHING ALONG THE KONA COAST

Landing on the southern shore of Kearake'kua, Mr. Bishop and I passed through the villages of Kiloa, Waipunaula, and Kalama, inviting

89

the people, as we went along, to attend a religious exercise. At the latter place we entered a large house, built by Karaimoku's mother, Kamauo-kalani, but at present belonging to Kekauonohi, his niece. It was the largest in the place, and was ninety-three feet by thirty in the inside. Here about three hundred people collected; and I preached to them from Psalm xxv. 8.

After the service, they seemed desirous to enter into conversation on what they had heard. One man stood up, and called out aloud, "I desire Jehovah, the good Lord, for my God! but we have no one to tell us about him."

SERVICES HAD TO BE REPEATED

In the afternoon we sent the head man word to collect the people, that they might hear the word of God again. It rained, but a considerable number soon assembled in the large house, and I preached to them from 1 Tim. i. 15.

Many kept arriving half an hour after the service had commenced, which induced me to recapitulate the discourse, yet they did not seem weary. When it was finished, the head man addressed the people, recommending them to attend to what they had heard, and proposed that henceforth they should abstain from all labour on the Sabbath, and pray to Jehovah and Jesus Christ; assuring them that such was his own intention.

After answering several inquiries, and encouraging them to adopt the proposal that had been made by the head man, we bade them farewell, and proceeded to another village.

Two large heaps of ti root, (a variety of dracaena, from the sweet root of which an intoxicating drink is made,) and one or two vessels of sugar-cane juice in a state of fermentation, preparatory to its being distilled, were, during the day, thrown away at this place, in consequence of some public remarks against intoxication.

EXPERIENCES AT KEEI

After leaving Kalama, we walked to Keei, a considerable village on the south point of Kearake'kua bay.

As we approached it, we passed over the ground where, about forty years ago, Tamehameha encamped with his warriors, previous to his decisive battles with Kivaraao, the son of Taraiopu.

On reaching the head man's house, about one hundred people soon collected before the door, and I preached to them from Psalm lxx. 4. concluding, as usual, with prayer.

We then went into the house prepared for our lodging, which the good people soon made very comfortable, by spreading some cocoa-nut leaves on the ground, and covering them with a clean mat.

The kind host then proposed to fetch a pig, and have it dressed for supper. We told him we had rather he would not do it on the Sabbath, but that, if agreeable, we should be glad to receive one in the morning.

After family worship, we laid down on the mats to repose, thankful for the opportunities of doing good which we had enjoyed, and for the encouraging attention manifested by the people.

CHAPTER V

In the morning of July the 21st, the party at Kamakau's walked through the village of Kaavaroa (Kowrowa in Cook's Voyages) to the sea-side. The water in some places is deep, and, along the whole extent of the north-west shore, a boat may pull in close to the rocks. The rocks which form the beach on this and the opposite side of the bay, are not, as was supposed by those who first described them, of black coral, but composed entirely of lava, porous, hard, and of a very dark colour, occasionally tinged with a ferruginous brown, bearing marks of having been in a state of fusion. Part of it has probably flowed through the cavern in which Captain Cook's body was deposited, as traces of a stream of lava from thence to the plain below are very distinct.

The steep rocks at the head of the bay are of the same kind of substance, but apparently more ancient; and judging from appearances, the lava of which they are composed had issued from its volcano before Kearake'kua existed; as part of the coast seems to have been rent from these rocks, and sunk below the level of the sea, which has filled up the indention thus made, and formed the present bay.

There are still a number of caves in the face of these rocks, which are seldom resorted to for security in a time of danger, but used as places of sepulture. Several were barricaded, to prevent any but the proprietors entering them, or depositing bodies there. The natives pointed out one in which the remains of Keoua, uncle of Tamehameha, were laid.

Having accomplished the object of their excursion, which was to procure some fragments of the rock on which Captain Cook had been killed, they prepared to return.

On their return, they exchanged a piece of blue cotton, about three yards in length, for four small idols. They were rudely-carved imitations of the human figure; one of them between three and four feet in length, the others not more than eighteen inches. Having breakfasted with Kamakau and his family, they took their leave, and passed over to the other side of the bay.

HAWAIIAN THEORIES OF THE HEREAFTER

The house in which Mr. Bishop and myself had lodged, was early crowded with natives. Morning worship was held in the native language, and a short address given to the people.

A very interesting conversation ensued, on the resurrection of the dead at the last day, which had been spoken of in the address. The people said they had heard of it by Kapihe, a native priest, who formerly resided in this village, and who, in the time of Tamehameha, told that prince, that at his death he would see his ancestors, and that hereafter all the kings, chief, and people of Hawaii, would live again.

I asked them how this would be effected, and with what circumstances it would be attended; whether they would live again on Hawaii, or in Miru, the Hades of the Sandwich Islands?

They said there were two gods, who conducted the departed spirits of their chiefs to some place in the heavens, where it was supposed the spirits of kings and chiefs sometimes dwelt, and afterwards returned with them to the earth, where they accompanied the movements, and watched over the destinies, of their survivors.

The name of one of these gods was Kaonohiokala, the eye-ball of the sun; and of the other, Kuahairo.

A REVELATION TO KAMEHAMEHA

Kapihe was priest to the latter, and, by pretended revelation, informed Tamehameha that when he should die, Kuahairo would take his spirit to the sky, and accompany it to the earth again, when his body would be reanimated and youthful; that he would have his wives, and resume his government in Hawaii; and that, at the same time, the existing generation would see and know their parents and ancestors, and all the people who had died would be restored to life.

These, they said, were all the particulars they knew; but added, that though at Kapihe's suggestion many valuable offerings were made to his god, he proved a false prophet, for Tamehameha died, and did not come to life again.

At eight o'clock, a small pig, nicely baked under ground, and a calabash full of potatoes, were brought in for breakfast. We were both too ill to partake of the bounty of our kind host, yet felt grateful for his attention.

MOKUOHAI, SITE OF KAMEHAMEHA'S DECISIVE BATTLE

At nine a.m. we were joined by our companions from Kaavaroa, and shortly after set out again on our tour.

Mr. Bishop went in the canoe, the rest of us walked on towards Honaunau, a considerable village about five miles distant.

Leaving Keei, we passed on Mokuohai, a spot celebrated as the place where, in the year 1780 or 1781, the great battle was fought between Kauikeouli, (called also as Kivaraao,) eldest son and successor of Taraiopu, and his cousin, Tamehameha, by which the latter though

93

before only possessed of two districts, became sovereign of the whole island.

This battle is considered by most of Tamehameha's friends (who frequently allude to it in talking of him) as the foundation of all his subsequent power and greatness in the Sandwich Islands.

AN EIGHT-DAY BATTLE

During seven successive days, a severe conflict was maintained, with doubtful success. On the morning of the eighth day, it was renewed with augmented fury on both sides, and continued raging until noon, when the death of Kauikeouli terminated the struggle in favour of his rival.

The circumstances attending his death were singular.

Keeaumoku, (the father of Kaahumanu, Piia, and Kuakini, present governor Hawaii), Tamehameha's principal general, with a few of his companions, had advanced a considerable distance beyond the main body of his warriors, and was completely surrounded by Kauikeouli's men.

After defending themselves for some time against superior numbers, all the associates of Keeaumoku were slain, he himself was dangerously wounded by a number of stabs with the pahoa, (the pahoa is a dagger, from eighteen inches to two feet long, made of wood or iron,) and fell in the midst of his foes. His enemies thought him mortally wounded, and were proceeding to despoil him of his ornaments, &c.

HOW THE BATTLE WAS WON

Kauikeouli approached, and called out to them to take care of the paraoa, a finely polished ornament, made of a whale's tooth, highly valued by the natives, and worn on the breast suspended by a necklace of curiously braided human hair, stooping down himself at the same time to untie it.

Keeaumoku, recovering from a swoon, and seeing Kauikeouli bending over him, made a sudden spring, and grasped him around his neck, or (as some of the natives say) by his long flowing hair, and being a man of uncommon stature and strength, held him down. Kauikeouli endeavoured, but in vain, to extricate himself from his grasp.

At this instant, Tamehameha and his attendants, having heard that Keeaumoku had fallen, hastened to the spot, and one of them, Narimaerua, perceiving the situation of Kauikeouli, rushed forward, and ran a spear through his body; another stabbed him with a pahoa. He fell upon the body of Keeaumoku, and instantly expired.

Keoua, his uncle, who fought near him, was about the same time wounded in the thigh by a spear, and obliged to quit the field.

As soon the the death of Kauikeouli was known, a panic spread through his men, and they quickly fled in every direction. Many jumped into the sea, and swam to some canoes lying off the place, and the rest fled to the mountains or the adjoining puhonua (place of refuge) at Honaunau, about four miles distant. Among these was Karaimoku, then a youth, now principal chief in the Sandwich Islands.

Looking one day at the drawing I had made of the puhonua, he pointed with his finger to the place by which he entered when fleeing thither for protection.

Tamehameha now remained master of the field, and before evening reached Honaunau, the former residence of the vanquished chiefs.

The scene of this sanguinary engagement was a large tract of rugged lava, the whole superficies of which had been broken up by an earthquake.

SCENES OF THE CONFLICT

Since leaving Keei, we had seen several heaps of stones raised over the bones of the slain, but they now became much more numerous.

As we passed along, our guide pointed out the place where Tairi, Tamehameha's war-god, stood, surrounded by the priests, and, a little further on, he shewed us the place where Tamehameha himself, his sisters, and friends, fought during the early part of the eighth day.

A few minutes after we had left it, we reached a large heap of stones overgrown with moss, which marks the spot where Kauikeouli was slain.

The numerous piles of stones which we saw in every direction, convinced us that the number of those who fell on both sides must have been considerable.

HAWAII A SCENE OF CONSTANT WARFARE

The Sandwich Islands, like many other parts of the world, have frequently felt the cruel scourge of war. Their traditionary history, so far as we have been able to trace it, is distinguished by nothing so much as accounts of the murderous and plundering expeditions of one island against another, or the sanguinary battles between the inhabitants of different parts of the same island.

The whole group have seldom, if ever, been united under one authority; but, in general, separate governments, and independent kings or chiefs, have existed in each of the large islands; and sometimes the six great divisions of Hawaii have been under as many distinct rulers or chieftains.

Their inclinations or interests often interfered, and almost every dispute terminated in an appeal to arms. Indeed, a pretext for war was seldom wanting, when one party thought themselves sufficiently powerful to invade with success the territories of their neighbours, and plunder their property.

HAWAIIAN METHOD OF WARFARE

Their modes of warfare must, therefore, necessarily exhibit much of their national character; and having during the course of the narrative already had occasion to describe two of their battles, some account of their system of war will probably be acceptable in this place.

Their armies were composed of individuals from every rank in society.

There was no distinct class of men trained exclusively to the use of arms, and warriors by profession, yet there have always been men celebrated for their courage and martial achievements; and there are many now living, who distinguished themselves by deeds of valour and strength in the frequent wars which were carried on during the former part of the late Tamehameha's reign; men who left their peaceful home and employment, as agriculturists or fishermen, to follow his fortunes in the field, and resumed their former pursuits on the cessation of hostilities.

HAWAIIAN WEAPONS OF WAR

Before the introduction of fire-arms and gunpowder, almost all the men were taught to use the various weapons employed in battle, and frequently engaged in martial exercises or warlike games.

One of the exercises consisted in slinging stones at a mark. They threw stones with great force and precision, and are supposed to have been able to strike a small stick at fifty yards' distance, four times out of five.

They also practised throwing the javelin, and catching and returning those thrown at them, or warding them off so as to avoid receiving any injury. In this latter exercise, they excelled to an astonishing degree.

We know some men who have stood and allowed six men to throw their javelins at them, which they would either catch, and return on their assailants, or so dexterously turn aside, that they fell harmless to the ground.

WRESTLING MATCHES AND SHAM FIGHTS

Wrestling was also practised by the more athletic youth, as a preparation to the single combats usual in almost every battle.

Sometimes they had sham fights, when large numbers engaged, and each party advanced and retreated, attacked and defended, and exercised all the maneuvers employed in actual engagement.

96

Admirably constituted by nature with fine-formed bodies, supple joints, strong and active limbs, accustomed also to a light and cumberless dress, they took great delight in these gymnastic and warlike exercises, and in the practice of them spent no inconsiderable portion of their time.

Whenever war was in contemplation, the poë kiro (diviners and priests) were directed to slay the accustomed victims, and consult the gods. Animals only were used on these occasions, generally hogs and fowls.

The priests offered their prayers and the diviners sacrificed the victims, observed the manner in which they expired, the appearance of thir entrails, and other signs.

Sometimes, when the animal was slain, they embowelled it, took out the spleen, and, holding it in their hands, offered their prayers. If they did not receive an answer, war was deferred. They also slept in the temple where the gods were kept, and, after the war-god had revealed his will by a vision or dream, or some other supernatural means, they communicated it to the king and warriors, and war was either determined or relinquished accordingly.

HUMAN SACRIFICES

If the expedition in contemplation was of any magnitude or importance, or the danger which threatened imminent, human sacrifices were offered, to ensure the co-operation of the war-gods in the destruction of their enemies.

They do not appear to have imagined these gods exerted any protecting influence over their devotees, but that their presence and their power destroyed the courage and strength of their enemies, and filled their hearts with terror and dismay.

Sometimes the priests proposed that human victims should be slain; sometimes the gods themselves were said to require them, to promise victory on condition of their being offered, and at other times they were slain after having consulted the gods as their oracle, and not having received a favourable answer, they were desirous to consult them again before they abandoned the enterprise.

METHOD OF OBTAINING HUMAN SACRIFICES AND OF KILLING

If any of their enemies had been taken captive, the victims were elected from among their number; if not, individuals who had broken tabu, or rendered themselves obnoxious to the chiefs, were fixed upon.

A message was sent to the chief under whose authority they were, and at the appointed time he sent his men, who generally despatched them with a stone or club, without any notice, and then carried them away to the temple.

Sometimes they were bound and taken alive to the heiau, and slain in the outer court, immediately before being placed on the altar.

It does not appear that they were slain in the idol's presence, or within the temple, but either on the outside or at the place where they were first taken; in both cases they appear to have endeavoured to preserve the body entire, or mangled as little as possible.

The victims were generally despatched by a blow on the head with a club or stone; sometimes, however, they were stabbed.

The number offered at a time varied according to circumstances, two, four, or seven, or ten, or even twenty, we have been informed, have been offered at once.

When carried into the temple, every article of clothing they might have on was taken off, and they were laid in a row with their faces downwards, on the altar immediately before the idol.

The priest then, in a kind of prayer, offered them to the gods; and if any offerings of hogs were presented at the same time, they were afterwards piled upon them, lying at right angles across the human bodies, where the whole were left to rot and putrefy together.

APPROBATION OF GODS PRELIMINARY TO WAR

War was seldom declared without the approbation of the gods, obtained through the medium of the priests, though it is probable the answer of the diviners was given with due regard to the previously known views of the king and chiefs.

Sometimes the question of war or peace was deliberated in a public meeting of chiefs and warriors, and these popular assemblies furnished occasion for the most powerful displays of native eloquence which, though never present at one of these councils, we should think, from the specimens we have heard repeated, was, like that of their neighbours of the southern isles, at once bold in sentiment, beautiful in imagery, and powerful in effect.

AN ELOQUENT ADDRESS

I never was more deeply affected than by the parting address of a warrior in the South Sea Islands, when he was taking leave of his friends, before going, as he expected, to battle.

Nothing can surpass their efforts on some of these occasions, when their addresses abound with figures like the following:

"Our ranks are rocks in the ocean, unmoved by the dashing waves; each warrior moves a sea porcupine, whom none dare handle.

98

"Let the king's troops advance, and they shall rise before his enemies as the lofty breadfruit rises before the slender grass.

"In the combat the warrior shall stand like the deep-rooted palm, and nod over the heads of their enemies, as the tall cocoa-nut nods over the bending reed."

On urging the attack by night,

"Our torches' glare shall surprise them like the lightning's flash; and our shouts, in the instantaneous onset, terrify like bursting thunder."

The effect was greatly heightened by the conciseness of their language, and the euphony with which it abounds; and probably on one side of the place where they were assembled, the rocks arose, and the waves dashed; while on the other, groves of stately bread-fruit trees appeared, or towering cocoa-nuts, seventy or eighty feet high, waved over their heads.

METHOD OF PREPARATION FOR WAR

When war was declared, the king and warrior chiefs, together with the priests, fixed the time and place for commencing, and the manner of carrying it on.

In the mean time, the Runapai (messengers of war) were sent to the districts and villages under their authority, to require the services of their tenants, in numbers proportionate to the magnitude of the expedition.

These were ordered to come with their weapons, candle nuts for torches, light calabashes for water, dried fish, or other portable provisions.

The summons was in general obeyed with alacrity, and as their spears, clubs, javelins, and slings, were usually suspended in some convenient part of every house, they armed with these, and soon joined the forces at the appointed rendezvous.

When the people en masse were required, the Tuahaua was sent, whose office it was to bring every individual capable of bearing arms.

TREATMENT OF SHIRKERS

Sometimes the Uruoki, another officer, was afterwards despatched; and if he found any lingering behind who ought to have been with the army, he cut or slit one of their ears, tied a rope around their body, and in this manner led them to the camp.

To remain at home when summoned to the field, was considered so disgraceful, the circumstances attending detection so humiliating, and the mark of cowardice, with which it was punished, so indelible, that it was seldom necessary to send round the last-named officer.

These messengers of war were sometimes called Rere, a word which signifies to fly, probably from the rapidity with which they conveyed the orders of the chiefs. They generally travelled at a running pace, and, in cases of emergency, are reported to have gone round the island of Hawaii in eight or nine days; a distance which, including the circuitous route they would take to call at different villages, exceeds three hundred miles.

When the different parties arrived at the place of rendezvous, the chief of the division or district, with some of inferior rank, waited on the king or commanding chief, and reported the number of warriors they had brought.

AN ENCAMPMENT—CHARACTER OF BATTLE FIELDS

They then selected a spot for their encampment, and erected their Hare-pai or Auoro, in which they abode till the army was collected.

The former were small huts, built with cocoa-nut leaves, or boughs and green ti leaves, which each party or family erected for their own accommodation, around that of their chief; and thus formed a small encampment by themselves.

The latter was a large open building, constructed with the same materials, in which the chief and his warriors all dwelt together.

Their camp was near an open space, and they generally selected the most broken and uneven ground, frequently rugged tracts of lava, as their fields of battle.

Sometimes they encamped on the banks of a river, or deep ravine, which lying between them and their enemies, secured them from sudden attack. But they do not appear to have thrown up lines or other artificial barriers around their camp; they did not, however, neglect to station piquets at all the passes by which they were likely to be approached.

FORTS AND REFUGES

Each party usually had a pari or pa-kaua, natural or artificial fortress, where they left their wives and children, and to which they fled if vanquished in the field.

These fortresses were either eminences of difficult ascent, and, by walling up the avenues leading to them, sometimes rendered inaccessible; or they were extensive enclosures, including a cave, or spring, or other natural means of sustenance or security.

The stone walls around the forts were composed of large blocks of lava, laid up solid, but without cement, sometimes eighteen feet high, and nearly twenty feet thick. On the tops of these walls the warrors fought with slings and stones, or with spears and clubs repelled their assailants.

When their pari was an eminence, after they had closed the avenues, they collected large stones and fragments of rock on the edges of the precipices overhanging the paths leading to the fortification, which they rolled down on the heads of their enemies.

NAVAL BATTLES

Sometimes they engaged in fleets amounting to upwards of one hundred canoes on each side.

At a distance they fought with slings and stones, and other missiles, and, at close quarters, with club and spear.

Their fleets were not lashed together like those of the Society islanders.

The Sandwich Islands not being surrounded with coral reefs, there is but little smooth water; and the roughness of the sea, most likely, induced them generally to select terra firma for their theatre of war.

FIGHTING IN OPEN, BY DAY—ORDER OF BATTLE

They do not appear to have practised many stratagems in war, seldom laid ambushes, generally sought open warfare, and but rarely attacked in the night.

Whenever they expected an action, they proceeded to hoonoho ka kaua, (fix the war, or set their army in battle array,) for which they had a regular system, and adopted various methods for attack and defence, according to the nature of the ground, force of the enemy, &c.

When about to engage in an open plain, their army, drawn up for battle, consisted of a centre and wings, the latter considerably in advance, and the line curved in form of a crescent.

The slingers, and those who threw the javelin, were in general distributed through the whole line.

Every chief led his own men to battle, and took his position according to the orders of the commanding chieftain, whose station was always in the centre.

The king generally commanded in person, or that authority was exercised by the highest chief among the warriors; occasionally, however, a chief inferior in rank, but distinguished by courage, or military talents and address, has been raised to the supreme command.

When they fought in a defile, or narrow pass, they advanced in a single column.

The first division, or advanced guard, was called the verau, or point, the name they also give to a bayonet. The other parts of the column were called by different names; the pohivi, or shoulder, was generally considered the strongest section. The chief who commanded was in the centre.

DESCRIPTION OF WEAPONS

Their weapons consisted of the pololu, a spear made of hard wood,

101

from sixteen to twenty feet long, and pointed at one end. The ihe, or javelin, about six feet in length, made of a species of hard red wood, resembling mahogany, called kauira, pointed and barbed. The raau parau, a weapon eight or nine feet long, between a club and spear, somewhat resembling a halbert, with which they were accustomed to thrust or strike, and the pahoa, or dagger, eighteen inches or two feet in length, made of the hard wood, sometimes pointed at both ends, and having a string attached to the handle, which passed around the wrist to prevent their losing it in action.

Besides these, they employed the sling, and their stones were very destructive. The slings were made of human hair, plaited, or the elastic fibres of the cocoa-nut husk; the stones they employed were about the size of a hen's egg, generally ponderous pieces of compact lava, from the bed of a stream or the sea-beach, where they had been worn smooth by the action of the water.

NO SHIELDS—WAR DRESS

They had no shields or weapons of defence, except the javelin, which they used in warding off those that might be thrown at them; they were very expert in avoiding a stone, if they saw it thrown, and the spearmen excelled in parrying the thrusts of their enemies' spears.

The warriors seldom went to battle with any other dress than a maro or narrow girdle round their loins.

Some, however, wore a quantity of cloth bound round their head, which was called ahupoonui, and the chiefs were frequently dressed in their war-cloaks and helmets.

HELMETS AND CLOAKS

The cloaks, though they gave the wearers an imposing appearance, must have proved an incumbrance, without affording much protection.

Some of the helmets were made of close wicker-work, exactly fitted the head, and were ornamented along the crown. But those worn by the high chiefs only, and called mahiori, though not more useful were peculiarly beautiful. They were made in the form of the Grecian helmet, with towering crest, and were thickly covered with the glossy red and yellow feathers of a small paroquet found in the mountains, (with whose feathers the war-cloaks were also ornamented,) and though they did not appear adapted to defend the head, any more than the cloaks were to guard the body, they increased the effect of the towering height and martial air of the chiefs, whose stature was generally above that of the common people.

102

The long cloaks reaching to the knees, or even to the ankles, were worn only by the king and principal chiefs.

The royal colour was yellow, and no one besides the king was allowed to wear a cloak made entirely of yellow feathers. Those of the other chiefs were of red and yellow rhomboidal figures intermingled or disposed in alternate lines, with sometimes a section of dark purple or glossy black.

Tippets were manufactured of the same materials, and worn by the inferior chiefs, or some of the principal warriors, whose rank did not entitle them to wear the cloak.

In addition to the helmet and cloak, the high chiefs occasionally wore a paraoa, or other ornament, like a breastplate, suspended from the neck by finely braided strings of human hair.

PRELIMINARIES AND DETAILS OF BATTLE

The diviners were consulted immediately before they engaged; they slew their victims, noticed also the face of the heavens, and passage of clouds over the sun, the appearance of the rainbow; and, if they augured well, the principal war-god was brought out in front of the whole army, and placed near the king.

The priest then addressed a prayer to the gods, urged them to exercise their power, and prove themselves, in the ensuing engagement, mightier than the gods of their enemies; promising, at the same time, hecatombs of victims in the event of victory.

The king, or commander-in-chief, now addressed the assembled warriors; and if they were to attack, gave the signal for the hoouta, or onset, and they rushed to hui, or mix in fight.

They did not employ any banners or colours, but in their warlike expeditions were attended by their idols.

FUNCTIONS OF THE BATTLE GODS

The national war-god was elevated above the ranks, and carried by the priest near the person of the king, or commander-in-chief. Nor was this the only idol borne to the battle: other chiefs of rank had their war-gods carried near them by their priest; and if the king or chief was killed or taken, the god himself was usually captured also.

The presence of their deities inspired the warriors with courage, who supposed their influence essential to victory.

A description of Tairi has already been given, and he may be taken as a sample; the image was four or five feet high, the upper part wicker-work, covered with red feathers, the face a hideous form, the mouth armed with triple rows of dog's or shark's teeth, the eyes of mother of

103

pearl, the head crowned with a helmet, the crest sometimes formed of long tresses of human hair. They were fixed on a small pillar or pedestal; were sometimes carried by the priests, or placed on the ground, upheld and defended by them.

APPEARANCE OF THE PRIEST HEVAHEVA

We have often conversed with Hevaheva, the priest of Tamehameha's war-god, and though there is nothing naturally repulsive in his countenance, we have been told, that, in the battle, he often distorted his face into every frightful form, and uttered most terrific and appalling yells, which were supposed to proceed from the god he bore or attended.

At times the whole army, except the reserve, engaged at once, but their battles were most commonly a succession of skirmishes, or partial engagements.

SINGLE COMBAT NOT UNUSUAL

The hooparau, single combat, was not unusual. A haughty and boastful warror would advance beyond the line of his companions, and toho or aa, (insult,) in opprobrious terms the whole army of his enemies.

A warrior from that army would hasten to meet him, and the encounter was continued till one was disabled or slain.

We do not know whether, like the Grecian heroes, these combatants addressed each other before engaging in the mortal strife, as did their neighbours in the southern seas. There the challenger, when he beheld his antagonist approaching, would exclaim:

"Who are you, that come to contend with me?—I am so and so, who slew such a one, whose name is famous to the farthest of these islands; the son of such a one, who achieved such an action: are you come to add to our fame?" &c. &c.

The other would answer, "I am such a one, the son of so and so, who performed such an action, celebrated in every island." And after much more rhodomontade, one would ask the other:

"Know you how to lift the spear?" or club; and immediately commence the combat.

We are not certain, but think it probable, that, like the Society Islanders, they had orators, whose duty it was to go through the camp, and through the ranks, on the day of battle, stimulating the men, by reciting, with most violent gesticulations, the warlike deeds of their ancestors, and the victories their island or district had formerly obtained.

Their battles were with confused noise, and boastful shouts.

BRUTAL BATTLE ETHICS

The first that either party slew, they called erehua; frequently the victor jumped upon the expiring body, or, spurning it contemptuously,

104

dedicated its spirit to his gods. He then cut or tore off the hair from the tops of the forehead, and, elevating it in the air, shouted aloud, He oho, a frontlet; and if it was a chief or warrior of note he had slain, his name was added.

He oho! He oho! was reiterated through the ranks of the victor, while he despoiled the fallen warrior of his ornaments, and then dragged the heana, slain body, to the king, or the priest, who, in a short address, offered the victim to his god.

The first offering they called urukoko, increasing blood.

The second slain was called maka-wai, face of water, and the third herua-oni, sand-dug. They were all likewise brought and offered to the gods on the field.

Their conflicts were sometimes continued for several successive days before either army retreated; and, on some occasions, both parties discontinued the contest as if by mutual consent, from despair of victory, or an evil omen revealed by the diviners. Such a battle was called rukurua, both beaten. This, however, was a rare occurrence; they generally fought till one of the armies was vanquished and fled.

NO MERCY TO VANQUISHED

When routed in the field, some fled to the pahu tapu, sacred enclosure, called also puhonua, or place of refuge; others repaired to their pari or fortress; and when these were distant, or the way to them intercepted, they all fled to the mountains, whither they were pursued by the victors for weeks, and even months, afterwards.

When discovered, they were cruelly massacred on the spot, or brought down to the king and chiefs.

When led to the king's presence, they usually prostrated themselves before him, and exclaimed, "E make pata, e ora paha,—i runa te aro? i raro te aro?" To die perhaps, to live perhaps,—upwards the face? or downwards the face?

If the king did not speak, or said "The face down," it was sentence of death, and some one in attendance either despatched the poor captive in his presence, or led him away to be slaughtered. But if the king said, "Upward the face," they were spared, though perhaps spared only to be slaves, or to be sacrificed when the priests should require human victims.

CAPTIVES PROPERTY OF VICTORS

The persons of the captives were the property of the victors, and their lives entirely at their disposal.

A chief taken in the field, or during the retreat, was sometimes spared, and allowed to return to his home.

105

The victors usually buried their dead; but the bodies of the slain, belonging to the vanquished, were generally left unburied on the field, and were devoured by hogs and dogs, or suffered to rot. Small heaps of stones were afterwards piled over their bones, or on the spot where they had fallen, probably as trophies of victory.

APPEALS FOR MERCY

When the king or any chief of high rank was known to be humane, or any of the vanquished had formerly been on terms of friendship with him, avoiding carefully the warriors, an individual, risking his life on the conqueror's clemency, would lie in wait for him in his walks, and prostrating himself in his path, supplicate his compassion, or rush into his house, and throw himself on the ground before him.

Though any one might have killed him, while on his way thither, none dare touch him within the king's enclosure, without his orders.

When the king did not speak, or directed the fugitive to be carried from his presence, which was very unusual, he was taken out and slain.

Generally the prince spoke to the individual who had thus thrown himself into his power; and if he did but speak, or only recognize him, he was secure. He might either join the retinue of the sovereign, or return to his own house. No one would molest him, as he was under maru, shade, or screening protection of the king.

These individuals, influenced by feelings of gratitude, generally attached themselves to the persons or interest of the prince by whom they had been saved, and frequently proved, through subsequent life, the most faithful attendants on his person, and steady adherents to his cause.

REAPPORTIONMENT OF LANDS AFTER WAR

When the vanquished were completely routed, or nearly cut off, their country was hoopahora, portioned out, by the conqueror, among the chiefs and warriors who had been his companions in the war, by whom it was settled.

The wives and children of those whom they had defeated were frequently made slaves, and attached to the soil for its cultivation, and, together with the captives, treated with great cruelty. But when there had been a great loss on both sides, or one party wished for peace, an ambassador with a young plantain tree, and a green branch of the ti plant, was sent with proposals for peace. If they were accepted, the preliminaries were arranged, and the chiefs and priests of both parties met to adjust the particulars.

106

When the conditions of peace were agreed to—they all repaired to the temple. There a pig was slain, its blood caught in a vessel, and afterwards poured on the ground, probably to signify that thus it should be done to those who broke the treaty. A wreath of mairi, a sweet-scented plant, was then woven by the leading chiefs of both parties, and deposited in the temple. Peace was ratified, feasting, dances, and public games followed. The warriors returned to their lands, and the king's heralds were sent round his districts to announce ua pau ka kaua, ended is the war.

The introduction of fire-arms, which so soon followed the discovery of the Sandwich Islands, increased the passion for conquest and plunder in the minds of the proud and turbulent chiefs by whom they were governed; and although the recent introduction and partial reception of Christianity has not induced them to discontinue the practice of war, it has already altered its ferocious and exterminating character, and the principles of clemency inculcated in the gospel have been most strikingly exemplified in the humane conduct of the chiefs by whom it has been embraced. After a late civil war in Tauai, when the captives were brought before Karaimoku, the chief against whom they had rebelled, he dismissed many of them with spelling books, and directed them to go home, and dwell in peace, cultivate their lands, learn to read and write, and worship the true God.

EFFECT OF CHRISTIANITY ON NATIVES

There is every reason to hope that Christianity, when more generally received, will subdue their restless and ambitious spirits; and under its influence they may be expected, like the southern islanders, to delight in the occupations of peace, and cease to learn the art, or find satisfaction in the practice, of war. Many most decisive and pleasing illustrations of the peaceful tendency of the principles of the Bible, have been given by the Southern Islanders.

One of these occurred under my own observation. In the year 1817 I visited the island of Tubuai, about 300 miles south of Tahiti. While there, two or three natives of the Paumotu or Paliser's Islands, which lie to the eastward of the Society Islands, came on board our vessel, and asked the captain for a passage to Tahiti. He inquired their business there? They said, that some weeks before, they left Tahiti, whither they had been on a visit, to return to their native islands, but that contrary winds drifted their canoe out of its course, and they reached the island of Tabuai; that shortly after their arrival, the natives of the island attacked them, plundered them of their property, and broke their canoe;

that they wished to go to Tahiti, and acquaint Pomare with their misfortune, procure another canoe, and prosecute their original voyage.

Two Europeans, who were on the island at the time, told me they were very peaceable in their behaviour; that the natives of Tubuai had attacked the strangers because they had tried to persuade them to cast away their idols, and had told them there was but one true God, viz. Jehovah.

Our captain, and some others who were present, asked why they did not resist the attack? inquiring, at the same time, if they were averse to war; knowing that their countrymen were continually engaged in most savage wars, and were also cannibals.

WHY THEY DID NOT FIGHT BACK

They said they had been taught to delight in war, and were not afraid of the natives of Tubuai; that if they had been heathens, they should have fought them at once; but that they had had been to Tahiti, and had embraced the new religion, as they called Christianity; had heard that Jehovah commanded those who worshipped Him to do no murder, and that Jesus Christ has directed his followers to love their enemies; that they feared it would be displeasing to God, should they have killed any of the Tubuaians, or even have indulged feelings of revenge towards them; adding, that they would rather lose their canoe and their property, than offend Jehovah, or disregard the directions of Jesus Christ.

Our captain gave them a passage. Pomare furnished them with a canoe; they returned for their companions, and subsequently sailed to their native islands.

When they arrived, they and other natives of the same islands who had also been to Tahiti, told their countrymen what they had learned there, and the changes they had witnessed; that Jehovah was the only God recognized at Tahiti, and that all was peace and good will.

God was pleased to accompany their plain narrative with such power to the hearts of their countrymen, that they abolished idolatry, erected places for the public worship of Jehovah, opened schoolhouses, became professedly Christian people; and the cruelties of their idolatry, cannibalism, and war, have ever since ceased among them.

These natives, in all probability, had never heard the question as to the lawfulness or unlawfulness of Christians engaging in war discussed or even named, but they had most likely been taught to commit to memory the decalogue, and our Lord's sermon on the mount, and hence resulted their noble forbearance at the island of Tubuai.

CHAPTER VI

IN AND ABOUT HONAUNAU.

Ever since Saturday last, I had suffered violent pain, probably induced by the bad water we had been obliged to drink since leaving Kairua; and shortly after passing over the battle ground, I found myself too ill to walk any further. I reclined about an hour on the rocks of lava, under the shade of a small shrub, and then travelled on slowly to Honaunau, which I reached about noon.

The town contains 147 houses, yet we could procure no better accommodation than what an open house for building canoes afforded. Here my companions spread a mat on the ground, and I laid down, grateful for the comfort the canoe shed afforded, as it screened me from the scorching rays of an almost vertical sun.

Towards the evening Mr. Thurston preached to the people of the place, who gave good attention.

I found myself much better the next morning, but too ill to resume the journey that day.

A WELL CULTIVATED SECTION.

After breakfast, Messrs. Thurston and Goodrich examined the inland part of the district, and found, after proceeding about two miles from the sea, that the ground was generally cultivated.

They passed through considerable groves of bread-fruit trees, saw many cocoa-nuts, and numbers of the prickly pear (cactus ficus indicus), growing very large, and loaded with fruit. They also found many people residing at the distance of from two to four miles from the beach, in the midst of their plantations, who seemed to enjoy an abundance of provisions, seldom possessed by those on the sea shore. They returned about noon.

Finding ourselves in want of cooking utensils, and a little tea and sugar, which, in order to lighten our baggage, we had left at Kairua, and perceiving our stock of medicines nearly expended, it was thought best that one of our number should return for them. Mr. Thurston accordingly left Honaunau in the canoe at 2 p.m. and reached Kairua about sunset. He returned about three the next morning, with most of the articles we needed.

The night of the 22d was a restless one with us all, on account of the swarms of vermin that infested our lodging. We should have been glad to have changed our quarters, but I was not yet well enough to proceed.

Another day's detention afforded us time for the more minute examination of whatever was interesting in the neighbourhood, and the more ample development of the object of our visit to the unenlightened people of the village; and those were the occupations of the day.

DESCRIPTION OF HALE O KEAWE.

Honaunau, we found, was formerly a place of considerable importance, having been the frequent residence of the kings of Hawaii for several successive generations.

The monuments and relics of the ancient idolatry with which this place abounds, were, from some cause unknown to us, spared amidst the general destruction of the idols, &c. that followed the abolition of the aitabu, in the summer of 1819.

The principal object that attracted our attention, was the Hare o Keave, (the House of Keave,) a sacred depository of the bones of departed kings and princes, probably erected for the reception of the bones of the king whose name it bears, and who reigned in Hawaii about eight generations back.

It is a compact building, twenty-four feet by sixteen, constructed with the most durable timber, and thatched with ti leaves, standing on a bed of lava that runs out a considerable distance into the sea.

It is surrounded by a strong fence of paling, leaving an area in the front, and at each end about twenty-four feet wide. The pavement is of smooth fragments of lava, laid down with considerable skill.

MANY IDOLS STILL IN PLACE.

Several rudely carved male and female images of wood were placed on the outside of the enclosure; some on low pedestals under the shade of an adjacent tree, others on high posts on the jutting rocks that hung over the edge of the water.

A number stood on the fence at unequal distances all around; but the principal assemblage of these frightful representatives of their former deities was at the south-east end of the enclosed space, where, forming a semicircle, twelve of them stood in grim array, as if perpetual guardians of "the mighty dead" reposing in the house adjoining.

A pile of stones was neatly laid up in the form of a crescent, about three feet wide, and two feet higher than the pavement, and in this pile the images were fixed. They stood on small pedestals, three or four feet high, though some were placed on pillars, eight or ten feet in height, and curiously carved.

110

Heiau and City of Refuge at Honaunau, Hawaii. The House was the "Haleokeawe" the Depository of the Bones of the Kings.

W.Ellis del.

J.Archer, jun.r sc.

The principal idol stood in the centre, the others on either hand; the most powerful being placed nearest to him: he was not so large as some of the others, but distinguished by the variety and superior carvings of his body, and especially of his head.

Once they had evidently been clothed, but now they appeared in the most indigent nakedness. A few tattered shreds round the neck of one that stood on the left hand side of the door, rotted by the rain and bleached by the sun, were all that remained of numerous and gaudy garments, with which their votaries had formerly arrayed them.

A large pile of broken calabashes and cocoa-nut shells lay in the centre, and a considerable heap of dried, and partly rotten, wreaths of flowers, branches of shrubs and bushes, and fragments of tapa, (the accumulated offerings of former days,) formed an unsightly mound immediately before each of the images.

The horrid stare of these idols, the tattered garments upon some of them, and the heaps of rotting offerings before them, seemed to us no improper emblems of the system they were designed to support; distinguished alike by its cruelty, folly, and wretchedness.

CONDITIONS INSIDE THE HOUSE.

We endeavoured to gain admission to the inside of the house, but were told it was tabu roa, (strictly prohibited,) and that nothing but a direct order from the king, or Karaimoku, could open the door.

However, by pushing one of the boards across the door-way a little on one side, we looked in, and saw many large images, some of wood very much carved, others of red feathers, with distended mouths, large rows of sharks' teeth, and pearl-shell eyes.

We also saw several bundles, apparently of human bones, cleaned, carefully tied up with cinet made of cocoa-nut fibres, and placed in different parts of the house, together with some rich shawls and other valuable articles, probably worn by those to whom the bones belonged, as the wearing apparel and other personal property of the chiefs is generally buried with them.

When we had gratified our curiosity, and I had taken a drawing of the building, and some of its appendages, we proceeded to examine other remarkable objects of the place.

CITY OF REFUGE AT HONAUNAU.

Adjoining the Hare o Keave to the southward, we found a Pahu tabu (sacred enclosure) of considerable extent, and were informed by our guide that it was one of the pohonuas of Hawaii, of which we had so often heard the chiefs and others speak. There are only two on the island; the one which we were then examining, and another at Waipio, on the north-east part of the island, in the district of Kohala.

These Puhonuas were the Hawaiian cities of refuge, and afforded an inviolable sanctuary to the guilty fugitive, who, when flying from the avenging spear, was so favoured as to enter their precincts.

This had several wide entrances, some on the side next the sea, the others facing the mountains. Hither the manslayer, the man who had broken a tabu, or failed in the observance of its rigid requirements, the thief, and even the murderer, fled from his incensed pursuers, and was secure.

To whomsoever he belonged, and from whatever part he came, he was equally certain of admittance, though liable to be pursued even to the gates of the enclosure.

Happily for him, those gates were perpetually open; and as soon as the fugitive had entered, he repaired to the presence of the idol, and made a short ejaculatory address, expressive of his obligations to him in reaching the place with security.

PROTECTION OF DEFEATED IN WAR.

Whenever war was proclaimed, and during the period of actual hostilities, a white flag was unfurled on the top of a tall spear, at each end of the enclosure, and, until the conclusion of peace, waved the symbol of hope to those who, vanquished in fight, might flee thither tor protection. It was fixed a short distance from the walls on the outside, and to the spot on which this banner was unfurled, the victorious warrior might chase his routed foes; but here, he must himself fall back; beyond it he must not advance one step, on pain of forfeiting his life.

The priests, and their adherents, would immediately put to death any one who should have the temerity to follow or molest those who were once within the pale of the pahu tabu; and, as they expressed it, under the shade or protection of the spirit of Keave, the tutelar deity of the place.

In one part of the enclosure, houses were formerly erected for the priests, and others for the refugees, who, after a certain period, or at the cessation of war, were dismissed by the priests, and returned unmolested to their dwellings and families; no one venturing to injure those, who, when they fled to the gods, had been by them protected.

We could not learn the length of time it was necessary for them to remain in the puhonua; but it did not appear to be more than two or three days. After that, they either attached themselves to the service of the priests, or returned to their homes.

The puhonua at Honaunau is capacious, capable of containing a vast multitude of people. In time of war, the females, children, and old

113

people of the neighbouring districts, were generally left within it, while the men went to battle. Here they awaited in safety the issue of the conflict, and were secure against surprise and destruction, in the event of a defeat.

The form of it was an irregular parallelogram, walled up on one side and at both ends, the other being formed by the sea-beach, except on the north-west end, where there was a low fence. On measuring it, we found it to be 715 feet in length, and 404 feet wide. The walls were twelve feet high and fifteen thick.

Holes were still visible in the top of the wall, where large images had formerly stood, about four rods apart throughout its whole extent.

Within this enclosure were three large heiaus, two of which were considerably demolished, while the other was nearly entire. It was a compact pile of stones, laid up in a solid mass, 126 feet by 65, and ten feet high.

Many fragments of rock, or pieces of lava, of two or more tons each, were seen in several parts of the wall, raised at least six feet from the ground.

The erection of such a place as the puhonua at Honaunau, under the circumstances and with the means by which alone it was reared, (as they had no machinery,) must have been an herculean task, and could not have been completed but by the labour of many hands.

ORIGIN OF CITY OF REFUGE.

We could not learn how long it had been standing, but were informed it was built for Keave, who reigned in Hawaii about 250 years ago. The walls and heiaus, indeed, looked as if it might claim such antiquity; but the house of Keave and the images must have been renewed since that time.

We had often passed over the ruins of deserted heathen temples, and the vestiges of demolished altars, in the Sandwich Islands, and I had frequently visited those in other groups of the Pacific; but the feelings excited on these occasions had always been those of deep melancholy and horror, at the human immolations and shocking cruelties which they had so often exhibited. Here, however, idolatry appeared at least in the form of clemency, and the sacred enclosure presented a scene unique among the ruins of paganism, which we contemplated with unusual interest.

Whether its establishment was originally projected by the priests, to attach to their interests all who might owe their lives to its institution, or by some mild and humane prince, anxious to diminish the barbarous cruelties of idolatry, and soften the sanguinary character of savage warfare; or whether derived traditionally from the Israelitish

114

cities of refuge, to which some of its features are strikingly analogous, —we do not pretend to determine.

However, we could not but rejoice that its abolition was so soon succeeded by the revelation of a refuge more secure,—that the white flag ceased not to wave till another banner was ready to be unfurled, on which was inscribed, "Look unto me, and be ye saved, all the ends of the earth."—Unto Jesus may they look, and may his name to them become the hope of glory.

> Sweet hope, it makes the coward brave,
> It makes a freeman of the slave,
>   And bids the sluggard rise:
> It lifts the worm of earth on high,
> Provides him wings, and makes him fly
>   To mansions in the skies.

DISCOMFORTS AT HONAUNAU AND KEOKEA.

Our accommodations at Honaunau were very indifferent. The house where we stayed, in addition to other unpleasant circumstances, being entirely open at one end, exposed us by night as well as by day to the unwelcome intrusion of hogs and dogs of every description.

As I was able to walk out on the 23d, we resolved to change our lodgings that evening; and about five o'clock in the afternoon we removed nearly half a mile, to a place called Keokea, where we put up in the best house we saw, in hopes of procuring at least a comfortable night's rest. In this, however, we were disappointed, for it rained heavily the greater part of the night, and the roof of the house not being water-proof, we were more than once obliged to shift our mats to different parts of the earthen floor.

SWEET POTATO LIQUOR.

This was not all; our host, and Makoa our guide, with almost a house full of natives besides, had been regaling themselves with an immense wooden bowl of fermented juice of the sweet potato, and were very noisy till midnight, when they lay down on their mats, but to our great annoyance continued either talking or singing until it was almost day. We frequently spoke to them, and asked them to be still. They answered, "Yes, yes, we will;" but in a few minutes were as boisterous as ever. We were not aware of the intoxicating nature of the simple juice of sweet potatoes when fermented, till we saw its effects on the party here.

But notwithstanding we were uncomfortable during our short stay at Honaunau, and the people less kind than we usually found them, it appeared to us a most eligible place for a missionary station, where

115

one or two devoted men might labour with a prospect of extensive usefulness.

The inhabitants, objects of the first attention with a missionary, are numerous, both in the town and neighbourhood.

The coast, for twenty miles to the northward, includes not less perhaps than forty villages, either on the shore or a short distance inland, and contains probably a population of 20,000 souls, among whom a missionary might labour with facility.

Though there is at present no chief of distinction residing here, as at Kairua, or Kearake'kua, yet the very circumstance of establishing a station here might lead one to remove hither; and the conduct of the people, we have no doubt, would alter materially as they became better acquainted with the missionaries, and their object in settling permanently among them. It is near Kearake'kua bay, the frequent resort of shipping, where supplies might be left; and the natives also told us, that fresh water in considerable quantities might be procured at a short distance. We had not an opportunity to examine the place where they said it was found; but should this prove a fact, Honaunau would possess an accommodation seldom met with on this side of the island.

Being sufficiently recovered to proceed on the journey, we left Keokea about eight o'clock on the morning of the 24th.

A VOLCANIC CURIOSITY.

After travelling half a mile, a singular appearance of the lava, at a small distance from the shore, attracted our attention, and, on examination, presented a curious phenomenon. It consisted of a covered avenue of considerable extent, from fifty to sixty feet in height, formed by the flowing of the lava, in some recent eruption, over the edge of a perpendicular pile of ancient volcanic rocks, from sixty to seventy feet high.

It appeared as if, at first, it had flowed over in one vast sheet, but had afterwards fallen more slowly, and in detached semifluid masses. These, cooling as they fell, had hardened and formed a pile, which, by continued augmentation from above, had ultimately reached the top, and united with the liquid lava there. It was evident that the lava had still continued to flow, along the outside of the arch thus formed, into the plain below, as we observed, in several places, the courses of unbroken streams, from the top of the cliff to the bed of smooth lava, that covered the beach for several miles.

The space at the bottom between the ancient rocks and more recently formed lava, was from six to twelve feet. On one side the lava rose, perpendicular and smooth, shewing distinctly the different and variously coloured masses of ancient lava of which it was composed; some of a bright scarlet, others brown and purple.

The whole pile appeared to have undergone since its formation the effects of violent heat. The cracks and hollows, horizontally between the different strata, or obliquely through them, were filled with lava of a florid red colour, and much less porous than the general mass. This last kind of lava must have been brought to a state of most perfect liquefaction, as it had filled up every crevice that was more than half an inch wide.

A MARVELOUS SIGHT.

It appeared highly glazed, and in some places we could discover small round pebbles, from the size of a hazel-nut to that of a hen's egg, of the same colour, and having the same vitreous covering, yet seeming to have remained solid, while the liquid lava, with which they were mixed, had been forced by subterranean fire into all the fissures of the ancient rock.

The pile on the other side, formed by the dripping of the liquid lava from the upper edge of the rocks, presented a striking contrast, but not a less interesting sight. It was generally of a dark purple or jet black colour, glittering in the rays of the sun, as if glazed over with a beautiful vitreous varnish.

On breaking off any fragments, we found them very porous, and considerably lighter than the ancient lava on the other side. Its varied forms baffled description, and were equal to the conceptions of the most fertile imagination.

The archway thus formed continued for about half a mile, occasionally interrupted by an opening in the pile of recent lava, caused by some projecting rock, or elevation in the precipice above. A spectacle awfully sublime and terrific must have been presented, when this burning stream rolled in one wide sheet, a fiery cascade, from the lofty steep down upon the smoking plain.

With what consternation and horror must it have filled the affrighted inhabitants of the surrounding villages, as they beheld its irresistible and devastating course, impressed as they were with the belief, that Pele, the goddess whom they had offended, had left her lightning, earthquake, and liquid fire, the instruments of her power abode in the volcano, and was in person visiting them with thunder, and vengeance.

As we passed along this vaulted avenue, called by the natives Keanaee, we beheld a number of caverns and tunnels, from some of which streams of lava had flowed. The mouths of others being walled up with stones, we supposed were used as sepulchres.

117

Mats, spread upon the slabs of lava, calabashes, &c. indicated some of them to be the habitations of men; others, near the openings, were used as workshops, where women were weaving mats, or beating cloth. Some, we also saw, used as storehouses, or depositories of sandal wood.

In many places the water filtered through the lava, and, around the spots where it had dropped on the ground, we observed a quantity of fine white spear-shaped crystals of a sharp nitrous taste.

Having walked a considerable distance along the covered way, and collected as many specimens of the lava as we could conveniently carry, we returned to the sea-shore. Mr. Harwood being indisposed, and unable to travel, and being myself but weak, we proceeded in the canoe to Kalahiti, where we landed about 2 p.m. and waited the arrival of our companions. The rest of the party travelled along the shore, by a path often tedious and difficult.

FURTHER REMARKABLE VOLCANIC FORMATIONS.

The lava frequently presented a mural front, from sixty to a hundred feet high, in many places hanging over their heads, apparently every moment ready to fall; while beneath them the long rolling billows of the Pacific chafed and foamed among the huge fragments of volcanic rocks, along which their road lay.

In many places the lava had flowed in vast torrents over the top of the precipice into the sea. Broad flakes of it, or masses like stalactites, hung from the projecting edge in every direction. The attention was also attracted by a number of apertures in the face of the rocks, at different distances from their base, looking like so many glazed tunnels, from which streams of lava had gushed out and fallen into the ocean below, probably at the same time that it had rolled down in a horrid cataract from the lofty rocks above.

They passed through two villages, containing between three and four hundred inhabitants, and reached Kalahiti about four in the afternoon. Here the people were collected for public worship, and Mr. Thurston preached to them from John vi. 38. They gave good attention, and appeared interested in what they heard.

The evening was spent in conversation on religious subjects, with those who crowded our lodgings.

CUSTOMS UPON DEATH OF A CHIEF.

At this place we observed many of the people with their hair either cut or shaved close on both sides of their heads, while it was left very long in the middle from the forehead to the back of the neck. When we inquired the reason of this, they informed us, that, according to the custom of their country, they had cut their hair, in the manner we

118

perceived, on account of their chief who had been sick, and who they had heard was dead.

The Sandwich islanders observe a number of singular ceremonies on the death of their kings and chiefs, and have been till very recently, accustomed to make these events occasions for the practice of almost every enormity and vice. The custom we noticed at this place is the most general. The people here had followed only one fashion in cutting their hair, but we have seen it polled in every imaginable form; sometimes a small round place only is made bald just on the crown, which causes them to look like Roman priests; at other times the whole head is shaved or cropped close, except round the edge, where, for about half an inch in breadth, the hair hangs down its usual length.

Some make their heads bald on one side, and leave the hair twelve or eighteen inches long on the other. Occasionally they cut out a patch, in the shape of a horse-shoe, either behind, or above the forehead; and sometimes we have seen a number of curved furrows cut from ear to ear, or from the forehead to the neck. When a chief who had lost a relative or friend had his own hair cut after any particular pattern, his followers and dependants usually imitated it in cutting theirs.

Not to cut or shave off the hair, indicates want of respect towards the deceased and the surviving friends. but to have it cut close in any form is enough. Each one usually follows his own taste, which produces the endless variety in which this ornamental appendage of the head is worn by the natives during a season of mourning.

KNOCKING OUT FRONT TEETH.

Another custom, almost as universal on these occasions, was that of knocking out some of the front teeth, practised by both sexes, though perhaps most extensively by the men.

When a chief died, those most anxious to shew their respect for him or his family would be the first to knock out with a stone one of their front teeth.

The chiefs related to the deceased, or on terms of friendship with him, were expected thus to exhibit their attachment; and when they had done so, their attendants and tenants felt themselves, by the influence of custom, obliged to follow their example. Sometimes a man broke out his own tooth with a stone; more frequently, however, it was done by another, who fixed one end of a piece of stick or hard wood against the tooth, and struck the other end with a stone, till it was broken off.

When any of the men deferred this operation, the women often performed it for them while they were asleep.

More than one tooth was seldom destroyed at one time; but the

119

mutilation being repeated on the decease of every chief of rank or authority, there are few men to be seen, who had arrived at maturity before the introduction of Christianity to the islands, with an entire set of teeth; and many by this custom have lost the front teeth on both the upper and lower jaw, which, aside from other inconveniences, causes a great defect in their speech.

Some, however, have dared to be singular; and though they must have seen many deaths, have parted with but few of their teeth. Among this number is Karaimoku, a chief next in authority to the king, not more than one of whose teeth are deficient.

Cutting one or both ears was formerly practised on these occasions; but as we never saw more than one or two old men thus disfigured, the custom appears to have been discontinued.

Another badge of mourning, assumed principally by the chiefs, is that of tatauing a black spot or line on the tongue, in the same manner as other parts of their bodies are tatued.

A SATURNALIA OF WICKEDNESS AND CRUELTY.

All these usages, though singular, are innocent compared with others, which, until very recently, were practised on every similar event.

As soon as the chief had expired, the whole neighbourhood exhibited a scene of confusion, wickedness, and cruelty, seldom witnessed even in the most barbarous society.

The people ran to and fro without their clothes, appearing and acting more like demons than human beings; every vice was practised, and almost every species of crime perpetrated.

Houses were burnt, property plundered, even murder sometimes committed, and the gratification of every base and savage feeling sought without restraint.

Injuries or accidents, long forgotten perhaps by the offending party, were now revenged with unrelenting cruelty. Hence many of the people of Maui, dreading their recurrence, when Keopuolani was thought to be near her end, took their effects into the enclosure belonging to the missionaries there, and requested permission to remain there, hoping to find a sanctuary within their premises amidst the general devastation which they expected would follow her decease.

MOURNING CUSTOMS IN SOUTH PACIFIC.

The inhabitants of several groups in the Pacific have mourning ceremonies somewhat resembling these.

The Friendly islanders cut off a joint of one of their fingers at the death of a chief, and, like the Society islanders, cut their temples, face, and bosoms, with shark's teeth.

120

The latter also, during their oto haa, or mourning, commit almost as many depredations as the Sandwich islanders. They have, however, one very delicate method of preserving the recollection of the dead, which the latter do not appear to employ; that is, of having a small portion of the hair of the deceased passed through a perforation in one of their ears, ingeniously braided in the form of an earring, and worn sometimes for life.

But the Sandwich islanders have another custom, almost peculiar to themselves, viz. singing at the death of their chiefs, something in the manner of the ancient Peruvians. I have been peculiarly affected more than once on witnessing this ceremony.

A MOURNING SONG.

A day or two after the decease of Keeaumoku, governor of Maui, and the elder brother of Kuakini, governor of Hawaii, I was sitting with the surviving relatives, who were weeping around the couch on which the corpse was lying, when a middle-aged woman came in at the other end of the large house, and having proceeded about half way towards the spot where the body lay, began to sing, in a plaintive tone, accompanying her song with affecting gesticulations, such as wringing her hands, grasping her hair, and beating her breasts. I wrote down her monody as she repeated it.

She described in a feeling manner the benevolence of the deceased, and her own consequent loss. One passage was as follows:

Ue, ue, ua mate tuu Arü,	Alas, alas, dead is my chief,
Ua mate tuu hatu e tuu hoa,	Dead is my lord and my friend;
Tuu hoa i ta wa o ta wi,	My friend in the season of famine,
Tuu hoa i paa ta aina,	My friend in the time of drought,
Tuu hoa i tuu ilihune,	My friend in my poverty,
Tuu hoa i ta uä e ta matani,	My friend in the rain and the wind,
Tuu hoa i ta vera o ta la,	My friend in the heat and the sun,
Tuu hoa i ta anu o ta mouna,	My friend in the cold from the mountain,
Tuu hoa i ta ino,	My friend in the storm,
Tuu hoa i ta marie,	My friend in the calm,
Tuu hoa i mau tai awaru,	My friend in the eight seas;*
Ue, ue, ua hala tuu hoa,	Alas, alas, gone is my friend,
Aohe e hoi hou mai.	And no more will return.

Other exhibitions of a similar kind I witnessed at Maui.

MOURNING FOR KEOPUOLANI.

After the death of Keopuolani, we frequently saw the inhabitants of a whole district, that had belonged to her, coming to weep on account of her death, They walked in profound silence, either in single file, or two or three abreast, the old people leading the van, and the children bringing up the rear.

---

* A figurative term for the channels between the different islands of the group.

They were not covered with ashes, but almost literally clothed in sack-cloth. No ornaments, or even decent piece of cloth, was seen on any one. Dressed only in old fishing nets, dirty and torn pieces of matting, or tattered garments, and these sometimes tied on their bodies with pieces of old canoe ropes, they appeared the most abject and wretched companies of human beings I ever saw.

When they were within a few hundred yards of the house where the corpse was lying, they began to lament and wail. The crowds of mourners around the house opened a passage for them to approach it, and then one or two of their number came forward, and standing a little before the rest, began a song or recitation, shewing her birth, rank, honours, and virtues, brandishing a staff or piece of sugar-cane, and accompanying their recitation with attitudes and gestures expressive of the most frantic grief. When they had finished, they sat down, and mingled with the thronging multitudes in their loud and ceaseless wailing.

MOURNING CUSTOMS AMONG COMMON PEOPLE.

Though these ceremonies were so popular, and almost universal on the decease of their chiefs, they do not appear to have been practised by the common people among themselves. The wife did not knock out her teeth on the death of her husband, nor the son his, when he lost his father or mother, neither did parents thus express their grief when bereaved of an only child. Sometimes they cut their hair, but in general only indulged in lamentations and weeping for several days.

Anxious to make ourselves acquainted with their reasons for these practices, we have frequently conversed with the natives respecting them.

The former, such as polling the hair, knocking out the teeth, tatauing the tongue, &c. they say is designed to shew the loss they have sustained, and perpetually to remind them of their departed friends.

Kamehamaru, queen of Rihoriho, who died on her recent visit to England, gave me a fine answer to this effect, on the occasion of the death of Keopuolani, her husband's mother.

TATOOING THE TONGUE.

A few days after the interment, I went into a house where a number of chiefs were assembled, for the purpose of having their tongues tataued; and the artist was performing this operation on hers when I entered. He first immersed the face of the instrument, which was a quarter of an inch wide, and set with a number of small fish-bones, into the colouring matter, placed it on her tongue, and giving it a quick and smart stroke with a small rod in his right hand, punctured the skin, and injected the dye at the same time. Her tongue bled much, and a few moments after I entered she made a sign for him to desist.

122

She emptied her mouth of the blood, and then held her hands to it to counteract the pain.

As soon as it appeared to have subsided a little, I remarked that I was sorry to see her following so useless a custom; and asked if it was not exceedingly painful? She answered, He eha nui no, he nui roa ra kuu aroha! Pain, great indeed; but greater my affection!

After further remarks, I asked some of the others why they chose that method of shewing their affectionate remembrance of the dead? They said, Aore roa ia e naro! That will never disappear, or be obliterated!

BURNING THE SKIN.

Another method, very generally practised by all classes on these occasions, was that of burning on their skin a large number of semi-circles disposed in different forms. It was not done by a heated iron, but having stripped the bark from a small branch of a tree, about an inch in diameter, they held it in the fire till one end of the bark was perfectly ignited, and in this state applied it to the face or bosom, which instantly raised the skin, and after the blister had subsided the scars remained a number of days.

We never found any apologists for the enormities practised on these occasions; and the only excuse they have ever given has been, that at the death of a great chief, the paroxysm of grief has been so violent as to deprive the people of their reason, hence they neither knew nor cared what they did, being hehena, frantic, or out of their senses through sorrow.

CHAPTER VII

CHANGE EFFECTED BY MISSIONARIES.

Since the introduction of the gospel by Christian missionaries, or rather since the death of Keopuolani in September, 1823, all the wicked practices, and most of the ceremonies usual on these occasions, have entirely ceased. Knocking out the teeth is discontinued; wailing, cutting the hair, and marking the tongue, is still practised; but all the evil customs have been most strictly forbidden by the principal chiefs.

We took leave of the friendly people of Kalahiti about nine a.m. on the 25th. Messrs. Thurston, Bishop, and Goodrich, continued their journey along the shore, and I went in the canoe in company with Mr. Harwood.

The coast, along which we sailed, looked literally ironbound. It was formed of steep rocks of porphyritic lava, whose surface wore the most rugged aspect imaginable.

FROM KALAHIKI TO KAPUA.

About two p.m. we reached Taureonanahoa, three large pillars of lava, about twenty feet square, and apparently sixty or eighty high, standing in the water, within a few yards of each other, and adjacent to the shore. Two of them were united at the top, but open at their base. The various coloured strata of black, reddish, and brown lava, being distinctly marked, looked like so many courses of masonry. We sailed between them and the main land; and about five in the afternoon landed at Kapua, a small and desolate-looking village, on the southwest point of Hawaii, and about twenty miles distant from Kalahiti. Here we had the canoe drawn up on the beach until our companions should arrive.

After leaving Kalahiti, Messrs. Thurston, Goodrich, and Bishop, proceeded over a rugged tract of lava, broken up in the wildest confusion, apparently by an earthquake, while it was in a fluid state. About noon they passed a large crater. Its rim, on the side towards the sea, was broken down, and the streams of lava issuing thence, marked the place by which its contents were principally discharged. The lava was not so porous as that at Keanaee, but, like much in the immediate vicinity of the craters, was of a dark red, or brown ferruginous colour, and but partially glazed over. It was exceedingly ponderous and compact, many

124

fragments had quite a basaltic shape, and contained quantities of olivin of a green and brown colour.

CANOEING THROUGH THE SURF.

For about a mile along the coast they found it impossible to travel without making a considerable circuit inland; they therefore procured a canoe, and passed along the part of the coast where the sea rolled up against the naked rocks; and about one p.m. landed in a very high surf. To a spectator on the shore their small canoe would have seemed every moment ready to be buried in the waves; yet, by the dexterity of the natives, they were safely landed with no other inconvenience than a slight wetting from the spray of the surf.

CAMPING AT HONOMALINO.

Mr. Thurston preached to the people at the place where they landed, after which they took some refreshment, and kept on their way over the same broken and rugged tract of lava till about six p.m. when they reached Honomalino. Here they were so much fatigued with the laborious travelling of the past day, that they were obliged to put up for the night. They procured a little sour poë, and only a small quantity of brackish water. Having conducted family worship with the people of the place, they laid themselves down to rest on their mats spread on the small fragments of lava, of which the floor of the house was composed.

Early the next morning the party at Honomalino proceeded to Kapua, and about eight a.m. joined those who had slept there.

A BARREN AND DESOLATE COUNTRY.

At this place we hired a man to go about seven miles into the mountains for fresh water; but he returned with only one calabash full; a very inadequate supply, as our whole company had suffered much from thirst, and the effects of the brackish water we had frequently drank since leaving Honaunau.

Nothing can exceed the barren and solitary appearance of this part of the island, not only from the want of fresh water, but from the rugged and broken tracts of lava of which it appears to be entirely composed.

Unwilling to spend the Sabbath in the desolate and almost forsaken village of Kapua, we prepared for a long day's journey, as we knew of no village before us containing more than five or six houses for nearly thirty miles' distance.

Before we left Kapua, we were so favoured as to procure water enough to fill our canteens, and about 10 a.m. resumed our journey. Messrs. Thurston, Bishop and Goodrich, walked on by the sea-side.

125

About noon they reached Kaulanamauna, and shortly after left Kona, and entered Kau.

Kona is the most populous of the six great divisions of Hawaii, and being situated on the leeward side, would probably have been the most fertile and beautiful part of the island, had it not been overflowed by floods of lava. It is joined to Kohala, a short distance to the southward of Towaihae bay, and extends along the western shore between seventy and eighty miles, including the irregularities of the coast.

The northern part, including Kairua, Kearake'kua, and Honaunau, contains a dense population; and the sides of the mountains are cultivated to a considerable extent; but the south part presents a most inhospitable aspect. The population is thin, consisting principally of fishermen, who cultivate but little land, and that at the distance of from five to seven miles from the shore.

ENTERING THE KAU DISTRICT.

The division of Kau commences at Kaulanamauna, runs down to the south point of the island, and stretches about forty miles along the south-east shore. On entering it, the same gloomy and cheerless desert of rugged lava spread itself in every direction from the shore to the mountains. Here and there at distant intervals they passed a lonely house, or a few wandering fishermen's huts, with a solitary shrub, or species of thistle, struggling for existence among the crevices in the blocks of scoriae and lava. All besides was "one vast desert, dreary, bleak, and wild."

In many places all traces of a path entirely disappeared; for miles together they clambered over huge pieces of vitreous scoriae, or rugged piles of lava, which, like several of the tracts they had passed in Kona, had been tossed in its present confusion by some violent convulsion of the earth.

VOLCANIC CONDITIONS IN KAU.

From the state of the lava covering that part of the country through which we have passed, we should be induced to think that eruptions and earthquakes had been, almost without exception, concomitants of each other; and the shocks must have been exceedingly violent, to cause what we every where beheld.

Slabs of lava, from nine to twelve inches thick, and from four to twenty or thirty feet in diameter, were frequently piled up edgewise or stood leaning against several others piled up in a similar manner. Some of them were six, ten, or twelve feet above the general surface fixed in the lava below, which appeared to have flowed round their base, and filled up the interstices occasioned by the separation of the different pieces.

One side of these rugged slabs generally presented a compact, smooth, glazed, and gently undulated surface, while the other appeared rugged and broken, as if torn with violence from the viscid mass to which it had tenaciously adhered. Probably these slabs were raised by the expansive force of the heated air beneath the sheet of lava.

KEAWAIKI—A PORT OF REFUGE.

After about eighteen miles of most difficult travelling they reached Keavaiti, a small opening among the rocks, where, in case of emergency, a canoe might land in safety. Here they found Mr. Harwood and myself waiting; for, after leaving Kapua, we had sailed along close to the shore, till the wind becoming too strong for us to proceed, we availed ourselves of the opening which Keavaiti afforded, to run the canoe ashore, and wait till the wind should abate, though in so doing we were completely wet with the surf, and spoiled the few provisions we had on board.

The wind was still too strong to allow the canoe to proceed on her voyage; and those who had travelled by land felt too much fatigued to go on without some refreshment and rest. Desirous of spending the Sabbath with the people at Tairitii, which was still fourteen or fifteen miles distant, we determined to rest a few hours, and then prosecute our journey by moonlight.

A number of conical hills, from 150 to 200 feet high, rose immediately in our rear, much resembling sand-hills in their appearance. On examination, however, we found them composed of volcanic ashes and cinders; but could not discover any mark of their ever having been craters.

HARD CONDITIONS AT KEAWAIKI.

When those of our party who had travelled by land had recovered a little from their fatigue, we partook of such refreshments as remained, and drank the little fresh water we had brought with us in the canoe. Being only about a quart between five persons, it was a very inadequate supply in such a dry and thirsty land, yet we drank it with thankfulness, hoping to procure some at Tairitii early on the following morning.

By the time we had finished our frugal meal, the shades of evening began to close around us. We called our little party together, and after committing ourselves, and those who travelled with us, to the watchful care of our merciful Father, we spread our mats on the small pieces of lava, and lay down to rest under the canopy of heaven. A pile of blocks of scoriae and lava, part of which we had built up ourselves, screened our heads from the winds.

The thermometer at sun-set stood at 73°, yet during the evening the land wind from the snow-covered top of Mouna Roa blew keenly down upon us. We slept, however, tolerably well till midnight, when the wind from the shore being favourable, and the moon having risen, we resumed our journey.

TRAVEL BY MOONLIGHT TO KAILIKII.

I went with Mr. Harwood in the canoe to Tairitii, which we reached a short time before daybreak; but the surf rolling high, we were obliged to keep off the shore until daylight enabled us to steer between the rocks to the landing place. Some friendly natives came down to the beach, and pointed out the passage to the steersman, by whose kind aid we landed in safety about half past five in the morning of the 27th. Our first inquiry was for water; Mauae, the governor's man, soon procured a calabash full, fresh and cool, of which we drank most copious draughts, then filled the canteens, and preserved them for those who were travelling along the shore.

LACK OF DRINKING WATER.

About half-past eight, Mr. Thurston hastily entered the house; his first salutation was, "Have you got any water?" A full canteen was handed to him, with which he quenched his thirst, exclaiming, as he returned it, that he had never in his life before suffered so much for want of water. When he first discovered the houses, about two miles distant, he felt his thirst so great, that he left his companions and hastened on, running and walking till he reached the place where those who arrived in the canoe were stopping.

After leaving Keavaiti, Messrs. Bishop, Goodrich, and Thurston travelled over the rugged lava, till the moon becoming obscured by dark heavy clouds, they were obliged to halt under a high rock of lava, and wait the dawn of day, for they found it impossible to proceed in the dark, without being every moment in danger of stumbling over the sharp projections of the rocks, or falling into some of the deep and wide fissures that intersected the bed of lava in every direction.

After waiting about an hour, they resumed their journey; and Messrs. Bishop and Goodrich reached Tairitii nearly half an hour after Mr. Thurston's arrival.

At 10 a.m. Mr. Thurston preached to the people of Tairitii, and the neighbouring village of Patini, all of whom are fishermen. They behaved with propriety, and appeared interested.

We had sent out Makoa, our guide, soon after our arrival, to inform the people that there would be a religious meeting, and invite their attendance. He had gone much further than we expected he would; and just as Mr. Thurston had finished his sermon, he returned, followed by a considerable company from an inland settlement, who, to use their own words, had come to hear about Jehovah and Jesus Christ. They seemed disappointed at finding the service over. As they said, they could not wait till the evening, they and the people of the village assembled in a large canoe-house, and Mr. Thurston preached again of salvation through Jesus Christ. They sat very quietly, and listened with apparent attention. After they had spent an hour or two in conversation with us, they returned, seemingly interested in what they had heard.

In the afternoon Mr. Thurston preached a third time. Between seventy and eighty were present. With most of those who have attended the public worship in this place, this day was probably the first time they ever heard of Jehovah the living God, or Jesus Christ the Saviour. We could not but desire and pray that the Holy Spirit might make the word spoken in this distant and desolate part of the earth, the power of God to the salvation of many that heard it.

A "SPOUTING HORN" AT KAILIKII.

July 28th.—During the whole of yesterday a most beautiful spouting of the water had attracted our attention, which we found was produced in a manner similar to that we had witnessed at Kairua. The aperture in the lava was about two feet in diameter, and every few seconds a column of water was thrown up with considerable noise, and a pleasing effect, to the height of thirty-five or forty feet.

The lava at this place was very ancient, and much heavier than what we had seen in Kona. The vesicles in it were also completely filled with olivin, which appeared in small, green, hard, transparent crystals, in such quantities as to give the rocks quite a green appearance; some of the olivin was brown.

In this neighbourhood we also discovered large masses of porphyritic lava, containing crystals of felspar and olivin in great quantities, and apparently black schorls.

LIMIT OF CANOE TRAVEL.

The trade-winds blowing along the shore very fresh, and directly against us, obliged us to leave our canoe at this place. Mauae and his companions having drawn it into an adjacent shed, took off the outrigger and left it, together with the mast, sails, and paddles, in the care of the man at whose house we had lodged; as he was also desirous to see the volcano, and, after an absence of several years, to revisit Kaimu, in the division of Puna, the place of his birth, he prepared to accompany us by land.

Hitherto we had travelled along the sea-shore, in order to visit the most populous villages in the districts through which we had passed.

But here receiving information that we should find more inhabitants a few miles inland, than nearer the sea, we thought it best to direct our course towards the mountains.

Makoa, our guide, procured men to carry our baggage, and at nine a.m. we left Tairitii. Our way lay over a bed of ancient lava, smooth, considerably decomposed, and generally covered with a thin layer of soil. We passed along the edge of a more recent stream of lava, rugged, black, and appalling in its aspect, compared with the tract we were walking over, which here and there showed a green tuft of grass, a straggling shrub, or a creeping convolvulus.

TRAMPING ALONG THE KAHUKU BLUFF.

After travelling about a mile, we reached the foot of a steep precipice. A winding path led to its top, up which we pursued our way, occasionally resting beneath the shade of huge overhanging rocks. This precipice is about three hundred feet high, and the rocks on fracture proved a dark grey kind of lava, more compact than that on the adjacent plain.

The whole pile appears to have been formed by successive eruptions from some volcano in the interior, as there appeared to be a thin layer of soil between some of the strata, or different inundations, which we supposed was produced by the decomposition of the lava on the surface of the lower stratum, before overflowed by the superincumbent mass.

The rocks appeared to have been rent in a line from the sea-shore towards the mountains, and probably the same convulsion which burst the rocks asunder, sunk the plain to its present level.

A CHANGE OF SCENE.

In half an hour we reached its summit. A beautiful country now appeared before us, and we seemed all at once transported to some happier island, where the devastations attributed to Nahoaarii, and Pele, deities of the volcanoes, had never been known.

The rough and desolate tract of lava, with all its distorted forms, was exchanged for the verdant plain, diversified with gently rising hills, and sloping dales, ornamented with shrubs, and gay with blooming flowers. We saw, however, no stream of water during the whole of the day; but, from the luxuriance of the herbage in every direction, the rains must be frequent or the dews heavy.

About noon we reached Kalehu, a small village, upwards of four miles from Tairitii. The kind cottagers brought us some fine watermelons, which afforded us a grateful repast while we rested during the heat of the noonday sun.

130

Between sixty and seventy persons collected around the house in which we were sitting, and as I was so far recovered as to be able to preach, I addressed them from Matt. i. 21. They seemed interested, and afterwards said, that they had heard good news. We remained about an hour, conversing on some of the first principles of the religion of Jesus Christ, and then resumed our journey over the same beautiful country, which was partially cultivated, and contained a numerous, though scattered, population.

The prospect was delightful. On one hand the Pacific dashed its mighty waves against the rocky shore, and on the other, the kuahivi (mountain ridges) of Kau, and snow-top'd Mouna Roa, rose in the interior, with lofty grandeur.

UPLAND TARO CULTIVATION.

The path led us through several fields of mountain taro, (a variety of the arum), a root which appears to be extensively cultivated in many parts of Hawaii. It was growing in a dry sandy soil, into which our feet sank two or three inches every step we took. The roots were of an oblong shape, generally from ten inches to a foot in length, and four or six inches in diameter. Seldom more than two or three leaves were attached to a root, and those of a light green colour, frequently blotched and sickly in their appearance. The inside of the root is of a brown or reddish colour, and much inferior to that of the arum esculentum, or lowland taro. It is, however, very palatable, and forms a prime article of food in those parts of the island, where there is a light soil, and but little water.

AN OVERNIGHT STOP AT KAULU.

Between three and four o'clock in the afternoon we reached Kauru, a small village environed with plantations, and pleasantly situated on the side of a wide valley, extending from the mountains to the south point of the island. As the men with our baggage had not come up, we waited about two hours, when Tuite, the head man of the village, arrived, and pressed us to spend the night at his house. We accepted his invitation, and proposed to him to collect the people of the village together, to hear about the true God. He consented, and a little before sunset about a hundred and fifty assembled in front of his house.

Mr. Thurston, after the usual devotional exercises, preached to them for about half an hour, and they paid great attention. During the evening, a baked pig, with some potatoes, and taro, was brought for our supper, of which we made a hearty repast.

131

At the request of Makoa, Tuite furnished men to carry our baggage to the next district, and soon after daylight on the 29th we left Kauru, and, taking an inland direction, travelled over a fertile plain, covered with a thin yet luxuriant soil. Sometimes the surface was strewed with small stones, or fragments of lava, but in general it was covered with brushwood.

The population in this part did not appear concentrated in towns and villages, as it had been along the sea-shore, but scattered over the whole face of the country, which appeared divided into farms of varied extent, and upon these the houses generally stood singly, or in small clusters, seldom exceeding four or five in number.

After walking six or seven miles, we entered the district of Papapohaku. When we had nearly passed through it, we sat down to rest, on a pile of stones by the way side. Between sixty and seventy natives soon collected around us; presenting a motley group. Most of the children were naked, or at best had only a narrow slip of tapa fastened round their loins.

DESCRIPTION OF PEOPLE OF PAPAPOHAKU.

Several of the men, on seeing us pass along the road, had left their work in the fields and gardens, and, although covered with dust and perspiration, had seated themselves in the midst, with their o-os in their hand. (This o-o is the principal implement of husbandry which a Hawaiian farmer uses. Formerly it was a sharp-pointed stick of hard wood; it is now usually pointed with iron. The best are made with broad socket chisels, into which they fix a handle four or six feet long.) Their only clothing was the maro, a narrow girdle worn round the loins, one end of which passes between the legs, and fastens in front.

The old men were most of them dressed in a kihei, as were also some of the women, but many of the latter wore only a pau of native cloth wound round their loins. Their black hair was in several instances turned up, and painted white all round the forehead, with a kind of chalk or clay, which is found in several parts of the island.

Many also wore a small looking-glass, set in a solid piece of wood, and suspended on the bosom by a handkerchief, or strip of native cloth, fastened round the neck, to which was sometimes added another article, considered equally useful, and not less ornamental; viz. a small wooden brass-tipped tobacco-pipe; the looking-glass and tobacco-pipe were sometimes combined in one ornament.

FOREIGNERS A CURIOSITY.

Most of these people had probably never seen so large a company of foreigners before; and their curiosity, as might be expected was unusually excited. Their countenances, however, indicated no feelings of jealousy, but manifested a degree of pleasure greater than ordinary.

After conversing with them some time on the objects of our tour, and their ideas of the true God, we proposed to them to listen to his word, and unite with us in worshipping him. They seated themselves on the grass. We sung a hymn, and I preached from Psalm cxxvii. 1. At the conclusion of our religious service we resumed our journey, several of the natives following us to the next village.

THE BEAUTIES OF WAIOHINU.

Our path running in a northerly direction, seemed leading us towards a ridge of high mountains, but it suddenly turned to the east, and presented to our view a most enchanting valley, clothed with verdure, and ornamented with clumps of kukui and kou trees. On the southeast it was open towards the sea, and on both sides adorned with gardens, and interspersed with cottages, even to the summits of the hills.

A fine stream of fresh water, the first we had seen on the island, ran along the centre of the valley, while several smaller ones issued from the rocks on the opposite side, and watered the plantations below. We drank a most grateful draught from the principal stream, and then continued our way along its margin, through Kiolaakaa, traveling towards the sea, till we reached Waiohinu, about ten miles from the place where we slept last night. Here we found a very comfortable house belonging to Pai, the head man, who invited us in, and kindly entertained us.

About noon, a hospitable dinner was prepared, of which, with the additional luxury of fresh water, we made a comfortable meal.

FIRST KNOWLEDGE OF JESUS CHRIST.

At two o'clock in the afternoon the people of the place were collected outside of the house; and when we had requested them to sit down, we conducted a religious exercise similar to that held in the morning. Much conversation followed, on the subject of religion. They said they had heard of Ieho (Jehovah) our God, but had never before heard of Jesus Christ; that, until now, they did not know there was a Sabbath day, on which they ought not to work, but that hereafter they would recollect and observe it. They wished, they said, to become good men, and to be saved by Jesus Christ.

Between three and four o'clock we took leave of them, and pursued our journey towards the sea-shore. Our road, for a considerable distance, lay through the cultivated parts of this beautiful valley: the mountain taro, bordered by sugar-cane and bananas, was planted in fields six or eight acres in extent, on the sides of the hills, and seemed to thrive

133

luxuriantly. On leaving the valley, we proceeded along by the foot of the mountains, in a line parallel with the sea, and about a mile and a half from it.

THE GAME OF PAHE DESCRIBED.

In our way we passed over a tahua pahe, or pahe floor, about fifty or sixty yards long, where a number of men were playing at pahe, a favourite amusement with farmers and common people in general. The pahe is a blunt kind of a dart, varying in length from two to five feet, and thickest about six inches from the point, after which it tapers gradually to the other end. These darts are made with much ingenuity, of a heavy wood. They are highly polished, and thrown with great force or exactness along the level ground, or floor of earth, previously prepared for the game.

Sometimes the excellence of the play consists in the dexterity with which the pahe is thrown. On these occasions two darts are laid down at a certain distance, three or four inches apart, and he who, in a given number of times, throws his dart most frequently between these two, without striking either of them, wins the game.

At other times it is a mere trial of strength; and those win who, in a certain number of times, throw their darts farthest. A mark is made in the ground, to designate the spot from which they are to throw it. The players, balancing the pahe in their right hand, retreat a few yards from this spot, and then springing forward to the mark, dart it along the ground with great velocity. The darts remain wherever they stop till all are thrown, when the whole party run to the other end of the floor, to see whose have been the most successful throws.

THE GAME OF MAIKA DESCRIBED.

This latter game is very laborious, yet we have known the men of whole districts engage in it at once, and have seen them playing several hours together, under the scorching rays of a vertical sun.

On the same tahua or floor they also play at another game, resembling the pahe, which they call maita or uru maita.

Two sticks are stuck in the ground only a few inches apart, at a distance of thirty or forty yards, and between these, but without striking either, the parties at play strive to throw their stone; at other times, the only contention is, who can bowl it farthest along the tahua or floor.

The uru, which they use instead of a dart, is a circular stone admirably adapted for rolling, being of compact lava, or a white alluvial rock, (found principally in the island of Oahu,) about three or four inches in diameter, an inch in thickness around the edge, but thicker, and consequently heavier, in the centre.

134

These stones are finely polished, highly valued, and carefully pre-served, being always oiled and wrapped up in native cloth after having been used. The people are, if possible, more fond of this game than the pahe; and the inhabitants of a district, not unfrequently challenge the people of the whole island, or the natives of one island those of all the others, to bring a man who shall try his skill with some favourite player of their own district or island.

On such occasions we have seen seven or eight thousand chiefs and people, men and women, assembled to witness the sport, which, as well as the pahe, is often continued for hours together.

Many of these amusements require great bodily exertion; and we have often been struck with the restless avidity and untiring effort with which they pursue even the most toilsome games.

Sometimes we have expressed our surprise that they should labour so arduously at their sport, and so leisurely at their plantations or houses, which, in our opinion, would be far more conducive to their advantage and comfort.

They have generally answered, that they built houses and cultivated their gardens from necessity, but followed their amusements because their hearts were fond of them.

GAMBLING CHIEF INCENTIVE OF GAMES.

There are some few who play merely for pleasure; but the greater part engage in it in hopes of gain.

Were their games followed only as sources of amusement, they would be comparatively harmless; but the demoralizing influence of the var-ious kinds of gambling existing among them is very extensive.

Scarcely an individual resorts to their games but for the purpose of betting; and at these periods all the excitement, anxiety, exultation, and rage, which such pursuits invariably produce, are not only visible in every countenance, but fully acted out, and all the malignant pas-sions which gambling engenders are indulged without restraint.

DESPERATE BETTING.

We have seen females hazarding their beads, scissors, cloth-beating mallets, and every piece of cloth they possessed, except what they wore, on a throw of the uru or pahe.

In the same throng might be frequently seen the farmer with his o-o, and other implements of husbandry; the builder of canoes, with his hatchets and adzes; and some poor man, with a knife, and the mat on which he slept,—all eager to stake every article they possessed on the success of their favourite player; and when they have lost all, we

135

have known them, frantic with rage, tear their hair from their heads on the spot.

This is not all; the sport seldom terminates without quarrels, sometimes of a serious nature, ensuing between the adherents of the different parties.

Since schools have been opened in the islands, and the natives have been induced to direct their attention to Christian instruction and intellectual improvement, we have had the satisfaction to observe these games much less followed than formerly; and we hope the period is fast approaching, when they shall only be the healthful exercises of children, and when the time and strength devoted to purposes so useless, and often injurious, shall be employed in cultivating their fertile soil, augmenting their sources of individual and social happiness, and securing to themselves the enjoyment of the comforts and privileges of civilized and Christian life.

The country appeared more thickly inhabited than that over which we had travelled in the morning. The villages, along the sea shore, were near together, and some of them extensive.

A RELIGIOUS DISCUSSION AT KAPAUKU.

After travelling about an hour, we came to Kapauku, a pleasant village belonging to Naihe. As we passed through it we found tall rows of sugar-cane lining the path on either side, and beneath their shade we sat down to rest.

A crowd of natives soon gathered around us; and after a little general conversation, we asked them who was their god? They said they had no god; formerly they had many, but now they had cast them all away.

We asked them if they had done well in abolishing them? They said, Yes, for the tabu occasioned much labour and inconvenience, and drained off the best of their property.

We asked them if it was a good thing to have no god, and to know of no being to whom they ought to render religious homage? They said perhaps it was, for they had nothing to provide for the great sacrifices, and were under no fear of punishment for breaking tabu; that now, one fire cooked their food, and men and women ate together the same kind of provisions.

We asked them if they would not like to hear about the true God, and the only Saviour? They said they had heard of Jesus Christ, by a boy belonging to Naihe, who came from Oahu about two months ago; but he had not told them much, and they should like to hear something more.

136

I then requested them to sit down, and preached to them on the way of salvation by Jesus Christ. When the service was ended, many involuntarily exclaimed, Nui roa maitai! E ake makou i kanaka makou no Jesu, a i ora roa ia ia. It is greatly good! We wish to become the people of Jesus Christ, and to be saved everlastingly by him.

We recommended them to think on his love, and to love him in return; to obey him; to keep the Sabbath-day, by abstaining from labour, and meeting together to talk about what they had heard; to ask God in prayer to teach them all his righteous will; and to send to Naihe their chief, or the missionaries at Oahu, for books, and a person to instruct them.

Bidding them farewell, we directed our course towards the shore, and in about half an hour came to Honuapo, an extensive and populous village, standing on a level bed of lava which runs out a considerable distance into the sea.

THE LEGEND OF KAWELOHEA.

As we approached this place, the natives led us to a steep precipice, overhanging the sea, and pointed out a rock in the water below, called Kaverohea. They seemed to regard both the place where we were, and the rock below, with strong feelings of superstition; at which we were not surprised, when they informed us, that formerly a jealous husband, who resided a short distance from the place, murdered his wife in a cruel manner with a stone, and afterwards dragged her down to the place where we stood, and threw her into the sea; that she fell on the rock which we saw, and, immediately afterwards, while he stood ruminating on what he had done, called out to him in the most affectionate and lamentable strains, attesting her innocence of the crime for which she had been murdered.

From the rock, which is still called by her name, they said her voice was often heard calling to her husband, and there her form was sometimes seen. They also informed us, that her lamentations were considered by them as ominous of some great disaster; as of war, or famine, or the death of a distinguished chief. We told them it was in imagination only that she was seen, and that her supposed lamentations were but the noise of the surf, or the whistling of the winds.

PRIMITIVE PEOPLE AT HONUAPO.

From the manner in which we were received at Honuapo, we should not think this village had been often visited by foreigners; for on our descending from the high land to the lava on which the town stands,

137

the natives came running out to meet us from all quarters, and soon gathered so thickly around us, that we found it difficult to proceed.

Boys and girls danced and hallooed before us; vast numbers walked by our side, or followed us, occasionally taking us by the hand, or catching hold of some part of our clothes.

They seemed surprised at our addressing them in their own tongue, but were much more so when Mauae, who preceded us with a large fan in his hand, told them we were teachers of religion,—that we had preached and prayed at every place where we had stopped, and should most likely do so there before we slept.

We passed through the town to the residence of the head man, situated on the farthest point towards the sea. He invited us to his house, procured us water to wash our feet with, and immediately sent to an adjacent pond for some fish for our supper. While that was preparing, the people assembled in crowds around the house, and a little before sun-set Mr. Thurston preached to them in the front yard. Upwards of 200 were present, and during the whole of the service, sat quietly and listened attentively.

TATOOING SIMILAR TO THAT OF NEW ZEALAND.

A number of the people at this place had one of their lips tataued, after the manner of some of the New Zealand tribes. There was more tatauing here than we had observed at any other place; but it was very rudely done, displaying much less taste and elegance than the figures on the bodies of either the New Zealanders, Tahitians, or Marquesians, which are sometimes really beautiful.

After the service, some of our number visited the ruins of a heiau, on a point of lava near our lodging. During the evening we made some inquiries respecting it, found it had been dedicated to Tairi, and was thrown down in the general destruction of idols in 1819.

STATUS OF IDOLATRY AND RELIGION.

They seemed to think it was well that idolatry had been prohibited by the king; said its frequent requisitions kept them very poor, and occasioned them much labour.

They were, as might be expected, almost entirely ignorant of the religion of Jesus Christ. And from what we saw and heard on first arriving among them, we should fear they were much degraded by immorality and vice.

One man only from this place had been at Honoruru, in Oahu, since the king had been favourably disposed towards Christianity; while there, he once attended the public worship in the native language, and heard about Jesus Christ, the God of the foreigners; but had given a very imperfect account of him.

138

Sketched by Mr. Ellis.

S. S. Jocelyn Sc.

A Missionary Preaching to Natives on the Lava at Kokukano.
(From the American Edition.)

The people seemed inclined to listen attentively to what was said about salvation through the Redeemer; and though fatigued by our journey and exercises with the people of the different places where we had stopped during the day, we esteemed it a privilege to spend the evening in conversation on a topic of so much interest and importance, and experienced no small degree of pleasure, while endeavouring to convey to their uninformed, but apparently inquiring minds, a concise and simple view of the leading doctrines and duties of our holy religion.

PEOPLE TALKED ALL NIGHT.

At a late hour, we asked them to unite with us in our evening worship, and afterwards lay down to rest. Many of the people in the house, however, continued talking till almost daylight. The attention given by the people to our instructions is not to be considered as evidencing their conversion to Christianity, or indicating any decisive change in their views or feelings, but are merely noticed as pleasing manifestations of their willingness to listen to the truths we are desirous to promulgate amongst them.

CHAPTER VIII

On the morning of the 30th, we arose much refreshed, but Makoa not having arrived with our baggage, we did not leave Honuapo so early as we could have wished.

Great numbers of the people crowded our house at an early hour, and, while breakfast was preparing, they were addressed from Psalm xcvi. 4. When the service was ended, the people were anxious to know more about these things; some time was therefore spent in conversation with them. We had seldom seen any who appeared more interested in the truths of the gospel, than the people of Honuapo.

About eight a.m. Makoa arrived, but without our baggage. The men who were bringing it, he said, could not be persuaded to come on last night, but had set out this morning, and would soon overtake us.

MAKOA FEARS VOLCANO GODS.

We now acquainted him with our intention to visit the volcano, and requested him to hasten on the men with our baggage, as we should want more things there than we could conveniently carry.

He objected strongly to our going thither, as we should most likely be mischievous, and offend Pele or Nahoaarii, gods of the volcano, by plucking the ohelo, (sacred berries,) digging up the sand, or throwing stones into the crater, and then they would either rise out of the crater in volumes of smoke, send up large stones to fall upon us and kill us, or cause darkness and rain to overtake us, so that we should never find our way back.

We told him we did not apprehend any danger from the gods; that we knew there were none; and should certainly visit the volcano.

If we were determined on going, he said, we must go by ourselves, he would go with us as far as Kapapala, the last village at which we should stop, and about twenty miles on this side of it; from thence he would descend to the sea-shore, and wait till we overtook him.

The governor, he said, had told him not to go there, and, if he had not, he should not venture near it, for it was a fearful place.

FROM HONUAPO TO HOKUKANO.

We waited till after nine o'clock, when, the men not arriving with our baggage, we proceeded on our way, leaving Makoa to wait for them, and come after us as far as Kapapala, where we expected to spend the night. As we walked through the village, numbers of the people came out of their houses, and followed us for a mile or two, when they gradually fell behind. When they designed to leave us, they would run on a little way ahead, sit down on a rock, give us their parting aroha as we passed, and continue to follow us with their eyes till we were out of sight.

After travelling some time over a wide tract of lava, in some places almost as rugged as any we had yet seen, we reached Hokukano. Here we found an excellent spring of fresh water, the first we had yet seen on our tour, though we had travelled upwards of a hundred miles.

While we were stopping to drink, and rest ourselves, many natives gathered around us from the neighbourhood. We requested them to accompany us to a cluster of houses a little further on, which they very cheerfully did; and here I addressed them, and invited all who were athirst, and whosoever would, to come and take of the water of life freely.

They sat quietly on the lava till the concluding prayer was finished, when several simultaneously exclaimed: "He mea maitai ke ora, e makemake au:" A good thing is salvation; I desire it. They then proposed several questions, which we answered apparently to their satisfaction, and afterwards kept on our way.

FISH PONDS AT HILEA.

We travelled over another rugged tract of lava about two hundred rods wide. It had been most violently torn to pieces, and thrown up in the wildest confusion; in some places it was heaped forty or fifty feet high. The road across it was formed of large smooth round stones, placed in a line two or three feet apart. By stepping along on these stones, we passed over, though not without considerable fatigue.

About half-past eleven we reached Hilea, a pleasant village belonging to the governor. As we approached it, we observed a number of artificial fish-ponds, formed by excavating the earth to the depth of two or three feet, and banking up the sides. The sea is let into them occasionally, and they are generally well stocked with excellent fish of the mullet kind.

We went into the house of the head man, and asked him to collect the people together, as we wished to speak to them about the true God. He sent out, and most of the people of the village, then at home, about two hundred in number, soon collected in his house, which was large, where Mr. Thurston preached to them. They appeared gratified with what they had heard, and pressed us very much to spend the day with

142

them. We could not consent to this, as we had travelled but a short distance since leaving Honuapo.

HOSPITALITY OF HILEA CHIEF.

The head man then asked us to stop till he could prepare some refreshment; saying, he had hogs, fish, taro, potatoes, and bananas in abundance. We told him we were not in need of any thing, and would rather go on. He said, probably the governor would be angry with him, banish him, or perhaps take off his head, when he should hear that he had not entertained his friends as they passed through the place. We ate a few ripe plantains which he placed before us, and then took our leave, assuring him that we would speak to the governor on the subject of taking off his head, &c. This seemed to satisfy him in some measure, and, after accompanying us a short distance, he gave us his aroha, and returned.

SCENE OF KEOUA'S FINAL DEFEAT.

As we left Hilea, our guide pointed out a small hill, called Makanau, where Keoua, the last rival of Tamehameha, surrendered himself up to the warriors under Taiana, by whom he had been conquered in two successive engagements. He was the younger brother of Kauikeouli, the eldest son and successor of Taraiopu.

After the battle of Keei, in which his brother was slain, he fled to Hiro, the large eastern division of the island. The warriors of Hiro, with those of Puna, and some part of Kau, on the south-east, together with those of part of Hamakua on the north-east, declared themselves in his favour, as the immediate descendant of Taraiopu. Among them he resided several years, undisturbed by Tamehameha, frequently making attacks on the northern and western parts of the island, in which, however, he was generally repulsed with loss.

Notwithstanding the defeats he had experienced, he was still desirous to obtain the sovereignty of the whole island, to the throne of which he considered himself the legitimate heir, and in the year 1789 marched from Hiro with all his forces, to attack Kau and Kona on the western shores.

A DESTRUCTIVE ERUPTION.

He took the inland road, and on his way across the island halted for the night in the vicinity of the volcano. An eruption took place that very night, and destroyed the warriors of two small villages, in all about eighty men. This was considered an ill omen.

He, however, continued his march, and shortly after reached Tairitii. Here he was met by a body of Tamehameha's warriors under Taiana, a chief of whom frequent mention is made in Meares's and Dixon's voyages.

An engagement took place, in which he was defeated, and obliged to retreat towards Hiro. The victorious party pursued, and overtook him at Puakokoki, in the division of Puna, where another battle was fought, in which his forces were totally routed, and almost all of them slain. He saved himself by flying to the mountains, attended by a few of his kahu, or faithful companions. Taiana and his warriors returned to Waiohinu, there to remain till the place of his retreat should be discovered.

SURRENDER OF KEOUA.

After some time, Keoua, Kaoreioku, his younger brother, and a few friends that were with them, came to Makanau. From hence he despatched a messenger to Taiana, requesting permission to pass to the sea-shore, in order that he might go and surrender himself to Tamehameha, who was then at Towaihae.

Taiana, and the rest of the warriors, agreed to allow him to pass unmolested through their camp, and Keaveaheuru, the father of Naihe, present chief of Kaavaroa, and Kamahoe, father of Hoapiri, two near relatives of Keoua, though attached to Tamehameha, went back to assure him of his safety, and of the friendly feelings of Tamehameha towards him.

KEOUA'S PROGRESS TO KAWAIHAE.

He accompanied them to Tairitii, where they embarked in Taiana's canoes, and directed their course along the western shores of Towaihae. On their way he stopped at several places, particularly Honomalino, Honaunau, Kaavaroa, Keauhou, and Kairua. The people at each of the places, at Honaunau in particular, crowded around him, brought him presents of food, hogs, tapa, and fruits, and, by every means in their power, demonstrated their attachment to him. Many of them wept, some on account of the joy they felt at seeing him again; others, from a foreboding fear of the result of his surrender to Tamehameha.

He stopped two nights at Paraoa, a small village a few miles to the southward of Towaihae, where he received the greatest assurances of Tamehameha's kind intentions; and on the morning of the third day, proceeded to Towaihae.

THE TREACHEROUS MURDER OF KEOUA.

Tamehameha, with his chiefs, was standing on the beach as his canoe came in sight, and, with most of the chiefs, intended to protect him; but Keeaumoku, a chief of the most sanguinary disposition, who

144

had grappled with his elder brother in the battle at Keei, had determined on his death; and fearing Tamehameha might frustrate his purpose, if the canoe was allowed to land, lie waded above his middle into the sea; and regardless of the orders of Tamehameha, and the expostulations of the other chiefs, caught hold of the canoe as it approached the shore, and either with his pahoa, or a long knife, stabbed Keoua to the heart as he sat in the stern. He also murdered seven of his companions and friends, who came in the same canoe.

In another canoe was Kaoreioku, his younger brother, and the father of Pauahi, one of the wives of Rihoriho, the late sovereign of the islands. Tamehameha gave strict orders to protect it, and their lives were spared.

Tamehameha, and many of the chiefs, particularly Keaveaheuru and Kamahoe, are reported to have regretted his death. Keeaumoku, however, justified his horrid act by saying, that if Keoua had been allowed to live, they should never have been secure.

THE REPRODUCTIVE PEBBLES OF NINOLE.

We had not travelled far before we reached Ninole, a small village on the sea-shore, celebrated on account of a short pebbly beach called Koroa, the stones of which were reported to possess very singular properties, amongst others, that of propagating their species.

The natives told us it was a wahi pana (place famous) for supplying the stones employed in making small adzes and hatchets, before they were acquainted with the use of iron; but particularly for furnishing the stones of which the gods were made, who presided over most of the games of Hawaii. Some powers of discrimination, they told us, were necessary to discover the stones which would answer to be deified.

THE MANUFACTURE OF GODS.

When selected, they were taken to the heiau, and there several ceremonies were performed over them. Afterwards, when dressed, and taken to the place where the games were practised, if the parties to whom they belonged were successful, their fame was established; but, if unsuccessful for several times together, they were either broken to pieces, or thrown contemptuously away.

When any were removed for the purpose of being transformed into gods, one of each sex was generally selected, and were always wrapped very carefully together in a piece of native cloth. After a certain time, they said a small stone would be found with them, which, when grown to the size of its parents, was taken to the heiau or temple, and afterwards made to preside at the games.

145

We were really surprised at the tenacity with which this last opinion was adhered to, not only by the poor people of the place, but by several others, with whom we have since conversed, and whom we should have supposed better informed. It required all the argument and ridicule that we could employ, to make them believe it could not possibly be so. Koroa was also a place of importance in times of war, as the best stones used in their slings were procured here.

GAME OF KANANE DESCRIBED.

This place is also celebrated as furnishing the small black and white stones used by the natives in playing at konane, a native game, resembling drafts, and apparently more intricate.

The konane board is generally two feet long, and contains upwards of two hundred squares, usually fourteen in a row. It is a favourite amusement with the old men; and we have known one game, commenced early in the morning, hardly concluded on the same day.

We examined some of the stones. The black ones appeared to be pieces of trap, or compact lava. The white ones were branches of white coral, common to all the islands of the Pacific. The angles of both were worn away, and the attrition occasioned by the continual rolling of the surf on the beach, had also given them a considerable polish.

AT PUNALUU—TRAVELING INLAND.

After travelling about two miles, we came to Punaruu, where the people of that and the next village, Wailau, collected together in a large house, and were addressed on the nature and attributes of the true God, and the way of salvation.

In general, speaking to the people in the open air was preferred, as we then had more hearers than when we addressed them in a house. But in the middle of the day we usually found it too hot to stand so long in the sun. The services which we held in the morning and evening were always out of doors.

We now left the road by the sea-side, and directed our course towards the mountains. Our path lay over a rich yellow-looking soil of decomposed lava, or over a fine black vegetable mould, in which we occasionally saw a few masses of lava partially decomposed, sufficient to convince us that the whole had once been overflowed, and that lava was the basis of the whole tract of country. There was but little cultivation, though the ground appeared well adapted to the growth of all the most valuable produce of the islands.

DOMESTIC LIFE OF NATIVES AT MAKAAKA.

After walking up a gentle ascent about eight miles, we came to a solitary hamlet, called Makaaka, containing four or five houses, in

146

which three or four families were residing. We entered one of them to take some refreshment and rest after the fatigue of travelling in the heat of the day. The people of the house, though poor, were hospitable, and gave us cheerfully a few roots of taro out of their own oven.

The house was large, and beneath one roof included their workshop, kitchen, and sleeping-room, without any intervening partitions.

On one side two women were beating native cloth, and the men were at work on a new canoe. In the same place were several larger ones, one upwards of sixty feet long, and between two or three feet deep, hollowed out of a single tree. The workmen told us they were making a pair of that size for Kaikioeva, guardian of the young prince Kauikeouli, whose tenants they were.

Near the south end of the house, which was quite open, was their fire-place, where a man was preparing a quantity of arum or taro for the oven. The roots were oblong, from six inches to a foot in length, and three or four inches in diameter. The substance of the root is somewhat like that of a potato, but more fibrous; and to the taste, before dressed, is exceedingly pungent and acrid.

METHODS OF COOKING DESCRIBED.

The tender leaves of this plant are sometimes wrapped up in plantain leaves, baked, and eaten by the natives; but in general the root only is used as an article of food.

The oven was a hole in the earth, three or four feet in diameter, and nearly a foot deep. A number of small stones were spread over the bottom, a few dried leaves laid on them, and the necessary quantity of sticks and firewood piled up, and covered over with small stones. The dry leaves were then kindled, and while the stones were heating, the man scraped off the skin or rind of the taro with a shell, and split the roots into two or three pieces.

When the stones were red-hot, they were spread out with a stick, the remaining fire-brands taken away; and when the dust and ashes, on the stones at the bottom, had been brushed off with a green bough, the taro, wrapped in leaves, was laid on them till the oven was full, when a few more leaves were spread on the taro; hot stones were then placed on these leaves, and a covering six inches thick of leaves and earth spread over the whole. In this state the taro remained to steam or bake about half an hour, when they opened their oven, and took out as many roots as were needed.

The arum or taro is an excellent vegetable, boiled as we are accustomed to dress potatoes, but is not so farinaceous and pleasant as when baked in a native oven.

147

Sometimes the natives broil their food on heated stones, or roast it before their fire; but these ovens are most generally used for cooking their several kinds of victuals. Potatoes and yams are dressed in the same manner as the taro; but pigs, dogs, fish, and birds, are wrapped in green leaves before they are put into the oven.

HOSPITALITY OF NATIVES.

We saw some Muscovy ducks feeding in the garden, and offered to purchase one; but they said they were rearing them for their landlord, and could not part with any; they furnished us, however, with a fowl, with which, and some biscuit we had with us, we made a tolerable meal.

We stopped about two hours, during which we did not omit to speak to the inhabitants respecting the Saviour.

We also offered to remunerate them for what we had received, but they refused to take any thing. We therefore made the children a present of a looking-glass and a few strings of beads, and then resumed our journey over the same verdant country, frequently crossing small valleys and water-courses, which, however, were all dry.

The surface of the country was covered with a light yellow soil, and clothed with tall grass, but the sides and bed of every watercourse we passed were composed of volcanic rock, a kind of basalt, or dark grey compact lava, with fine grains of olivin, the different strata lying in a direction gently inclined towards the sea.

KAALAALA AND KAPAPALA THICKLY SETTLED.

The land, though very good, was but partially cultivated, till we came to Kaaraara, where we passed through large fields of taro and potatoes, with sugar-cane and plantains growing very luxuriantly.

Maruae, the chief of the place, came down to the road side as we passed by, and asked us to stay for the night at his house; but as Kapapala was only four miles distant, we thought we could reach it before dark, and therefore thanked him, and proposed to walk on. As our boys were tired with their bundles, we asked him to allow a man to carry them to Kapapala. He immediately ordered one to go with us, and we passed on through a continued succession of plantations, in a high state of cultivation.

VOLCANIC MANIFESTATION.

During the whole of the time we had been travelling on the high land, we had perceived a number of columns of smoke and vapour, rising at a considerable distance, and also one large steady column, that seemed little affected by the wind; and this, we were informed, arose from the great crater at Kirauea. The smaller columns were emitted

148

at irregular intervals of several seconds between each. On inquiry we learned, that they arose from deep chasms in the earth, and were accompanied by a hot and sulphureous vapour.

CONDITIONS AT KAPAPALA.

About seven o'clock in the evening we reached Kapapala, and directed our weary steps to the house of Tapuahi, the head man. He kindly bade us welcome, spread a mat in the front of his house for us to sit down upon, and brought us a most agreeable beverage, a calabash full of good cool fresh water.

The thermometer at sun-set stood at 70°, and we sat for some time talking with the people around us. The air from the mountains, however, soon began to be keen. We then went into the house, and, although we were in a tropical climate, in the month of July, we found a fire very comfortable. It was kindled in a hollow place in the centre of the earthen floor, surrounded by large square stones, and gave both light and heat. But as there was only one aperture, which, as in the houses of the ancient Britons, answered the triple purpose of a door, a window, and a chimney, the smoke was sometimes rather troublesome.

A PIG MEMBER OF THE FAMILY.

Few of the Hawaiian females are without some favourite animal. It is usually a dog. Here, however, we observed a species of pet that we had not seen before. It was a curly-tailed pig, about a year and a half old, three or four feet long, and apparently well fed. He belonged to two sisters of our host, who formed part of his family, and joined the social circle around the evening hearth.

In the neighbourhood of Kapapala we noticed a variety of the paper-mulberry, somewhat different from that generally cultivated, which grew spontaneously, and appeared indigenous. Large quantities of the dried bark of this plant, tied up in bundles, like hemp or flax, were piled up in the house where we lodged. It is used in manufacturing a kind of tapa, called mamake, prized throughout the islands on account of its strength and durability.

About eight o'clock a pig was baked, and some taro prepared by our host for supper. At our particular request he was induced to partake of it, though contrary to the etiquette of his country.

When we had finished, Tapuahi and his household assembled for family worship, after which we retired to rest. We had travelled more than twenty miles, and two of our number had since the morning spoken four times to the people.

Soon after sunrise on the 31st, the people of the place were collected around our house. I requested them to sit down in front, and, after singing a hymn, preached to them a short and plain discourse. Mr.

149

Thurston concluded the service with prayer. The people remained in the place for nearly an hour, and made many inquiries.

VOLCANIC ACTIVITY AT PONAHOHOA.

After breakfast three of our number went to visit the places where we had seen the columns of smoke rising yesterday. After travelling about five miles, over a country fertile and generally cultivated, we came to Ponahohoa. It was a bed of ancient lava, the surface of which was decomposed; and in many places shrubs and trees had grown to a considerable height.

As we approached the places whence the smoke issued, we passed over a number of fissures and deep chasms, from two inches to six feet in width.

The whole mass of rocks had evidently been rent by some violent convulsion of the earth, at no very distant period; and when we came in sight of the ascending columns of smoke and vapour, we beheld immediately before us a valley, or hollow, about half a mile across, formed by the sinking of the whole surface of ancient lava, to a depth of fifty feet below its original level.

Its superficies was intersected by fissures in every direction; and along the centre of the hollow, two large chasms, of irregular form and breadth, were seen stretching from the mountain towards the sea in a south-and-by-west direction, and extending either way as far as the eye could reach.

The principal chasm was in some places so narrow that we could step over it, but in others it was ten or twelve feet across. It was from these wider portions that the smoke and vapours arose.

As we descended into this valley, the ground sounded hollow, and in several places the lava cracked under our feet. Towards the centre it was so hot that we could not stand more than a minute in the same place.

THE GUIDE FEARS PELE.

As we drew near one of the apertures that emitted smoke and vapour, our guide stopped, and tried to dissuade us from proceeding any further, assuring us he durst not venture nearer for fear of Pele, the deity of the volcanoes.

We told him there was no Pele of which he need be afraid; but that if he did not wish to accompany us, he might go back to the bushes at the edge of the valley, and await our return. He immediately retraced his steps, and we proceeded on, passing as near some of the smoking fissures, as the heat and sulphureous vapour rising from them would admit.

We looked down into several, but it was only in three or four that

150

Masked Paddlers Bearing Gifts to Captain Cook, Kealakekua Bay, 1778

we could see any bottom. The depth of these appeared to be about fifty or sixty feet, and the bottoms were composed of loose fragments of rocks and large stones, that had fallen in from the top or sides of the chasm.

Most of them appeared to be red-hot; and we thought we saw flames in one, but the smoke was generally so dense, and the heat so great, that we could not look long, nor see very distinctly the bottom of any of them.

DETAILS OF ERUPTION.

Our legs, hands, and faces, were nearly scorched by the heat. Into one of the small fissures we put our thermometer, which had stood at 84°; it instantly rose to 118°, and, probably, would have risen much higher, could we have held it longer there.

After walking along the middle of the hollow for nearly a mile, we came to a place where the chasm was about three feet across, at its upper edge, though apparently much wider below, and about forty feet in length; and from which a large quantity of lava had been recently vomited. It had been thrown in detached semifluid pieces to a considerable distance in every direction, and from both sides of the opening had flowed down in a number of smaller streams.

The appearance of the tufts of long grass through which it had run; the scorched leaves still remaining on one side of a tree, while the other side was reduced to charcoal, and the strings of lava hanging from some of the branches like stalactites; together with the fresh appearance of the shrubs, partially overflowed, and broken down,— convinced us the lava had been thrown out only a few days before. It was highly scoriaceous, of a different kind from the ancient bed of which the whole valley was composed, being of a jet-black colour, and bright variegated lustre, brittle, and porous; while the ancient lava was of a gray or reddish colour, compact, and broken with difficulty.

VOLUMES OF SMOKE AND VAPOR.

We found the heat to vary considerably in different parts of the surface; and at one of the places, where a quantity of lava had been thrown out, and from which a volume of smoke continually issued, we could stand several minutes together, without inconvenience. We at first attributed this to the subterranean fires having become extinct beneath, but the greater thickness of the crust of ancient lava, at that place, afterwards appeared to us the most probable cause, as the volumes of smoke and vapour which constantly ascended, indicated the vigorous action of fire below.

I took a drawing of this place; and when we had collected as many specimens of the lava as we could conveniently carry back to our lodgings, we returned to our guide, whom we found waiting at the spot where we first entered the hollow.

DATE OF PONAHOAHOA ERUPTION.

As he was a resident in Kapapala, and owned a small garden near, we endeavoured to learn from him something of the history of the phenomenon before us.

He told us that the two large chasms were formed about eleven moons ago; that nothing else had been visible till nearly two moons back, when a slight earthquake was experienced at Kapapala, and the next time he came by, the ground had fallen in, forming the hollow that we saw, which also appeared full of fissures.

About three weeks ago, as he was going to his plantation, he said, he saw a small flame issuing from the apertures, and a quantity of smoking lava all around; the branches of the trees that stood near were also broken and burnt, and several of them still smoking.

VOLCANO AT PONAHOAHOA, KAU.

Having gratified our curiosity, we prepared to leave this infant volcano, for such to us it appeared. Although the surface, at least, of the whole country around had a volcanic origin, it seems to have remained undisturbed a number of years, perhaps ages. The lava is decomposed, frequently a foot in depth, and is mingled with a prolific soil, fertile in vegetation, and profitable to its proprietors; and we felt a sort of melancholy interest in witnessing the first exhibitions of returning action after so long a repose in this mighty agent, whose irresistible energies will, probably, at no very remote period, spread desolation over a district now smiling in verdure, repaying the toils, and gladdening the heart, of the industrious cultivator.

Ponahohoa, the place we had visited, is situated in the district of Kapapala, in the north-east part of the division of Kau, and is, as near as we could judge, from ten to twelve miles from the sea-shore, and about twenty miles from the great volcano at the foot of Mouna Roa.

The road by which we returned lay through a number of fields of mountain taro, which appears to be cultivated here more extensively than the sweet potato.

USES OF THE WILIWILI TREE.

On the edge of one of these fields we sat down in the grass to rest, beneath a clump of beautiful trees, the Erythrina corollodendrum; a tree we frequently met with in the mountains, sometimes covered with beautiful flowers, and always affording an agreeable shade. It is called by the natives oviriviri, or viriviri. Its branches are much used in erecting fences, on account of the readiness with which they take root

153

when planted in the ground. The wood is also employed for making the carved stools placed under their canoes, when drawn on the beach, or laid up in their houses. The best kind of surf-boards are also made of this wood, which is lighter than any other the natives possess.

On our way back, we also passed several hills, whose broad base and irregular tops shewed them originally to have been craters. They must be very ancient, as they were covered with shrubs and trees. From them must have come the then molten, but now indurated, flood over which we were travelling.

OTHER VOLCANIC ACTIVITY.

Several small columns of smoke were seen rising near them from fissures recently made.

About two p.m. we reached our lodgings, and dismissed the man who had shewed us the way, with a remuneration for his trouble.

Mr. Harwood, who had arrived during our absence, informed us, that on reaching Kaaraara last night, he took up his lodging with Maruae, the chief of the place, by whom he had been hospitably entertained. Mauae, and his two companions, who had also slept at Kaaraara, arrived with him, but nothing had been heard of Makoa, or our baggage; and we began to suspect he would not follow us, even so far as he had promised.

TRAVELLERS FROM KEALAKOMO.

Between three and four o'clock in the afternoon of the 31st of July, a party of travellers, consisting of four men and a woman, entered the house in which we were stopping, and sat down to rest. We soon learned that they belonged to Kearakomo, in Puna, whither they were going, by a road that also led to the great volcano; and having before experienced the great inconvenience of travelling without a guide over a country of which we were entirely ignorant, it appeared desirable that some of us at least should go with them. We expressed our intention to accompany them. They were pleased, and told us they would wait till we were ready.

No tidings had yet been received of Makoa, or our baggage, our biscuit was nearly expended, and being without even a change of linen, we did not think it expedient to leave this place altogether before our baggage should arrive, especially as we knew it would be several days before we should reach any of the villages on the shores of Puna. Messrs. Bishop and Goodrich, therefore, thought best to wait at least another day, while the rest of us should proceed with the travellers.

Having made this arrangement, we immediately packed up our provisions, which were but a scanty supply, and filled our canteens with water. The natives filled their calabashes; and about five p.m. Messrs.

154

Thurston, Harwood, and myself, left Kapapala, in company with the people of Puna.

A CAVE RESIDENCE AT KAPUAHI.

We proceeded a short distance to a place called Kapuahi, (the hearth of fire,) where we stopped at the entrance of a large cave, arched over by a thick crust of ancient lava. Here two or three families, consisting of men, women, and children, were residing. Its interior was rather dark, as the entrance was the only aperture that admitted any light; yet the inhabitants of this dreary abode seemed cheerful and contented, and perhaps felt themselves favoured by Pele, in having a permanent abode furnished free of labour or expense.

The women were employed in making mats, and beating tapa; the children were playing among the fragments of lava on the outside, and the men were preparing an oven in which to bake some taro. We wished to purchase a few fowls of them, but they had none to dispose of. They gave us, however, two or three roots of taro, and a draught of excellent spring water. Bidding them farewell, we pursued our way over a beautiful country, gradually sloping towards the right, and meeting the ocean, at a distance of from ten to fifteen miles, and rising more abruptly on the left, where it was crowned with the woods, which extended like a vast belt round the base of the greater part of Mouna Roa.

A CAVE LODGING AT KEAPUANA.

After travelling between three and four miles, we reached Keapuana, a large cavern, frequently used as a lodging-place by weary or benighted travellers. The sun was nearly down, and the guides proposed to halt for the night in the cave, rather than proceed any further, and sleep in the open air. The proposal was agreed to, and when we had gathered a quantity of fern leaves and grass for our bed, and collected some fuel for the evening fire, we descended about fourteen feet to the mouth of the cavern, which was probably formed in the same manner as those we had explored in the vicinity of Kairua. The entrance, which was eight feet wide and five high, was formed by an arch of ancient lava, several feet in thickness.

The interior of the cavern was about fifty feet square, and the arch that covered it, ten feet high. There was an aperture at the northern end, about three feet in diameter, occasioned by the falling in of the lava, which admitted a current of keen mountain air through the whole of the night.

While we were clearing out the small stones between some of the blocks of lava that lay scattered around, a large fire was kindled near the entrance, which, throwing its glimmering light on the dark volcanic sides of the cavern, and illuminating one side of the huge masses of lava

155

exhibited to our view the strange features of our apartment, which resembled, in no small degree, scenes described in tales of romance.

When we had cleared a sufficient space, we spread our beds of fern-leaves and grass on the rough floor of the cavern, and then mingled with the cheerful circle who were sitting round the fire. We sung a hymn in the native language, and afterwards committed ourselves and fellow-travellers to the kind keeping of Him, whose wakeful eye and watchful care no dark cavern can exclude.

FIRST VIEW OF KILAUEA'S FIRES.

While the natives were sitting round the fire, Mr. Thurston and I ascended to the upper region, and walked to a rising ground at a small distance from the mouth of the cavern, to try if we could discern the light of the volcano. The wind blew fresh from the mountains; the noise of the rolling surf, to which we had been accustomed on the shore, was not heard; and the stillness of the night was only disturbed by the chirping of the insects in the grass. The sky was clear, except in the eastern horizon, where a few light clouds arose, and slowly floated across the expanse of heaven.

On looking towards the north-east, we saw a broad column of light rising to a considerable elevation in the air, and immediately above it some bright clouds, or thin vapours, beautifully tinged with red on the under side. We had no doubt that the column of light arose from the large crater, and that its fires illuminated the surrounding atmosphere. The fleecy clouds generally passed over the luminous column in a south-east direction. As they approached it, the side towards the place where we stood became generally bright; afterwards the under edge only reflected the volcanic fire; and in a little time each cloud passed entirely away, and was succeeded by another.

We remained some time to observe the beautiful phenomenon occasioned by the reflection of the volcanic fire, and the more magnificent spectacle presented by the multitude and brilliancy of the heavenly bodies. The season was solemn and delightful.

156

CHAPTER IX

Refreshed by a comfortable night's sleep, we arose before daylight on the morning of the first of August, and after stirring up the embers of our fire, rendered, with grateful hearts, our morning tribute of praise to our almighty Preserver.

As the day began to dawn, we tied on our sandals, ascended from the subterraneous dormitory, and pursued our journey, directing our course towards the column of smoke, which bore E. N. E. from the cavern.

The path for several miles lay through a most fertile tract of country, covered with bushes, or tall grass and fern, frequently from three to five feet high, and so heavily laden with dew, that before we had passed it, we were as completely wet as if we had walked through a river.

The morning air was cool, the singing of birds enlivened the woods, and we travelled along in Indian file nearly four miles an hour, although most of the natives carried heavy burdens, which were tied on their backs with small bands over their shoulders, in the same manner that a soldier fastens on his knapsack. Having also ourselves a small leather bag containing a bible, inkstand, note-book, compass, &c. suspended from one shoulder, a canteen of water from the other, and sometimes a light port-folio, of papers, with specimens of plants besides, our whole party appeared, in this respect at least, somewhat en militaire.

STOPPED BY A CHASM.

After travelling a short distance over the open country, we came to a small wood, into which we had not penetrated far, before all traces of a path entirely disappeared. We kept on some time, but were soon brought to a stand by a deep chasm, over which we saw no means of passing. Here the natives ran about in every direction searching for marks of footsteps, just as a dog runs to and fro when he has lost the track of his master.

After searching about half an hour, they discovered a path, which led some distance to the southward, in order to avoid the deep chasm in the lava.

SUGAR CANE REFRESHMENT.

Near the place where we crossed over, there was an extensive cavern. The natives sat down on the top of the arch by which it was formed, and began eating their sugar-cane, a portable kind of provision usually carried on their journeys, while we explored the cavern in hopes of finding fresh water. In several places drops of water, beautifully clear, constantly filtered through the vaulted arch, and fell into calabashes placed underneath to receive it. Unfortunately for us, these were all nearly empty. Probably some thirsty traveller had been there but a short time before.

A SANDY DESERT.

Leaving the wood, we entered a waste of dry sand, about four miles across. The travelling over it was extremely fatiguing, as we sunk in to our ankles at every step. The sand was of a dark olive colour, fine and sparkling, parts of it adhering readily to the magnet, and being raised up in heaps in every direction, presented a surface resembling, colour excepted, that of drifted snow.

It was undoubtedly volcanic; but whether thrown out of any of the adjacent craters in its present form, or made up of small particles of decomposed lava, and the crystalline olivin we had observed so abundant in the lava of the southern shore, and drifted by the constant trade-wind from the vast tract of lava to the eastward, we could not determine.

When we had nearly passed through it, we sat down on a heap of lava to rest and refresh ourselves, having taken nothing since the preceding noon. About ten o'clock, Messrs. Bishop and Goodrich reached the place where we were sitting. They had heard by some travellers, that two or three days would elapse before Makoa would overtake them, and deeming it inexpedient to wait so long, had procured a guide, and early this morning set out from Kapapala to follow the rest of the party.

VOLCANIC FORMATIONS DESCRIBED.

Having refreshed ourselves, we resumed our journey, taking a northerly direction towards the columns of smoke, which we could now distinctly perceive. Our way lay over a wide waste of ancient lava, of a black colour, compact and heavy, with a shining vitreous surface, sometimes entirely covered with obsidian, and frequently thrown up, by the expansive force of vapour or heated air, into conical mounds, from six to twelve feet high, which were, probably, by the same power rent into a number of pieces, from the apex to the base. The hollows between the mounds and long ridges were filled with volcanic sand, and fine particles of olivin, or decomposed lava.

This vast tract of lava resembled in appearance an inland sea, bounded by distant mountains. Once it had certainly been in a fluid state, but appeared as if it had become suddenly petrified, or turned into a glassy stone, while its agitated billows were rolling to and fro.

158

Not only were the large swells and hollows distinctly marked, but in many places the surface of these billows was covered by a smaller ripple, like that observed on the surface of the sea at the first springing up of a breeze, or the passing currents of air which produce what the sailors call a cat's-paw. The billows may have been raised by the force which elevated the mounds or hills, but they look as if the whole mass, extending several miles, had, when in a state of perfect fusion, been agitated with a violent undulating or heaving motion.

A HARD ROAD.

The sun had now risen in his strength, and his bright rays, reflected from the sparkling sand, and undulated surface of the vitreous lava, dazzled our sight and caused considerable pain, particularly as the trade-wind blew fresh in our faces, and continually drove into our eyes particles of sand.

This part of our journey was unusually laborious, not only from the heat of the sun and the reflection from the lava, but also from the unevenness of its surface, which obliged us constantly to tread on an inclined plane, in some places as smooth and almost as slippery as glass, where the greatest caution was necessary to avoid a fall. Frequently we chose to walk along on the ridge of a billow of lava, though considerably circuitous, rather than pass up and down its polished sides. Taking the trough, or hollow between the waves, was found safer, but much more fatiguing, as we sunk every step ankle-deep into the sand.

The natives ran along the ridges, stepping like goats from one ridge to another. They, however, occasionally descended into the hollows, and made several marks with their feet in the sand at short distances, for the direction of two or three native boys with our provisions, and some of their companions, who had fallen behind early in the morning, not being able to keep up with the foremost party.

CRATERS AND ACTIVE VOLCANIC CRACKS.

Between eleven and twelve we passed a number of conical hills on our right, which the natives informed us were craters. A quantity of sand was collected round their base, but whether thrown out by them, or drifted thither by the wind, they could not inform us.

In their vicinity we also passed several deep chasms, from which, in a number of places, small columns of vapour arose, at frequent and irregular intervals. They appeared to proceed from Kirauea, the great volcano, and extended towards the sea in a south-east direction. Probably they are connected with Ponahohoa, and may mark the course of a vast subterraneous channel leading from the volcano to the shore.

159

Sketched by Mr Ellis.

S. S. Everton Jr.

The South End of the Volcano of Kirauea in 1823.

(From the American Edition of Journal. See Engraving from the same sketch in English Edition.)

W. Ellis. del.

J. Archer junr. sc.

The Burning Chasms at Ponahohoa, about 20 Miles Makai of Kilauea. Aftermath of the Lava Flow of 1823.

The surface of the lava on both sides was heated, and the vapour had a strong sulphureous smell.

DEPOSITS OF PUMACE LAVA.

We continued our way beneath the scorching rays of a vertical sun till about noon, when we reached a solitary tree growing in a bed of sand, spreading its roots among the crevices of the rocks, and casting its grateful shade on the barren lava. Here we threw ourselves down on the sand and fragments of lava, stretched out our weary limbs, and drank the little water left in our canteens.

In every direction we observed a number of pieces of spumous lava, of an olive colour, extremely cellular, and as light as sponge. They appeared to have been drifted by the wind into the hollows which they occupied.

The high bluff rocks on the north-west side of the volcano were distinctly seen; the smoke and vapours driven past us, and the scent of the fumes of sulphur, which, as we approached from the leeward, we had perceived ever since the wind sprung up becoming very strong, indicated our proximity to Kirauea.

EATING OHELO BERRIES.

Impatient to view it we arose, after resting about half an hour, and pursued our journey. In the way we saw a number of low bushes bearing beautiful red and yellow berries in clusters, each berry being about the size and shape of a large currant. The bushes on which they grew were generally low, seldom reaching two feet in height; the branches small and clear, leaves alternate, obtuse with a point, and serrated; the flower was monopetalous, and, on being examined, determined the plant to belong to the class decandria, and order monogynia.

The native name of the plant is ohelo. The berries looked tempting to persons experiencing both hunger and thirst, and we eagerly plucked and ate all that came in our way. They are juicy, but rather insipid to the taste.

NATIVE FEARS OF PELE.

As soon as the natives perceived us eating them, they called out aloud, and begged us to desist, saying we were now within the precincts of Pele's dominions, to whom they belonged, and by whom they were rahuiia, (prohibited,) until some had been offered to her, and permission to eat them asked. We told them we were sorry they should feel uneasy on this account,—that we acknowledged Jehovah as the only divine proprietor of the fruits of the earth, and felt thankful to him for them, especially in our present circumstances.

162

Some of them then said, "We are afraid. We shall be overtaken by some calamity before we leave this place."

We advised them to dismiss their fears, and eat with us, as we knew they were thirsty and faint. They shook their heads, and perceiving us determined to disregard their entreaties, walked along in silence.

KILAUEA DESCRIBED.

We travelled on, regretting that the natives should indulge notions so superstitious, but clearing every ohelo bush that grew near our path, till about two p.m. when the Crater of Kirauea suddenly burst upon our view.

We expected to have seen a mountain with a broad base and rough indented sides, composed of loose slags or hardened streams of lava, and whose summit would have presented a rugged wall of scoria, forming the rim of a mighty caldron. But instead of this, we found ourselves on the edge of a steep precipice, with a vast plain before us, fifteen or sixteen miles in circumference, and sunk from 200 to 400 feet below its original level.

The surface of this plain was uneven, and strewed over with large stones and volcanic rocks, and in the centre of it was the great crater, at the distance of a mile and a half from the precipice on which we were standing.

Our guides led us round towards the north end of the ridge, in order to find a place by which we might descend to the plain below.

NATIVE TRIBUTE TO PELE.

As we passed along, we observed the natives, who had hitherto refused to touch any of the ohelo berries, now gather several bunches, and, after offering a part to Pele, eat them very freely. They did not use much ceremony in their acknowledgment; but when they had plucked a branch, containing several clusters of berries, they turned their faces towards the place whence the greatest quantity of smoke and vapour issued, and, breaking the branch they held in their hand in two, they threw one part down the precipice, saying at the same time,

"E Pele, eia ka ohelo 'au; e taumaha aku wau ia oe, e ai hoi au tetahi."
"Pele, here are your ohelos: I offer some to you, some I also eat."

Several of them told us, as they turned round from the crater, that after such acknowledgments they might eat the fruit with security.

DESCENDING INTO KILAUEA.

We answered we were sorry to see them offering to an imaginary deity the gifts of the true God; but hoped they would soon know better, and acknowledge Jehovah alone in all the benefits they received.

We walked on to the north end of the ridge, where, the precipice

163

being less steep, a descent to the plain below seemed practicable. It required, however, the greatest caution, as the stones and fragments of rock frequently gave way under our feet, and rolled down from above; but, with all our care, we did not reach the bottom without several falls and slight bruises.

The steep which we had descended was formed of volcanic matter, apparently a light red and gray kind of lava, vesicular, and lying in horizontal strata, varying in thickness from one to forty feet. In a small number of places the different strata of lava were also rent in perpendicular or oblique directions, from the top to the bottom, either by earthquakes, or other violent convulsions of the ground connected with the action of the adjacent volcano.

ON THE EDGE OF THE PIT.

After walking some distance over the sunken plain, which in several places sounded hollow under our feet, we at length came to the edge of the great crater, where a spectacle, sublime and even appalling, presented itself before us—

"We stopped, and trembled."

Astonishment and awe for some moments rendered us mute, and, like statues, we stood fixed to the spot, with our eyes riveted on the abyss below.

Immediately before us yawned an immense gulf, in the form of a crescent, about two miles in length, from north-east to south-west, nearly a mile in width, and apparently 800 feet deep.

A FLOOD OF BURNING LAVA.

The bottom was covered with lava, and the south-west and northern parts of it were one vast flood of burning matter, in a state of terrific ebullition, rolling to and fro its "fiery surge" and flaming billows.

Fifty-one conical islands, of varied form and size, containing so many craters, rose either round the edge or from the surface of the burning lake.

Twenty-two constantly emitted columns of gray smoke, or pyramids of brilliant flame; and several of these at the same time vomited from their ignited mouths streams of lava, which rolled in blazing torrents down their black indented sides into the boiling mass below.

The existence of these conical craters led us to conclude, that the boiling caldron of lava before us did not form the focus of the volcano; that this mass of melted lava was comparatively shallow; and that the basin in which it was contained was separated, by a stratum of solid matter, from the great volcanic abyss, which constantly poured out its melted contents through these numerous craters into this upper reservoir.

164

We were further inclined to this opinion, from the vast columns of vapour continually ascending from the chasms in the vicinity of the sulphur banks and pools of water, for they must have been produced by other fire than that which caused the ebullition in the lava at the bottom of the great crater; and also by noticing a number of small craters, in vigorous action, situated high up the sides of the great gulf, and apparently quite detached from it.

The streams of lava which they emitted rolled down into the lake, and mingled with the melted mass there, which, though thrown up by different apertures, had perhaps been originally fused in one vast furnace.

800 FEET DOWN TO THE LAKE.

The sides of the gulf before us, although composed of different strata of ancient lava, were perpendicular for about 400 feet, and rose from a wide horizontal ledge of solid black lava of irregular breadth, but extending completely round.

Beneath this ledge the sides sloped gradually towards the burning lake, which was, as nearly as we could judge, 300 or 400 feet lower. It was evident that the large crater had been recently filled with liquid lava up to this black ledge, and had, by some subterranean canal, emptied itself into the sea, or upon the low land on the shore; and in all probability this evacuation had caused the inundation of the Kapapala coast, which took place, as we afterwards learned, about three weeks prior to our visit.

ROARING OF VAST FURNACE.

The gray, and in some places apparently calcined, sides of the great crater before us; the fissures which intersected the surface of the plain on which we were standing; the long banks of sulphur on the opposite side of the abyss; the vigorous action of the numerous small craters on its borders; the dense columns of vapour and smoke that rose at the north and south end of the plain; together with the ridge of steep rocks by which it was surrounded, rising probably in some places 300 or 400 feet in perpendicular height, presented an immense volcanic panorama, the effect of which was greatly augmented by the constant roaring of the vast furnaces below.

After the first feelings of astonishment had subsided, we remained a considerable time contemplating a scene, which it is impossible to describe, and which filled us with wonder and admiration at the almost overwhelming manifestation it affords of the power of that dread Being who created the world, and who has declared that by fire he will one day destroy it. We then walked along the west side of the crater, and in half an hour reached the north end.

While walking over the plain, which was covered with a thin layer of what appeared like indurated sand, but which we afterwards found to be decomposed lava, the natives requested us not to kaha, a heru ka one, strike, scratch, or dig the sand, assuring us it would displease Pele, and be followed by an irruption of lava, or other expression of vengeance from this goddess of the volcano, of whose power and displeasure they had manifested the greatest apprehensions ever since our approach to Kirauea. It appears singular that similar ideas respecting the consequences of disturbing the earth in the vicinity of volcanoes, should prevail here, as among the natives of the New Hebrides.

SIMILAR SUPERSTITIONS AT NEW HEBRIDES.

Forster, in this account of a visit to a place somewhat resembling this, in the island of Tanna, speaking of their making a hole, and burying their thermometer, says, "The natives, who observed that we stirred in the solfatarra, (as he called the places where the smoke and vapour issued,) desired us to leave it, telling us it would take fire, and resemble the volcano, which they called Assoor. They seemed to be extremely apprehensive of some mischance, and were very uneasy as often as we made the least attempt to disturb the sulphurous earth."— Forst. Voy. vol. ii. page 308.

FRESH WATER ENCOUNTERED.

At the north end of the crater we left the few provisions and little baggage that we had, and went in search of water, which we had been informed was to be found in the neighbourhood of a number of columns of vapour, which we saw rising in a northerly direction. About half a mile distant, we found two or three small pools of perfectly sweet, fresh water; a luxury which, notwithstanding the reports of the natives, we did not expect to meet with in these regions of fire. It proved a most grateful refreshment to us after travelling not less than twenty miles over a barren thirsty desert.

These pools appeared great natural curiosities. The surface of the ground in the vicinity was perceptibly warm, and rent by several deep irregular chasms, from which steam and thick vapours continually arose. In some places chasms were two feet wide, and from them a volume of steam ascended, which was immediately condensed by the cool mountain air, and driven, like drizzling rain, into hollows in the compact lava on the leeward side of the chasms.

166

The pools, which were six or eight feet from the chasms, were surroundel and covered by flags, rushes, and tall grass. Nourished by the moisture of the vapours, these plants flourished luxuriantly, and, in their turn, sheltered the pools from the heat of the sun, and prevented evaporation.

We expected to find the water warm, but in this we were also agreeably disappointed.

EXPLORING NORTH OF THE CRATER.

When we had quenched our thirst with water thus distilled by nature, we directed the natives to build a hut in which we might pass the night, in such a situation as to command a view of the burning lava; and while they were thus employed, we prepared to examine the many interesting objects around us. Mr. Bishop returned, with a canteen of water, to meet Mr. Harwood, who had not yet come up.

Mr. Thurston visited the eastern side of the great crater, and I went with Mr. Goodrich to examine some extensive beds of sulphur at the north-east end.

After walking about three-quarters of a mile over a tract of decomposed lava, covered with ohelo bushes and ferns, we came to a bank about a hundred and fifty yards long, and in some places upwards of thirty feet high, formed of sulphur, with a small proportion of red clay or ochre. The ground was very hot; its surface rent by fissures; and we were sometimes completely enveloped in the thick vapours that continually ascended from these cracks.

THE SULPHUR BANKS.

A number of apertures were visible along the whole extent of the bank of sulphur; smoke and vapours arose from these fissures also; and the heat of the sulphur around them was more intense than in any other part. Their edges were fringed with fine crystals, in various combinations, like what are called flowers of sulphur.

We climbed about half way up the bank, and endeavoured to break off some parts of the crust, but soon found it too hot to be handled. However, by means of our walking sticks, we detached some curious specimens. Those procured near the surface were crystallized in beautiful acicular prisms, of a light yellow colour; while those found three or four inches deep in the bank, were of an orange yellow, generally in single or double tetrahedral pyramids, and fully an inch in length.

A singular hissing and cracking noise was heard among the crystals, whenever the outside crust of the sulphur was broken and the atmospheric air admitted. The same noise was produced among the fragments broken off, until they were quite cold. The adjacent stones and pieces of clay were frequently incrusted, either with sulphate of ammonia, or volcanic sal ammoniac. Considerable quantities were also found in the crevices of some of the neighbouring rocks, which were much more pungent than that exposed to the air.

Along the bottom of the sulphur bank we found a number of pieces of tufa, or clay-stone, which appeared to have been fused, extremely light and cellular. It seemed as if sulphur, or some other inflammable substance, had formerly occupied the cells in these stones.

A thick fog now came over, which, being followed by a shower of rain, obliged us to leave this interesting laboratory of nature, and return to our companions.

On the eastern side of the crater, we saw banks of sulphur less pure, but apparently more extensive, than those we had visited; but their distance from us, and the unfavourable state of the weather, prevented our examining them.

FLOCKS OF WILD GEESE.

On our way to the sulphur banks, we saw two flocks of wild geese, which came down from the mountains, and settled among the ohelo bushes, near the pools of water. They were smaller than the common goose, had brown necks, and their wings were tipped with the same colour. The natives informed us there were vast flocks in the interior, although they were never seen near the sea.

Just as the sun was setting we reached the place where we had left our baggage, and found Messrs. Bishop and Harwood sitting near the spot, where the natives, with a few green branches of trees, some fern leaves, and rushes, had erected a hut.

MORE SUPERSTITIOUS FEARS OF PELE.

We were none of us pleased with the site which they had chosen. It was at the north-east end of the crater, on a pile of rocks overhanging the abyss below, and actually within four feet of the precipice. When we expressed our disapprobation, they said it was the only place where we might expect to pass the night undisturbed by Pele, and secure from earthquake and other calamity, being the place in which alone Pele allowed travellers to build a hut.

We told them it was unnecessarily near, and, being also unsafe, we wished to remove.

They answered, that as it was within the limits prescribed by Pele for safe lodging, they should be unwilling to sleep any where else, and had not time to build another hut for us.

We then directed them to collect a quantity of fire-wood, as we expected the night would be cold, although the thermometer then stood at 69°. We were the more anxious to have the fuel collected before the shades of night should close upon us, as travelling in some places was extremely dangerous.

DANGEROUS GROUND UNDERFOOT.

The ground sounded hollow in every direction, frequently cracked, and, in two instances, actually gave way while we were passing over it. Mr. Bishop was approaching the hut, when the lava suddenly broke under him. He instantly threw himself forward, and fell flat on his face over a part that was more solid.

A boy, who followed me with a basket to the sulphur banks, and walked about a yard behind Mr. Goodrich and myself, also fell in. There was no crack in the surface of the lava over which he was walking, neither did it bend under his weight, but broke suddenly, when he sunk in up to his middle. His legs and thighs were considerably bruised, but providentially he escaped without any other injury.

The lava in both places was about two inches in thickness, and broke short, leaving the aperture regular and defined, without even cracking the adjoining parts. On looking into the holes, we could see no bottom, but on both sides, at a short distance from the aperture, the lava was solid, and they appeared to have fallen into a narrow chasm covered over by a thin crust of lava, already in a state of decomposition.

MR. THURSTON'S ADVENTURE.

When night came on, we kindled a good fire, and prepared our frugal supper. Mr. Thurston, however, had not yet returned, and, as the darkness of the night increased, we began to feel anxious for his safety. The wind came down from the mountains in violent gusts, dark clouds lowered over us, and a thick fog enveloped every object; even the fires of the volcano were but indistinctly seen.

The darkness of the night advanced, but no tidings reached us of Mr. Thurston. About seven o'clock we sent out the natives with torches and firebrands, to search for him. They went as far as they durst, hallooing along the border of the crater, till their lights were extinguished, when they returned, without having seen or heard any thing of him. We now increased our fire, hoping it might serve as a beacon to direct him to our hut. Eight o'clock came, and he did not appear.

We began seriously to fear that he had fallen into the crater itself, or some of the deep and rugged chasms by which it was surrounded. A native, who accompanied Mr. Goodrich on a subsequent visit to the volcano, fell into one of these chasms; he was severely bruised by the fall, and could only be extricated from his perilous situation by a rope lowered down from the surface. In this state of painful suspense we remained till nearly half-past eight, when we were happily relieved by his sudden appearance. He had descended, and walked along the dark ledge of lava on the east side of the crater, till a chasm obliged him to ascend. Having with difficulty reached the top, he travelled along the southern and western sides, till the light of our fire directed him to our encampment. The extent of the crater, the unevenness of the path, the numerous fissures and rugged surface of the lava, and the darkness of the night, had prevented his earlier arrival.

A STRENUOUS CAMP.

We now partook with cheerfulness of our evening repast, and afterwards, amidst the whistling of the winds around, and the roaring of the furnace beneath, rendered our evening sacrifice of praise, and committed ourselves to the secure protection of our God. We then spread our mats on the ground, but as we were all wet through with the rain, against which our hut was but an indifferent shelter, we preferred to sit or stand round the fire, rather than lie down on the ground.

THE VOLCANO AT NIGHT.

Between nine and ten, the dark clouds and heavy fog, that since the setting of the sun had hung over the volcano, gradually cleared away, and the fires of Kirauea, darting their fierce light athwart the midnight gloom, unfolded a sight terrible and sublime beyond all we had yet seen.

The agitated mass of liquid lava, like a flood of melted metal, raged with tumultuous whirl. The lively flame that danced over its undulating surface, tinged with sulphureous blue, or glowing with mineral red, cast a broad glare of dazzling light on the indented sides of the insulated craters, whose roaring mouths, amidst rising flames, and eddying streams of fire, shot up, at frequent intervals, with very loud detonations, spherical masses of fusing lava, or bright ignited stones.

The dark bold outline of the perpendicular and jutting rocks around, formed a striking contrast with the luminous lake below, whose vivid rays, thrown on the rugged promontories, and reflected by the overhanging clouds, combined to complete the awful grandeur of the imposing scene.

A MAGNIFICENT PHENOMENON.

We sat gazing at the magnificent phenomena for several hours, when we laid ourselves down on our mats, in order to observe more leisurely their varying aspect; for, although we had travelled upwards of twenty miles since the morning, and were both weary and cold, we felt but little disposition to sleep. This disinclination was probably increased by our proximity to the yawning gulf, and our conviction that the detachment of a fragment from beneath the over-hanging pile on which we were

170

reclining, or the slightest concussion of the earth, which every thing around indicated to be no unfrequent occurrence, would perhaps precipitate us, amidst the horrid crash of falling rocks, into the burning lake immediately before us.

NATIVE VIEWS CONCERNING KILAUEA.

The natives, who probably viewed the scene with thoughts and feelings somewhat different from ours, seemed, however, equally interested. They sat most of the night talking of the achievements of Pele, and regarding with a superstitious fear, at which we were not surprised, the brilliant exhibition. They considered it the primeval abode of their volcanic deities. The conical craters, they said, were their houses, where they frequently amused themselves by playing at Konane (the game resembling drafts, described on page 146); the roaring of the furnaces and the crackling of the flames were the kani of their hura, (music of their dance,) and the red flaming surge was the surf wherein they played, sportively swimming on the rolling wave. Swimming in the sea, when the weather is tempestuous and the surf high, is a favourite amusement throughout the Sandwich and other islands in the Pacific.

NATIVE TRADITIONS CONCERNING VOLCANO.

As eight of the natives with us belonged to the adjoining district, we asked them to tell us what they knew of the history of this volcano, and what their opinions were respecting it. From their account, and that of others with whom we conversed, we learned, that it had been burning from time immemorial, or, to use their own words, "mai ka po mai," from chaos till now, (the Hawaiian traditions, like those of the ancients, refer to night, or a chaotic state, the origin of the world, and almost all things therein, the greater part of their gods not excepted; the present state they call the Ao marama, Day, or state of light; they speak of creation as a transition from darkness to light; and when they wish to express the existence of any thing from the beginning, they say it has been so mai ka po mai, from the night, or state of darkness or confusion, till now;) and had overflowed some part of the country during the reign of every king that had governed Hawaii: that in earlier ages it used to boil up, overflow its banks, and inundate the adjacent country; but that, for many kings' reigns past, it had kept below the level of the surrounding plain, continually extending its surface and increasing its depth, and occasionally throwing up, with violent explosion, huge rocks or red-hot stones. These eruptions, they said, were always accompanied by dreadful earthquakes, loud claps of thunder, with vivid and quick-succeeding lightning. No great explosion, they added, had taken place since the days of Keoua; but many places near

171

the sea had since been overflowed, on which occasions they supposed Pele went by a road under ground from her house in the crater to the shore.

These few facts were gathered from their accounts of its origin and operation; but they were so incorporated with their traditions of its supernatural inhabitants, and fabulous stories of their romantic adventures, that we found no small difficulty in distinguishing fiction from fact.

MYTHOLOGY OF THE VOLCANO.

Among other things, we were told, that though, according to the traditions preserved in their songs, Kirauea had been burning ever since the island emerged from night, it was not inhabited till after the Tai-a-kahina'rii, sea of Kahina'rii, or deluge of the Sandwich Islands. Shortly after that event, they say, the present volcanic family came from Tahiti, a foreign country, to Hawaii.

The names of the principal individuals were: Kamoho-arii, the king Moho; moho sometimes means a vapour, hence the name might be the king of steam or vapour—Ta-poha-i-tahi-ora, the explosion in the place of life — Te-ua-a-te-po, the rain of night — Tanehetiri, husband of thunder, or thundering tane (Tane is the name of one of their gods, as well as the name of the principal god formerly worshipped by the Society islanders; in both languages the word also means a husband) — and Te-o-ahi-tama-taua, fire-thrusting child of war; these were all brothers, and two of them, Vulcan-like, were deformed, having hump backs— Pele, principal goddess—Makore-wawahi-waa, fiery-eyed canoe-breaker — Hiata-wawahi-lani, heaven-rending cloud-holder — Hiata-noholani, heaven-dwelling cloud-holder—Hiata-taarava-mata, quick glancing eyed cloud-holder, or the cloud-holder whose eyes turn quickly and look frequently over her shoulders — Hiata-hoi-te-pori-a-Pele, the cloud-holder embracing or kissing the bosom of Pele—Hiata-ta-bu-enaena, the red-hot mountain holding or lifting clouds—Hiata-tareiia, the wreath or garland-encircled cloud-holder—and Hiata-opio, young cloud-holder.

These were all sisters, and, with many others in their train, on landing at Hawaii, are said to have taken up their abode in Kirauea. Something of their characters may be inferred from the few names we have given. Whenever the natives speak of them, it is as dreadful beings.

VOLCANO THE ABODE OF THE GODS.

This volcano is represented as having been their principal residence ever since their arrival, though they are thought to have many other dwellings in different parts of the island, and not a few on the tops of the snow-covered mountains. To these some of them frequently remove. Sometimes their arrival in a district was foretold by the priests of the heiaus there, and always announced by the convulsive trembling

172

of earth, the illuminating fire in their houses, (craters,) the flashes of lightning, and the roar of awful thunder.

OFFERINGS TO THE VOLCANO GODS.

They never journeyed on errands of mercy; to receive offerings, or execute vengeance, were the only objects for which they left their palace. "Nui wale," said the people with whom we were talking, "ka kanaka i make ia rakou," (alluding to those destroyed by the inundations,) Great indeed is the number of men slain by them; ua rau, ua rau, ua rau, ka puaa i tioraia na rakou, (this is a figurative expression signifying a great number, as we are accustomed to hear of thousands, and thousands, and thousands,) four hundreds, four hundreds, four hundreds of hogs have been thrown to them. (Vast numbers of hogs, some alive, others cooked, were thrown into the craters during the time they were in action, or when they threatened an eruption; and also, during an inundation, many were thrown into the rolling torrent of lava, to appease the gods, and stay its progress.)

VENGEANCE OF THE VOLCANO GODS.

The whole island was considered as bound to pay them tribute, or support their heiaus, and kahu, (devotees;) and whenever the chiefs or people failed to send the proper offerings, or incurred their displeasure by insulting them or their priests, or breaking the tabu (sacred restrictions) of their domains in the vicinity of the craters, they filled Kirauea with lava, and spouted it out, or, taking a subterranean passage, marched to some one of their houses (craters) in the neighbourhood where the offending parties dwelt, and from thence came down upon the delinquents with all their dreadful scourges.

If a sufficient number of fish were not taken to them by the inhabitants of the sea-shore, they would go down, and with fire kill the fish, fill up with pahoehoe (lava) the shallow places, and destroy all the fishing grounds.

COMBAT BETWEEN KAMAPUAA AND PELE.

We were told that several attempts had been made to drive them off the islands, and that once they were nearly overpowered by Tamapuaa, the Centaur of Hawaii, a gigantic animal, half hog and half man. He travelled from Oahu to countries beyond the heavens, viz. beyond the visible horizon, the boundary where they supposed the heavens to be, in form of a hollow cone, joined to the sea.

He also visited Kirauea, and made proposals to become the guest and suitor of Pele, the elder sister. When she saw him standing on the edge of the crater, she rejected his proposals with contempt, calling him a hog, the son of a hog. On her ascending from the crater to drive him away, a fierce combat ensued.

Pele was forced to her volcano, and threatened with destruction from the waters of the sea, which Tamapuaa poured into the crater till it was almost full, and the fires were nearly extinct. Pele and her companions drank up the waters, rose again from the craters, and finally succeeded in driving Tamapuaa into the sea, whither she followed him with thunder, lightning, and showers of large stones.

DESTRUCTION OF KEOUA'S ARMY.

They also related the account of the destruction of part of Keoua's camp by a violent eruption of the volcano, which, from their description, must have been sudden and awful.

Pele, they said, was propitious to Tamehameha, and availed herself of the opportunity afforded by the contiguous encampment of Keoua to diminish his forces and aid the cause of his rival.

We asked why Keoua was unpopular with Pele. They said, "we do not exactly know. Some say, he had not sent sufficient offerings to the heiaus; others, that he had no right to make war against Tamehameha, as he had before concluded a treaty of peace with him; and others, that he had broken the tabu of the place by eating the ohelos, marking and disturbing the sand, or pulling up a sacred kind of grass growing in the neighbourhood."

THE EXPLOSIVE ERUPTION OF 1790.

Whatever was the cause, Pele, they said, was "huhu roa," exceedingly angry, and, soon after sun-set, repeatedly shook the earth with the most violent heaving motion, sent up a column of dense black smoke, followed by the most brilliant flames.

A violent percussion was afterwards felt, streams of bright red lava were spouted up, and immense rocks in a state of ignition thrown to a great height in the air. A volley of smaller stones, thrown with much greater velocity and force, instantly followed the larger ones, and struck some of them, when the latter frequently burst with a report like thunder, accompanied by the most vivid flashes of lightning.

Many of Keoua's people were killed by the falling fragments of rocks, and many were actually buried beneath the overwhelming mass of ashes and lava. Some of the natives say, the warriors of two districts, about eighty men, perished on this occasion.

Not intimidated by this event, which many considered as a premonition of his fate, Keoua continued his march, and the volcano continued its action, confining, however, its operation within the boundaries of Kirauea.

174

We had heard the account several times before, with some little variation as to the numbers killed, and the appearance of Pele to Keoua, in the column of smoke as it rose from the crater, and, with the exception of this last circumstance, believe it to be true.

Frequently during the night the natives thought they saw some one or other of the deities, but immediately afterwards they doubted. At these times, if we asked them where they saw Pele, they would sometimes point to the red lava, at others to the variegated flame; and on our saying we could not perceive any distinct form, they generally answered by assuring us, that during the night some one or other of them would certainly be seen.

We jocosely requested them to inform us as soon as any appeared; and even to awake us, should we happen to be asleep. At the same time we told them, that when we considered their ignorance of the true God, and of the causes by which the action of volcanoes was sustained, we were not surprised at their supposing them to be the habitations of their deities, and their operations those of supernatural beings.

As far as their language and mental capability admitted, we endeavoured to explain some of the causes of volcanic fire; and illustrated them by the force of gunpowder, with the effects of which the natives are familiar; assuring them that the expansive force of steam is much greater than that of gunpowder.

Our principal solicitude, however, was to lead their minds to God, who created the world, and whose almighty power controls the elements of nature in all their diversified operations; but of whom, though they beheld the wondrous works of his hand, they were lamentably ignorant.

After two or three hours' sleep, we arose before it was day, and, gathering round our fire, sang our morning hymn of praise, in which we were joined by the natives who were with us. The sun had now risen, and, as we had no provisions left, we felt it necessary to prepare for our departure. Mr. Goodrich walked along the north side of the crater, in order to enable us to form as accurate an opinion as possible of its actual dimensions; and, from the observations of Mr. Goodrich and Mr. Thurston, as well as those the rest of us made when we walked along the north and east sides, we think the crater is not less than five, or five-and-a-half, miles in circumference.

The following extract of a letter from Mr. Chamberlain is copied from a recent American publication:

"Mr. Goódrich and myself visited the volcano again, and, with a line, measured the upper edge of the crater, and found it to be seven miles and a half in circumference. We then descended, and measured the side of the ledge, and satisfied ourselves, that, at the depth of 500 or 600 feet, the circumference is at least five miles and a half. We did not get the exact depth of it, but judge it not less than one thousand feet. We had good opportunities for forming a judgment."

In a letter to Professor Silliman of New Haven, Mr. Goodrich corroborates the above, and states also, that he walked across the bottom, where the lava was hard, the surface of which, though apparently smooth as seen from the top, was raised in hills or sunk in valleys; that dense sulphureous fumes and gases, very suffocating, some of them resembling muriatic gas, ascended from almost all parts of the bottom, making in their escape a "tremendous roaring, like the discharge of steam from the boiler of a steam engine;" at one place the florid lava was boiling like a fountain, and spouting up lava forty or fifty feet into the air.—Philosophical Magazine for September, 1826.

DEPTH OF THE CRATER.

We regret that we had not means for ascertaining more accurately its depth.

We lowered down a line one hundred feet from the edge of the plain on which our hut was erected, but it did not appear to reach near half-way to the black ledge of lava; and judging the proportion below to be equal to that above, it could not be less than 700 or 800 feet to the liquid lava.

We also threw down some large stones, which after several seconds struck on the sides, and then bounded down to the bottom, where they were lost in the lava. When they reached the bottom they appeared like pebbles, and we were obliged to watch their course very steadily to perceive them at all.

A SECOND VISIT TO KILAUEA.

In company with Dr. Blatchely, Messrs. Chamberlain and Ely, American missionaries, and a gentleman resident in Oahu, I have since visited Kirauea, when we again endeavoured to measure its circumference.

Mr. Chamberlain walked round the northern end from east to west, as near the edge as it was prudent to go, and, numbering his paces, made that part of it 3 1/16 miles; from which, we think, the above estimate does not exceed the actual extent of the crater.

176

We also lowered down a line 230 feet long, but it did not reach the horizontal ledge of lava. The fissures in the vicinity of the sulphur banks, and pools of water, were more numerous, and the smoke and vapour that ascended from them greater in quantity, than during our first visit.

CHANGES AT THE VOLCANO.

The volcano was much more quiescent; but some violent convulsions had taken place in the interim, for several masses of rock had fallen from the high precipices in the neighbourhood. The fires in the south and west parts burned but feebly; and though there was but little fire in the north and east sections of the volcano, it was evident that the whole of the lava in this part had been in a state of agitation since we had seen it.

Some of the small craters, on the southern sides of the great abyss, were extinguished; but several new craters had been formed on the opposite side, and bore marks of having been in vigorous action but a very short period before.

Soon after leaving our encampment this morning, we came to the pools of water, where we filled our canteens.

THE JOURNEY FROM KILAUEA TO HILO.

Here also our party separated; Messrs. Goodrich and Harwood proceeding across the interior through the villages of Ora to Waiakea, in the division of Hiro, while the rest of us passed along the east side of the crater, towards the sea-shore.

The path was in many places dangerous, lying along narrow ridges, with fearful precipices on each side, or across deep chasms and hollows that required the utmost care to avoid falling into them, and where a fall would have been fatal, as several of the chasms seemed narrowest at the surface.

In one place, we passed along for a considerable distance under a high precipice, where, though the country was perfectly level at the top, or sloped gradually towards the sea, the impending rocks towered some hundred feet above us on our left, and the appalling flood of lava rolled almost immediately beneath us on our right.

LAVA SPECIMENS AND PELE'S HAIR.

On this side we descended to some small craters on the declivity, and also to the black ledge; where we collected a number of beautiful specimens of highly scoriacious lava, the base approaching to volcanic glass. It was generally of a black or red colour, light, cellular, brittle, and shining.

We also found a quantity of volcanic glass drawn out into filaments as fine as human hair, and called by the natives rauoho o Pele, (hair of Pele). It was of a dark olive colour, semi-transparent, and brittle, though some of the filaments were several inches long. Probably it had been produced by the bursting of igneous masses of lava, thrown out from the craters, or separated in fine-spun threads from the boiling fluid, when in a state of perfect fusion, and, borne by the smoke or vapour above the edges of the crater, had been wafted by the winds over the adjacent plain; for we also found quantities of it at least seven miles distant from the large crater.

LAVA CONES AND TUNNELS.

We entered several small craters, that had been in vigorous action but a very short period before, marks of most recent fusion presenting themselves on every side. Their size and height were various, and many, which from the top had appeared insignificant as mole-hills, we now found twelve or twenty feet high. The outside was composed of bright shining scoriacious lava, heaped up in piles of most singular form. The lava on the inside was of a light or dark red colour, with a glazed surface, and in several places, where the heat had evidently been intense, we saw a deposit of small and beautifully white crystals.

We also entered several covered channels, or tunnels, down which the lava had flowed into the large abyss. They had been formed by the cooling of the lava on the sides and surface of the stream, while it had continued to flow on underneath. As the size of the current diminished, it had left a hard crust of lava of unequal thickness over the top, supported by walls of the same material on each side. Their interior was beautiful beyond description.

DESCRIPTION OF LAVA CAVES.

In many places they were ten or twelve feet high, and as many wide at the bottom. The roofs formed a regular arch, hung with red and brown stalactitic lava, in every imaginable shape, while the floor appeared like one continued glassy stream. The winding of its current and the ripple of its surface were so entire, that it seemed as if, while in rapid motion, the stream of lava had suddenly stopped, and become indurated, even before the undulations of the surface had subsided.

We traced one of these volcanic chambers to the edge of the precipice that bounds the great crater, and looked over the fearful steep, down which the fiery cascade had rushed. In the place where it had fallen, the lava had formed a spacious basin, which, hardening as it cooled, had retained all those forms which a torrent of lava, falling several hundred feet, might be expected to produce on the viscid mass below.

178

In the neighbourhood we saw several large masses of basaltic rock, of a dark gray colour, weighing probably from one to four or five tons, which although they did not bear any marks of recent fire, must have been ejected from the great crater during some violent eruption as the surrounding rocks in every direction presented a very different appearance; or they might have been thrown out in a liquid state, combined with other matter that had formed a rock of a less durable kind, which, decomposing more rapidly, had been washed away, and left them in detached masses scattered on the plain.

They were hard, and, when fractured, appeared a lava of basalt, containing very fine grains of compact felspar and augite; some of them contained small particles of olivin.

We also saw a number of other rocks in a state of decomposition, which proved to be a species of lava, containing globules of zeolite. The decomposition of these rocks appeared to have formed the present surface of much of the west, north, and east parts of the plain immediately surrounding the crater.

When we had broken off specimens of these, and of some red earthy-looking stones, which seemed to have the same base as the other, but to have lost their compact texture, and to have experienced a change of colour, from a further degree of decomposition, we passed along to the east side, where I took a sketch of the south-west end of the crater.

KILAUEA-IKI DESCRIBED.

As we travelled on from this spot, we unexpectedly came to another deep crater, nearly half as large as the former. The native name of it is Kirauea-iti, (little Kirauea). It is separated from the large crater by an isthmus nearly a hundred yards wide. Its sides, which were much less perpendicular than those of the great crater, were covered with trees and shrubs, but the bottom was filled with black lava, either fluid or scarcely cold, and probably supplied by the great crater, as the trees, shrubs, and grass on its sides, shewed it had remained many years in a state of quiescence. Though this was the only small one we saw, our companions informed us there were many in the neighbourhood.

They also pointed out to us the ruins of Oararauo, an old heiau, which crowned the summit of a lofty precipice on our left. It was formerly a temple of Pele, of which Kamakaakeakua, (the eye of god,) a distinguished soothsayer, who died in the reign of Tamehameha, was many years priest.

Large offerings were frequently made of hogs, dogs, fish, and fruits, but we could not learn that human victims were ever immolated on its

179

altars. These offerings were always cooked in the steaming chasms, or the adjoining ground. Had they been dressed any where else, or prepared with other fire, they would have been considered polluted, and have been expected to draw down curses on those who presented them.

CONDITIONS IN THE VICINITY OF KILAUEA.

The ground throughout the whole plain is so hot, that those who come to the mountains to procure wood for building, or to cut down trees and hollow them out for canoes, always cook their own food, whether animal or vegetable, by simply wrapping it in fern leaves, and burying it in the earth.

The east side of the plain was ornamented with some beautiful species of filices; also with several plants much resembling some of the varieties of cycas, and thickly covered with ohelo bushes, the berries of which we ate freely as we walked along, till, coming to a steep precipice, we ascended about 300 feet, and reached the high land on the side towards the sea, which commanded a fine view of Mouna Roa, opposite to which we had been travelling ever since we left Punaruu.

The mountain appeared of an oval shape, stretching along in a southwest direction, nearly parallel with the south-east shore, from which its base was generally distant twenty or thirty miles.

A ridge of high land appeared to extend from the eastern point to the south-west shore. Between it and the foot of Mouna Roa was a valley, as near as we could judge, from seven to twelve miles wide.

MAUNA LOA SNOW CAPPED.

The summit of Mouna Roa was never free from snow, the higher parts of the mountain's side were totally destitute of every kind of vegetation; and by the help of a telescope we could discover numerous extinguished craters, with brown and black streams of indurated lava over the whole extent of its surface.

The foot of the mountain was enriched on this side by trees and shrubs, which extended from its base six or seven miles towards the summit.

FIRST WHITES TO VISIT KILAUEA.

The volcano of Kirauea, the largest of which we have any account, and which was, until visited by us, unknown to the civilized parts of the world, is situated in the district of Kapapala, nearly on the boundary line between the divisions of Kau and Puna, twenty miles from the sea-shore.

We could form no correct estimate of its elevation above the level of the sea; the only means we had of judging being the difference of temperature in the air, as shewn by our thermometer, which, on the shore, was usually at sunrise 71°, but which, in the neighbourhood of the volcano, was, at the same hour, no higher than 46°.

180

From the isthmus between Kirauea-nui, or Great Kirauea, and Little Kirauea, the highest peak of Mouna-Kea bore by compass N. N. W. and the centre of Mouna-Roa W. S. W.

The uneven summits of the steep rocks, that, like a wall, many miles in extent, surrounded the crater and all its appendages, shewed the original level of the country, or perhaps marked the base, and formed as it were the natural buttresses of some lofty mountain, raised in the first instance by the accumulation of volcanic matter, whose bowels had been consumed by volcanic fire, and whose sides had afterwards fallen into the vast furnace, where, reduced a second time to a liquefied state, they had been again vomited out on the adjacent plain.

SPECULATIONS CONCERNING THE VOLCANO.

But the magnificent fires of Kirauea, which we had viewed with such admiration, appeared to dwindle into insignificance, when we thought of the probable subterranean fires immediately beneath us.

The whole island of Hawaii, covering a space of four thousand square miles, from the summits of its lofty mountains, perhaps 15,000 or 16,000 feet above the level of the sea, down to the beach, is, according to every observation we could make, one complete mass of lava, or other volcanic matter, in different stages of decomposition.

Perforated with innumerable apertures in the shape of craters, the island forms a hollow cone over one vast furnace, situated in the heart of a stupendous submarine mountain, rising from the bottom of the sea; or possibly the fires may rage with augmented force beneath the bed of the ocean, rearing through the superincumbent weight of water the base of Hawaii, and, at the same time, forming a pyramidal funnel from the furnace to the atmosphere.

CAPT. KING CONCERNING KEA AND LOA.

In Cook's Voyages, Captain King, speaking of Mouna-Kaah, (Kea,) remarks that it "may be clearly seen at fourteen leagues' distance."

Describing Mouna-Roa, and estimating it according to the tropical line of snow, he observes, "This mountain must be at least 16,020 feet high, which exceeds the height of the Pico de Teyde, or Peak of Teneriffe, by 724 feet, according to Dr. Heberden's computation, or 3680 according to that of Chevalier de Borda. The peaks of Mouna Kaah appeared to be about half a mile high; and as they are entirely covered with snow, the altitude of their summits cannot be less than 18,400 feet. But it is probable that both these mountains may be considerably higher; for in insular situations, the effects of the warm sea air must necessarily remove the line of snow, in equal latitudes, to a greater height, than where the atmosphere is chilled on all sides by an immense tract of perpetual snow."

181

CHAPTER X

LEAVING THE VOLCANO.

Though we left our encampment at daybreak, it was eleven o'clock in the forenoon before we took our final leave of Kirauea.

The path by which we descended towards the sea was about south-east-by-east. On the high lands in the vicinity of the crater, we found the ground covered with strawberry plants, on some of which were a few berries, but the season for them appeared to be gone by. The plants and vines were small, as was also the fruit, which in its colour and shape resembled the hautboy strawberry, though in taste it was much more insipid.

Strawberries, as well as raspberries, are indigenous plants, and are found in great abundance over most of the high lands of Hawaii; though we do not know of their existence in any other islands of the group.

The ground over which we walked was composed of ancient lava, of a light brown colour, broken into small pieces, resembling coarse dry gravel, to the depth of two or three inches, below which it was one solid mass of lava. The surface was covered with ohelo bushes, and a few straggling ferns and low shrubs, which made travelling much more agreeable than when we approached the volcano.

KEANAKAKOI CRATER.

Within a few miles of Kirauea, we passed three or four high and extinct craters. One of them, Keanakakoi, the natives told us, sent forth, in the days of Riroa, king of Hawaii about fourteen generations back, most of the lava over which we were travelling. The sides of these craters were generally covered with verdure, while the brown irregular-shaped rocks on their indented summits frowned like the battlements of an ancient castle in ruins.

We occasionally passed through rather extensive shrubberies of bushes and small trees growing in the decomposed lava and sand, and striking their roots among the cracks which were filled up with the same material.

DESCRIPTION OF APPROACHES TO PUNA.

As we approached the sea, the soil became more generally spread over the surface, and vegetation more luxuriant:

About two p.m. we sat down to rest. The natives ran to a spot in the neighbourhood, which had formerly been a plantation, and brought

182

a number of pieces of sugar-cane, with which we quenched our thirst, and then walked on through several plantations of the sweet potato, belonging to the inhabitants of the coast, until about three o'clock, when we reached the edge of the high ground, which, at a remote period, probably formed the south-east coast.

We stopped at a solitary cottage, where we procured a copious draught of fresh water, to us a most grateful beverage, as we had travelled ever since the morning without any refreshment, except a few berries and a piece of sugar-cane.

We descended 300 or 400 feet, by a narrow winding path, covered with overhanging trees, and bordered by shrubs and grass. We then walked over a tract of lava, broken and decomposed, and about four or five miles wide, at the end of which another steep appeared.

These steep precipices form concentric ridges of volcanic rock round the greater part of this side of the island. Down this we descended, by following the course of a rugged current of ancient lava, for about 600 feet perpendicular depth, when we arrived at the plain below, which was one extended sheet of lava, without shrub or bush, stretching to the north and south as far as the eye could reach, and from four to six miles across, from the foot of the mountain to the sea.

POOR WATER AT KEALAKOMO.

The natives gave us the fabulous story of the combat between Pele and Tamapuaa, as the origin of this flood of lava.

This vast tract of lava was black, shining, and cellular, though not very brittle, and was more homogeneous than that which covered the southern shores of the island.

We crossed it in about two hours, and arrived at Kearakomo, the second village in the division of Puna. We stopped at the first house we came to, and begged some water. The natives brought us a calabash-full, of which we drank most hearty draughts, though it was little better than the water of the sea, from which it had percolated through the vesicles of the lava into the hollows from nine to twelve feet distant from the ocean. It barely quenched our thirst while we were swallowing it, but it was the best we could procure, and we could hardly refrain from drinking at every hollow to which we came.

ACCOMMODATIONS BAD—NATIVES DRUNK.

After walking about a mile along the beach, we came to a house, which our guide pointed out as our lodgings. It was a miserable hut, and we asked if we could not find better accommodations, as we intended to spend the Sabbath in the village? Mauae told us it was the only one in the place that was not crowded with people, and he thought the most comfortable one we could procure.

The village is populous, and the natives soon thronged around us. To our great regret, two-thirds of them appeared to be in a state of intoxication, a circumstance we frequently had occasion to lament, in the villages through which we passed. Their inebriation was generally the effect of an intoxicating drink made of fermented sugar-cane juice, sweet potatoes, or ti root.

MAKING LIQUOR FROM THE TI PLANT.

The ti plant is common in all the South Sea islands, and is a variety of dracaena, resembling the dracaena terminalis, except in the colour of its leaves, which are of a lively shining green. It is a slow-growing plant, with a large woody fusiform root, which, when first dug out of the ground, is hard and fibrous, almost tasteless, and of a white or light yellow colour.

The natives bake it in large ovens underground, in the same manner as they dress the arum and other edible roots. After baking, it appears like a different substance altogether, being of a yellowish brown colour, soft though fibrous, and saturated with a highly saccharine juice. It is sweet and pleasant to the taste, and much of it is eaten in this state, but the greater part is employed in making an intoxicating liquor much used by the natives.

They bruise the baked roots with a stone, and steep them with water in a barrel or the bottom of an old canoe, till the mass is in a state of fermentation. The liquor is then drawn off, and sometimes distilled, when it produces a strong spirit; but the greater part of it is drank in its fermented state without any further preparation.

The root is certainly capable of being used for many valuable purposes. A good beer may be made from it; and in the Society Islands, though never able to granulate it, we have frequently boiled its juice to a thick syrup, and used it as a substitute for sugar, when destitute of that article.

OTHER USES OF THE TI PLANT.

We should think it an excellent antiscorbutic, and as such, useful to ships on long voyages.

Captains visiting the Society Islands frequently procure large quantities of it to make beer with during their voyage, as it will keep good six weeks or two months after it is baked. It is not so plentiful in the Sandwich Islands as it was before the natives used it for the above purpose, but in some of the other islands of the Pacific it is abundant, and may be easily procured.

On my return in the American ship Russell, Captain Coleman, we procured a quantity that had been baked, at Rurutu, near the Society Islands, and brought it round Cape Horn. It lasted five or six weeks, and would probably have kept longer, as the only change we perceived during that time was a slight degree of acidity in the taste. Cattle, sheep, and goats, are fond of the leaves; and as they contain more nutriment than any other indigenous vegetable, and may be kept on board ships several weeks, they are certainly the best provender that can be procured in the islands for stock taken to sea.

TI LEAVES USED AS FLAGS OF TRUCE.

Other parts of the dracaena are also useful. The natives frequently plant the roots thickly around their enclosures, interweave the stems of the plant, and form a valuable permanent hedge.

The branch was always an emblem of peace, and in times of war, borne, together with a young plantain tree, as a flag of truce by the messengers who passed between the hostile parties.

The leaves, woven together by their stalks, formed a short cloak, which the natives wore in their mountainous journeys; they also make the most durable thatch for the sides and roofs of their best houses, are employed in constructing their tents in war, and temporary abodes during their inland excursions.

About sunset we sent to the head man of the village for some refreshment, but he was intoxicated; and though we had walked upwards of twenty miles since morning, and had subsisted on but scanty fare since leaving Kapapala, we could only procure a few cold potatoes, and two or three pieces of raw salt fish.

SUPERSTITIOUS FEAR OF PELE.

Multitudes crowded around our hut; and with those that were sober we entered into conversation. When they learned that we had been to Kirauea, they were unwilling to believe we had broken the sulphur banks, eaten the ohelo berries, descended to the craters, or broken any fragments of lava from them, as they said Pele ma, Pele and her associates, would certainly have avenged the insult. However, when our boys shewed them the ohelo berries, with the specimens of sulphur and lava that we had brought away, they were convinced that we had been there, but said we had escaped only because we were haore, foreigners. No Hawaiian, they added, would have done so with impunity, for Pele was a dreadful being.

The apprehensions uniformly entertained by the natives, of the fearful consequences of Pele's anger, prevented their paying very frequent visits to the vicinity of her abode; and when, on their inland journeys, they had occasion to approach Kirauea, they were scrupulously attentive to every injunction of her priests, and regarded with a degree of superstitious veneration and awe, the appalling spectacle which the crater and its appendages presented.

185

The violations of her sacred abode, and the insults to her power, of which we had been guilty, appeared to them, and to the natives in general, acts of temerity and sacrilege; and, notwithstanding the fact of our being foreigners, we were subsequently threatened with the vengeance of the volcanic deity, under the following circumstances.

A PRIESTESS OF PELE THREATENS VENGEANCE.

Some months after our visit to Kirauea, a priestess of Pele came to Lahaina, in Maui, where the principal chiefs of the islands then resided. The object of her visit was noised abroad among the people, and much public interest excited. One or two mornings after her arrival in the district, arrayed in her prophetic robes, having the edges of her garments burnt with fire, and holding a short staff or spear in her hand, preceded by her daughter, who was also a candidate for the office of priestess, and followed by thousands of the people, she came into the presence of the chiefs; and having told who she was, they asked what communications she had to make.

She replied, that, in a trance or vision, she had been with Pele, by whom she was charged to complain to them that a number of foreigners had visited Kirauea; eaten the sacred berries; broken her houses, the craters; thrown down large stones, &c. to request that the offenders might be sent away; and to assure them, that if these foreigners were not banished from the islands, Pele would certainly, in a given number of days, take vengeance by inundating the country with lava, and destroying the people. She also pretended to have received, in a supernatural manner, Rihoriho's approbation of the request of the goddess.

PELE'S PRIESTESS REPUDIATED BY KAAHUMANU.

The crowds of natives who stood waiting the result of her interview with the chiefs, were almost as much astonished as the priestess herself, when Kaahumanu and the other chiefs ordered all her paraphernalia of office to be thrown into the fire; told her the message she had delivered was a falsehood, and directed her to return home, cultivate the ground for her subsistence, and discontinue her journeys of deception among the people.

This answer was dictated by the chiefs themselves.

The missionaries at the station, although they were aware of the visit of the priestess, and saw her, followed by the thronging crowd, pass by their habitation on her way to the residence of the chiefs, did not think it necessary to attend or interfere, but relied entirely on the enlightened judgment and integrity of the chiefs, to suppress any attempts that might be made to revive the influence of Pele over the people; and in the result they were not disappointed, for the natives returned

186

to their habitations, and the priestess soon after left the island, and has not since troubled them with the threatenings of the goddess.

KAPIOLANI'S VISIT TO KILAUEA.

On another occasion, Kapiolani, a pious chief-woman, the wife of Naihe, chief of Kaavaroa, was passing near the volcano, and expressed her determination to visit it.

Some of the devotees of the goddess met her, and attempted to dissuade her from her purpose; assuring her that though foreigners might go there with security, yet Pele would allow no Hawaiian to intrude.

Kapiolani, however, was not to be thus diverted, but proposed that they should all go together; and declaring that if Pele appeared, or inflicted any punishment, she would then worship the goddess, but proposing that if nothing of the kind took place, they should renounce their attachment to Pele, and join with her and her friends in acknowledging Jehovah as the true God.

They all went together to the volcano; Kapiolani, with her attendants, descended several hundred feet towards the bottom of the crater, where she spoke to them of the delusion they had formerly laboured under in supposing it inhabited by their false gods; they sung a hymn, and after spending several hours in the vicinity, pursued their journey. What effect the conduct of Kapiolani, on this occasion, will have on the natives in general, remains yet to be discovered.

RECENT VOLCANIC ACTIVITY AT KEALAALA AND MAHUKA.

The people of Kearakomo also told us, that no longer than five moons ago, Pele had issued from a subterranean cavern, and overflowed the low land of Kearaara, and the southern part of Kapapala. The inundation was sudden and violent, burnt one canoe, and carried four more into the sea.

At Mahuka, the deep torrent of lava bore into the sea a large rock, according to their account, near a hundred feet high, which, a short period before, had been separated by an earthquake from the main pile in the neighbourhood. It now stands, they say, in the sea, nearly a mile from the shore, its bottom surrounded by lava, its summit rising considerably above the water.

We exceedingly regretted our ignorance of this inundation at the time when we passed through the inland parts of the above-mentioned districts, for had we known of it then, we should certainly have descended to the shore, and examined its extent and appearance.

We now felt convinced that the chasms we had visited at Ponahohoa, and the smoking fissures we afterwards saw nearer Kirauea, marked the course of a stream of lava, and thought it probable that though the lava

187

nad burst out five months ago, it was still flowing in a smaller and less rapid stream.

Perhaps the body of lava that had filled Kirauea up to the black ledge which we saw, between three and four hundred feet above the liquid lava, at the time we visited it, had been drawn off by this subterranean channel, though the distance between the great crater and the land overflowed by it, was not less than thirty or thirty-five miles.

A NIGHT AND DAY AT KEALAKOMO.

When the day began to close, and we wished the natives to retire, we told them that to-morrow was the sacred day of Jehovah, the true God, and directed them to come together early in the morning, to hear his word, and unite with us in his worship. We then spread our mats upon some poles that lay at one end of the house, and, as we had no lamp, and could procure no candle-nuts, we laid ourselves down as soon as it became dark, and, notwithstanding our uncomfortable lodging place, slept very soundly till day-break.

"Welcome, sweet day of rest," was the language of our hearts, as on the morning of the 3d we beheld the Sabbath's early light dawn on the desolate shores of Puna, and saw the bright luminary of day, emblem of the Sabbath's Lord, rise from the eastern wave of the extended Pacific.

After the fatiguing journey, and unusual excitement, of the past week, a day's rest was necessary, and we were happy to spend it in the populous, though desolate-looking village of Kearakomo, as it afforded us an opportunity of unfolding the Saviour's love to many of its inhabitants, and inviting them to seek that everlasting rest and happiness reserved for his followers in the heavenly world.

SUNDAY MORNING SERVICES WITH THE NATIVES.

Between six and seven o'clock, about two hundred of the people collected in front of our house. We sung a hymn; one of our number preached to them a discourse, which occupied rather more than half an hour; and another concluded the service with prayer. They were all sober, and appeared attentive. Several proposed questions to us; and when we had answered them, we directed them to return to their houses, to abstain from fishing and other ordinary employments, and, when the sun was over their heads, (the manner of expressing midday,) to come together again, and hear more about Jehovah and Jesus Christ. Many, however, continued talking with the natives belonging to our company, and gazing at us through most of the day.

HOSPITALITY OF NATIVES.

About nine a.m. a friend of Mauae brought us a bundle of potatoes

188

and a fowl. We procured another; our native boys cooked them in an oven of stones under ground, and they made us a good breakfast. All that we wanted was fresh water, that which we were obliged to drink being extremely brackish. For it, however, and our other refreshments, we felt thankful; and considered the inconvenience of wanting fresh water very trifling, compared with the pleasure which passing a Sabbath among the poor benighted people around, imparted, in declaring to them the love of God, and inviting them to partake of the bread which came down from heaven, and to drink of the fountain of the water of life.

FURTHER SERVICES AND HOSPITALITY.

At 12 o'clock, about three hundred of the people again assembled near our dwelling, and we held a religious exercise similar to that which they had attended in the morning.

The head man of the village was present during the service. He came into our house after it was over, and told us all his provisions were at his farm, which was some distance inland, and that tomorrow he intended to bring us a pig, and some potatoes. We thanked him, but told him probably we should proceed on our way early in the morning. He went away, and in a short time returned with a raw salted albacore, and a basket of baked sweet potatoes, which he said was all he could furnish us with to-day.

We spent the afternoon in conversation with those who crowded our hut, and wished to inquire more fully about the things of which they had heard.

Between five and six in the evening, the people again collected for worship in front of our house, when they were addressed from Isaiah lx. 1. "Arise, shine, for thy light is come." They listened with attention to the advantages of Christian light and knowledge, contrasted with pagan ignorance and misery, and several exclaimed at the close of the service, Oia no. Poereere makou. E ake makou i hoomaramarama ia. "So it is. We are dark. We desire to be enlightened."

FRESH WATER A LUXURY.

In the evening, we were so favoured as to procure a calabash-full of fresh water from the caves in the mountains, where it had filtered through the strata of lava, and was received into vessels placed there for that purpose. It tasted bitter, from standing long in the calabashes; but yet it was a luxury, for our thirst was great, notwithstanding the quantities of water we had drank during the day.

About sunset we ate some of our raw fish and half-baked potatoes. When it began to grow dark, we concluded the day with prayer, imploring the gracious influences of the Holy Spirit to follow our feeble attempts to declare his truth, and make it effectual to the spiritual welfare of the people.

We afterwards lay down upon our mats, but passed an uncomfortable night, from the swarms of vermin which infested the house, and the indisposition induced by the nature of the food and water we had taken since leaving the volcano.

We held worship with the people of the village at sunrise on the 4th, and after a short address, in which we earnestly recommended them to give themselves up to the Saviour, we bade them farewell, and set out again on our journey.

Leaving Kearakomo, we travelled several miles in a north-easterly direction along the same bed of lava that we had crossed on Saturday evening.

WHY NATIVES LIVE ALONG THE SHORE.

The population of this part of Puna, though somewhat numerous, did not appear to possess the means of subsistence in any great variety or abundance; and we have often been surprised to find the desolate coasts more thickly inhabited than some of the fertile tracts in the interior; a circumstance we can only account for, by supposing that the facilities which the former afford for fishing, induce the natives to prefer them as places of abode; for they find that where the coast is low, the adjacent water is generally shallow.

We saw several fowls and a few hogs here, but a tolerable number of dogs, and quantities of dried salt fish, principally albacores and bonitos. This latter article, with their poë and sweet potatoes, constitutes nearly the entire support of the inhabitants, not only in this vicinity, but on the sea-coasts of the north and south parts of the island.

DRIED FISH AN ARTICLE OF COMMERCE.

Besides what is reserved for their own subsistence, they cure large quantities as an article of commerce, which they exchange for the vegetable productions of Hiro and Mamakua, or the mamake and other tapas of Ora and the more fertile districts of Hawaii.

When we had passed Punau, Leapuki, and Kamomoa, the country began to wear a more agreeable aspect. Groves of coca-nuts ornamented the projecting points of land, clumps of kou-trees appeared in various directions, and the habitations of the natives were also thickly scattered over the coast.

THE HEIAU OF WAHAULA.

At noon we passed through Pulana, where we saw a large heiau called Wahaura, Red Mouth, or Red-feather Mouth, built by Tamehameha, and dedicated to Tairi, his war-god. Human sacrifices, we were informed, were occasionally offered here.

190

Shortly after, we reached Kupahua, a pleasant village, situated on a rising ground, in the midst of groves of shady trees, and surrounded by a well-cultivated country. Here we stopped, and, having collected the people of the village, I preached to them. They afterwards proposed several interesting inquiries connected with what they had heard, and said it was a good thing for us to aroha, or have compassion on them. They also asked when we would come again.

AT KALAPANA—RESIDENCE OF PRIEST KAPIHI.

Leaving this interesting place, we passed on to Kalapana, a small village on the sea-shore, distinguished as the residence of Kapihi, the priest, who, in the days of Tamehameha, told the king, that after death he and all his ancestors would live again on Hawaii.

We saw a large heiau, of which he was chief priest, but did not see many people in the houses as we passed by. Kapihi had many disciples, who believed, or pretended to believe, his predictions.

Frequent offerings were made to Kuahairo, his god, at other parts of the island more frequently visited by the king, and this probably drew away many of the people from Kalapana.

AT KAIMU—ROYAL RECEPTION TO MAUAE.

About three p.m. we approached Kaimu. This was the birth-place of Mauae, and the residence of most of his relations. He was a young man belonging to the governor, who had been sent with the canoe, and who, since leaving Honuapo, had acted as our guide. He walked before us as we entered the village. The old people from the houses welcomed him as he passed along, and numbers of the young men and women came out to meet him, saluted him by touching noses, and wept for joy at his arrival. Some took off his hat, and crowned him with a garland of flowers; others hung round his neck wreaths of a sweet-scented plant resembling ivy, or necklaces composed of the nut of the fragrant pandanus odoratissime.

When we reached the house where his sister lived, she ran to meet him, threw her arms around his neck, and having affectionately embraced him, walked hand in hand with him through the village.

Multitudes of young people and children followed, chanting his name, the names of his parents, the place and circumstances of his birth, and the most remarkable events in the history of his family, in a lively song, which, he afterwards informed us, was composed on the occasion of his birth. The following fragments of the commencement, which I afterwards wrote down from the mouth of one of his aged relatives who was with us, will suffice as a specimen, as the whole is too long for insertion:

191

Inoa o Mauae a Para,	Name of Mauae,[1] (son) of Para,
He aha matou auanei	How shall we declare?
O Mauae, te wahine horua nui,	O Mauae, woman famous at horua,
Wahine maheai pono.	Woman tilling well the ground.
Tuu ra te Ravaia	Give the fisherman,
I ta wahine maheai,	To the woman (who) tilleth the ground;
I pono wale ai ta aina o orua.	Happy will be the land of you two.
I ravaia te tane,	A fisherman the husband,
I mahe ai te wahine,	The wife a tiller of the ground.
Mahe te ai na te ohua,	Cultivated food for the aged, and the young;
I ai na te puari.	Food for the company of favourite warriors.
Malama te ora na te hoapiriwale.	Regarded the life of the friend.
E Mahe ai na Tuitelani.	Cultivated for Tuitelani.[3]
Owerawahie i uta i Tapapala.	Burnt were the woods inland of Tapapala.
Tupu mau ua ore te pari.	Long parched had been the precipice.
Oneanea te aina o Tuaehu.	Lonely was the land of Tuaehu.
Ua tu ra te manu i te pari Oharahara.	The bird perched on Oharahara rocks.
Ewaru te po, ewaru te ao,	Eight the nights, eight the days,
Ua pau te aho o na hoa maheai,	Gone was the breath of those who help the tillage,
I te tanu wale i te rau, a maloa.	With planting herbs (they) were fatigued;
Ua mate i he la,	Fainting under the sun,
Ua tu nevaneva.	(They) looked anxiously around.
I ta matani, ua ino auaurere,	By the wind, the flying scudding tempest,
Ua tu ta repo i Hiona:	Thrown up was the earth (or dust) at Hiona:
Pura ta onohi i ta u i ta repo.	Red were the eye-balls with the dust.
O Tauai, O Tauai, aroha wale	O Tauai,[4] O Tauai, loved he
Te aina i roto o te tai,	The land in the midst of the sea,
E noho marie oe I roto o te tai,	Thou dwellest quietly in the midst of the sea,
E hariu ai te aro i rehua.	And turnest thy face to the pleasant wind,
Pura ta onohi i ta matani,	Red were the eye balls with the wind,
Ta tatau ta iri onionio,	(Of those) whose skin was spotted with tatau,
Ta repo a Tau i Pohaturoa,	The sand of Taii (lay) at Pohaturoa,[5]
Te a i Ohiaotalani.	The lava at Ohiaotalani.[6]
Ma tai te aranui e hiti ai	By the sea was the road to arrive
I te one i Taimu,	At the sandy beach of Taimu,
Ma uta i ta tuahivi,	Inland by the mountain ridges,
Te aranui i hunaia.	The path that was concealed.
Narowale Tirauea i te ino.	His was Tirauea[7] by the tempest.
Noho Pele i Tirauea,	Pele[8] abode in Tirauea,
I tahu mau ana i te rua.	In the pit, ever feeding the fires.

---

[1]Mother of the young man. [2]Horua, a native game. [3]Name of a chief. [4]Atooi.
[5]Districts. [6]North peak of the volcano. [7]The great volcano. [8]Goddess of volcanoes.

They continued chanting their song, and thus we passed through their plantations, and groves of cocoanut trees, till we reached his father's house, where a general effusion of affection and joy presented itself, which it was impossible to witness without delight.

MAUAE'S FAMILY REUNION.

A number of children, who ran on before, had announced his approach; his father, followed by his brothers and several other relations, came out to meet him, and, under the shade of a wide-spreading kou-tree, fell on his neck, and wept aloud for some minutes; after which they took him by the hand, and led him through a neat little garden into the house.

He seated himself on a mat on the floor, while his brothers and sisters gathered around him; some unloosed his sandals, and rubbed his limbs and feet; others clasped his hand, frequently saluting it by touching it with their nose; others brought him a calabash of water, or a lighted tobacco pipe.

One of his sisters, in particular, seemed much affected; she clasped his hand, and sat for some time weeping by his side. At this we should have been surprised, had we not known it to be the usual manner, among the South Sea Islanders, of expressing unusual joy or grief. In the present instance, it was the unrestrained expression of joyful feelings. Indeed, every one seemed at a loss how to manifest the sincere pleasure which his unexpected arrival, after several years' absence, had produced.

WELL PROVIDED FOR WITH FOOD AND FRESH WATER.

On first reaching the house, we had thrown ourselves down on a mat, and remained silent spectators, not, however, without being considerably affected by the interesting scene.

We had been sitting in the house about an hour, when a small hog, baked under-ground, with some good sweet potatoes, was brought in for dinner, of which we were kindly invited to partake. As there was also plenty of good fresh water here, we found ourselves more comfortably provided for than we had been since leaving Kapapala on Thursday last.

At six o'clock in the evening, we sent to collect the people of the village to hear preaching. Between three and four hundred assembled, under a clump of shady cordia trees, in front of the house, and I preached to them from Psalm xxii. verses 27 and 28.

Our singing appeared to interest them, as well as other parts of the service, and at the conclusion several exclaimed, "Jehovah is a good God; I desire him for my God."

About this time Makoa arrived with our baggage. We were glad to see him, and inquired where he had been during the past week? He said he remained only one night at Honuapo, and followed on the next morning; observing, at the same time, we must have travelled fast, or he should have been here before us, as he had not gone round by the volcano, but had proceeded in a straight line from Kapapala to Kearakomo.

NATIVE TRADITIONS CONCERNING THE VOLCANO.

The evenings we spent with the people of the place in conversation on various subjects, but principally respecting the volcano which we had recently visited. They corroborated the accounts we had before heard, by telling us it had been burning from time immemorial, and added, that eruptions from it had taken place during every king's reign, whose name was preserved in tradition, or song, from Akea, first king of the island, down to the present monarch.

Kaimu, the district where we were, was overflowed in the days of Arapai, but how many generations it was since he reigned, we could not learn, as they were not agreed about it among themselves.

They also repeated the account of the inundation of Kearaara, and the low land of Kapapala, five moons ago, and some of them told us they had seen the large rock carried out into the sea at Mahuka. Like the people of Kearakomo, they believed Kirauea to be the abode of supernatural beings.

They recapitulated the contest between Pele and Tamapuaa, and related the adventures of several warriors, who, with spear in hand, had opposed the volcanic demons when coming down on a torrent of lava. They could not believe that we had descended into the crater, or broken off pieces of Pele's houses, as they called the small craters, until the specimens of lava, &c. were produced, when some of them looked very significantly, and none of them cared much to handle them.

We tried to convince them of their mistake in supposing Kirauea was inhabited, and unfolded to them, in as simple a manner as possible, the nature of volcanoes, and of their various phenomena, assuring them, at the same time, that they were under the sovereign control of Jehovah, the only true God. Some said, "Ae paha," "Yes, perhaps;" others were silent.

PREACHING AND TALKING AT KAIMU.

Numbers of the people were present at our evening worship, which we conducted in their language.

After a very comfortable night's rest, we arose at daybreak on the 5th.

At sun-rise the people assembled more numerously than they had done on the preceding evening, and I preached to them from these words,—"Herein is love, not that we loved God, but that he loved us,

194

and sent his Son to be the propitiation for our sins." They appeared to listen with interest, and numbers sat down under the kou-trees, talking among themselves on the subject, for a long time after the services had closed.

After breakfast we walked through the district, entered several of the cottages, and talked with the people.

GREAT EARTHQUAKE AT KAIMU IN 1823.

We also examined the effects of an earthquake experienced in this place about two months before. We were informed that it took place about ten o'clock in the evening. The ground, after being agitated some minutes with a violent tremulous motion, suddenly burst open, for several miles in extent, in a direction from north by east, to south by west, and emitted, in various places at the same instant, a considerable quantity of smoke and luminous vapour, but none of the people were injured by it.

A stone wall, four feet thick and six feet high, enclosing a garden at the north end of the village, was thrown down.

A chasm about a foot wide marked distinctly its course; this was generally open, though in some places it seemed as if the earth had closed up again.

AN EARTHQUAKE CHASM.

We entered a house, sixteen feet by twelve in the inside, through which it had passed. Ten persons, viz. one man, six women, and three children, were asleep here at the time it occurred. They were lying on both sides of the house, with their heads towards the centre; some of them every near the place where the ground was rent open. The trembling of the ground, they said, awoke them, but before they could think what it was that had disturbed them, the earth opened with a violent percussion; a quantity of sand and dust was thrown up with violence, and smoke and steam were at the same time emitted.

After a short interval, a second percussion was felt, vapour again arose, and at the opposite end of the house to that in which they were lying, they saw a light blue flame, which almost instantly disappeared.

We asked them if they were not alarmed? They said they were at first, but after remaining awake some time, and finding the shock was not repeated, they lay down and slept till morning, when they filled up the fissure with grass and earth!

We examined the aperture, that still remained open at one end of the house, and found its sides perpendicular, and its breadth one foot and eleven inches. The north-west corner of the house was broken by the shock.

195

We next traced its course through the fields of potatoes. In some places the ground seemed hardly disturbed, yet it sunk six or eight inches beneath our tread. At other places we saw apertures upwards of two feet wide. The potatoes that were growing immediately in the direction of the fissure, were all spoiled. Several roots of considerable size were thrown out of the ground, and, according to the representations of the natives, appeared as if they had been scorched.

At the south end of the village, it had passed through a small well, in which originally there was seldom more than eighteen inches' depth of water, though since that period there has been upwards of three feet.

The crack was about ten inches wide, running from north to south across the bottom of the well. The water has not only increased in quantity, but suffered a great deterioration in quality, being now very salt; and its rising and falling with the ebbing and flowing of the tide, indicates its connexion with the waters of the ocean, from which it is distant about 300 yards.

Convulsions of this kind are common over the whole island: they are not, however, so frequent in this vicinity as in the northern and western parts, and are seldom violent, except when they immediately precede the eruption of a volcano.

The superstitions of the natives lead them to believe they are produced by the power of Pele, or some of the volcanic deities, and consider them as requisitions for offerings, or threatenings of still greater calamities.

DESCRIPTION AND POPULATION OF KAIMU AND MAKENA.

In the afternoon, Messrs. Thurston and Bishop walked over to Makena, a pleasant village about a mile to the southward of Kaimu, where they collected about one hundred people, to whom Mr. Thurston preached in one of their houses. A greater number would probably have attended, but for the rain which fell during most of the afternoon. Mr. Bishop numbered the houses in the village, and found them, including Makena, to be 145.

Kaimu is pleasantly situated near the sea shore, on the S. E. side of the island, standing on a bed of lava considerably decomposed, and covered over with a light and fertile soil. It is adorned with plantations, groves of cocoa-nuts, and clumps of kou-trees. It has a fine sandy beach, where canoes may land with safety; and, according to the houses numbered to-day, contains about 725 inhabitants.

Including the villages in its immediate vicinity, along the coast, the population would probably amount to 2000; and, if water could be procured near at hand, it would form an eligible missionary station.

196

There are several wells in the village, containing brackish water, which has passed from the sea, through the cells of the lava, undergoing a kind of filtration, and is collected in hollows scooped out to receive it.

The natives told us, that, at the distance of about a mile there was plenty of fresh water.

KAIMU NATIVES SOBER AND INDUSTRIOUS.

The extent of cultivation in the neighbourhood, together with the decent and orderly appearance of the people, induced us to think they are more sober and industrious than those of many villages through which we have passed.

The rain continuing through the afternoon, prevented our preaching to the people, but many, influenced probably by motives of curiosity, collected in the house where we lodged, in conversation with whom we passed the evening.

Their ignorance and superstition awakened lively sympathy in our minds. They are still "without God in the world," and are satisfied with their state.

RELIGIOUS BELIEFS AND THEORIES.

Like the inhabitants of Honuapo and Kapauku, and most of those we had conversed with on the subject, they rejoiced in the abolition of the national idolatry. Its general features precluded their ever contemplating it with pleasure or satisfaction, and every memento that remains, only serves to awaken the recollection of its cruelty, and the oppressive bondage under which they were enslaved while it continued. From this they feel themselves emancipated, and seem also to enjoy, in some degree, the social and domestic comfort resulting from their dwelling together in one house, sitting down to the same repast, and eating the same kind of food. But though they approved of the destruction of the national idols, many were far from having renounced idolatry, and were in general destitute of all knowledge of that dispensation of grace and truth which came by Jesus Christ. They related many tales about their gods, and seemed firm believers in the existence of deities in the volcanoes.

NATIVE THEORIES CONCERNING LIFE AFTER DEATH.

Respecting family idols, the natives in general suppose that after the death of any member of a family, the spirit of the departed hovers about the places of its former resort, appears to the survivors sometimes in a dream, and watches over their destinies; hence they worship an image with which they imagine the spirit is in some way connected.

We endeavoured to convince them of their mistake respecting the objects of their worship, spoke to them of Jehovah, the only being to whom religious homage should be rendered, and of that life and immortality revealed in the sacred scriptures.

Before we retired, we wrote a letter to the governor, informing him of our progress, the hospitality of the people in general, and the kind attention we had received from Mauae, who intended to return from this place to Kairua.

At daybreak on the 6th, Mauae and his family united with us in our morning worship, after which we recommended him to improve the time he might spend here, in teaching his brothers and sisters to read and write, in telling them of the true God, and persuading them, and the people of the place, to avoid intoxication and every other vice, and to regard the sabbath-day by refraining from labour and amusement. He promised to try what he could do; and, when we had taken leave of the family, he walked with us through the village, pointed out the best road, then gave us his parting aroha, and returned to his house.

DISCUSSIONS WITH THE NATIVES AT KEOUOHANA.

After travelling nearly two hours, we arrived at Keouohana, where we sat down to rest beneath the shade of some cocoa-nut trees.

Makoa, our guide, spoke to the head man, and he directed the people to collect near his house. About 100 soon assembled, and when we had explained to them in few words, the object of our visit, we requested them to sit down, and listen to the tidings we had brought. They immediately obeyed.

We sang a hymn in their language, after which an address was given, and the service concluded in the usual manner. As soon as it was finished, they began to talk about what we had told them. Some said it was very good: they had never heard before of a God who had sent his Son to save men. Others said, it was very well for the haore (foreigners) to believe it, but Tane, Rono, Tanaroa, and Tu, were the gods of the Sandwich Islanders.

Makoa, who was a chief speaker among them on such occasions, said they must all attend to the new word, must forsake thieving and drunkenness, infanticide and murder, and do no work on the la tabu, (day sacred;) adding, at the same time, that the king had received the palapala, books, &c. and went to church on the sacred day, as did also Kuakini, the governor.

The head man brought us some ripe plantains, of which we ate a few, and then proceeded on our way, leaving them busy in conversation about the news they had heard; which, in all probability, were "strange things" to their ears.

198

After travelling a mile and a half along the shore, we came to Kehena, a populous village; the people seemed, from the number of their canoes, nets, &c. to be much engaged in fishing. Their contrivance for launching and landing their canoes, was curious and singular.

The bold coast is formed of perpendicular or overhanging rocks, from forty to sixty feet high, against which, this being the windward part of the island, the swell beats violently.

In one place, where there were a few low rocks about thirty feet from the shore, they had erected a kind of ladder. Two long poles, one tied to the end of the other, reached from these rocks to the top of the cliffs. Two other poles, tied together in the same manner, were fixed parallel to the first two, and about four or five feet distant from them. Strong sticks, eight or ten feet long, were laid across these at right angles, and about two or three inches apart, which being fastened to the long poles with ië, (the tough fibrous roots of a climbing sort of plant, which they find in the woods,) formed the steps of this ingenious and useful ladder.

LANDING OF THE CANOES.

The canoes of the place were light and small, seldom carrying more than one man in each. A number were just landing, as we arrived at the place. Two men went down, and stood close to the water's edge, on the leeward or southern side of the rock.

The canoes were paddled up one at a time. The person in each, then watching a convenient opportunity, rowed swiftly to shore, when the rolling billow carried the canoe upon the rock, and it was seized by two men who stood there to receive it. At the same instant that it was grasped on each side by the men on the rock, the one in the canoe, who steered it, jumped into the sea, swam to the shore, and assisted them in carrying it up the ladder to the top of the cliff, where they placed it upon curiously carved stools, made of the wood of the erythrina, and returned to the rock to await the arrival of another canoe. In this way five or six were brought up while we stood looking at them, and I took a sketch of their useful contrivance.

We then walked to the house of the head man, which was large, and contained several families. A number of people soon gathered round us; and when they had expressed their wishes to hear what we had to say, I addressed them on the subject of our religion.

HOSPITABLE RECEPTION AT KAMAILI.

Leaving Kehena, we walked on to Kamaili, a pleasant village, standing in a gently sloping valley, cultivated and shaded by some large cocoa-nut trees. Here we stopped to take breakfast, having travelled about four hours and a half. The hospitable inhabitants, at the request of our guide, soon brought us some fresh fish, a nice pig, with potatoes and taro, and a calabash of good water.

The people who were not employed on their plantations, or in fishing, afterwards assembled, and were addressed from Psalm lxvii. 7. Considerable conversation followed, and they detained us some time to answer their questions, or to explain more fully the things that had been spoken. It was truly gratifying to notice the eagerness with which they proposed their inquiries. After spending about half an hour in endeavouring to satisfy 200 or 300 of them, we took leave, and pursued our journey.

Our path from Kaimu had been smooth and pleasant, but shortly after leaving Kamaili, we passed a very rugged tract of lava nearly four miles across. The lava seemed as if broken to pieces as it cooled; it had continued to roll on like a stream of large scoria, or cinders. Our progress across it was slow and fatiguing.

On our way, our guide pointed out Karepa, an ancient heiau, formerly dedicated to Tu and Rono, and built in the days of Teavemau-hiri, or Tanakini, king of this part of the island. We could not learn whether this was the heiau of Rono, in which the bones of Captain Cook were deposited, and worshipped.

MEETING THE NATIVES AT OPIHIKAO.

About half-past one, we arrived at Opihikao, another populous village, situated within a short distance of the sea. The head man, Karaikoa, brought out a mat, spread it under the umbrageous shade of a kou-tree in front of his door, and invited us to sit down and rest, as the sun was vertical, and travelling laborious. We seated ourselves beside him, and, so soon as he learned from Makoa the nature of our errand, he sent of his own accord, and collected the people to hear what we had to say to them.

When they had assembled, we stood up and sung a hymn, after which one of our number preached to them from Job xxi. 15. It was undoubtedly the first time most, if not all of them, had attended a meeting of the kind; and the preacher was frequently interrupted by several, who exclaimed, "Owau kahi e malama ia Jehova,—e ake au i ora ia Jesu Kraist:" I am one that will serve Jehovah;—I desire to be saved by Jesus Christ.

We invited them to ask us any question respecting what they had heard; and, in answering those they proposed, we spent some time after the service was concluded.

We then proceeded about two miles, principally through cultivated grounds, to Kauaea. About 300 people, excited by curiosity, soon collected around us, to whom Mr. Thurston preached.

We afterwards sat down and talked with them, and then resumed our journey through the district of Malama, the inland part of which was inundated by a volcanic eruption about thirty years since. The part over which we passed, being nearer the sea than that which the lava had overflowed, was covered with soil, and smiling with verdure.

AT KEAHIALAKA.

Near five p.m. we reached Keahialaka, the residence of Kinao, chief or governor of Puna. We found him lying on a couch of sickness, and felt anxious to administer to his comfort, yet did not like at so early an hour to halt altogether for the night. I therefore remained with the sick chief, while Messrs. Thurston and Bishop went on to a village at the east point, about two miles distant.

When they reached Pualaa, the above-mentioned village, they were kindly welcomed by the head man, who soon had the people of the place collected at their request, and to them Mr. Thurston proclaimed the news of salvation through Jesus Christ. The chief furnished the travellers with a hospitable supper and comfortable lodgings.

DISCUSSIONS WITH A SICK CHIEF.

Just before the setting of the sun, I preached to the people at the village where I was staying, and spent the evening with the chief, who was afflicted with a pulmonary complaint, and almost reduced to a skeleton, earnestly recommending him to fly to Jesus, the great physician of souls. He seemed at first much attached to the superstitions of his ancestors, said he had performed every ceremony that he thought likely to be of any avail, and would do any thing to live; but added, E make paha auanei, Perhaps I must soon die.

The love of the Saviour, and his suitableness to the situation of the poor chief, were pointed out, and he was requested rather to seek unto Him for the salvation of his soul, than to priests, and the incantations of sorcerers, for the prolongation of his mortal life, which, although of infinitely less moment than the well-being of his soul, was yet entirely beyond their power. He listened attentively, and at a late hour requested me to pray for him to Jesus Christ. The family collected during the time of prayer, at the close of which the chief lay down on his mat, but said he could not sleep.

We were fatigued with the labours of the day, though we had not travelled so far as usual. The country had been much more populous than any we had passed since leaving Kona, and we felt thankful for the opportunities that we had this day enjoyed of speaking to so many about those things which concern their everlasting peace. May the Holy Spirit water the seed this day sown!

Messrs. Thurston and Bishop conducted the usual worship with the people, who, at an early hour the next morning, crowded the house where they had lodged,—I spent some time in endeavoring to inform the dark mind of the dying chief, on points of the last importance, again directed him to that compassionate Saviour, who invites all to come unto him, receives even those who apply at the eleventh hour, and is able to save to the uttermost those who trust in his mercy. I afterwards prayed with him and his family, and then bade them farewell.

SUPERSTITIONS OF THE NATIVES CONCERNING SICKNESS.

The situation of Kinao was affecting. He appeared in the midst of his days, probably not more than thirty or forty years of age; and though formerly robust and healthy, he was now pale, emaciated, and reduced almost to a skeleton. Enveloped in all the darkness of paganism, and perhaps agitated with fearful uncertainties respecting a future state, he clung eagerly to life, yet seemed to feel a conviction of his approaching end daily increasing. Like his countrymen in general, he supposed his disease inflicted in consequence of the prayers of some malicious enemy, or the vindictive displeasure of the gods of his country; hence he had consulted the sorcerers, expended on them his property, and attended to all their injunctions, if by any means his life might be spared.

The popular superstitions of the islanders lead them to imagine, that an individual who possesses the means of employing a sorcerer, may afflict with painful disease, and even occasion the death of, any person against whom he may indulge feelings of hatred or revenge.

They also believe that the sorcerers, by certain incantations, can discover the author or cause of the disease, and refer it back to the party with whom it originated. So prevalent are these notions, that the people generally believe every individual, who does not meet his death by some act of violence, is destroyed by the immediate power of an unpropitious deity, by poison, or the incantations of the sorcerers employed by some cruel enemy.

POWERS AND CEREMONIES OF THE SORCERERS.

This belief gives the sorcerers great influence among the middling and lower orders; and in times of protracted sickness, their aid is almost invariably sought by all who can procure a dog and a fowl for the sacrifice, and a piece or two of tapa as a fee for the priest.

202

A dog and a fowl are all that are necessary for the ceremony; but the offerings to the god, and the fees to the priest, are regulated according to the wealth or rank of the individuals on whose behalf the aid of sorcery is employed.

The ceremonies performed are various; but the most general is the kuni ahi, broiling fire, a kind of anaana, or sorcery, used to discover the person whose incantation has induced the illness of the party for whom it is performed.

When a chief wishes to resort to it, he sends for a priest, who, on his arrival, receives a number of hogs, dogs, and fowls, together with several bundles of tapa.

Before he commences any of his operations, all persons, except the parties immediately concerned, retire from the house, which the priest tabu's, and prohibits strangers from entering.

He then kindles a small fire somewhere near the couch of the invalid, and covers it with stones. This being done, he kills one of the dogs by strangling it, and cuts off the head of one of the fowls, muttering all the while his prayers to the god he invokes.

INCANTATIONS OF THE SORCERERS.

The dog, fowl, and pig, if there be one, are then cut open, embowelled, and laid on the heated stones, the priest continuing his incantations, and watching, at the same time, the offerings broiling on the fire.

A small part only of these offerings are eaten by the priest, the rest remain on the fire until consumed, when the priest lies down to sleep; and if his prayers are answered, he informs the poor sufferer, on awaking, who or what is the cause of his sickness.

Additional presents are then made to the god, and other prayers offered, that the sickness may seize the person whose incantations in the first instance caused it, or, if in consequence of any delinquency towards the god on the part of the sufferer, that he would abate his anger, and remove the disease.

But if, during his sleep, the priest has no revelation or dream, he informs his employers, on awaking, that he has not succeeded, and that another kuni ahi must be prepared, before he can satisfy them respecting the cause of the sickness. On such occasions the unsuccessful priest is often dismissed, and another sent for, to try his influence with the god.

Different priests employ different prayers or incantations, and are careful to keep the knowledge of them confined to their families, as each one supposes, or wishes the people to think, his own form the best; hence we have often heard the natives, when talking on the subject,

say, "He pule mana ko me," A powerful prayer has such a one:—
and the priest or sorcerer who is supposed to have most influence with
the god, is most frequently employed by the people, and hence derives
the greatest emoluments from his profession.

Though Uri is the principal god of the sorcerers, each tribe has its
respective deities for these occasions. Thus the poor deluded people
are led to imagine that the beings they worship are continually exerting
their power against each other; or that the same god who, when a small
offering only was presented, would allow sickness to continue till death
should destroy the victim of his displeasure, would, for a larger offering,
restrain his anger and withdraw the disease.

The sorcerers were a distinct class among the priests of the island,
and their art appears to claim equal antiquity with the other parts of
that cruel system of idolatry by which the people have been so long
oppressed; and though it has survived the destruction of the national
idolatry, and is still practised by many, it is entirely discontinued by
the principal chiefs in every island, and by all who attend to Christian
instruction.

CHAPTER XI

It was about eight o'clock in the morning of the 7th when I joined Messrs. Thurston and Bishop at Pualaa, where we took breakfast, and afterwards spent the forenoon in conversation with the natives who thronged around us.

Two or three old men, whom we afterwards learned were priests, seemed to dispute what we said about Jehovah's being the only true God, and the Christian the only true religion. They said they thought their taö (traditions) respecting Tu, Tanaroa, Rono, or Orono, and Tairi, were as authentic as the accounts in our book, though ours, from the circumstance of their being written, or, as they expressed it, "hana paia i ka palapala," (made fast on the paper,) were better preserved, and more akaaka, clear, or generally intelligible.

To this we replied at some length, after which the old men ceased to object, but continued to withhold their assent. Numbers sat around, and seemed interested in the discussion. We continued talking to them on the subject of their traditions, one of which we wrote down as they repeated it.

LAVA FLOW DURING TIME OF CAPT. COOK.

About half-past eleven we took leave of them, and directed our way across the eastern point. A most beautiful and romantic landscape presented itself on our left, as we travelled out of Pualaa. The lava was covered with a tolerably thick layer of soil, and the verdant plain, extending several miles towards the foot of the mountains, was agreeably diversified by groups of picturesque hills, originally craters, but now clothed with grass, and ornamented with clumps of trees.

The natives informed us, that three of these groups, Honuaura, Malama, and Mariu, being contiguous, and joined at their base, arrested the progress of an immense torrent of lava, which, in the days of Taraiopu, the friend of Captain Cook, inundated all the country beyond them. We soon left this cheerful scenery, and entered a rugged tract of lava, over which we continued our way till about two p.m., when we reached Kapoho.

DESCRIPTION OF KAPOHO AND GREEN LAKE CRATER.

A cluster, apparently of hills three or four miles round, and as many hundred feet high, with deep indented sides, overhung with trees, and clothed with herbage, standing in the midst of the barren plain of lava, attracted our attention.

We walked through the gardens that encircled its base, till we reached the S. E. side, where it was much lower than on the northern parts. Here we ascended what appeared to us to be one of the hills, and, on reaching the summit, were agreeably surprised to behold a charming valley opening before us. It was circular, and open towards the sea.

The outer boundary of this natural amphitheatre was formed by an uneven ridge of rocks, covered with soil and vegetation. Within these there was a smaller circle of hills, equally verdant, and ornamented with trees. The sides of the valley, which gradually sloped from the foot of the hills, were almost entirely laid out in plantations, and enlivened by the cottages of their proprietors.

In the centre was an oval hollow, about half a mile cross, and probably two hundred feet deep, at the bottom of which was a beautiful lake of brackish water, whose margin was in a high state of cultivation, planted with taro, bananas, and sugar-cane.

The steep perpendicular rocks, forming the sides of the hollow, were adorned with tufts of grass, or blooming pendulous plants, while, along the narrow and verdant border of the lake at the bottom, the bread-fruit, the kukui, and the ohia trees, appeared, with now and then a lowly native hut standing beneath their shade.

A SCENE OF BEAUTY.

We walked to the upper edge of the rocks that form the side of the hollow, where we viewed with pleasure this singularly beautiful scene.

The placid surface of the lake, disturbed only by the boys and girls diving and sporting in its waters, the serpentine walks among the luxuriant gardens along its margin, the tranquil occupations of the inhabitants, some weaving mats, others walking cheerfully up and down the winding path among the steep rocks, the sound of the cloth-beating mallet from several directions, and the smiling gaiety of the whole, contrasted strongly with the panorama we had recently beheld at Kirauea. Yet we felt persuaded, that this now cheerful spot had once presented a similar spectacle, less extended, but equally grand and appalling.

TRADITIONS OF THE NATIVES CONCERNING KAPOHO.

The traditions of the people informed us, that the valley itself was originally a crater, the indented rocks along the outer ridge forming its rim, and the opening towards the sea its mouth. But had tradition been silent, the volcanic nature of the rocks, which were basaltic, or of compact lava in some parts and cellular in others, the structure of the

206

large basin in which we were standing, and the deep hollow in the centre which we were viewing, would have carried conviction to the mind of every beholder, that it had once been the seat of volcanic fires.

We asked several natives of the place, if they had any account of the king in whose reign it had burned; or if they knew any songs or traditions, in which it was stated how many kings had reigned in Hawaii, or how many chiefs had governed Puna, either since it first broke out, or since it became extinct; but they could give us no information on these subjects.

They told us the name of the place was Kapoho (the sunken in,) and of the lake, Ka wai a Pele (the water of Pele).

The saltness of the water in this extinguished volcano proves the connexion of the lake with the sea, from which it is about a mile distant; but we could not learn that it was at all affected by the rising or falling of the tides.

GAME OF HORUA, OR SLEDDING, DESCRIBED.

The natives also told us that it was one of the places from which the volcanic goddess threw rocks and lava after Kahavari, for refusing his papa, or sledge, when playing at horua.

The horua has for many generations been a popular amusement throughout the Sandwich Islands, and is still practised in several places. It consists in sliding down a hill on a narrow sledge, and those who, by strength or skill in balancing themselves, slide farthest, are considered victorious.

The papa, or sledge, is composed of two narrow runners, from seven to twelve or eighteen feet long, two or three inches deep, highly polished, and at the foremost end tapering off from the under side to a point at the upper edge. These two runners are fastened together by a number of short pieces of wood laid horizontally across. To the upper edge of these short pieces two long tough sticks are fastened, extending the whole length of the cross pieces, and about five or six inches apart.

Sometimes a narrow piece of matting is fastened over the whole upper surface, except three or four feet at the foremost end, though in general only a small part for the breast to rest on is covered.

At the foremost end there is a space of about two inches between the runners, but they widen gradually towards the hinder part, where they are distant from each other four or five inches.

The person about to slide grasps the small side-stick firmly with his right hand, somewhere about the middle, runs a few yards to the brow of the hill, or starting-place, where he grasps it with his left hand, and at the same time with all his strength throwing himself forward, falls flat upon it, and slides down the hill, his hands retaining their hold of the side-sticks, and his feet being fixed against the hindermost cross-piece of the sledge.

Much practice and address are necessary, to assume and keep an even balance on so narrow a vehicle, yet a man accustomed to the sport will throw himself, with velocity and apparent ease, 150 or 200 yards down the side of a gradually sloping hill.

GAME OF HOLUA AT KULA.

About three o'clock we resumed our journey, and soon reached Kula, a romantic spot, where Kahavari took leave of his sister.

The hill on which he was sliding when he incurred the displeasure of the terrible goddess, the spot where he rested, and first saw her pursuing him, were visible; and the traditionary story of his encounter with Pele is so interesting, that we think we shall be pardoned for inserting it.

In the reign of Keariikukii, an ancient king of Hawaii, Kahavari, chief of Puna, and one of his punahele, (favourite companions,) went one day to amuse themselves at the horua on the sloping side of a hill, which is still called Ka horua-ana o Kahavari, (the sliding place of Kahavari).

Vast numbers of the people collected at the bottom of the hill, to witness the game; and a company of musicians and dancers repaired to the spot, to add to the amusement of the spectators. The buskined youths had begun their dance, and, amidst the sound of the drums and the songs of the musicians, the horua commenced between Kahavari and his favourite.

KAHAVARI'S ADVENTURE WITH PELE.

Pele, the goddess of the volcano, came down from Kirauea to witness the sport.

She stood on the top of the hill, in the form of a woman, and challenged Kahavari to slide with her. He accepted the offer, and they set off together down the hill. Pele, less acquainted with the art of balancing herself on the narrow sledge than her rival, was beaten, and Kahavari was applauded by the spectators as he returned up the side of the hill.

Before they started again, Pele asked him to give her his papa. He, supposing from her appearance that she was no more than a native woman, said, Aore, no! "Are you my wife, that you should obtain my sledge?" and, as if impatient at being delayed, adjusted his papa, ran a few yards to take a spring, and then, with all his strength, threw himself upon it, and shot down the hill.

208

Pele, incensed at his answer, stamped on the ground, and an earthquake followed, which rent the hill in sunder. She called, and fire and liquid lava arose, and, assuming her supernatural form, with these irresistible ministers of vengeance, she followed down the hill.

When Kahavari reached the bottom of the hill, he arose, and, on looking behind, saw Pele, accompanied by thunder and lightning, earthquake, and streams of burning lava, closely pursuing him. He took up his broad spear, which he had stuck in the ground at the beginning of the game, and, accompanied by his friend, fled for his life.

The musicians, dancers, and crowds of spectators, were instantly buried beneath the fiery torrent, which bearing on its foremost wave the enraged goddess, continued to pursue Kahavari and his friend.

They ran till they came to an eminence, called Buukea. Here Kahavari threw off his tuiraï, cloak of netted ti leaves, and proceeded towards his house, which stood near the shore.

KAHAVARI ABANDONS MOTHER, WIFE AND CHILDREN.

He met his favourite hog Aroipuaa, saluted him by touching noses, and ran to the house of his mother who lived at Kukii, saluted her by touching noses, and said, Aroha ino oe, eia ihonei paha oe e make ai, ke ai mainei Pele: Compassion great to you, close here perhaps is your death; Pele comes devouring.

Leaving her, he met his wife, Kanakawahine. He saluted her. The burning torrent approached, and she said, "Stay with me here, and let us die together." He said, "No; I go, I go."

He then saluted his two children Paupouru and Kaohe, and said, "Ke ue nei au ia orua," I grieve for you two.

The lava rolled near, and he ran till a deep chasm arrested his progress. He laid down his spear, and on it walked safely over. His friend called out for his help; he held out his spear over the chasm; his companion took hold of it, and he drew him securely over.

KAHAVARI ESCAPES.

By this time Pele was coming down the chasm with accelerated motion. He ran till he reached the place where we were sitting.

Here he met his sister Koae, but had only time to say, Aroha oe! "Alas for you!" and then ran on to the sea-shore. His younger brother had just landed from his fishing canoe, and had hastened to his house to provide for the safety of his family, when Kahavari arrived; he and his friend leaped into the canoe, and with his broad spear paddled out to sea.

Pele perceiving his escape, ran to the shore, and hurled after him, with prodigious force, huge stones and fragments of rock, which fell thickly around, but did not strike his canoe.

A SPECIMEN OF HAWAIIAN TRADITIONS.

When they had paddled a short distance from the shore, the Kumu-kahi (east wind) sprung up. He fixed his broad spear upright in the canoe, which answering the double purpose of mast and sail, he soon reached the island of Maui. Here they rested one night, and proceeded to Ranai. On the day following he removed to Morokai, and from thence to Oahu, the abode of Koronohairaau his father, and Kanewa-hinekeaho his sister, to whom he related his disastrous perils, and with whom he took up his permanent abode.

The above tale is a tolerable specimen of most of their traditions, though it is among the least marvellous of the many fabulous stories we have met with, and the truth may easily be separated from the fiction. A sudden and unexpected eruption of a volcano, when a chief and his people were playing at horua, is probably its only foundation.

ILLUSTRATION OF LOW STATUS OF WOMEN.

It exhibits, however, much of the general character of the people, the low estimation in which the females were held, and the wretched state of their social and domestic society, in which those fond attachments, that in civilized and Christian life endear the different members of kindred and family to each other, appear scarcely to have existed.

The absence of relative affections shewn by Kahavari, who, notwithstanding the entreaties of his wife, could leave her, his children, his mother, and his sister, to certain destruction, meets with no reprehension; neither is any censure passed on his unjust seizure of the canoe belonging to his brother, who was engaged in saving his own family, while his adroitness in escaping the dreadful calamity of which he had been the sole cause, is applauded in terms too indelicate to be recorded.

The natives pointed out a number of rocks in the sea, which, they said, were thrown by Pele to sink the canoe in which Kahavari escaped.

KAHAVARI'S HILL—A RUGGED COUNTRY.

After travelling a short distance, we saw the Bu o Kahavari, (Hill of Kahavari,) the place where he stopped, after sliding down-hill, and perceived the goddess pursuing him. It was a black frowning crater, about 100 feet high, with a deep gap in its rim on the eastern side, from which the course of the current of lava could be distinctly traced.

Our way now lay over a very rugged tract of country. Sometimes for a mile or two we were obliged to walk along on the top of a wall four feet high and about three feet wide, formed of fragments of lava that had been collected from the surface of the enclosures which these walls surrounded. We were, however, cheered with a beautiful prospect; for the land, which rose gradually towards the mountains, a few miles to the westward of us, presented an almost enchanting appearance.

The plain was covered with verdure; and as we advanced, a woody eminence, probably some ancient crater, frequently arose from the gently undulated surface, while groups of hills, clothed with trees of various foliage, agreeably diversified the scene.

The shore, which was about a mile to the eastward of us, was occasionally lined with the spiral pandanus, the waving cocoa-nut grove, or the clustering huts of the natives.

AT KAHUWAI AND HONOLULU.

At half-past four we reached Kahuwai, where we sat down and took some refreshment, while Makoa was engaged in bringing the people of the place together. About one hundred and fifty assembled around the door, and were addressed.

After conversing some time, we travelled in an inland direction to Honoruru, a small village situated in the midst of a wood, where we arrived just at the setting of the sun.

Whilst the kind people at the house where we put up were preparing our supper, we sent and invited the inhabitants of the next village to come and hear the word we had to speak to them. They soon arrived; the large house in which we had taken up our lodgings was filled, and a discourse was delivered from John xii. 46. "I am come a light into the world," &c.

RELIGIOUS SERVICES AT WAIAKAHIULA.

We afterwards spent a hour in conversation and prayer with the people of these sequestered villages, who had perhaps never before been visited by foreigners, and then lay down on our mats to rest.

We arose early on the 8th, and Mr. Thurston held morning worship with the friendly people of the place. Although I had been much indisposed through the night, we left Honoruru soon after six a.m. and, travelling slowly towards the sea-shore, reached Waiakaheula about eight, where I was obliged to stop, and lie down under the shade of a canoe-house near the shore. Messrs. Thurston and Bishop walked up to the settlement about half a mile inland, where the former preached to the people.

BISHOP TRAVELS THROUGH KEAAU TO WAIAKEA.

We had seen the eastern division of Hiro yesterday afternoon; and Mr. Bishop hoping to reach Waiakea in a few hours, left Mr. Thurston and the natives with me, and proceeded thither. He was much deceived as to the distance; for it was three o'clock in the afternoon when he arrived at Kaau (Keaau), where the natives tried to persuade him to stay till morning, as they did not think he could reach Waiakea before night. However, he kept on with increased speed, in hopes of getting at least a sight of Waiakea before dark. But in this he was disappointed, for the sun sunk behind Mouna-Kea, and darkness overshadowed the landscape before he had passed the wilderness of pandanus, that stretched along the eastern shore, between Kaau and Hiro. He began to think of resting for the night beneath the shelter of the surrounding bushes; but the path becoming more beaten, indicated his approach to a village. Encouraged by this, he pursued his way, about nine in the evening reached Waiakea, and entered the house of Maaro, where he found Messrs. Goodrich and Harwood, by whom he was gladly welcomed.

Being somewhat recovered by noon, I was able to proceed with Mr. Thurston. The country was populous, but the houses stood singly, or in small clusters, generally on the plantations, which were scattered over the whole country. Grass and herbage were abundant, vegetation in many places luxuriant, and the soil, though shallow, was light and fertile.

KEAAU DESCRIBED.

Soon after five p.m. we reached Kaau, the last village in the division of Puna. It was extensive and populous, abounding with well-cultivated plantations of taro, sweet potatoes, and sugar-cane; and probably owes its fertility to a fine rapid stream of water, which, descending from the mountains, runs through it into the sea. It was the second stream we had seen on the island.

Having quenched our thirst, we passed over it by stepping on some large stones, and directed our way to the house of the head man, where we put up for the night. He was absent in the mountains, with most of his people, and Makoa could procure us no provisions. We, however, succeeded in purchasing a fowl and some potatoes, and made a comfortable supper. While our boys were preparing it, Mr. Thurston preached to a considerable number of people, who had collected outside of the house. We were afterwards joined in evening worship by the family, who at night furnished us with a comfortable and clean mat for our bed, an accommodation we did not always enjoy.

Early on the 9th the house was crowded with natives, and a little before sun-rise morning worship was performed as usual.

Some of the natives observed, in conversation, "We shall never obtain the things of which you have told us, for we are a wicked and unbelieving people."

212

Before we left the place, the people offered for sale some curious deep oval baskets, with covers, made of the fibrous roots of ie. We purchased two, intending to preserve them as specimens of native ingenuity.

Leaving the village of Kaau, we resumed our journey, and after walking between two and three hours, stopped in the midst of a thicket to rest, and prepare some breakfast.

The natives produced fire by rubbing two dry sticks, of the hibiscus tiliaceus, together; and having suspended over it a small iron pot, in gipsy style, upon three sticks, soon prepared our food. At half-past ten we resumed our walk, and passing about two miles through a wood of pretty large timber, came to the open country in the vicinity of Waiakea. At one p.m. we reached the house of the chief, where we were welcomed by our companions, and Maaro, the chief, who, though very ill, was glad to see us.

LOCATED AT WAIAKEA.

As our party was now all together, and intended to spend several days in his district, we applied to him for lodgings, and he directed one of his men to conduct us to a comfortable house by the sea-side, where he said we could be accommodated so long as we should find it necessary or agreeable to stay. We removed into it, and employed the afternoon in narrating the incidents of our respective journeys, and preparing for the coming Sabbath.

It was exactly a week since Messrs. Goodrich and Harwood had parted from us at Kirauea, the great volcano. They had travelled over a pleasant and not uneven country, well wooded, and abounding with ohelos and strawberries, till they reached the inland district of Ora (Olaa). They purchased a hog and vegetables of the people, and had the hog dressed that evening. The next day was the Sabbath; Mr. Goodrich was unable to preach in the native language. The people of the place, however, were induced to abstain from working on that holy day. They arrived at Waiakea on Wednesday evening, and ever since had been hospitably entertained by Maaro.

OLAA DESCRIBED

In company with Messrs. Chamberlain, Ely, and Blatchely, I have since travelled from this place to the volcano, and during that journey had an opportunity of preaching at most of the villages of Ora.

The distance is probably between thirty and forty miles, and the ascent gradual from the shore to the volcano. The soil is generally rich

213

and fertile, and the face of the country, though more uniform than some parts which we passed over, on leaving the southern shore, is varied by occasional undulations.

We travelled through two or three extensive woods, in which were many large trees, and saw also several pools and small currents of excellent fresh water.

The construction of the swineherds' houses at the village of Ka-pu-o-ka-ahi, (the hill of the fire), was singular. There were no walls, nor upright posts along the sides, but the rafters were fixed in the ground, united at the top, and thatched about half way down.

RASPBERRY, OHELO AND STRAWBERRIES

In the neighbourhood of this village we also saw hedges of raspberry bushes, which the natives informed us bore white berries, and were abundant in the mountains, though they would not grow nearer the shore.

Nine or ten miles from the sea, we met with ohelo bushes, and after we had travelled about twenty miles, we found strawberry plants in abundance, and saw several in blossom, although it was in the month of January. The latter plant, as well as the raspberry, is found in all the higher parts of Hawaii, which induces us to think them both indigenous.

RELIGIOUS INTEREST BY NATIVES

It was six months after our tour along the coast, that we passed through the villages of Ora, and we were gratified to find that several of the people, at different places, had received some general ideas of the true God, from the reports of those natives who had heard us preach when travelling along the shore, and had subsequently visited these inland districts.

At one place where we halted for the night, on our return from the volcano, I preached to the people in the evening, and natives afterwards maintained an interesting conversation on religious subjects till midnight.

Among other things, respecting the salvation of the soul through Jesus Christ, they said, "Our forefathers, from time immemorial, and we, ever since we can remember any thing, have been seeking the ora roa (enduring life), or a state in which we should not die, but we have never found it yet; perhaps this is it, of which you are telling us."

NATIVES COLLECTING SANDAL WOOD

During the same journey we overtook Maaro, the chief of Waiakea, and three or four hundred people, returning with sandal wood, which they had been cutting in the mountains. Each man carried two or three pieces, from four to six feet long, and about three inches in diameter.

214

The bark and sap had been chipped off with small adzes, and the wood appeared lighter in colour than what is usually sold at Oahu, probably from its having been but recently cut down.

The sandal wood is the same as in the East Indies, and is probably the santalum album. It is a tolerably heavy and solid wood, and after the sap, or part next the bark, is taken off, is of a light yellow or brown colour, containing a quantity of aromatic oil. Although a plant of slow growth, it is found in abundance in all the mountainous parts of the Sandwich Islands, and is cut in great quantities by the natives, as it constitutes their principal article of exportation.

It is brought down to the beach in pieces from a foot to eighteen inches in diameter, and six or eight feet long, to small sticks not more than an inch thick and a foot and a half long.

It is sold by weight, and the merchants, who exchange for it articles of European or Chinese manufacture, take it to the Canton market, where it is bought by the Chinese for the purpose of preparing incense to burn in their idol temples.

HILO A RAINY DISTRICT

In the evening, many natives, attracted by curiosity, came to our house. We conversed some time with them, and when they went away, invited them to attend public worship on the morrow.

Dense fogs and heavy rains are more frequent at Waiakea, and over the whole division of Hiro, than in any other part of the island. We were, therefore, not surprised at beholding, on the morning of the 10th, the district and coast enveloped in mist, and experiencing frequent showers of rain through the earlier part of the day. Between nine and ten in the forenoon, however, the fog cleared off, and the sun shone brightly on the glowing landscape.

Shortly after ten o'clock, the chiefs, and people in considerable numbers, assembled in a large house adjacent to that in which we resided, agreeably to the invitation given them last evening. The worship commenced as usual, and I preached from the text, "Happy is that people whose God is the Lord." The attention was not so good as that generally given by the congregations we had addressed. Many, however, quietly listened till the services was over.

A CONTROVERSY WITH A PRIESTESS OF PELE

As we arose to depart, an old woman, who during the discourse sat near the speaker, and had listened very attentively, all at once exclaimed, "Powerful are the gods of Hawaii, and great is Pele, the goddess of Hawaii, she shall save Maaro," (the sick chief who was present).

215

Another began to chant a song in praise of Pele, to which the people generally listened, though some began to laugh.

We supposed they were intoxicated, and therefore took no notice of them; but on our leaving the house, some of our people told us they were not ona i ka ruma (intoxicated or poisoned with rum), but inspired by the akua (goddess) of the volcano; or that one of them was Pele herself, in the form of one of her priestesses.

On hearing this, I turned back into the house, and when the song was ended, immediately entered into conversation with the principal one, by asking her if she had attended to the discourse that had been delivered there?

She answered that she had listened, and understood it.

I then asked if she thought Jehovah was good, and those happy who made him their God?

She answered, "He is your good God, (or best God), and it is right that you should worship him; but Pele is my deity, and the great goddess of Hawaii. Kirauea is the place of her abode. Ohiaotelani (the northern peak of the volcano) is one corner of her house. From the land beyond the sky, in former times, she came."

She then went on with the song which she had thus begun, giving a long account of the deeds and honours of Pele. This she pronounced in such a rapid and vociferous manner, accompanied by such violent gestures, that only here and there a word could be understood. Indeed, towards the close, she appeared to lose all command of herself.

When she had done, I told her she was mistaken in supposing any supernatural being resided in the volcano; that Pele was a creature of their own invention, and existed only in the imagination of her kahu, or devotees: adding, that volcanoes, and all their accompanying phenomena, were under the powerful control of Jehovah, who, though uncreated himself, was the Creator and Supporter of heaven and earth, and every thing she beheld.

JEHOVAH NOT THE ONLY GOD

She replied, that it was not so. She did not dispute that Jehovah was a God, but that he was not the only God.

Pele was a goddess, and dwelt in her, and through her would heal the sick chief then present. She wished him restored, and therefore came to visit him.

I said I also wished Maaro to recover, but if he did recover, it would be by the favour of Jehovah, and that I hoped he would acknowledge him, and seek to him alone, as he was the only true Physician, who could save both body and soul, making the latter happy in another world,

216

when this world, with all its volcanoes, mountains, and oceans, should cease to exist.

I then advised her, and all present, to forsake their imaginary deity, whose character was distinguished by all that was revengeful and destructive, and accept the offers Jehovah had made them by his servants, that they might be happy now, and escape the everlasting death that would overtake all the idolatrous and wicked.

AN IMPERSONATOR OF PELE

Assuming a haughty air, she said, "I am Pele; I shall never die; and those who follow me, when they die, if part of their bones be taken to Kirauea, (the name of the volcano), will live with me in the bright fires there."

I said, Are you Pele?

She replied, Yes: and was proceeding to state her powers, &c. when Makoa, who had till now stood silent, interrupted her, and said, "It is true you are Pele, or some of Pele's party; and it is you that have destroyed the king's land, devoured his people, and spoiled all the fishing grounds.

Ever since you came to the islands, you have been busied in mischief; you spoiled the greater part of the island, shook it to pieces, or cursed it with barrenness, by inundating it with lava.

You never did any good; and if I were the king, I would throw you all into the sea, or banish you from the islands. Hawaii would be quiet if you were away."

This was rather unexpected, and seemed to surprise several of the company.

However, the pretended Pele said, "Formerly we did overflow some of the land, but it was only the land of those that were rebels, or were very wicked people. (Broke the restrictions of the tabu, or brought no offerings). Now we abide quietly in Kirauea."

RUM WORSE THAN PELE

She then added, "It cannot be said that in these days we destroy the king's people." She mentioned the names of several chiefs, and then asked who destroyed these?

Not Pele, but the rum of the foreigners, whose God you are so fond of. Their diseases and their rum have destroyed more of the king's men, than all the volcanoes on the island.

I told her I regretted that their intercourse with foreigners should have introduced among them diseases to which they were strangers before, and that I hoped they would also receive the advantages of

217

Christian instruction and civilization, which the benevolent in those countries by which they had been injured, were now anxious to impart: that intoxication was wholly forbidden by Jehovah, the God of Christians, who had declared that no drunkard should enter the kingdom of heaven.

I then said, I was sorry to see her so deceived, and attempting to deceive others; told her she knew her pretensions were false, and recommended her to consider seriously the consequences of idolatry, and cease to practise her fatal deceptions; to recollect that she would one day die; that God had given her an opportunity of hearing of his love to sinners in the gift of his Son; and that if she applied to him for mercy, although now an idolatrous priestess, she might be saved; but if she did not, a fearful doom awaited her.

"I shall not die," she exclaimed, "but ora no," (live spontaneously).

After replying to this, I retired; but the spectators, who had manifested by their countenances that they were not uninterested in the discussion, continued in earnest conversation for some time.

The name of the priestess we afterwards learned was Oani. She resided in a neighbouring village, and had that morning arrived at Waiakea on a visit to Maaro.

THREATS BY PRIESTS OF PELE

When the national idolatry was publicly abolished in the year 1819, several priests of Pele denounced the most awful threatenings, of earthquakes, eruptions, &c. from the gods of the volcanoes, in revenge for the insult and neglect then shewn by the king and chiefs. But no fires afterwards appearing in any of the extinguished volcanoes, no fresh ones having broken out, and those then in action having since that period remained in a state of comparative quiescence, some of the people have been led to conclude, that the gods formerly supposed to preside over volcanoes had existed only in their imagination.

The fearful apprehensions which they had been accustomed to associate with every idea of Pele and her companions, have in a great measure subsided, and the oppressive power of her priests and priestesses is consequently diminished.

PELE STILL DREADED

There are, however, many who remain in constant dread of her displeasure, and who pay the most submissive and unhesitating obedience to the requisitions of her priests.

This is no more than was to be expected, particularly in this part of the island, where the people are far removed from the means of instruction, the example and influence of the principal chiefs, and more enlightened part of the population; and it appears a matter of surprise, that in the course of three years only, so many should have relinquished their superstitious notions respecting the deities of the volcanoes, when we consider their ignorance, and their early impressions, and recollect that while resting at night, perhaps on a bed of lava, they are occasionally startled from their midnight slumbers by the undulating earthquake, and are daily reminded of the dreadful power of this imaginary goddess "by almost every object that meets their view, from the cliffs which are washed by the waves of the sea, even to the lofty craters, her ancient seat above the clouds, and amid perpetual snows."

Until this morning, however, none of the servants of Pele had ever publicly opposed her pretended right to that homage and obedience which it was our object to persuade and invite them to render to Jehovah alone; and though it was encouraging to notice, that, by many of the people present, the pretensions of Oani were disregarded, it was exceedingly painful to hear an idolatrous priestess declaring that the conduct of those, by whom they had been sometimes visited from countries called Christian, had been productive of consequences more injurious and fatal to the unsuspecting and unenlightened Hawaiians, than these dreadful phenomena in nature, which they had been accustomed to attribute to the most destructive of their imaginary deities, and to know also that such a declaration was too true to be contradicted.

NATIVES INCLINED TOWARD CHRISTIANITY

A number of people, after they left the place of public worship, came to our house, and conversed on the blessedness of those who worship and obey Jehovah. They all said it was good, and that if the king were to come or send them word, they would build a house for a missionary, a school-house, and chapel, and also observe the Sabbath-day.

In the afternoon Mr. Thurston preached at the same place to an attentive congregation. In company with Mr. Bishop, I walked over to Ponahawai, where Makoa collected upwards of one hundred people at the head man's house, to whom I preached from Rom. x. 13. "Whosoever shall call upon the name of the Lord shall be saved." The whole assembly gave good attention, frequently interrupting me while speaking, by their exclamations.

A gray-headed old man, who sat near the door, listened with apparent interest during the whole service, and when, towards the close, it was stated that those who in faith called on the Lord, would in another world obtain everlasting life, he exclaimed, "My days are almost ended, that cannot be for me,—can an old man live for ever?" He was told that Jesus was willing to save the souls of all who with humility and

219

sincerity come to him, both old and young; that he would reanimate their bodies in the resurrection; and that he would give eternal life to as many as believed on his name.

We have more than once had occasion to notice with peculiar interest the impression made on an adult heathen, when some of the sublime and important doctrines of religion are for the first time presented to his mind.

Accustomed to contemplate the gods of his ancestors as the patrons of every vice, and supernatural monsters of cruelty, deriving satisfaction from the struggles and expiring agonies of the victim offered in sacrifice, he is surprised to hear of the holy nature of God, and the condescending love of Christ; but the idea of the resurrection of the body, the general judgment, and the eternal happiness or misery of all mankind, affects him with a degree of astonishment never witnessed in countries where the Christian religion prevails, and in which, notwithstanding the lamentable ignorance existing in different portions of the community, there are few who have not some moral perceptions, which have enlarged with the growth of intellect, and the more extended observations of riper years.

But the heathen, whose mental powers have reached maturity before the truth has been presented, experiences very different sensations; and we have seen the effects produced at these times exhibited in various ways: sometimes by most significant gestures, at other times by involuntary exclamations, or penetrating looks fixed on the speaker; and occasionally, as was the case this afternoon, by their actually interrupting us to inquire, "How can these things be?" or declaring in their own beautiful and figurative language, that the tidings they had heard "broke in upon their minds like the light of the morning."

When the exercises were ended, they congratulated each other on the news they had heard; said it was good, and added, "Let us all attend to it; who is there that does not desire eternal life in the other world?" They afterwards made many inquiries about the Sabbath-day, prayer, &c. and asked if they should not be visited again. We told them it was probable that, before long, teachers would come and reside permanently among them.

DESCRIPTION OF A CHIEF'S HOUSEHOLD

On our way home, we called on Maaro, whom we found very ill. One of his children was also sick, and seemed near dying. We regretted that we had no medicine proper to administer either to the suffering chief or his child.

220

The wretched picture of uncivilized society, which this family exhibited, powerfully affected our minds. Maaro's house, like that of the chiefs in general, was large, and accommodated many of his friends and dependents.

On one side near the door, he lay on a mat which was spread on the ground. Two or three domestics sat around, one of them holding a small calabash of water, and another with a kahiri was fanning away the flies.

Near the centre of the house, on another mat, spread also on the ground, lay the pale emaciated child, its features distorted with pain, and its feeble voice occasionally uttering the most piteous cries. A native girl sat beside it, driving away the flies, and holding a cocoanut shell in her hand, containing a little poë, with which she had been endeavouring to feed it.

INDIFFERENCE OF FAMILY TO SICKNESS

In the same place, and nearly between the father and the child, two of Maaro's wives, and some other chief women, were seated on the ground, playing at cards, laughing and jesting over their game.

We tried to enter into conversation with them, but they were too intent on the play to pay any attention to what we said.

The visitors or attendants of the chief sat in groups in different parts of the house, some carelessly singing, others engaged in earnest conversation.

We could not forbear contrasting the scene here presented, with a domestic circle in civilized and Christian society, under similar circumstances, where all the alleviations which the tenderest sympathy could impart, would be promptly tendered to the suffering individuals.

But here, alas! ignorance, cruel idolatry, and familiarity with vice, appeared to have destroyed natural affection, and all the tender sympathies of humanity, in their bosoms.

The wife beheld unmoved the sufferings of her husband, and the amusement of the mother was undisturbed by the painful crying of her languishing child.

TREATMENT OF THE SICK IN TAHITI

The state of domestic society in Tahiti and the neighbouring islands, only a few years ago, was even more affecting. There the sick were often removed from the house in which they had been accustomed to reside, and placed in a miserable hut a few yards distant, and were sometimes starved to death, or murdered, or buried alive, from motives of covetousness or idleness; children frequently declaring it was too much trouble to attend to the wants of their parents.

But what a pleasing change has the introduction of Christianity effected among them!

So far from being unwilling to take care of their sick relatives and friends, a number of individuals, at several of the missionary stations, annually devote a part of the produce of their labour, to erect houses, purchase medicine, and provide for the comfort of those who are sick and indigent.

It is impossible for any people to be more attentive and kind than they now are. Many a time the friend of some one who had been taken ill has called me up at midnight to ask for medicine; and often have I seen a wife or a sister supporting in her lap the head of a sick and perhaps dying husband or brother, night after night, yet refusing to leave them, though almost exhausted with fatigue.

DISCUSSIONS WITH MAARO, CHIEF OF WAIAKEA

Leaving Maaro, we returned through a highly cultivated part of the district. Every thing in nature was lovely, and the landscape around awakened emotions very different from those excited during our visit to the abode of sickness which we had just left.

The wretchedness of the people, we trust, will ere long be ameliorated; for the gospel, which produced the favourable change above alluded to, among the natives of the Society Islands, has at length reached these shores; and there is every reason to expect that its humane spirit and principles, when once imbibed by the people, will result in corresponding effects.

The morning of the 11th was cloudy, with rain, which did not clear off till about 10 a.m. The greater part of the day we employed in examining the district and harbour. We were highly gratified with the fertility of the soil, and the luxuriance of the verdure.

PROPOSAL TO SEND MISSIONARIES TO HILO

In the afternoon we waited on Maaro the chief, to ask his opinion respecting missionaries settling permanently in his neighbourhood. He said, perhaps it would be well; that if the king and chiefs approved of it, he should desire it.

We asked if he would patronize and protect missionaries and their families, provided the king and chiefs approved of their settling at Waiakea. He answered, "Yes, certainly," and, at the same time, pointed out several places where they might build their houses."

We told him that the king, Karaimoku, Kaahumanu, and the governor, approved of instructors coming to teach the people of Waiakea; but that we were also desirous to obtain his opinion, before any arrangements were made for their removal from Oahu. He again repeated that he thought it would be a good thing; and that if the missionaries came with the approbation of the king and chiefs, he should be glad to witness their arrival.

We then took leave of Maaro, and the chiefs that were with him. Messrs. Thurston and Bishop walked to the opposite side of the bay, where we had held a religious exercise yesterday, and here Mr. Thurston preached to an attentive congregation of about sixty people. The head man afterwards expressed a strong desire to be instructed, and said all the people would like to learn the palapala, and keep the Sabbath-day.

DISCUSSIONS WITH NATIVES ABOUT MISSIONARIES

While they were on the western shore, I visited several houses on the eastern side of the settlement, and entered into conversation with the people on the subject of missionaries coming to reside at Waiakea.

In general they approved, saying they had dark minds, and needed instruction. Some, however, seemed to doubt the propriety of foreigners coming to reside permanently among them. They said they had heard that in several countries where foreigners had intermingled with the original natives, the latter had soon disappeared; and should missionaries come to live at Waiakea, perhaps the land would ultimately become theirs, and the kanaka maore (aborigines) cease to be its occupiers.

I told them, that had been the case in some countries; but that the residence of missionaries among them, so far from producing it, was designed and eminently calculated to prevent a consequence so melancholy.

At the same time I remarked, that their sanguinary wars, their extensive and cruel practice of infanticide, their frequent intoxication, and their numerous diseases, partly gendered by vicious habits, had, according to their own account, diminished the population of the island three-fourths within the last forty years; and, from the destructive operation of these causes, there was every reason to fear the Hawaiian people would soon be annihilated, unless some antidote was found, some barrier opposed, to their depopulating effects.

None, I added, were so strong as moral restraints; none so efficacious as instruction and civilization; and, above all, the principles and doctrines of the Bible, which they could not become acquainted with but by the residence of missionaries among them.

Such, I informed them, was the opinion of the friends of missions, who, anxious to ameliorate their wretched condition, preserve from oblivion the remnant of the people, place them among the nations of the earth, and direct them to the enjoyment of civilized life, and the participation of immortality and happiness in another world, had sent

223

them the word of God, and missionaries to unfold to them, in their own language, its divine and invaluable truths.

At the close of this interview, some again repeated, that it would be a good thing for missionaries to come; others expressed doubt and hesitation.

Many of the people, during their intercourse with foreigners, have been made acquainted with the leading facts in the history of South America and the West Indies; and hence the natives of this place, in all probability, derived the ground of their objection.

STATUS OF NATIVES COMPARED WITH SOCIETY ISLANDERS

The houses of the natives whom we had visited today, like most in this part of the island, where the pandanus is abundant, were covered with the leaves of this plant, which, though it requires more labour in thatching, makes the most durable dwellings.

The inhabitants of Waiakea are peculiarly favoured in having woods producing timber, such as they use for building, within three or four miles of their settlement, while the natives in most parts of the islands have to fetch it from a much greater distance.

In neatness and elegance of appearance their houses are not equal to those of the Society Islanders, even before they were instructed by Europeans, but in point of strength and durability they sometimes exceed them.

STYLES AND METHODS OF BUILDING HAWAIIAN HOUSES

There is also less variety in the form of the Sandwich Island dwellings, which are chiefly of two kinds, viz. the hale noho, (dwelling house), or halau, (a long building), nearly open at one end, and, though thatched with different materials, they are all framed in nearly the same way.

They begin to build a house by planting in the ground a number of posts, six or eight inches in diameter, in a row, about three or four feet apart, which are to support one side of the house. When these are fixed in a straight line, they erect a parallel row, to form the opposite side.

In the small houses, these posts are not more than three or four feet high, while in the larger ones they are twelve or fourteen feet in height, and proportionably stout. Those used in the chiefs' houses are round, straight, and smooth, being prepared with great care, but in general they are fixed in the ground without even having the bark stripped off.

Grooves are cut in the top of the posts, along which small poles are laid horizontally, instead of wall-plates, and tied to the posts with the fibrous roots of the ie, a tough mountain plant.

A high post, notched at the top, is next fixed in the middle at each end, and supports the ridge-pole, on which the tops of the rafters rest, while, at the lower end, they are fixed on the wall-plate, each .rafter being placed exactly above the post which supports the horizontal pole, or wall-plate.

When the rafters are fixed, small poles are laid along, where they cross each other above the ridge-pole; sometimes poles are fastened across like tie-beams, about half-way up the roof, and the separate parts of the whole frame are tied together with strong cinet, made of the roots of the ie plant, or fibres of cocoa-nut husk.

The space between the posts at the sides and ends is now closed up with sticks, larger than a common-sized walking-stick, which are tied with cinet in horizontal lines, two or three inches apart, on the outside of the posts, and extending from the ground to the top of the roof. A large house, in this stage of its erection, has a singular appearance.

If the sides and roof are of plantain leafstalks, and the leaves of the pandanus, or of ti leaves, each leaf is woven around the horizontal sticks, which gives it a neat appearance, resembling a kind of coarse matting on the inside, while the ends of the leaves hang down without. But if they are covered with grass, which is most commonly the case, it is bound up in small bundles, and these are tied to the small sticks along the side of the wall of the house, with cinet or cord.

They always begin at the bottom, and tie on the grass with the roots upward, and inclined towards the inside, and continue one row above another from the ground to the top of the roof.

The roof and sides are always of the same material, except where the latter are of plantain or ti leaves. The corners and ridge are sometimes covered with fern-leaves, with which they can secure these parts better than with grass, &c.

ABSENCE OF WINDOWS IN HOUSES

The shell is now finished, and generally, except in the lowness of the sides and steepness of the roof, looks much like a hay-rick, particularly as until recently they never thought of making windows, and had only one aperture, which was the entrance.

A large portion of the lower part of that end of the halau which faces the sea, is usually open.

The houses of this kind were probably originally erected for the construction and preservation of canoes, for which purpose they are still sometimes used, though frequently occupied as dwellings.

In the common dwelling-house, the door is frequently on one side. In the old houses the doors are always low.

225

Since foreigners have resided among them, and built houses with doors and windows, the natives have enlarged their doors, though there are yet but few that can be entered without stooping.

Some of them also begin to think windows a convenience, but they by no means fall in with our ideas of uniformity in the disposition of them.

Sometimes we have seen a house forty or fifty feet long, with the door at one end, and a small window at the other, half way up to the top of the roof.

Again, we have entered a house of equal dimensions, and in some parts of it we have seen an aperture within a foot or a foot and a half of the floor, generally near their sleeping-places. This, as well as the other, they call a buka makani, (wind hole), and assign as a reason for placing it in such a situation, that they sometimes find it close in their houses, and like to have the wind blow on them as they lie on their mats.

INTERIOR ARRANGEMENT OF DWELLINGS

The shell of the house being finished, they proceed to fit up the inside, which is soon accomplished, as they have neither partitions nor chambers, and, however large the house may be, but one room and one floor. In preparing the latter, they sometimes level the ground, and spread grass over it, which they cover with large mats made of the leaves of the pandanus. But the best floors are those formed with pebbles, or small fragments of lava, which are always dry, and less likely to be infested with vermin than those covered with grass.

The size and quality of a dwelling varies according to the rank and means of its possessor, those of the poor people being mere huts, eight or ten feet square, others twenty feet long, and ten or twelve feet wide, while the houses of the chiefs are from forty to seventy feet long.

Their houses are generally separate from each other; even in their most populous villages, however near the houses may be, they are always distinct buildings.

METHODS OF ERECTION OF HOUSES

Although there are professed house-carpenters who excel in framing, and others who are taught to finish the corners of the house and ridge of the roof, which but few understand, yet, in general, every man erects his own house. If it be of a middling or large size, this, to an individual or a family, is a formidable undertaking, as they have to cut down the trees in the mountains, and bring the wood from six to ten miles on their shoulders, gather the leaves or grass, braid the cinet, &c. before they can begin to build.

But when a chief wants a house, he requires the labour of all who hold lands under him; and we have often been surprised at the despatch with which a house is sometimes built.

We have known the natives come with their materials in the morning, put up the frame of a middling-sized house in one day, cover it in the next, and on the third day return to their lands.

Each division of people has a part of the house allotted by the chief, in proportion to its number; and it is no unusual thing to see upwards of a hundred men at a time working on one house.

DURABILITY OF GRASS HOUSES

A good house, such as they build for the chiefs, will keep out the wind and rain, and last from seven to ten years. But, in general, they do not last more than five years; and those which they are hired to build for foreigners, not much more than half that time.

In less than twelve months after my own grass house was built, the rain came through the roof from one end to the other, every time there was a heavy shower.

In some of the islands the natives have recently covered their houses with mud; this, however, does not appear to render them more durable.

TOOLS USED BY NATIVES

Before they were visited by foreigners, the only tool employed in building was a stone adze, formed of a kind of basalt, or compact lava; and though they now use an axe in felling the trees, the adze is still their favourite tool, and many of them use no other.

The stone adze is, however, exchanged for one made with a plane iron, bent, and tied securely to a handle of light wood. This they prefer to the European adze, which they say is too heavy.

Sometimes they use a saw, chisel, and gimlet, in framing their houses, but they are not yet adepts in the use of these tools; we have often seen them throw down the saw, and take up their adze to finish that which they had commenced cutting with a saw.

IMPROVEMENTS IN DWELLINGS

Their habitations, though rude, discover, concerning their circumstances and means, a greater degree of industry, and attention to comfort, than is usually manifested by uncivilized nations; and within the last few years great improvements have been made in their houses.

Karaimoku has erected in the island of Oahu, a stone house, sixty feet by thirty, three stories high, with a spacious cellar underneath. The inside of the house he has formed into apartments, which, by foreign workmen whom he employed, have been finished in a highly respectable

227

manner. The front, which faces the south, is screened by a wide veranda enclosed with light railing, and ascended by a handsome flight of stairs.

SUPERSTITIONS CONNECTED WITH HOUSE BUILDING—HOW FURNISHED

While idolatry existed, a number of superstitious ceremonies were performed, before they could occupy their houses. Offerings were made to the gods, and presents to the priest, who entered the house, uttered prayers, went through other ceremonies, and slept in it before the owner took possession, in order to prevent evil spirits from resorting to it, and to secure its inmates from the effects of incantation.

When the house was finished, it was soon furnished. A sleeping-mat spread on the ground, and a wooden pillow, a wicker basket or two to keep their tapa or native cloth in, a few calabashes for water and poë, and some wooden dishes, of various size and shape, together with a haka, were all they required.

This latter article was sometimes like a stand used by us for hanging hats and coats on. It was often made with care, and carved, but more frequently it was a small arm of a tree, with a number of branches attached to it. These were cut off within a foot of the main stem, which was planted in some convenient part of the house, and upon these natural pegs they used to hang their calabashes, and other vessels containing food.

METHODS OF EATING

They generally sat on the ground, and took their food near the door of their house: sometimes, however, they took their meals in the more luxurious manner of some of the eastern nations, lying nearly in a horizontal posture, and resting on one arm, or reclining on a large cushion or pillow placed under the breast for that purpose; in this manner the late king, with the members of his family, and many of the principal chiefs, were accustomed frequently to take their evening meal.

Their intercourse with foreigners of late years has taught many of the chiefs to prefer a bedstead to the ground, and a mattress to a mat, to sit on a chair, eat at a table, use a knife and fork, &c. This we think advantageous, not only to those who visit them for purposes of commerce, but to the natives themselves, as it increases their wants, and consequently stimulates to habits of industry.

CHAPTER XII

CANOE HIRED FOR PASSAGE TO LAUPAHOEHOE

Having been informed by our guide that travelling along the coast to the northward would be tedious and difficult, on account of the numerous deep ravines that intersected the whole extent of Hiro and Hamakua, it seemed desirable to take a canoe as far as Laupahoehoe, by which we should avoid some of the most difficult parts of the coast.

As soon as the rain had ceased, and the fog cleared off, on the morning of the 12th I waited on Maaro, to inquire if he could furnish us with one. The chief said, he had not a double canoe at his command, or he would cheerfully provide one. I therefore walked on to Pueo, on the western shore, where, for six dollars, I hired one of Kapapa, chief of the place, to take us between twenty and twenty-five miles.

TOLL CHARGED FOR CROSSING WAILUKU RIVER

Returning from Pueo, I visited Wairuku, a beautiful stream of water flowing rapidly over a rocky bed, with frequent falls, and many places eligible for the erection of water-mills of almost any description. Makoa and the natives pointed out a square rock in the middle of the stream, on which, during the reign of Tamehameha, and former kings, a toll used to be paid by every traveller who passed over the river.

Whenever any one approached the stream, he stood on the brink, and called to the collector of the toll, who resided on the opposite side. He came down with a broad piece of board, which he placed on the rock above mentioned. Those who wished to cross met him there, and deposited on the board whatever articles had been brought; and if satisfactory, the person was allowed to pass the river. It did not appear that any uniform toll was required; the amount, or value, being generally left to the collector.

The natives said it was principally regulated by the rank or number of those who passed over.

In order the better to accommodate passengers, all kinds of permanently valuable articles were received. Some paid in native tapa and mats, or baskets, others paid a hog, a dog, some fowls, a roll of tobacco, or a quantity of dried salt fish.

MARKET FAIRS HELD AT HILO

The river of Wairuku was also distinguished by the markets or fairs held at stated periods on its banks. At those times the people of Puna,

229

and the desolate shores of Kau, even from the south point of the island, brought mats, and mamake tapa, which is a remarkably strong black or brown native cloth, for the manufacture of which the inhabitants of Ora, and some of the inland parts of Puna, are celebrated throughout the whole group of the Sandwich Islands. It is made of a variety of the morus papyrifera, which grows spontaneously in those parts. These, together with vast quantities of dried salt fish, were ranged along on the south side of the ravine.

The people of Hiro and Hamakua, as far as the north point, brought hogs, tobacco, tapa of various kinds, large mats made of the pandanus leaves, and bundles of ai pa, which were collected on the north bank. Ai pai, (hard food). A kind of food made of baked taro, pounded together without water. When properly prepared, it is wrapped in green ti leaves, and tied up in bundles containing from twenty to forty pounds each; in this state it will remain several months without injury. From bank to bank the traders shouted to each other, and arranged the preliminaries of their bargains. From thence the articles were taken down to the before-mentioned rock in the middle of the stream, which in this place is almost covered with large stones. Here they were examined by the parties immediately concerned, in the presence of the collectors, who stood on each side of the rock, and were the general arbiters, in the event of any disputes arising. To them also was committed the preservation of good order during the fair, and they, of course, received a suitable remuneration from the different parties.

On the above occasions, the banks of the Wairuku must often have presented an interesting scene, in the bustle of which these clerks of the market must have had no inconsiderable share.

According to the account of the natives, this institution was in force till the accession of Rihoriho, the late king, since which time it has been abolished.

In the afternoon I called on Maaro, and found him very ill, and averse to conversation. His wives sat in the same room playing at cards, and apparently too intent on their game to be easily diverted.

A CASE OF INFANTICIDE—JUSTIFIED BY KAMEHAMEHA

About twelve years ago, a shocking instance of infanticide occurred in this district, exhibiting, in a most affecting manner, the unrestrained violence of malignant passion, and the want of parental affection, which so often characterize savage life.

A man and his wife, tenants of Mr. Young, who has for many years held, under the king, the small district of Kukuwau, situated on the centre of Waiakea bay, resided not far from Maaro's house. They had one child, a fine little boy. A quarrel arose between them on one occasion

230

respecting this child. The wife refusing to accede to the wishes of the husband, he, in revenge, caught up the child by the head and the feet, broke its back across his knee, and then threw it down in expiring agonies before her.

Struck with the atrocity of the act, Mr. Young seized the man, led him before the king, Tamehameha, who was then at Waiakea, and requested that he might be punished.

The king inquired, "To whom did the child he has murdered belong?"

Mr. Young answered, that it was his own son.

"Then," said the king, "neither you nor I have any right to interfere; I cannot say any thing to him."

PREVALENCE OF INFANTICIDE IN HAWAII

We have long known that the Sandwich Islanders practised infanticide, but had no idea of the extent to which it prevailed, until we had made various inquiries during our present tour, and had conversed with Karaimoku, Kapiolani, the governor, and several other chiefs, who, though formerly unwilling to converse on the subject, have, since their reception of Christianity, become more communicative.

It prevails throughout all the islands, and, with the exception of the higher class of chiefs, is, as far as we could learn, practised by all ranks of the people.

However numerous the children among the lower orders, parents seldom rear more than two or three, and many spare only one; all the others are destroyed sometimes shortly after birth, generally during the first year of their age.

The means by which it is accomplished, though numerous, it would be improper to describe. Kuakini, the governor of the Island, in a conversation I had with him at Kairua, enumerated many different methods, several of which frequently proved fatal to the mother also. Sometimes they strangle their children, but more frequently bury them alive.

INFANTICIDE IN SOCIETY ISLANDS

Among the Society Islanders, who, while they were idolaters, probably practised infanticide more than any other natives in the Pacific, if the intended victim survived only one day, and frequently not more than a few hours, it was generally saved.

Depraved as they were, they could not afterwards sacrifice to a barbarous custom an innocent babe, who seemed to look with confidence to its mother or its nurse, and unconsciously smiled upon those who stood by: hence the parties interested in the child's destruction, which were the parents themselves, or their relations, generally strangled it soon after its birth.

231

But among the Sandwich Islanders, the infant, after living a week, a month, or even a year, was still insecure, as some were destroyed when nearly able to walk.

It is painful to think of the numbers thus murdered. All the information we have been able to obtain, and the facts that have come to our knowledge in the neighbourhood where we resided, afford every reason to believe, that from the prevalence of infanticide two-thirds of the children perished.

We have been told by some of the chiefs, on whose word we can depend, that they have known parents to murder three or four infants where they have spared one. But even supposing that not more than half the children were thus cut off, what an awful spectacle of depravity is presented! how many infants must have been annually sacrificed to a custom so repugnant to all the tenderest feelings of humanity, that, without the clearest evidence, we should not believe it would be found in the catalogue of human crimes.

REASONS FOR INFANTICIDE

The reasons they give for this practice manifest a degree of depravity no less affecting.

Among the Marquesians, who inhabit a group of islands to the southeast of Hawaii, we are told that children are sometimes, during seasons of extreme scarcity, killed and eaten by their parents, to satisfy hunger.

With the Society Islanders, the rules of the Areoi institutions, and family pride, were the principal motives to its practice.

If the rank or family of the mother was inferior to that of the father, his relations or friends usually destroyed the child.

More frequently, however, the mother's rank was superior to that of the father. In this case, her relations, in order to avoid the degradation which they supposed it would entail on their family or class in society, almost invariably murdered the child.

The regulations of the Areoi society were not only abominable and vicious, but exceedingly cruel, and, excepting the chiefs, the members usually destroyed their offspring; and the rearing of any was considered a degradation.

The reason generally assigned for this was, that nursing children quickly diminished the personal charms of the mother.

Excepting the latter, which operates in a small degree, none of these motives actuate the Sandwich Islanders; those, however, by which they are influenced are equally criminal.

Some of the natives have told us that children were formerly sacrificed to the sharks infesting their shores, and which through fear they had deified; but as we have never met with persons who have ever offered any, or seen others do it, this possibly may be only report.

LAZINESS PRINCIPAL REASON FOR INFANTICIDE

The principal motive with the greater part of those who practise it, is idleness; and the reason most frequently assigned, even by the parents themselves, for the murder of their children, is, the trouble of bringing them up.

In general they are of a changeable disposition, fond of a wandering manner of life, and find their children a restraint, preventing them, in some degree, from following their roving inclinations.

Like other savage nations, they are averse to any more labour than is absolutely necessary. Hence they consider their children a burden, and are unwilling to cultivate a little more ground, or undertake the small additional labour necessary to the support of their offspring during the helpless periods of infancy and childhood.

In some cases, when the child has been sickly, and the parents have grown tired of nursing and attending it, they have been known, in order to avoid further attendance and care, to bury it at once; and we have been credibly informed that children have been buried alive, merely because of the irritation they have discovered.

BURIED ALIVE IN FLOOR OF HOUSE

On these occasions, when the child has cried more than the parents, particularly the mother, could patiently bear, instead of clasping the little sufferer to her bosom, and soothing by caresses the pains which, though unable to tell them, it has probably felt, she has, to free herself from this annoyance, stopped its cries by thrusting a piece of tapa into its mouth, dug a hole in the floor of the house, and, perhaps within a few yards of her bed, and the spot where she took her daily meals, has relentlessly buried, in the untimely grave, her helpless babe.

The Society Islanders buried the infants they destroyed among the bushes, at some distance from their houses; but many of the infants in the Sandwich Islands are buried in the houses in which both parents and child had resided together.

In the floors, which are frequently of earth or pebbles, a hole is dug, two or three feet deep, into which they put the little infant, placed in a broken calabash, and having a piece of native cloth laid upon its mouth to stop its cries. The hole is then filled up with earth, and the inhuman parents themselves have sometimes joined in treading down the earth upon their own innocent but murdered child.

INDIFFERENCE OF NATIVES CONCERNING INFANTICIDE

The bare recital of these acts of cruelty has often filled our minds

233

with horror, while those who have been engaged in the perpetration of them, have related all their tragic circumstances in detail with apparent unconcern.

What an affecting view does this practice exhibit of human nature, unaided by the light of revelation, uninfluenced by the mild spirit of true religion, and under the debasing influence of cruel superstition.

To what an abject state of moral degradation must a people, in many respects extremely interesting, be reduced, to perpetrate, without compunction, such atrocities; and what a painful and humiliating demonstration do they afford of the truth of the scripture declaration, that "the dark places of the earth are full of the habitations of cruelty."

Instinct teaches animals to take care of their offspring; even the savage tiger roams the forest to provide for her young, or fearlessly meets death in their defence. But here, where so many advantages combine to increase the comforts of the inhabitants, infants are destroyed by a parent's hand.

How great are the obligations of those whose lot is cast in countries favoured with the Bible, to whose domestic society Christianity imparts so much happiness. And how consoling to know, that its principles, wherever imbibed, will produce, even in the most barbarous communities, such a delightful transformation of character, that the lion and leopard shall become harmless as the lamb and the kid, "and they shall neither hurt nor destroy."

CHRISTIANITY TERMINATED INFANTICIDE IN SOCIETY ISLANDS

When the natives of the Society Islands embraced the Christian religion, they immediately refrained from this practice. The infants, spared as they grew up, kindled and cherished in their parents' bosoms emotions they had never before experienced. They became, in general, exceedingly fond of their children.

I have seen a mother or a father, who have been known to have murdered several children, fondling and nursing a little babe with a degree of tenderness, that, without witnessing it, I could not believe would have been felt by individuals so hardened and insensible as they had formerly been.

As parental affection increased, they began to view with abhorrence a crime, their former familiarity with which was now surprising even to themselves; and, in order to mark their sense of its enormity, the very first article in the code of laws proposed by the chiefs, and adopted by the people in most of the Society Islands, shortly after their reception of Christianity, is a prohibition of infanticide, annexing the punishment of death to its perpetration under any circumstances whatever.

234

In the Sandwich Islands, although not abolished, we have reason to believe it prevails less extensively now than it did four or five years ago.

The king, and some of the chiefs, especially Karaimoku, since they have attended to the precepts of Christianity, and have been made acquainted with the direct prohibitions of it in the Bible, have readily expressed in public their conviction of its criminality, and that committing it is in fact pepehi kanaka, (to kill man), under circumstances which aggravate its guilt. They have also been led to see its impolicy with respect to their resources, in its tendency to depopulate the islands, and render them barren or unprofiitable, and, from these views, have lately exerted themselves to suppress it.

Karaimoku, regent of the islands, has more than once forbidden any parents to destroy their children, and has threatened to punish with banishment, if not with death, any who shall be found guilty of it.

ONLY RECENTLY THAT CHIEFS HAVE OPPOSED INFANTICIDE

After we left Kairua, on our present tour, Kuakini, the governor, published among all the people under his jurisdiction, a strict prohibition of this barbarous custom. It is, however, only recently that the chiefs have endeavoured to prevent it, and the people do not very well brook their interference; so that, notwithstanding their efforts, it is still practised, particularly in remote districts, but in general privately, for fear of detection and punishment.

The check, however, which infanticide has received from the humane and enlightened policy of the chiefs, is encouraging. It warrants the most sanguine expectations, that as Christianity advances among the Hawaiians, this, and other customs equally degrading to their character, and destructive of their race, will be entirely laid aside, as has been the case among the Tahitians; and there is every reason to presume, that the pleasing change, which has resulted from the general reception of the gospel among the latter, will, under the divine blessing, be ultimately realized by the Sandwich Islanders.

May that happy period soon arrive! for if the total abolition of this cruel practice (though amongst the least of its benevolent objects) be the only advantage which the establishment of a Christian Mission in these distant islands shall confer on their inhabitants, yet, in rescuing every year, through all the succeeding generations of this reviving nation, multitudes from a premature death, the liberal assistance of its friends and the labours of its several members will be most amply rewarded.

KAHUNAS ATTEMPT TO CURE CHIEF

On the morning of the 13th we examined some of the eastern parts

235

of the bay. I also visited Maaro. On arriving at the house in which I had left the sick chief yesterday, the natives told me that he had been removed, that the house where he then was, was tabu, and the tabu would be broken if I should go there. They refused to tell where he was, but did not attempt to prevent my going in search for him.

After travelling a mile and a half inland, I reached the house in which he lay, and was immediately invited to enter. The number of small sticks, with the leaves of the ti plant fastened round them, which I saw fixed in different parts of the house, particularly around the mat on which the chief was reclining, induced me to think they had been performing some incantation for his recovery, or were preparing for one.

I asked one who sat by, and who, I supposed, was a kahuna, (doctor), what remedies they were using for his recovery; but they gave me no answer. The chief seemed to have less pain than yesterday, and was much more communicative. He said the native doctors had brought him there in order to try the effect of medicines, which he trusted would give relief.

A WARNING AGAINST INCANTATION

I told him it was right to use every lawful means for the recovery of health; but cautioned him particularly against having recourse to the incantations of the priests, or making any offerings to their former gods, as that was not only foolish and useless, but offensive to God the author of all our mercies, with whom alone were the issues of life and death.

He made no reply, but turned the conversation, by saying he regretted that he was not able to furnish us with a canoe, and that his sickness had not allowed him to be more with us.

I told him we wished to have had more frequent opportunities of telling him of Jesus Christ; and endeavouring to impress his mind with the necessity of an early application for the pardon of his sins, and the salvation of his spirit. When I left him, he said he would think of these things, and, should he get better, would attend to instruction, and use his influence to induce his people to attend.

THE PRACTICE OF MEDICINE AND SORCERY

Maaro was attended by two or three natives, who were called kahuna rapaau mai, the name given to those who undertake to cure diseases, from kahuna, a priest, or one expert in his profession, rapaau, to heal, or to apply medicine, and mai, disease.

Although among the Sandwich Islanders there are none who exclusively devote themselves to this employment, there are many who pretend to great skill in the discovery and cure of diseases. They are

236

usually, as their name imports, priests or sorcerers, and seldom administer medicine unaccompanied by some superstitious ceremony.

The knowledge of the art is frequently communicated from father to son, and thus continued in one family. In their practice they have different departments, and those who are successful in removing internal complaints are most esteemed.

Febrile disorders are not so prevalent as in many tropical climates, but asthmatic and pulmonary affections are frequent, and the latter generally baffle all their skill.

HAWAIIAN MEDICINES AND MEDICAL TREATMENT

We are not aware that they admit into their materia medica any but vegetable substances, which are variously prepared; sometimes baked, or heated in a cocoa-nut shell, but often applied after being simply bruised with a stone. In the selection and employment of these, they certainly manifest an acquaintance with the medicinal properties of a number of indigenous herbs and roots, which is commendable, and may hereafter be turned to a good account.

Several of their applications, simply as they are prepared, are, however, very powerful, and sometimes fatal in their effects. They had till lately no means of employing a warm bath, but frequently steamed their patients on an oven of heated stones, or placed them over the smoke of a fire covered with green succulent herbs.

They have also a singular method of employing friction by rolling a stone or cannon shot over the part in pain.

I went one day into a house belonging to Karaimoku, where a chief was lying on his face, and the kahuna, or his attendant, was rolling a cannon shot of twelve or fourteen pounds weight backwards and forwards along his back, in order to alleviate the pain.

OCULISTS AND SURGERY

There were also among them oculists, who were celebrated for curing diseases of the eye, and who were sometimes sent for by persons residing many miles distanct. But in surgery they seem to be far behind the Society Islanders.

Their operations were usually performed with no small degree of roughness and insensibility; and from what I have seen, I am strongly inclined to think that the sense the natives have of pain is less than ours, or their powers of endurance greater.

In setting a broken leg or an arm, they were frequently successful. Not so, however, when they attempted, as was sometimes the case, more difficult operations.

They relate, that when some of their warriors have had the bones of their head fractured by a blow or a stone in battle, they have removed the pieces of bone, fitted in a piece of cocoa-nut shell, covered the skin over, and that the patient has recovered; but although they say there are persons living on whom it has been performed, I never saw one, and can hardly credit their having recovered, though I believe they performed the operation.

DISPOSITION OF NATIVES TOWARD FOREIGN MEDICINE AND TREATMENT

The chiefs, and many of the natives, who are accustomed to associate with foreigners, have entirely discarded the native doctors; and in times of sickness apply to the physician connected with the American mission, to the surgeon on shore, or one belonging to any ship in harbour, and shew a decided preference for foreign medicine.

The great body of the people, however, are generally averse to our remedies, and prefer the attendance of the native doctors. The employment is somewhat profitable, and the fee, which is either a piece of cloth, a mat, a pig, or dog, &c. is usually paid before the kahuna undertakes the case.

NATIVE TRADITION OF ORIGIN OF ART OF MEDICINE

In conversation on this subject with the governor at Kairua, I once asked him what first induced them to employ herbs, &c. for the cure of diseases.

He said that, many generations back, a man called Koreamoku obtained all their medicinal herbs from the gods, who also taught him the use of them: that after his death he was deified, and a wooden image of him placed in the large temple at Kairua, to which offerings of hogs, fish, and cocoa-nuts were frequently presented.

Oronopuha and Makanuiairono, two friends and disciples of Koreamoku, continued to practise the art after the death of their master, and were also deified after death, particularly because they were frequently successful in driving away the evil spirits by which the people were afflicted and threatened with death. This is the account they have of the first use of herbs medicinally; and to these deified men the prayers of the kahuna are addressed, when medicine is administered to the sick.

DESCRIPTION OF WAIAKEA OR BYRON'S BAY

During the day we examined various parts of the district on the western side, and sounded in several places along the channel leading into the bay. The district of Waiakea, and the bay of the same name, the Whye-a-te-a Bay of Vancouver, form the southern boundary of the division of Hiro, are situated on the north-east coast of Hawaii, and distant about twenty or twenty-five miles from the eastern point of the island. Recently in some of the public journals this bay has been called

238

Byron's Bay, having been visited and explored by Captain Lord Byron, on his late voyage to the Sandwich Islands in his majesty's ship Blonde.

The highest peak of Mouna-Kea bears due west from the sandy beach, at the bottom or south end of the bay.

In the centre, or rather towards the south-east side, is a small island connected with the shore by a number of rocks, and covered with cocoa-nut trees. South-west of this small island the native vessels usually anchor, and are thereby sheltered from all winds to the eastward of north-east. The bottom is good across the whole extent of the bay, but the western side is more exposed to the prevailing trade-winds.

There is a shoal extending perhaps two miles from the above mentioned island. It is therefore necessary in going into the harbour to keep near the western shore, which is very bold; the water is deep, and the passage free from rocks.

RIVERS EMPTYING INTO BAY

There are three streams of fresh water, which empty themselves into the bay. One on the western angle is called Wairuku. It rises near the summit of Mouna-Kea, and, after taking a circuitous course for several miles, runs rapidly into the sea.

Two others, called Wairama and Waiakea, rise in springs, boiling up through the hollows of the lava, at a short distance from the shore, fill several large fish-ponds, and afterwards empty themselves into the sea. Waiakea, on the eastern side of the bay, is tolerably deep, and is navigated by canoes and boats some distance inland.

PRODUCTS OF WAIAKEA

The face of the country in the vicinity of Waiakea is the most beautiful we have yet seen, which is probably occasioned by the humidity of the atmosphere, the frequent rains that fall here, and the long repose which the district has experienced from volcanic eruptions.

The light and fertile soil is formed by decomposed lava, with a considerable portion of vegetable mould. The whole is covered with luxuriant vegetation, and the greater part of it formed into plantations, where plantains, bananas, sugar-cane, taro, potatoes, and melons, grow to the greatest perfection.

Groves of cocoa-nut and breadfruit trees are seen in every direction loaded with fruit, or clothed with umbrageous foliage. The houses are mostly larger and better built than those of many districts through which we had passed. We thought the people generally industrious; for in several of the less fertile parts of the district we saw small pieces of lava thrown up in heaps, and potato vines growing very well in the midst of them, though we could scarcely perceive a particle of soil.

239

There are plenty of ducks in the ponds and streams, at a short distance from the sea, and several large ponds or lakes literally swarm with fish, principally of the mullet kind. The fish in these ponds belong to the king and chiefs, and are tabued from the common people.

Along the stone walls which partly encircle these ponds, we saw a number of small huts, where the persons reside who have the care of the fish, and are obliged frequently to feed them with a small kind of mussel, which they procure in the sands round the bay.

The district of Waiakea, though it does not include more than half the bay, is yet extensive. Kukuwau in the middle of the bay is its western boundary, from which, passing along the eastern side, it extends ten or twelve miles towards Kaau, the last district in the division of Puna.

RECOMMENDED AS A MISSION STATION

Taking every circumstance into consideration, this appears a most eligible spot for a missionary station. The fertility of the soil, the abundance of fresh water, the convenience of the harbour, the dense population, and the favourable reception we have met with, all combine to give it a stronger claim to immediate attention than any other place we have yet seen, except Kairua.

There are 400 houses in the bay, and probably not less than 2000 inhabitants, who would be immediately embraced in the operations of a missionary station here, besides the populous places to the north and south, that might be occasionally visited by itinerant preachers from Waiakea.

INTERVIEW WITH THREE MARQUESANS

In the afternoon I preached in front of the house where we held our worship on the last Sabbath. There were three Marquesans present, who arrived here but a few weeks ago. After the service was ended, they said it was maitai, or good.

I asked them from what island they came. They said "Fatuhiva," (La Magdalena), and that there were seven white men and two negroes living on their island, but they did not tell them any thing concerning Jehovah or Jesus Christ.

I then asked them if they thought their countrymen would receive and protect Christian teachers, "Yes," they all answered, "we are sure they would." "But you kill and eat white people; missionaries would not be safe among you." They seemed affected by this observation, and, after a moment's pause, exclaimed, "O, no! O, no! you would not injure us, and should never be injured by us."

240

These strangers, possessing all the vivacity natural to their country-men, could not fail to excite in our minds strong feelings of interest; and we can but hope a Christian mission will soon be established in those islands. Many advantages might be expected to result from it; and, among others, the security of vessels touching there for refreshments.

MISSIONARY EFFORT IN TAHITI AND MARQUESAS

The natives of these islands have frequently sent to Tahiti for teachers, and, since the above was written, they have been visited by Mr. Crook, a missionary, who was in 1797 stationed among them, but who is now labouring in Tahiti. The natives of Tahuata were favourably disposed towards instruction, and three native teachers from the Society Islands were left among them, preparatory to the establishment of a permanent mission in the Marquesas.

It is truly distressing to hear so frequently of the murderous quarrels which take place between the natives of the Marquesas, and other islands in the Pacific, and the crews of ships visiting them; which, we think, would be in a great degree prevented, were missionaries permanently residing among them.

The natives are sometimes exceedingly deceitful and treacherous in their dealings with foreigners, and the conduct of the latter is not always such as to inspire confidence.

The missionaries in the Society Islands have often been the means of preventing the consequences to which the misunderstanding of the natives and foreigners would in all probability have led.

A DISHONEST CAPTAIN

Once in particular, about four years ago, a captain, who had never visited them before, and has not been there since, touched at a small island to the south-west of Tahiti, bargained with the natives for a num-ber of hogs, agreeing to give in exchange for them tools or clothing.

The natives carried to the ship, which was lying off and on, five or six large hogs in a canoe; they were hoisted in, when, instead of return-ing the stipulated articles, the captain threw down into their canoe a bundle of old iron, principally iron hoops, cast loose the rope by which they held on to the ship, and sailed away.

The natives returned to the shore; a council was held, in which it was agreed to take revenge on the first ship that should arrive. In the interim, however, a missionary from one of the Society Islands, whom they had long known, visited them, and being made acquainted with the circumstances, dissuaded them from their purpose, promised to make up their loss, and thus, in all probability, the death of several innocent persons was prevented.

While we were engaged in worship at Waiakea, Messrs. Bishop and Thurston went over to Pueho, on the western shore, and Mr. Thurston preached to about 100 of the people at the house of Kapapa, the head man. When the service was ended, Kapapa accompanied them to the east side of the bay, in the double canoe which had been hired to convey us to Laupahoehoe.

As we intended to leave Waiakea early in the morning, I paid a farewell visit to Maaro this evening. The chief seemed more indisposed than when I last saw him, was restless, and apparently in much pain.

After spending some time in religious conversation with Maaro and his household, I took leave of them, and enjoyed a pleasant walk back through the lonely village.

The noise of the rolling surf on the distant beach was occasionally heard; the passing breeze caused a frequent rustling among the slender leaves of the cocoa-nut groves; while the rapid stream rippled over its pebbly bed in several places close by the path. The glimmering lights in the native huts shed their enlivening rays through the thick foliage of the surrounding gardens, and the beating of the drum, and the sound of the hura, with transient intervals between, broke upon the ear from several directions.

These last, though far more agreeable than the drunken halloo, the savage war-cry, or the horrid yell from the mysterious and dark heiau, I yet could not but hope would soon be exchanged for the words of inspired truth, read aloud from the holy scriptures, the cheerful hymn of praise, or the solemn language of family devotion, so frequently heard from the lowly Tahitian cottage, during an evening walk through the happy villages of the Society Islands.

TRAVEL BY CANOE TO LAUPAHOEHOE

At daybreak on the 14th, after morning worship with the people who crowded our house, we made arrangements for our departure. Mr. Harwood remained, to return to Oahu in the brig Inore, lying at anchor in the bay, as he would thereby be enabled to transact some business for the mission, and also avoid travelling over the ravines of Hiro and Hamakua.

Soon after six a.m. we embarked on board our canoe, and passed over the reef to the deep water on the western side of the bay. The weather was calm, and the men laboured with their paddles till about eight, when the maranai (east wind) sprung up, and wafted us pleasantly along the shore. We found our double canoe very convenient, for it had a pora (or stage) raised in the middle, which provided a comfortable seat, and also kept our packages above the spray of the sea.

242

The pora is formed by tying slight poles to the iako, or cross pieces that connect the two canoes together, from the foremost iako to the one nearest the stern. The cross pieces are not straight, but bent like a bow, and form an arch between the two canoes, which raises the pora or stage at least two feet higher than the sides of the canoe.

When the breeze sprang up, four of the men laid down their paddles, and attended to the sail, while one man sat in the stern of each canoe with a large paddle to steer.

Our canoe, though made of heavy wood, was thin, and consequently light, and, as the wind increased, seemed at a rapid rate to skim along the tops of the waves; dashing through the crested foam with a degree of velocity, which, but for the confidence we reposed in the skill and address of our pilots, would have excited no small degree of apprehension for our safety.

The canoes of the Sandwich Islands appear eminently calculated for swiftness, being long, narrow, generally light, and drawing but little water.

SIZE AND FINISH OF CANOES

A canoe is always made out of a single tree; some of them are upwards of seventy feet long, one or two feet wide, and sometimes more than three feet deep, though in length they seldom exceed fifty feet.

The body of the canoe is generally covered with a black paint, made by the natives with various earthy and vegetable materials, in which the bark, oil, and burnt nuts of the kukui tree are the principal ingredients.

On the upper edge of the canoe is sewed, in a remarkably neat manner, a small strip of hard white wood, from six to eight inches in width, according to the size and length of the canoe. These strips meet and close over the top at both stem and stern, and shoot off much water that would otherwise enter the canoe.

SPEED OF HAWAIIAN CANOES—SAILING AND PADDLING

All the canoes of these islands are remarkably strong and neatly made; and though not so large as those of New Zealand, the Society Islands, or some of the other islands to the southward, are certainly better made; and would probably paddle or sail faster than any of them.

One man will sometimes paddle a single canoe faster than a good boat's crew could row a whale-boat. Their tackling is simple and convenient; the mast generally has a notch cut at the lower end, and is placed on one of the cross pieces to which it is tied; the sails they now use, are made of mats, and cut in imitation of the sprit-sails of foreign boats, which, they say, they find much better than the kind of sail they had when first visited by foreigners.

When sailing with a fresh breeze, the ropes from the lower corners of the sails are always loosened, and held in the hands of persons whose only business it is to keep them properly trimmed.

Their paddles, which are large and strong, are generally four or five feet long, have an oval-shaped blade and round handle, and are made of the same hard and heavy wood employed in building their canoes. They are not handsome, and their weight must make paddling very laborious.

Neither the canoes nor paddles of the Sandwich Islanders are carved like those of many islands in the Pacific. Their canoes are, nevertheless, remarkably neat, and sometimes handsome.

DESCRIPTION OF HILO DISTRICT

The country, by which we sailed, was fertile, beautiful, and apparently populous. The numerous plantations on the eminences and sides of the deep ravines or valleys, by which it was intersected, with the streams meandering through them into the sea, presented altogether a most agreeable prospect. The coast was bold, and the rocks evidently volcanic. We frequently saw the water gushing out of hollows in the face of the rocks, or flowing in cascades from the top to the bottom.

After sailing pleasantly for several hours, we approached Laupahoehoe: we had proceeded upwards of twenty miles, and had passed not less than fifty ravines or valleys, but we had not seen a spot where we thought it would be possible to land without being swamped; and although we knew we had arrived at the end of our voyage, we could discover no place by which it seemed safe to approach the shore, as the surf was beating violently, and the wind blowing directly towards the land.

LANDING AT LAUPAHOEHOE

However, when we came within a few yards of the surf, we perceived an opening in the rocks, just wide enough to admit our canoe. Into this our pilots steered with uncommon address and precision; and before we could look round, we found our canoe on a sandy beach, a few yards long, entirely defended by rocks of lava from the rolling surf on the outside.

It was one p.m. when we landed, and walked up to the house of the head man, where we had a few fish and some potatoes, that we had brought with us, prepared for dinner. After the people of the place had been spoken to on the subject of religion, they said they had heard there were missionaries living at Oahu, teaching the king to read, and write, and pray. They had also heard of Jehovah, but not of Jesus Christ. It was compassionate in the great God, they added, to think of them, and send his word among them.

After remaining an hour or two, we proposed to proceed, but could not prevail on Makoa to go any further that night. He said we had come far enough for one day, and had better stay till the morning. He also complained of being tired with bailing out the canoe. We knew this was only an excuse, and that the principal reason why he wished to stop was because the head man of the place had invited us to remain, and had told us that if we would spend the night there, he would have a pig and some taro cooked. Makoa could not agree to lose the benefit of this offer; but as we were refreshed, and thought it best to proceed, we thanked the chief for his kindness, and, finding our guide determined to stay, we took each a blanket for a covering at night, and resumed our journey.

FROM LAUPAHOEHOE TO HUMUULA

Leaving Laupahoehoe, we ascended the north side of the deep ravine, at the bottom of which the village is situated. We reached the top after climbing between 400 and 500 feet, and beheld a beautiful country before us. Over this we travelled about five miles in a W. N. W. direction towards the foot of Mouna-Kea, and after passing three deep ravines, reached Humuula shortly before sun-set.

This retired little village is situated on the edge of a wood, extending along the base of Mouna-Kea. We directed our steps to the principal house in the village, and invited the people of the neighbourhood to meet us there. They soon collected, and listened with apparent interest to a short discourse. Many continued with us till a late hour in conversation, which to them is usually a source of no small gratification.

HAWAIIAN CUSTOM TO TALK AND SING ALL NIGHT

We have several times during our tour been kept awake by the natives in the houses where we lodged, who have continued talking and singing till near daybreak. Circumstances the most trivial sometimes furnish conversation for hours. Their songs also afford much amusement, and it is no unusual thing for the family to entertain their guests with these, or for strangers to gratify their host by reciting those of their own island or neighbourhood.

More than once, when we have entered a house, some of the inmates have shortly afterwards commenced a song, accompanied occasionally by a little drum, or the beating of the raau hura, musical stick; and the natives, who formerly visited Hawaii from the Society Islands, excited no small degree of interest by reciting the songs of their country.

245

It is probable that many of the fabulous tales and songs so popular among them, have originated in the gratification they find in thus spending their time. This kind of amusement is common to most of the South Sea Islands.

HABITS OF SONG, CONVERSATION AND GOSSIP IN THE PACIFIC

The Sandwich Islanders equal the Marquesans, the most lively natives of the Pacific, in the number of their songs, and exceed the Society Islanders; but their conversational powers are inferior to those of the latter, who are perhaps the most loquacious of them all.

An acquaintance with every body's business used almost to be cultivated as an accomplishment; and inquiries, which to us would appear most officious, were only common civilities. To meet a party, and not ask where they came from, or where they were going, what was their business, and when they intended to return, would be considered indicative of displeasure towards the party thus neglected, or at least of want of interest in their welfare.

HOSPITALITY OF HAWAIIANS AND SOUTH SEA ISLANDERS

Our hostess, who was a widow, treated us kindly, and between seven and eight brought in for supper a small baked pig, and a large dish of taro. This was the more grateful, as it had not been required by Makoa in the governor's name, but was furnished by the genuine hospitality which characterizes the South Sea Islanders, though not practised so much by the Hawaiians as by some other tribes in the Pacific, and we believe much less now than when the Sandwich Islands were first discovered, or during the earlier visits they received.

They are still, however, a hospitable people, and even the poorest would generally share their scanty dish of potatoes with a stranger.

Not to entertain a guest with what they have, is, among themselves, considered reproachful; and there are many, who, if they had but one pig or fowl in the yard, or one root of potatoes in the garden, would cheerfully take them to furnish a repast for a friend. This generous disposition is frequently abused, and encourages the rambling manner of life of which many are so fond.

HAWAIIAN SOCIAL CUSTOMS

It is not unusual for a family, when they have planted their field with sweet potatoes, &c. to pay a visit for four or five months to some friend in a distant part of the island. When the crop is ripe they travel home again, and in return are most likely visited by a friend, who will not think of leaving them so long as any of their provisions remain unconsumed. This, however, is only the case where friendship has previously existed between the parties.

246

A transient visitor on arriving among them will generally have an entertainment provided, of which the persons who furnish it seldom partake. The family with which we lodged were, however, induced to join us this evening at supper, though contrary to their ideas of propriety.

Whenever we have remarked to the natives that their conduct in this respect is unsocial, they have usually answered, "Would it be right for us to present food to our friends, and then sit down and eat of it ourselves?"

Connected with this, another custom, equally at variance with our views of hospitality, is practised by the guests, who invariably carry away all that remains of the entertainment, however abundant it may have been. Hence, whenever a pig, &c. has been dressed for us, and our party have finished their meal, our boys always put the remainder into their baskets, and carried it away. To this we often objected: but they usually replied, "It is our custom; and if we don't take it, the people will think you are dissatisfied with what they have provided."

The entertainment given to strangers or visitors is regulated by the means of the host, or the rank of the guests.

SOCIAL CUSTOMS OF SOCIETY ISLANDERS

In the Society Islands their feasts were formerly characterized by a degree of prodigality extremely oppressive to the people who had to furnish the provisions.

I once saw in the island of Raiatea upwards of fifty large baked hogs, and a proportionate quantity of poë, yams, &c. served up at one time for a party of chiefs on a visit from the Georgian or Windward Islands.

DOGS THE PRINCIPAL MEAT

In this respect the Sandwich Islanders are not behind their southern neighbours, but in their feasts the flesh of the dog constitutes the principal meat.

I have seen nearly two hundred dogs cooked at one time; and during the last visit which Taumuarii, late king of Tauai, and Kaahumanu his queen, paid Kuakini, the governor of this island, a feast was prepared for them by the latter, at which Auna was present, and counted four hundred baked dogs, with fish and hogs, and vegetables in proportion.

Sometimes the food is spread out on the ground, which is previously covered with grass or green leaves; the party sit down around it, and the chiefs distribute it among them, after the servants have carved it with a knife, or with a piece of bamboo cane, which, before visited by foreigners, was the only kind of knife they possessed.

247

The serrated edge of the hard bamboo cane, when but recently split, is very sharp; and we have often been surprised at the facility with which they cut up a large hog with no other instrument.

The head of a hog, or at least the brains, were always offered to the principal chief of the party; particular parts were given to the priests, if any were present; while the backbone and the tail were the usual perquisites of the person who carved.

In general, however, when such large presents of food are made, each hog or dog when baked is put into a distinct basket, and piled up in heaps in the court-yard, in front of the house where the chief is residing; the fish, dogs, and vegetables, in separate heaps.

When collected, the chief comes out to look at it, and those who have brought it retire. He then calls his stewards—directs them to select a portion for his own table—distributes some among the chiefs in the neighbourhood, in which the chief who has provided the feast is frequently included—and divides the rest among his own followers, who sometimes amount to two or three hundred.

CHAPTER XIII

DOG FARMS

Numbers of dogs, of rather a small size, and something like a terrier, are raised every year as an article of food. They are mostly fed on vegetables; and we have sometimes seen them kept in yards, with small houses to sleep in.

A part of the rent of every tenant who occupies land, is paid in dogs for his landlord's table.

Though often invited by the natives to join them in partaking of the baked dog, we were never induced to taste of one. The natives, however, say it is sweeter than the flesh of the pig, and much more palatable than that of goats or kids, which some refuse to touch, and few care to eat.

These feasts are much less frequent than formerly, particularly among those chiefs who have opportunities for frequent intercourse with foreigners, several of whom now spread their table in the European manner, and invite their friends to dine, or entertain their guests at home, and treat them as members of their family while they remain under their roof.

Several members of the family we had lodged with, united with us in our morning worship on the 15th, after which we breakfasted together.

While thus engaged, Makoa arrived with our baggage, and about eight a.m. we were ready to proceed. Unwilling that our hostess should suffer by her kindness, we presented her with as much blue cotton cloth as would amply pay for the supper she had generously furnished last evening, and then set out on our journey.

TRAMPING FROM HILO TO HAMAKUA

The wide-extended prospect which our morning walk afforded, of the ocean, and the shores of Hamakua on our right, was agreeably diversified by the occasional appearance of the snow-capt peaks of Mouna-Kea, seen through the openings in the trees on our left. The body of the mountain was hid by the wood, and the different peaks only appeared like so many distinct hills at a great distance. The highest peak bore S. W. by S. from Humuula.

The high land over which we passed was generally woody, though the trees were not large. The places that were free from wood, were covered with long grass and luxuriant ferns. The houses mostly stood singly, and were scattered over the face of the country.

A rich field of potatoes or taro, five or six acres sometimes in extent, or large plantations of sugar-cane and bananas, occasionally bordered our path. But though the soil was excellent, it was only partially cultivated. The population also appeared less than what we had seen inhabiting some of the most desolate parts of the island.

About 10 a.m. we reached the pleasant and verdant valley of Kaura, which separates the divisions of Hilo and Hamakua.

HOW BOUNDARIES ARE MARKED

The geographical divisions of Hawaii, and the other islands of the group, are sometimes artificial, and a stone image, a line of stones somewhat distant from each other, a path, or a stone wall, serves to separate the different districts, or larger divisions, from each other. They are, however, more frequently natural, as in the present instance, where a watercourse, winding through the centre of the valley, marked the boundary of these two divisions. The boundary of the smaller districts, and even the different farms, as well as the large divisions, are definitely marked, well understood, and permanent.

Each division, district, village, and farm, and many of the sites of houses, have a distinct name, which is often significant of some object or quality distinguishing the place.

WORSHIP OF PELE STILL PRACTISED

On descending to the bottom of the valley, we reached a heiau dedicated to Pele, with several rude stone idols, wrapped up in white and yellow cloth, standing in the midst of it. A number of wreaths of flowers, pieces of sugar-cane, and other presents, some of which were not yet faded, lay strewed around, and we were told that every passing traveller left a trifling offering before them.

Once in a year, we were also informed, the inhabitants of Hamakua brought large gifts of hogs, dogs, and fruit, when the priests and kahu of Pele assembled to perform certain rites, and partake of the feast.

This annual festival, we were told, was designed to propitiate the volcanic goddess, and secure their country from earthquakes, or inundations of lava. Locks of human hair were among the offerings made to Pele. They were frequently presented to this goddess by those who passed by the crater of Kirauea, on which occasions they were thrown into the crater, a short address being made at the same time to the deity supposed to reside there.

250

We ventured to deviate from the custom of travellers in general; yet, though we presented no offerings, we did not proceed to pull down the heiau, and irritate the people by destroying their idols, but entered into conversation with them on the folly of worshipping such senseless things, and pointed out the more excellent way of propitiating the favour of Jehovah, the true God, with sacrifices of thanksgiving and praise, placing all their hopes in his mercy, and depending for security on his providence.

They took what we said in good part, and answered, that though the stones could not save them, the being whom they represented, or in honour of whom they were erected, was very powerful, and capable of devouring their land, and destroying the people. This we denied; and told them that volcanoes, and all their powers, were under the control of that God, whom we wished them to choose for their God and Saviour.

When a drawing had been taken of this beautiful valley, where kukui trees, plantains, bananas, and ti plants were growing spontaneously with unusual richness of foliage and flower, we took leave of the people, and, continuing our journey, entered Hamakua.

DESCRIPTION OF THE HILO DISTRICT

Hiro, which we had now left, though not so extensive and populous as Kona, is the most fertile and interesting division on the island.

The coast from Waiakea to this place is bold and steep, and intersected by numerous valleys or ravines; many of these are apparently formed by the streams from the mountains, which flow through them into the sea. The rocks along the coast are volcanic, generally a brown vesicular lava. In the sides and bottoms of some of the ravines, they were occasionally of very hard compact lava, or a kind of basalt.

This part of the island, from the district of Waiakea to the northern point, appears to have remained many years undisturbed by volcanic eruptions. The habitations of the natives generally appear in clusters at the opening of the valleys, or scattered over the face of the high land. The soil is fertile, and herbage abundant.

The lofty Mouna-Kea, rising about the centre of this division, forms a conspicuous object in every view that can be taken of it. The base of the mountain on this side is covered with woods, which occasionally extend within five or six miles of the shore.

CLIMATE OF HILO AND HAMAKUA

While the division of Kona, on the leeward side of the island, is often several months without a shower, rain is frequent in this and the adjoining division of Hamakua, which form the centre of the windward coast, and is doubtless the source of their abundant fertility. The climate is warm. Our thermometer was usually 71° at sun-rise; 74° at noon; and 72° or 73° at sun-set. Notwithstanding these natural advantages, the inhabitants, excepting at Waiakea, did not appear better supplied with the necessaries of life than those of Kona, or the more barren parts of Hawaii. They had better houses, plenty of vegetables, some dogs, and a few hogs, but hardly any fish, a principal article of food with the natives in general.

THRU KEARAKAHA, MANIENIE AND TOUMOARII

About mid-day we came to a village called Kearakaha, where we collected the people, and preached to them. They listened attentively, and conversed very freely afterwards on what had been said.

Leaving Kearakaha, we continued our walk to Manienie, where we dined, and rested two or three hours. During our stay we addressed the people as usual.

Shortly after four in the afternoon we left Manienie, and travelled over a well-cultivated tract of country, till we reached Toumoarii, where we put up for the night, as we were considerably fatigued with our day's journey, having crossed nearly twenty ravines, some of which were from 300 to 400 feet deep. The people collected in front of the head man's house, for religious worship; and the service was concluded with singing and prayer just as the sun was setting.

We spent the evening in conversation with the people of the house. Many of them exclaimed, "Makemake au ia Jesu Kraist. Aroha nui o Jesu!" I desire Jesus Christ; great is Jesus' love.

MAKOA AS A RELIGIOUS TEACHER

Makoa, as usual, excited much interest among the natives by the accounts he gave of our journey, &c. This evening he turned theologian, and while we were at supper, we heard him telling a party around him in another part of the house, that heaven was a place where there was neither salt fish, nor calabashes of poë. Indeed, added he, we shall never want any there, for we shall never be hungry. But in order to get there, much is to be done. A man that wishes to go there, must live peaceably with his neighbours; must never be idle; and, moreover, must be a kanaka opu nui ore, i. e. must not be a glutton.

We arose at day-light on the 16th, and shortly after left Taumoarii. We had not travelled more than four or five miles when we reached Kaahua. After breakfast, we proceeded on our journey over a country equal in fertility to any we had passed since leaving Waiakea. The houses were in general large, containing usually three or four families each. Mr. Goodrich was indisposed through the day, which obliged us to travel but slowly.

Near noon we stopped at Koloaha, and, while he reclined beneath the shade of an adjoining grove of trees, I addressed the assembled natives on the subject of religion.

After remaining about two hours, we walked to another village, where Mr. Thurston spoke to the people, who gave good attention.

We then kept on our way till we reached Malanahae, where a congregation of the people assembled, with whom we conversed some short time, then bade them farewell, and about three p.m. reached Kapulena, where we preached to upwards of 100 of the people.

At this place we thought it best to form ourselves into two parties, in order that we might preach to the natives along the northern parts of the island, and examine the interior between this place and Towaihae. It was therefore arranged that Messrs. Bishop and Goodrich should spend the Sabbath here, and on Monday morning pass over to Waimea, and thence to Tawaihae, while Mr. Thurston and myself travelled through the villages on the northern shores.

THE PARTY SEPARATES

On Monday morning Messrs. Bishop and Goodrich commenced their journey to Waimea. Having procured a man to carry their baggage, they left Kapulena, and, taking an inland direction, passed over a pleasant country, gently undulated with hill and dale. The soil was fertile, the vegetation flourishing, and there was considerable cultivation, though but few inhabitants.

THRU WAIMEA AND KAWAIHAE—MEETING WITH JOHN YOUNG

About noon they reached the valley of Waimea, lying at the foot of Mouna-Kea, on the northwest side. Here a number of villages appeared on each side of the path, surrounded with plantations, in which plantains, sugar-cane, and taro, were seen growing unusually large. At 4 p.m. they obtained a view of the ocean, and kept on their way towards Towaihae.

When they had travelled several miles the sun went down, and, no houses being near, they spread their blankets on the ground, and slept comfortably in the open air.

At break of day on the 19th they began to descend, and, after walking about two hours, reached Towaihae, where they were hospitably received by Mr. Young, with whom they spent the day.

Having heard that a schooner from Oahu was at Keauhou, they left Towaihae in the evening in a canoe belonging to Mr. Young, and proceeded to Kairua, where the schooner was lying at anchor.

It was about 5 o'clock in the afternoon of the 16th, when Mr. Thurston and myself left Kapulena. Wishing to spend the Sabbath in the populous village of Waipio, we travelled fast along the narrow paths bordered with long grass, or through the well-cultivated plantations of the natives.

The Sandwich Islanders have no idea of constructing their roads or foot-path in a straight line. In many parts, where the country was level and open, the paths from one village to another were not more than a foot wide, and very crooked. We often had occasion to notice this, but never passed over any so completely serpentine as those we travelled this evening.

The sun had set when we reached the high cliff that formed the southern boundary of Waipio. Steep rocks, not less than five hundred feet high, rose immediately opposite. Viewed from the great elevation at which we stood, the charming valley, spread out beneath us like a map, with its numerous inhabitants, cottages, plantations, fishponds, and meandering streams, (on the surface of which the light canoe was moving to and fro), appeared in beautiful miniature.

WAIPIO DESCRIBED

Makoa led the way down the steep cliffs. The descent was difficult, and it was quite dark before we reached the bottom. A party of natives, returning from a fishing excursion, ferried us across the stream that ran along near the place where we descended, and we directed our steps towards the house of Haa, head man of the village.

He received us courteously, ordered a clean mat to be spread for us to recline on, and water for us to drink; some of his attendants also handed us a large wooden tobacco-pipe, which is usually passed round when strangers arrive; this last compliment, however, we begged leave to decline.

Makoa seated himself by the side of the chief, and gave him a brief outline of our tour—our object—and the instructions given to the people. In the mean time, fish was prepared for supper by a fire of sandal wood, which, instead of filling the house with disagreeable smoke, perfumed it with a fragrant odour. After family worship in the native language, we retired to rest.

The next morning unveiled to view the extent and beauty of the romantic valley. Its entrance from the sea, which was blocked up with sand-hills, fifty or sixty feet high, appeared to be a mile or a mile and a half wide.

The summits of the hills, which bordered the valley, seemed 600 feet above the level of the sea. They were nearly perpendicular, yet they

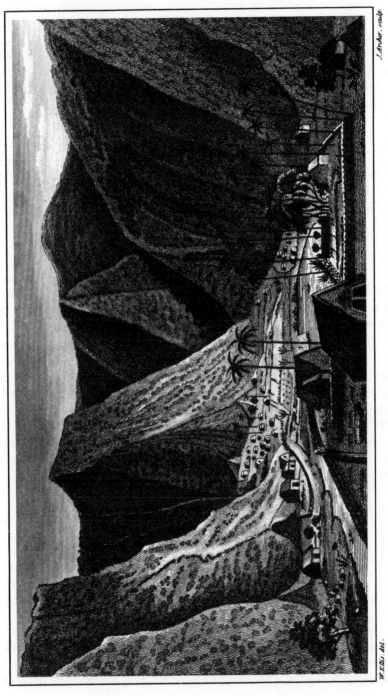

W.Ellis. del.   J.Archr. sculp.

The Valley of Waipio, in Hawaii, from the Sand Hills on the Beach.

were mostly clothed with grass, and low straggling shrubs were here and there seen amidst the jutting rocks.

A number of winding paths led up their steep sides, and, in several parts, limpid streams flowed, in beautiful cascades, from the top to the bottom, forming a considerable stream, which, meandering along the valley, found a passage through the sand-hills, and emptied itself into the sea.

A CONTINUOUS AND POPULOUS GARDEN

The bottom of the valley was one continued garden, cultivated with taro, bananas, sugar-cane, and other productions of the islands, all growing luxuriantly. Several large ponds were also seen in different directions, well stocked with excellent fish.

A number of small villages, containing from twenty to fifty houses each, stood along the foot of the mountains, at unequal distances on each side, and extended up the valley till projecting cliffs obstructed the view.

Morning worship was attended by our host and his family, and about half-past ten the people of the neighbourhood assembled in front of the house. Mr. Thurston preached to them, and was encouraged by the attention given.

In the afternoon he walked up the north side of the valley, and preached to congregations of about 100 persons, in three different villages. I proceeded about a mile and a half along the south side of the valley, to the village of Napopo, containing forty-three houses, and preached to the natives. After the service, the people complained of their great ignorance, and wished they might be visited again.

At five p.m. I returned, and addressed the people in the place where Mr. Thurston had preached in the morning. About 300 were present, and listened attentively.

DISCUSSIONS WITH A CHIEF

The chief with whom we lodged made many inquiries respecting the way of salvation through Jesus Christ. He also asked about the change which had taken place in the Society Islands; and afterwards observed, that Hawaii was a dark land, and would not soon attend to its true interests. He and his family cheerfully united in the devotional exercises of the day, and by his conversation manifested, for an untutored native, an unusual degree of intelligence.

In the evening, as we sat around the door, the voice of wailing and lamentation broke upon the ear. On inquiry, it was found to proceed from a neighbouring cottage, where a woman, who had been some time ill, had just expired. This circumstance led to a conversation on death

256

and a future state, and the necessity of habitual preparedness for the eventful change which awaits all mankind.

While we were talking, the moon arose, and shed her mild light upon the valley; her beams were reflected by the rippling stream, and the small lake beautified the scene. All was serene and still, save the chirping insects in the grass. The echo of the cloth-mallet, which had been heard through the day in different parts of the valley, had now ceased. Though generally a pleasant sound, especially when heard in a solitary valley, indicating the industry of the natives, it had on this day, which was the Sabbath, called forth the most affectionate solicitude for the interesting people of the place; and we could not but desire the speedy arrival of that time, when the sacred hours of the Sabbath should be employed in spiritual and devotional exercises. That, however, is not to be expected in the present circumstances of the people, for

"The sound of the church-going bell
These valleys and rocks never heard:
Never sigh'd at the sound of a knell,
Nor smiled when a Sabbath appear'd."

And probably until this day their inhabitants had not been informed, that "in six days they should labour and do all their work, and that the seventh is the Sabbath of the Lord their God," which he requires them to sanctify by sacred worship and holy rest.

MAKOA GIVES POINTERS ON HAOLE MEDICINE

On the morning of the 18th, while some medicine was preparing, Haa inquired of what kind it was, when Makoa, who was sitting by, observed that it was very strong medicine; that if a native only smelt it, his breath would be taken away: (he referred probably to a bottle of hartshorn, of which he had once smelt). "If we were to be taken sick on a journey, we should rest a few days before we thought of continuing it: but they are stronge people, very unlike us; for frequently, after being ill all night, they get up in the morning, take medicine, and then walk all day as if nothing were the matter with them."

HAWAIIAN METHODS OF INTERMENT

We were desirous of witnessing the interment of the person who died last night, but were disappointed; it was, as most of their funerals are, performed in secret.

A few particulars, relative to their mode of burying, we have been able to gather from the people of this place and other parts of the island.

The bones of the legs and arms, and sometimes the skull, of their kings and principal chiefs, those who were supposed to have descended from the gods, or were to be deified, were usually preserved, as already

257

noticed. The other parts of the body were burnt or buried, while these bones were either bound up with cinet, wrapped in cloth, and deposited in temples for adoration, or distributed among the immediate relatives, who, during their lives, always carried them wherever they went. This was the case with the bones of Tamehameha; and it is probable that some of his bones were brought by his son Rihoriho on his recent visit to England, as they supposed that so long as the bones of the deceased were revered, his spirit would accompany them, and exercise a super-natural guardianship over them.

They did not wash the bodies of the dead, as was the practice with some of the South Sea Islanders.

The bodies of priests, and chiefs of inferior rank, were laid out straight, wrapped in many folds of native tapa, and buried in that posture; the priests generally within the precincts of the temple in which they had officiated.

DIFFERENT BURIAL METHODS

A pile of stones, or a circle of high poles, surrounded their grave, and marked the place of their interment. It was only the bodies of priests, or persons of some importance, that were thus buried.

The common people committed their dead to the earth in a most singular manner. After death, they raised the upper part of the body, bent the face forwards to the knees, the hands were next put under the hams, and passed up between the knees, when the head, hands, and knees were bound together with cinet or cord. The body was afterwards wrapped in a coarse mat, and buried the first or second day after its decease.

They preferred natural graves whenever available, and selected for this purpose caves in the sides of their steep rocks, or large subter-ranean caverns.

SEPULCHRAL CAVES

Sometimes the inhabitants of a village deposited their dead in one large cavern, but in general each family had a distinct sepulchral cave.

Their artificial graves were either simple pits dug in the earth, or large enclosures. One of the latter, which we saw at Keahou, was a space surrounded with high stone walls, appearing much like an ancient heiau or temple. We proposed to several natives of the village to accompany us on a visit to it, and give us an outline of its history; but they appeared startled at the thought, said it was a wahi ino, (place evil), filled with dead bodies, and objected so strongly to our approach-ing it, that we deemed it inexpedient to make our intended visit.

Occasionally they buried their dead in sequestered places, at a short distance from their habitations, but frequently in their gardens, and sometimes in their houses. Their graves were not deep, and the bodies were usually placed in them in a sitting posture.

BURIALS ARE SECRET AND WITHOUT CEREMONY

No prayer was offered at the grave, except occasionally by the inhabitants of Oahu.

All their interments are conducted without any ceremony, and are usually managed with great secrecy. We have often been surprised at this, and believe it arises from the superstitious dread the people entertain respecting the places where dead bodies are deposited, which they believe resorted to by the spirits of those buried there.

Like most ignorant and barbarous nations, they imagine that apparitions are frequently seen, and often injure those who come in their way.

Their funerals take place in the night, to avoid observation; for we have been told, that if the people were to see a party carrying a dead body past their houses, they would abuse them, or even throw stones at them, for not taking it some other way, supposing the spirit would return to and fro to the former abode of the deceased by the path along which the body had been borne to the place of interment.

BONES THROWN TO PELE AND THE SHARKS

The worshippers of Pele threw a part of the bones of their dead into the volcano, under the impression that the spirits of the deceased would then be admitted to the society of the volcanic deities, and that their influence would preserve the survivors from the ravages of volcanic fire.

The fishermen sometimes wrapped their dead in red native cloth, and threw them into the sea, to be devoured by the sharks. Under the influence of a belief in the transmigration of souls, they supposed the spirit of the departed would animate the shark by which the body was devoured, and that the survivors would be spared by those voracious monsters, in the event of their being overtaken by any accident at sea.

The bodies of criminals who had broken tabu, after having been slain to appease the anger of the god whose tabu, or prohibition, they had broken, were buried within the precincts of the heiau.

The bones of human sacrifices, after the flesh had rotted, were piled up in different parts of the heiau in which they had been offered.

CHANGES IN BURIAL METHODS INTRODUCED BY MISSIONARIES

Idolatry, since 1819, has been abolished, and all ceremonies connected therewith have ceased; the other heathenish modes of burying their dead are only observed by those who are uninstructed, and are not professed worshippers of the true God: those who are, inter their dead in a manner more resembling the practice of Christians.

259

The corpse is usually laid in a coffin, which, previous to interment, is borne to the place of worship, attended by the relatives in mourning habiliments, where a short service is performed; it is then carried to the grave; after being deposited there, sometimes the spectators are addressed by the missionary, on other occasions a short prayer only is offered, and, as the friends retire, the grave is filled up.

After breakfast, Mr. Thurston walked about five miles up the valley, in order to estimate its population, and preach to the people. The whole extent was well cultivated, and presented in every direction the most beautiful prospects. At one of the villages where he stopped, about 100 people collected, to whom he preached the word of salvation.

TALES OF HUMAN SACRIFICES

I spent the morning in taking a drawing of the valley from the sand-hills on the beach; and in examining some large heiaus in the neighbourhood, in reference to which the natives taxed our credulity by the legendary tales they related respecting the numbers of victims which had on some occasions been offered.

In the days of Umi, they said, that king, after having been victorious in battle over the kings of six of the divisions of Hawaii, was sacrificing captives at Waipio, when the voice of Kuahiro, his god, was heard from the clouds, requiring more men; the king kept sacrificing, and the voice continued calling for more, till he had slain all his men except one, whom, as he was a great favourite, he refused at first to give up; but the god being urgent, he sacrificed him also, and the priest and himself were all that remained. Upwards of eighty victims, they added, were offered at that time, in obedience to the audible demands of the insatiate demon.

We have heard the same account at other places, of eighty victims being slain at one time; and though perhaps the account may exceed the number actually immolated, the tradition serves to shew the savage character of the gods, who, in the opinion of the natives, could require such prodigal waste of human life.

CITY OF REFUGE OF PAKARANA AT WAIPIO

In the afternoon we visited Pakarana, the Puhonua, or place of refuge, for all this part of the island. It was a large enclosure, less extensive, however, than that at Honaunau. The walls, though of great antiquity, were of inferior height and dimensions. In the midst of the enclosure, under a wide-spreading pandanus, was a small house, called Ke Hale o Riroa, (The House of Riroa), from the circumstance of its containing the bones of a king of that name, who was the grandson of Umi, and, according to their traditions, reigned in Hawaii about fifteen generations back.

260

We tried, but could not gain admittance to the pahu tabu, or sacred enclosure. We also endeavoured to obtain a sight of the bones of Riroa, but the man who had charge of the house told us we must offer a hog before we could be admitted; that Tamehameha, whenever he entered, had always sent offerings; that Rihoriho, since he had become king, had done the same, and that no one could be admitted on other conditions.

Fining us unwilling to comply, yet anxious to see the bones, they directed us to a rudely carved stone image, about six feet high, standing at one corner of the wall, which they said was a tii, or image of Riroa.

We talked some time with the people around, who were principally priests, on the folly of deifying and worshipping departed mortals. The only answer, however, which they made was, Pela no i Hawaii nei: So it is in Hawaii here.

SANDAL WOOD COLLECTING

During the afternoon great numbers of men belonging to the valley returned with loads of sandal wood, which they had been cutting in the neighbouring mountains. The wood was much superior to that which we had seen at Waiakea, being high coloured, strongly scented, and sometimes in large pieces nearly a foot in diameter.

At five o'clock in the afternoon, about 300 of the natives of the place assembled for public worship in front of the head man's house, where they were addressed from Luke xiv. 23. The people were attentive, and frequently interrupted the speaker by their exclamations.

Some said, "Jehovah is a good God: the living God is a good God; great is his love."

After the service, they sat talking on what they had heard, and occasionally making inquiries, till the sun had set, and the moon had nearly reached the mid-heaven. The chief, in particular, seemed much interested, and, during the evening, he and several others expressed themselves very desirous that a missionary should come and reside with them, that they might be instructed fully in all these things.

LARGE POPULATION AT WAIPIO

According to the number of houses which we have seen, in all 265, there are at least 1325 inhabitants in this sequestered valley, besides populous villages on each side along the coast, which might be easily visited. This circumstance, together with the fertility of the soil, the abundance of water, the facility with which, at most seasons of the year, supplies can be forwarded by water from Kairua or Towaihae, combine to render this an eligible spot for a missionary station; but notwithstanding all these favourable circumstances, together with the great desire of the people to be instructed in the important principles of Christianity, it is much to be feared that, unless the funds of the Parent

Societies are increased, this inviting field, as well as several others, must long remain destitute of moral culture.

WAIPIO CELEBRATED IN HAWAIIAN HISTORY

The valley of Waipio is a place frequently celebrated in the songs and traditions of Hawaii, as having been the abode of Akea and Miru, the first kings of the island; of Umi and Riroa, kings who make a prominent figure in their history.

It is also noted as the residence of Hoakau, king of this part of the island, who appears to have been one of the Neros of the Sandwich Islands, and whose memory is execrable among the people, on account of his cruelties; and of whom it is reported, that if a man was said to have a fine-looking head, he would send his servants to behead the individual, and bring his head before him, when he would wantonly cut, and otherwise disfigure it. He is said also to have ordered a man's arm to be cut off, and brought to him, only because it was tataued in a manner more handsome than his own.

DISCUSSION ON THE SOUL, RESURRECTION AND GENERAL JUDGMENT

An interesting conversation was carried on this evening with respect to the separate existence of the soul, the resurrection of the body, and the general judgment at the last day.

The account of the raising of the widow's son, and the calling of Lazarus from the grave after he had been dead four days, seemed greatly to interest the natives.

We afterwards endeavoured to learn from them something respecting their opinions of a state of existence after death. But all they said upon the subject was so contradictory, and mixed with fiction, that it could not be discovered whether they had any definite idea of the nature, or even the existence, of such a state.

HAWAIIAN VIEWS CONCERNING LIFE AFTER DEATH

Some said that all the souls of the departed went to the Po, (place of night), and were annihilated, or eaten by the gods there.

Others said, that some went to the regions of Akea and Miru.

Akea, they said, was the first king of Hawaii. At the expiration of his reign, which terminated with his life at Waipio, the place where we then were, he descended to a region far below, called Kapapahanau-moku, (the island-bearing rock, or stratum—compounded of Ka papa, the rock, or stratum of rock; hanau, to bear or bring forth; and moku, an island), and founded a kingdom there.

Miru, who was his successor, and reigned in Hamakua, descended, when he died, to Akea, and shared the government of the place with him. Their land is a place of darkness; their food lizards and butter-

262

flies. There are several streams of water, of which they drink, and some said there were large Kahiris, and wide-spreading kou-trees, beneath which they reclined. (Though the Kahiris were usually small, resembling the one represented in the plate of the native dance at Kairua, they were sometimes upwards of twenty feet high; the handle twelve or fifteen feet long, beautifully covered with tortoise shell and the ivory of whales' teeth; and the upper part formed with red, yellow, or black feathers, fastened on a kind of wicker-work, and resembling a cylinder twelve or thirteen inches in diameter. These, however, are only used on state occasions, when they are carried in processions instead of banners, and are fixed in the ground near the tent or house in which the king or principal personages may remain on such occasions). But to most of the questions that were asked, they said they could give no answer, as they knew nothing about it; none had ever returned in open daylight, to tell them any thing respecting it; and all they knew was from visions or dreams of the priests.

MESSAGES FROM THE OTHER WORLD

Sometimes, they said, when a recently liberated spirit arrived in the dominions of Miru, the Pluto of Hawaii, he (viz. Miru) would ask it what the kings above were doing, and what were the principal pursuits of the people? and when he had answered, he was sent back to the ao marama (state of day or light) with a message from Miru to them, to iho nui mai ma nei, (to descend altogether to this place). The person so sent would appear to the priests in a dream, deliver his message, and then return to the lower regions.

This account accorded with the report of the late Tamehameha's appearing to a man in the division of Kona, of which we had before heard.

A MESSAGE FROM KAMEHAMEHA AFTER DEATH

A short time ago, a man in the southern part of Kona retired to rest as usual. In the middle of the night, it is said, he was conducted by a spirit to the lower regions where he saw Tamehameha, who asked him by whom Hawaii was governed; and made several inquiries respecting his son, Rihoriho, and his other children. Tamehameha then requested the man to return, deliver a certain message to Kuakini, and also to Rihoriho the king, promising his favour if he obeyed, but threatening severely, should he fail to do as he had directed him.

The man returned to his house, related where he had been, but instead of setting off immediately to Kairua, he remained to dress a hog, and prepare food for the journey. The delay was severely punished, for he died before the food he had stopped to prepare was cooked.

263

This story probably originated with those who were fearful lest some of the institutions and principles of the late king should be disregarded by his successors. It serves, however, to exhibit the popular notions of the people, and the great influence Tamehameha had over them.

HAWAIIAN AND SOCIETY ISLAND TRADITIONS OF HADES

The account given this evening of the Hawaiian hades, afforded another proof of the identity between the traditions of the Sandwich and Society Islanders. For among the latter, the spirits of the Areois, and priests of certain idols, were not eaten by the gods after the death of their bodies, but went to Miru, (pronounced by both, Meru), where they lived much in the same way as the departed kings and heroes of Hawaii were supposed to do; or joining hands, they formed a circle with those that had gone before, and danced in one eternal round.

At daylight, on the 19th, numbers of the people collected around the house where we had lodged, with whom we held morning worship.

Haa, the chief of the place, beneath whose friendly roof we had been most hospitably entertained, then accompanied us to the beach, where he had prepared a canoe to convey us to the next district. Shortly after six a.m. we gave him the parting hand, with sincere thanks for his kindness, after which we seated ourselves in the canoe, and, in the midst of many expressions of good will, from those who had come down to the beach to bid us farewell, we were safely launched through the surf.

We left Waipio, deeply impressed with a sense of the kind treatment we had received, and with feelings of sympathy for the mental darkness and degradation of the interesting people by whom it was inhabited. We could not but hope that they would soon enjoy the constant light of Christian instruction, and participate in every Christian privilege. A wide field of usefulness is here presented to a Christian missionary, and we sincerely hope the directors of missionary operations will have means sufficient at their disposal to send a missionary to this, and every other place where the people are so anxious to be instructed.

DOWN THE COAST FROM WAIPIO

The shore, along which the canoe was paddled, was extremely bold and romantic. In many places the mountains rose almost perpendicularly 500 or 600 feet above the sea. Their steep sides were nearly destitute of verdure, as it was the dry season, yet, at unequal distances of a quarter or half a mile from each other, beautiful waterfalls and varied cascades flowed from the top into the ocean below. The rocks seemed composed of various strata of vesicular lava, and in several places the water was seen oozing out between the strata in the face of the rocks some hundred feet below their summits.

Large stones and fragments of rocks in some places lay scattered along the base of the precipice, just above the water's edge; but frequently the mountain sides seemed to descend perpendicularly to a great depth under water.

We saw several groups of natives passing along on the large stones at the foot of the mountains, and whenever they came to a place where the deep waters extended to the base of the precipice, they all jumped into the sea, and swam perhaps fifty or sixty yards, till they came to another ledge of rocks, upon which they would climb, and pursue their journey.

SHIPPING SANDAL WOOD AT WAIMANU

After proceeding pleasantly along for five or six miles, we arrived at Waimanu a little before eight o'clock.

We found Arapai, the chief, and a number of his men, busy on the beach shipping sandal-wood on board a sloop belonging to the governor, then lying at anchor in a small bay off the mouth of the valley. He received us kindly, and directed two of his men to conduct us to his house, which was on the opposite side.

The valley, though not so spacious or cultivated as Waipio, was equally verdant and picturesque; we could not but notice the unusual beauty of its natural scenery. The glittering cascades and waterfalls, that rolled down the deep sides of the surrounding mountains, seemed more numerous and beautiful than those at Waipio.

SURFING AT WAIMANU

As we crossed the head of the bay, we saw a number of young persons swimming in the surf, which rolled with some violence on the rocky beach.

To a spectator nothing can appear more daring, and sometimes alarming, than to see a number of persons splashing about among the waves of the sea as they dash on the shore; yet this is the most popular and delightful of the native sports.

There are perhaps no people more accustomed to the water than the islanders of the Pacific; they seem almost a race of amphibious beings. Familiar with the sea from their birth, they lose all dread of it, and seem nearly as much at home in the water as on dry land.

CHILDREN SWIM AS SOON AS THEY WALK

There are few children who are not taken into the sea by their mothers the second or third day after their birth, and many who can swim as soon as they can walk.

The heat of the climate is, no doubt, one source of the gratification they find in this amusement, which is so universal, that it is scarcely possible to pass along the shore where there are many habitations near, and not see a number of children playing in the sea.

Here they remain for hours together, and yet I never knew of but one child being drowned during the number of years I have resided in the islands.

CHILDREN'S WATER GAMES

They have a variety of games, and gambol as fearlessly in the water as the children of a school do in their playground.

Sometimes they erect a stage eight or ten feet high on the edge of some deep place, and lay a pole in an oblique direction over the edge of it, perhaps twenty feet above the water; along this they pursue each other to the outermost end, when they jump into the sea.

Throwing themselves from the lower yards, or bowsprit, of a ship, is also a favourite sport, but the most general and frequent game is swimming in the surf. The higher the sea and the larger the waves in their opinion the better the sport.

SURF BOARDING

On these occasions they use a board, which they call papa he naru, (wave sliding-board), generally five or six feet long, and rather more than a foot wide, sometimes flat, but more frequently slightly convex on both sides. It is usually made from the wood of the erythrina, stained quite black, and preserved with great care. After using, it is placed in the sun till perfectly dry, when it is rubbed over with cocoa-nut oil, frequently wrapped in cloth, and suspended in some part of their dwelling house.

Sometimes they choose a place where the deep water reaches to the beach, but generally prefer a part where the rocks are ten or twenty feet under water, and extend to a distance from the shore, as the surf breaks more violently over these.

When playing in these places, each individual takes his board, and, pushing it before him, swims perhaps a quarter of a mile or more out to sea.

They do not attempt to go over the billows which roll towards the shore, but watch their approach, and dive under water, allowing the billow to pass over their heads.

GOING IN ON THE SURF

When they reach the outside of the rocks, where the waves first break, they adjust themselves on one end of the board, lying flat on their faces, and watch the approach of the largest billow; they then poise themselves on its highest edge, and, paddling as it were with their hands and feet, ride on the crest of the wave, in the midst of the spray

266

and foam, till within a yard or two of the rocks or the shore; and when the observers would expect to see them dashed to pieces, they steer with great address between the rocks, or slide off their board in a moment, grasp it by the middle, and dive under water, while the wave rolls on, and breaks among the rocks with a roaring noise, the effect of which is greatly heightened by the shouts and laughter of the natives in the water.

Those who are expert frequently change their position on the board, sometimes sitting and sometimes standing erect in the midst of the foam.

The greatest address is necessary in order to keep on the edge of the wave: for if they get too forward, they are sure to be overturned; and if they fall back, they are buried beneath the succeeding billow.

CANOE SURFING—WHOLE VILLAGES, INCLUDING CHIEFS, SURFING

Occasionally they take a very light canoe; but this, though directed in the same manner as the board, is much more difficult to manage.

Sometimes the greater part of the inhabitants of a village go out to this sport, when the wind blows fresh towards the shore, and spend the greater part of the day in the water. All ranks and ages appear equally fond of it.

We have seen Karaimoku and Kakioeva, some of the highest chiefs in the island, both between fifty and sixty years of age, and large corpulent men, balancing themselves on their narrow board, or splashing about in the foam, with as much satisfaction as youths of sixteen.

They frequently play at the mouth of a large river, where the strong current running into the sea, and the rolling of the waves towards the shore, produce a degree of agitation between the water of the river and the sea, that would be fatal to an European, however expert he might be; yet in this they delight: and when the king or queen, or any high chiefs, are playing, none of the common people are allowed to approach these places, lest they should spoil their sport.

KAUMUALII AN EXPERT SURFER

The chiefs pride themselves much on excelling in some of the games of their country; hence Taumuarii, the late king of Tauai, was celebrated as the most expert swimmer in the surf, known in the islands.

FEAR OF SHARKS

The only circumstance that ever mars their pleasure in this diversion is the approach of a shark. When this happens, though they sometimes fly in every direction, they frequently unite, set up a loud shout, and make so much splashing in the water, as to frighten him away. Their fear of them, however, is very great; and after a party return from this amusement, almost the first question they are asked is, "Were there any sharks?"

The fondness of the natives for the water must strike any person visiting their islands; long before he goes on shore, he will see them swimming around his ship; and few ships leave without being accompanied part of the way out of the harbour by the natives, sporting in the water; but to see fifty or a hundred persons riding on an immense billow, half immersed in spray and foam, for a distance of several hundred yards together, is one of the most novel and interesting sports a foreigner can witness in the islands.

INSPECTING WAIMANU

When we arrived at the house of Arapai, we were welcomed by his wife and several members of his family.

Mr. Thurston walked up to the head of the valley, to number the houses and speak to the people. At one of the villages through which he passed, about 150 of the inhabitants assembled, to whom he preached. The people were interested, and several of them followed him down to the the chief's house near the beach. Shortly after his return, the chief came home, and some breakfast of salt fish and taro was provided, of which we partook with the family.

THE FURNISHINGS OF CHIEF ALAPAI'S HOUSE

Arapai is evidently a chief of some importance. We saw several large double canoes in his out-houses. The number of his domestics was greater than usual; his house was large, well built, and stocked with a number of useful articles, among which we noticed some large and handsomely stained calabashes, marked with a variety of devices.

The calabash is a large kind of gourd, sometimes capable of holding four or five gallons. It is used to contain water and other fluids, by the natives of all the islands in the South Sea; but the art of staining it is peculiar to the Sandwich Islanders, and is another proof of their superior powers of invention and ingenuity.

When the calabash has grown to its full size, they empty it in the usual manner, by placing it in the sun till the inside is decayed, and may be shaken out. The shell, which remains entire, except the small perforation made at the stalk for the purpose of discharging its contents, and serving as a mouth to the vessel, is, when the calabash is large, sometimes half an inch thick.

DECORATION OF CALABASHES

In order to stain it, they mix several bruised herbs, principally the stalks and leaves of the arum, and a quantity of dark ferruginous earth, with water, and fill the vessel with it. They then draw with a piece of

268

hard wood or stone on the outside of the calabash, whatever figures they wish to ornament it with. These are various, being either rhomboids, stars, circles, or wavy and straight lines, in separate sections, or crossing each other at right angles, generally marked with a great degree of accuracy and taste.

After the colouring matter has remained three or four days in the calabashes, they are put into a native oven and baked. When they are taken out, all the parts previously marked appear beautifully brown or black, while those places, where the outer skin had not been broken, retain their natural bright yellow colour. The dye is now emptied out, and the calabash dried in the sun; the whole of the outside appears perfectly smooth and shining, while the colours imparted by the above process remain indelible.

USES OF THE CANDLE NUT

Large quantities of kukui, or candle nuts, hung in long strings in different parts of Arapai's dwelling. These are the fruit of the aleurites triloba; a tree which is abundant in the mountains, and highly serviceable to the natives.

It furnishes a gum, which they use in preparing varnish for their tapa, or native cloth.

The inner bark produces a permanent dark-red dye, but the nuts are the most valuable part; they are heart-shaped, about the size of a walnut, and are produced in abundance.

Sometimes the natives burn them to charcoal, which they pulverize, and use in tatauing their skin, painting their canoes, surf-boards, idols, or drums; but they are generally used as a substitute for candles or lamps. When designed for this purpose, they are slightly baked in a native oven, after which the shell, which is exceedingly hard, is taken off, and a hole perforated in the kernel, through which a rush is passed, and they are hung up for use, as we saw them at this place.

When employed for fishing by torch-light, four or five strings are enclosed in the leaves of the pandanus, which not only keeps them together, but renders the light more brilliant.

When they use them in their houses, ten or twelve are strung on the thin stalk of the cocoa-nut leaf, and look like a number of peeled chestnuts on a long skewer.

The person who has charge of them lights a nut at one end of the stick, and holds it up, till the oil it contains is consumed, when the flame kindles on the one beneath it, and he breaks off the extinct nut with a short piece of wood, which serves as a pair of snuffers.

Each nut will burn two or three minutes, and, if attended, give a tolerable light. We have often had occasion to notice, with admiration, the merciful and abundant provision which the God of nature has made for the comfort of those insulated people, which is strikingly manifested by the spontaneous growth of this valuable tree in all the islands; a great convenience is hereby secured, with no other trouble than picking up the nuts from under the trees.

The tree is large, the leaves and wood remarkably white; and though the latter is not used by the Sandwich Islanders, except occasionally in making fences, small canoes are frequently made of it by the Society Islanders.

In addition to the above purposes, the nuts are often baked or roasted as an article of food, which the natives eat with salt.

The nut contains a large portion of oil, which, possessing the property of drying, is useful in painting; and for this purpose quantities are carried by the Russian vessels to their settlements on the northwest coast of America.

A FAREWELL SERVICE AT WAIMANU

Before we prepared for our departure, we requested that the people of the place might assemble to hear the word which we had to speak to them. About 200 collected, and were addressed from John vi. 40. They gave good attention, particularly the wife of Arapai, who was afflicted with an affection of the spine, which prevented her walking without support. She called us to her after the service, and told us she had incurred the displeasure of the gods by eating a fish that was tabu, or sacred, and that the disease which rendered her a cripple was her punishment. She said she had felt great pleasure on hearing the invitation of Jesus Christ, desired to go to him and obey his word, inquiring at the same time very earnestly, if we thought he could and would save her. We told her that eating the tabu fish was not the cause of her suffering, and encouraged her to repair, by faith, to Him who was able and willing to heal her body if he saw fit, and who would assuredly save her soul, if she applied in a right manner; repeating several of the most precious promises of our blessed Lord to those that are weary and heavy laden with sin, and desire salvation through his mercy.

Numbers of the people crowded round us when the service was ended, and with earnestness besought us to sit down and repeat several of the truths they had heard respecting the name and attributes of Jehovah, his law, and the name and offices of Jesus Christ the only Saviour. They also requested to be more particularly informed in what manner they should pray to him, and how they should know when the Sabbath-day came.

We told them to go to Jehovah in prayer, as a child went to its parents, assuring them they would find him more ready to attend to them, than the fondest earthly parent was to listen to his most beloved child. This did not satisfy them; we, therefore, after observing that God did not regard so much the words, as the desires of the heart, mentioned several expressions of praise, confession, and petition—which the natives repeated after us till they could recite them correctly.

The chief then sent for a youth, about sixteen years of age, of whom he seemed very fond, and after he and his wife had requested him to attend very particularly to what he should hear, they requested us to repeat to him what we had told them. We did so; the youth evidently tried to treasure up the words in his memory; and when he could repeat correctly what had been told him, the parents appeared highly pleased.

Indeed, the greater part of the people seemed to regard the tidings of ora roa ia Jesu, (endless life by Jesus), as the most joyful news they had ever heard; "breaking upon them," to use the expressions of the natives on another occasion, "like light in the morning."

The chief's wife in particular exclaimed aloud, "Will my spirit never die? and can this poor weak body live again?"

TRIP FROM WAIMANU TO HONOKANE

When we departed, she rose up, and, by the help of two sticks, walked down to the beach with us. Here we took an affectionate leave, and then stepped into a canoe, which Arapai had provided to convey us as far as Honokane, the first village in the division of Kohala.

As the canoe pushed off from the shore, we again bade them farewell. When we saw the interesting group standing on the beach, we could not but feel the most lively concern for their welfare, and involuntarily besought the great Redeemer, that his holy Spirit might be poured out upon them, that the seed sown among them might take root in their hearts, and produce an abundant harvest to his praise.

FORMATION OF LAUPAHOEHOE NO. 2

After leaving Waimanu, we passed by Laupahoehoe, a second village of that name on this part of the coast, where, according to the accounts of the natives, about eight or nine months before, an immense mass of rocks had suddenly fallen down. The mountain that remained appeared nearly 600 feet high. The face next the sea was perpendicular, and as smooth as a compact piece of masonry. The rock appeared volcanic, and the different strata of highly vesicular lava were very distinct. In several places we saw the water oozing from the face of the rock 200 or 300 feet from the summit.

The mass that had fallen lay in ruins at the base, where it had formed two considerable hills, filled up a large fish-pond and part of the sea, presenting altogether a scene of wide-spread desolation.

271

The original surface of the ground appeared to have been broken by an earthquake, as some parts were rent by deep chasms, others sunk down six or twelve feet lower than the rest. The shrubs and grass were growing luxuriantly on the upper or original, and lower or fallen surface, while the perpendicular space between them indicated that the latter had recently sunk down from the former.

Wrecks of houses were seen in several places, some partly buried by the ruins, other standing just on the edge of the huge rocks that had fallen from above. Several houses were standing in the neighbourhood, but all seemed deserted.

The natives say that in the evening when the accident took place, a mist or fog was seen to envelop the summits of the precipice, and that after the sun had set, a luminous appearance, like a lambent flame, was observed issuing from and playing about the top, which made them think it was a forerunner of Pele, or volcanic fire. A priest of Pele and his family, residing in one of the villages below, immediately offered his prayer to the goddess, and told the inhabitants that no harm would befall them.

About ten o'clock at night, however, the whole side of the mountain, for nearly half a mile in extent along the shore, fell down with a horrid crash.

Part of two small villages were destroyed, and several of the inhabitants killed, but the natives did not agree as to the numbers; some said twenty were killed, others only eighteen.

The people with whom we talked on the spot, and at other places subsequently, could not recollect having heard the natives who escaped say any thing about an earthquake at the time.

TRAILS ALONG KOHALA MOUNTAIN BLUFFS

We did not land at this place, but passed close to the shore, and continued to sail along at the base of steep mountains, 500 or 600 feet high; and although nearly perpendicular, they were intersected here and there by winding paths, which we at first thought could be travelled only by goats, but up which we afterwards saw one or two groups of travellers pursuing their steep and rugged way.

About noon we passed Honokea, a narrow valley which separates the divisions of Hamakua and Kohala, and shortly after reached Hono-kane, the second village in the latter.

DESCRIPTION OF HAMAKUA DISTRICT

The division of Hamakua, on the N. E. side of the island, is, during the greater part of the year, singularly romantic in its appearance, particularly as seen from a vessel four or five miles out at sea.

272

The coast is bold and steep, and the cliffs, from three to five hundred feet high, partially covered with shrubs and herbage, intersected by numerous deep ravines and valleys, frequently in a high state of cultivation, while the whole coast is ornamented with waterfalls and cascades of every description. I once beheld three-and-twenty at one time from a ship's deck, some rolling in one continued stream from the summit of the cliffs to the sea, others foaming and winding among the ledges of rock that arrested their progress, sparkling among the verdant shrubs that fringed their borders, and altogether presenting a most delightful spectacle.

EXPERIENCES AT HONOKANE

We landed at Honokane, and went through the village to the house of Ihikaina, chief woman of the place, and sister to Arapai, the chief of Waimanu, from which this district is distant about twenty miles. Ihikaina received us kindly, and for our refreshment provided a duck, some vegetables, and a small quantity of excellent goat's milk, large flocks of which are reared by some of the natives for the supply of ships touching at the islands for refreshments.

The valley contained fifty houses. A number of the people collected round the door of the house, and listened to a short address.

GREAT LAND SLIDE NEAR POLOLU

About 4 p.m. we left Honokane, and passed on to Pololu. On our way we walked over a long tract of fragments of rocks, occasioned by the falling down of a side of the mountain, which took place at the same time that the mass of rocks fell at Laupahoehoe, which we had passed in the forenoon.

It was impossible, without considerable emotion, to walk over these rocks; some of them were broken in small pieces, others in blocks of several tons weight, each lying exactly as it had fallen, the fractures fresh, and the surface hardly discoloured, while the steep side of the mountain from which they had fallen looked as smooth and even as if the mass below had been separated from it only a few minutes before.

In some places between Honokane and Pololu, we had to walk in the sea, where the water was up to the knees, but by watching the surf we passed by without much inconvenience.

POLOLU DESCRIBED

Pololu is a pleasant village, situated in a small cultivated valley, having a fine stream of water flowing down its centre, while lofty mountains rise on either side.

The houses stand principally on the beach, but as we did not see many of the inhabitants, we passed on, ascended the steep mountain

273

on the north side, and kept on our way. The country was fertile, and seemed populous, though the houses were scattered, and more than three or four seldom appeared together. The streams of water were frequent, and a large quantity of ground was cultivated on their banks, and in the vicinity.

About sun-set we passed the residence of Mr. Parker, an American, who has resided a number of years on the island, and cultivated a considerable tract of ground. As he was in the mountains shooting wild cattle for the king and Karaimoku, we did not stop at his farm. During our journey this day, we passed by 458 houses; but as we travelled part of the way six or eight miles from the shore, in order to avoid the frequent and deep ravines, it is probable there were several villages which we did not see.

HOSPITABLE CUSTOMS OF THE HAWAIIANS

About seven in the evening we reached Halaua, the residence of Miomioi, a friend and favourite of the late king Tamehameha. He gave us a hearty welcome, with the accustomed courtesy of a Hawaiian chief, saying, "Our house is large, and there are plenty of sleeping mats for us."

The hospitality of the chiefs, both of the Society and Sandwich Islands, is always accompanied with a courtesy of behaviour peculiarly gratifying to those who are their guests, and indicating a degree of refinement seldom witnessed among uncivilized nations.

The usual salutation is Aroha (attachment), or Aroha nui (attachment great); and the customary invitation to partake of some refreshment is, "The food (a kakou) belonging to you and us is ready; let us eat together"; always using the pronoun kakou, or kaua, which includes the person addressed, as well as the speaker.

On entering a chief's house, should we remark, Yours is a strong or convenient house, he would answer, "It is a good house for (or belonging to) you and me."

If, on entering a house, or examining a fine canoe or piece of cloth, we should ask who it belongs to, another person would tell us the possessor's name; but if we happened to inquire of the owner himself, he would invariably answer, "It is yours and mine." The same desire to please is manifested in a variety of ways.

The manner in which they frequently ask a favour of each other is singular, usually prefacing it with, "I rea oe," If pleasing to you. Hence we often have a message or note to the following effect: "If pleasing to you, I should like a sheet of writing paper or a pen; but if it would not give you pleasure to send it, I do not wish it."

274

Soon after we had entered his house, a salt flying-fish was broiled for supper. A large copper boiler was also brought out, and tea was made with some dried mint, which, he said, he had procured many months ago from ships at Towaihae.

He supped at the same time, but, instead of drinking tea, took a large cocoanut shell full of ava. If an opinion of its taste might be formed by the distortion of his countenance after taking it, it must be a most nauseous dose. There seemed to be about half a pint of it in the cup; its colour was like thick dirty calcareous water.

As he took it, a man stood by his side with a calabash of fresh water, and the moment he had swallowed the intoxicating dose, he seized the calabash, and drank a hearty draught of water, to remove the unpleasant taste and burning effect of the ava.

USE OF AWA SUBSTITUTED BY LIQUOR

The ava has been used for the purpose of inebriation by most of the South Sea Islanders, and is prepared from the roots and stalks of a species of pepper plant, the piper methysticum of Forster, which is cultivated for this purpose in many of the islands, and being a plant of slow growth, was frequently tabued from the common people.

The water in which the ava had been macerated, was the only intoxicating liquor with which the natives were acquainted before their intercourse with foreigners, and was, comparatively speaking, but little used, and sometimes only medicinally, to cure cutaneous eruptions and prevent corpulency.

But since they have been so much visited by shipping, the case is very different. They have been taught the art of distillation; and foreign spirits in some places are so easily obtained, that inebriety, with all its demoralization, and attendant misery, is ten times more prevalent than formerly. This is a circumstance deeply to be deplored, especially when we recollect the immediate cause of its prevalence.

CHIEF'S HOUSE DESCRIBED

The chief's house was large, and one end of it was raised, by leaves and mats, about a foot higher than the rest of the floor, and partially screened from the other parts of the house. This was his own sleeping place, but he ordered a new mat to be spread, and obligingly requested us to occupy it. We did so, and enjoyed a comfortable night's rest.

After an early breakfast with Miomioi and his family, I embraced the opportunity of addressing his people on the subject of religion, before they separated to pursue their various avocations. About fifty, were present and listened with silent attention.

Miomioi, though not so tall and stout in person as many of the chiefs, appeared a remarkably active man, and soon convinced us he had been accustomed to delight in war. His military skill had probably recommended him to the notice and friendship of Tamehameha, and had secured for him the occupancy of the district of Halaua, the original patrimony of that prince.

Every thing in his house seemed to be preserved with care, but particularly his implements of war. Spears, nearly twenty feet long, and highly polished, were suspended in several places, which he was very careful to show us; remarking, that Tamehameha always required every man to keep his weapons in order, so as to be ready for war at the shortest notice, and shewing, at the same time, an evident satisfaction at the degree of care with which his own were preserved.

Considering his natural disposition, the circumstances and principles under which he had been brought up, his total ignorance of the gospel of peace, and the influence of a superstition which gave greater importance to war than any other human pursuit, we did not censure his complacency in exhibiting to us these instruments of death, but it was very affecting to think of numerous bodies of men meeting together with an intention to murder each other—And we may cherish the hope that the principles of Christianity, when embraced by the Hawaiians, will produce that cultivation of peace, and that aversion to war, which so happily prevail among the Society Islanders, and of which, since their reception of the gospel, they have given so many illustrations.

KAMEHAMEHA'S HOME

Between seven and eight, Miomioi, dressed in a blue jacket and trowsers, shoes and stockings, and a sailor's red cap on his head, conducted us down to the village on the sea-shore, where he pointed out to us several places remarkable by their connexion with the early history of Tamehameha.

Halaua is a large district on the north-east coast of the island, and, if not the birth-place of Tamehameha, was the land which he inherited from his parents, and, with the exception of a small district in the division of Kona, the only land he possessed in Hawaii prior to the death of Taraiopu, and the celebrated battle of Keei, which took place shortly afterwards.

DESCRIPTION OF KAMEHAMEHA

Tamehameha seems to have been early distinguished by enterprise, energy, decision of character, and unwearied perseverance in the accomplishment of his objects. Added to these, he possessed a vigorous constitution, and an unrivalled acquaintance with all the warlike games and athletic exercises of his country. To these qualities of mind and body he was probably indebted for the extensive power and protracted dominion which he exercised over the Sandwich Islands.

In early life he associated with himself a number of youthful chiefs of his own age and disposition, into whom he had the happy art of instilling, on all occasions, his own spirit, and inspiring them with his own resolution; by these means he most effectually secured their attachment and co-operation.

ENGINEERING WORK BY KAMEHAMEHA

Great undertakings appear to have been his delight, and achievements deemed by others impracticable were those which he regarded as most suitable exercises of his prowess.

Miomioi led the way to a spot, where, in a small bay, the original coast had been a perpendicular pile of rocks at least 100 feet high. Here Tamehameha and his companions, by digging through the rocks, had made a good road, with a regular and gradual descent from the high ground to the sea, up and down which their fishing canoes could be easily drawn.

At another place, he had endeavoured to procure water by digging through the rocks, but after forcing his way through several strata, the lava was so hard that he was obliged to give up the undertaking. Probably he had no powder with which to blast the rocks, and not the best tools for working through them.

REMINISCENCES OF KAMEHAMEHA

A wide tract of country in the neighbourhood was divided into fields of considerable size, containing several acres each, which he used to keep in good order, and well stocked with potatoes and other vegetables. One of these was called by his name. He was accustomed to cultivate it with his own hands. There were several others, called by the names of his principal friends or companions, which, following his example, they used to cultivate themselves; the others were cultivated by their dependants.

As the chief walked through the village, he pointed out the houses in which Tamehameha formerly resided, and several groves of noni trees, the morinda citrifolia, that he had planted, as Miomioi remarked, before his beard was grown.

Tamehameha was undoubtedly a prince possessing shrewdness and great strength of character. During his reign, the knowledge of the people was much enlarged, and their comforts in some respects increased; their acquisition of iron tools facilitated many of their labours; the introduction of fire-arms changed their mode of warfare; and in many

277

cases, cloth of European manufacture was substituted for that made of native bark. But these improvements appear to be rather the result of their intercourse with foreigners, than of any measures of their sovereign; though the encouragement he gave to all foreigners visiting the islands, was, no doubt, advantageous in these respects.

He has been called the Alfred of the Hawaiians; but he appears rather to have been their Alexander, ambition and a desire of conquest having been his ruling passions during the greater part of his life, though towards its close avarice superseded them.

It has been stated that he projected an invasion of the Society Islands, but the report, from many conversations on the subject with the natives, appears destitute of all foundation.

KAMEHAMEHA'S HEIAU AT KOHALA

Miomioi also pointed out the family heiau of Tamehameha, of which Tairi was the god, and the heiau was called Hare o Tairi, House of Tairi. It was an insignificant pile of stones, on a jutting point of volcanic rocks. Miomioi, however, said that the tabu was very strictly observed, and the punishments incurred by breaking it invariably inflicted on the transgressor; adding, at the same time, that Tamehameha always supposed his success, in every enterprise, to be owing to the strict attention he paid to the service and requirements of his god. Many persons, he said, had been burnt on the adjoining hills, for having broken the tabu enjoined by the priests of Tairi.

The Tabu formed an important and essential part of their cruel system of idolatry, and was one of the strongest means of its support.

PRACTICE OF THE TABU IN POLYNESIA

In most of the Polynesian dialects, the usual meaning of the word tabu is, sacred. It does not, however, imply any moral quality, but expresses a connexion with the gods, or a separation from ordinary purposes, and exclusive appropriation to persons or things considered sacred.

Those chiefs who trace their genealogy to the gods, are called arii tabu, chiefs sacred, from their supposed connexion with the gods; and a temple is called a wahi tabu, place sacred, because devoted exclusively to the abode and worship of the gods.

It is a distinct word from rahui, to prohibit, as the ohelo berries at Kirauea were said to be prohibited, being tabu na Pele, sacred for Pele, and is opposed to the word noa, which means general or common. Hence the system, which prohibited females from eating with the men, and from eating, except on special occasions, any fruits or animals ever offered in sacrifice to the gods, while it allowed the men to partake of them, was called the Ai tabu, eating sacred, but the present state of things is called the Ai moa, eating generally, or having food in common.

278

This appears to be the legitimate meaning of the word tabu, though the natives, when talking with foreigners, use it more extensively, applying it to every thing prohibited or improper. This, however, is only to accommodate the latter, as they use kaukau (a word of Chinese origin) instead of the native word for eat, and pikaninny, for small, supposing they are thereby better understood.

The tabu separating whatever it was applied to from common use, and devoting it to the above purposes, was one of the most remarkable institutions among the South Sea Islanders; and though it prevailed, with slight variations, in the different groups of the Pacific, it has not been met with in any other part of the world.

TABU WAS PRIMARILY A RELIGIOUS CEREMONY

Although employed for civil as well as sacred purposes, the tabu was entirely a religious ceremony, and could be imposed only by the priests.

A religious motive was always assigned for laying it on, though it was often done at the instance of the civil authorities; and persons called kiaimoku, (island keepers), a kind of police officers, were always appointed by the king to see that the tabu was strictly observed.

The antiquity of the tabu was equal to the other branches of that superstition of which it formed so component a part, and its application was both general and particular, occasional and permanent.

WHAT TABU APPLIED TO

The idols, temples, persons, and names of the king, and members of the reigning family; the persons of the priests; canoes belonging to the gods; houses, clothes, and mats of the king and priests; and the heads of men who were the devotees of any particular idol,—were always tabu, or sacred.

The flesh of hogs, fowls, turtle, and several other kinds of fish, cocoa-nuts, and almost every thing offered in sacrifice, were tabu to the use of the gods and the men; hence the women were, except in cases of particular indulgence, restricted from using them.

Particular places, as those frequented by the king for bathing, were also rendered permanently tabu.

Sometimes an island or a district was tabued, when no canoe or person was allowed to approach it. Particular fruits, animals, and the fish of certain places, were occasionally tabu for several months from both men and women.

The seasons generally kept tabu were, on the approach of some great religious ceremony; immediately before going to war; and during the sickness of chiefs. Their duration was various, and much longer in ancient than modern times.

Tradition states, that in the days of Umi there was a tabu kept thirty years, during which the men were not allowed to trim their beards, &c. Subsequently there was one kept five years.

Before the reign of Tamehameha, forty days was the usual period; during it, ten or five days, and some-only times one day.

The tabu seasons were either common or direct.

COMMON AND STRICT TABUS

During a common tabu, the men were only required to abstain from their usual avocations, and attend at the heiau when the prayers were offered every morning and evening. But during the season of strict tabu, every fire and light on the island or district must be extinguished; no canoe must be launched on the water, no person must bathe; and, except those whose attendance was required at the temple, no individual must be seen out of doors; no dog must bark, no pig must grunt, no cock must crow,—or the tabu would be broken, and fail to accomplish the object designed.

DOGS, PIGS AND CHICKENS KEPT THE TABU

On these occasions they tied up the mouths of the dogs and pigs, and put the fowls under a calabash, or fastened a piece of cloth over their eyes.

All the common people prostrated themselves, with their faces touching the ground, before the sacred chiefs, when they walked out, particularly during tabu; and neither the king nor the priests were allowed to touch any thing,—even their food was put into their mouths by another person.

The tabu was imposed either by proclamation, when the crier or herald of the priests went round, generally in the evening, requiring every light to be extinguished, the path by the sea to be left for the king, the paths inland to be left for the gods, &c. The people, however, were generally prepared, having had previous warning; though this was not always the case.

HOW THE TABU WAS MADE KNOWN

Sometimes it was laid on by fixing certain marks called unu unu, the purport of which was well understood, on the places or things tabued.

280

CHAPTER XIV

SANDAL WOOD COLLECTING IN KOHALA

Having seen the most remarkable places in the village, we took leave of Miomioi, and proceeded in a N. N. W. direction. The soil was fertile, and vegetation abundant. The coast towards the N. W. point of the island is frequently broken by snug little bays or inlets, which are invaluable to the inhabitants, on account of the facilities they afford for fishing. The tract we passed over today seemed more populous than that through which we had travelled yesterday, but we found most of the villages destitute of inhabitants, except a few women who had charge of some of the houses. On inquiry, we learned that a short time ago the people of Kohala had received orders from the king to provide a certain quantity of sandal-wood, and that they were absent in the mountains, cutting it.

TRADITIONS OF PAAO, A WHITE PRIEST

At noon we stopped at Kapaau, an inland village, where, with some difficulty, we collected a congregation of about fifty, principally women, to whom a short discourse was addressed. When we had remained some time for rest and conversation, we resumed our journey, and proceeded towards the north point of the island, near which we passed through the district of Pauepu, in which formerly stood a temple called Mokini, celebrated in the historical accounts of the Hawaiians, as built by Paao, a foreign priest, who resided in Pauepu, and officiated in this temple.

A tradition preserved among them states, that in the reign of Kahoukapu, a kahuna (priest) arrived at Hawaii from a foreign country; that he was a white man, and brought with him two idols or gods, one large, and the other small; that they were adopted by the people, and placed among the Hawaiian gods; that the above-mentioned temple of Mokini was erected for them, where they were worshipped according to the direction of Paao, who became a powerful man in the nation. The principal event preserved of his life, however, respects a child of Kahoukapu, whose mother was a woman of humble rank, but which was spared at the solicitations of Paao. After his death, his son, Opiri, officiated in his temple; and the only particular worthy of note in their account of his life, is his acting as interpreter between the king and a party of white men who arrived at the island.—We forbear making any comment on the above, though it naturally originates a variety of interesting inquiries.

283

We heard a similar account of this priest at two other places during our tour, viz. at Kairua, and at the first place we visited after setting out.

TALES OF ADVENTURES OF KANA

During our journey today we also passed another place, celebrated as the residence of the brother of Kana, a warrior; in comparison with the fabulous accounts of whom, the descriptions in the Arabian Nights' Entertainments are tame. He is described as having been so tall, that he could walk through the sea from one island to another; stand with one foot on the island of Oahu, and the other on Tauai, which is seventy miles distant.

The tale which recounts his adventures, states, that the Hawaiians, on one occasion, offended a king of Tahiti; who, in revenge, deprived them of the sun; that after the land had remained some time in darkness, Kana walked through the sea to Tahiti, where Kahoaarii, who according to their traditions made the sun, then resided. He obtained the sun, returned, and fixed it in the heavens, where it has remained ever since.

Various other adventures, equally surprising, are related. The numerous tales of fiction preserved by oral tradition among the people, and from the recital of which they derive so much pleasure, prove that they are not deficient in imagination; and lead us to hope, that their mental powers will be hereafter employed on subjects more consistent with truth, and productive of more pure and permanent gratification.

TRADITIONS OF VOYAGES TO MARQUESAS AND TAHITI

In this part of the island there is another tradition very generally received by the natives, of a somewhat more interesting character; and as it may tend to illustrate the history of the inhabitants, and the means by which the islands were peopled, I shall introduce it in this place.

These traditions respect several visits, which in remote times some of the natives made to Nuuhiva and Tahuata, two islands in the Marquesan group, and to Tahiti, the principal of the Society Islands.

One of these accounts the natives call, "The Voyage of Kamapiikai," in which they state that Kamapiikai (child running or climbing the sea—from kama, a child, pii, to run or climb, and kai, the sea) was priest of a temple in Kohala, dedicated to Kanenuiakea.

The exact period of their history when he lived, we have not been able to ascertain; but it is added, that the god appeared to him in a vision, and revealed to him the existence, situation, and distance of Tahiti, and directed him to make a voyage thither. In obedience to the communication, he immediately prepared for the voyage, and, with about forty of his companions, set sail from Hawaii in four double canoes.

284

After an absence of fifteen years, they returned, and gave a most flattering account of Haupokane, the country which they had visited. We know of no island in the neighbourhood called by this name, which appears to be a compound of Haupo, sometimes a lap, and Kane, one of their gods. Among other things, they described the one rauena, a peculiar kind of sandy beach, well stocked with shell-fish, &c. The country, they said, was inhabited by handsome people, whose property was abundant, and the fruits of the earth delicious and plentiful. There was also a stream or fountain, which was called the wai ora roa, (water of enduring life).

OTHER VOYAGES TO TAHITI

Kamapiikai made three subsequent voyages to the country he had discovered, accompanied by many of the Sandwich Islanders. From the fourth voyage they never returned, and were supposed to have perished at sea, or to have taken up their permanent residence at Tahiti. Many were induced to accompany this priest to the country he visited, for the purpose of bathing in the life-giving waters, in consequence of the marvellous change they were reported to produce in those who used them; for it was said, that however infirm, emaciated, or deformed they might be when they went into the water, they invariably came out young, strong, and handsome.

Without making further remarks, these traditions furnish very strong evidence that the Sandwich Islanders were acquainted with the existence of the Marquesan and Society Islands long before visited by Captain Cook; and they also warrant the inference, that in some remote period the Sandwich Islanders have visited or colonized other islands in the Pacific.

About three p.m. we reached Owawarua, a considerable village on the north-west coast, inhabited mostly by fishermen. Here we tried to collect a congregation, but only three women and two small children remained in the place, the rest having gone to Waimea to fetch sandal wood for Karaimoku.

From Owawarua we passed on to Hihiu, where we had an opportunity of speaking to a small party of natives.

HAWAIIAN FISHERIES AND FISHING METHODS

In these villages we saw numbers of canoes and many large fishing nets, which are generally made with a native kind of flax, very strong and durable, but produced by a plant very different from that called the phormium tenax, which furnishes the flax of New Zealand, and bearing a nearer resemblance to the plant used by the natives of the Society Islands, called roa, the urtica argentea, or candicans of Parkinson.

In taking fish out at sea, they commonly make use of a net, of which they have many kinds, some very large, others mere hand-nets; they occasionally employ the hook and line, but never use the spear or dart which is a favourite weapon with the southern islanders.

Quantities of fish were spread out in the sun to dry, in several places, and the inhabitants of the northern shores seem better supplied with this article than those of any other part of the island.

The shores of Hawaii are by no means so well stocked with fish as those of the Society Islands, for though the natives of the former appear equally skilful and industrious, they have not from the sea either that variety or abundance of fish which their southern neighbours enjoy.

The numerous coral reefs and shoals, and lagoons of salt water, which surround the latter islands, while very rare among these, is the probable occasion of the difference in this respect.

The industry of the Hawaiians in a great degree makes up the deficiency, for they have numerous small lakes and ponds, frequently artificial, wherein they breed fish of various kinds, and in tolerable abundance.

FROM KOHALA TO KAWAIHAE BY CANOE

Being considerably fatigued, and unable to find any fresh water in the village, we procured a canoe to take us to Towaihae, from which we were distant about twenty miles.

Though we had numbered, in our journey today, 600 houses, we had not seen any thing like four hundred people, almost the whole population being employed in the mountains cutting sandal wood.

It was about seven o'clock in the evening when we sailed from Hihiu, in a single canoe. The land breeze was light, but the canoe went at a tolerably rapid rate, and about eleven at night we reached Towaihae, where we were kindly received by Mr. Young. By him we were informed that Messrs. Bishop and Goodrich had arrived at Towaihae on the preceding Tuesday, and had gone to Kairua, expecting to obtain a passage to Oahu, in a native vessel called the pilot-boat.

THOUSANDS OF MEN PACKING SANDAL WOOD

Before daylight on the 22d we were roused by vast multitudes of people passing through the district from Waimea with sandal wood, which had been cut in the adjacent mountains for Karaimoku, by the people of Waimea, and which the people of Kohala, as far as the north point, had been ordered to bring down to his storehouse on the beach, for the purpose of its being shipped to Oahu.

There were between two and three thousand men, carrying each from one to six pieces of sandal wood, according to their size and weight. It was generally tied on their backs by bands made of ti leaves, passed over the shoulders and under the arms, and fastened across their breast. When they had deposited the wood at the storehouse, they departed to their respective homes.

AT THE KAWAIHAE WARM SPRINGS

Between seven and eight in the morning, we walked to the warm springs, a short distance to the southward of the large heiaus, and enjoyed a most refreshing bathe.

These springs rise on the beach a little below high-water mark, of course they are overflowed by every tide; but at low tide, the warm water bubbles up through the sand, fills a small kind of cistern, made with stones piled close together on the side towards the sea, and affords a very agreeable bathing place.

The water is comfortably warm, and is probably impregnated with sulphur; various medicinal qualities are ascribed to it by those who have used it.

SALT PONDS AT KAWAIHAE

The natives of this district manufacture large quantities of salt, by evaporating the sea water. We saw a number of their pans, in the disposition of which they display great ingenuity. They have generally one large pond near the sea, into which the water flows by a channel cut through the rocks, or is carried thither by the natives in large calabashes. After remaining there some time, it is conducted into a number of smaller pans about six or eight inches in depth, which are made with great care, and frequently lined with large evergreen leaves, in order to prevent absorption. Along the narrow banks or partitions between the different pans, we saw a number of large evergreen leaves placed. They were tied up at each end, so as to resemble a shallow dish, and filled with sea water, in which the crystals of salt were abundant.

USE OF SALT IN HAWAII AND SOCIETY ISLANDS

Although salt was never made by the Society Islanders, who used as a substitute the sea water, in a cocoa-nut shell-full of which they always dipped their food before eating it, it has ever been an essential article with the Sandwich Islanders, who eat it very freely with their food, and use large quantities in preserving their fish.

They have, however, besides what they make, salt lakes, which yield them large supplies. The surplus thus furnished, they dispose of to vessels touching at the islands, or export to the Russian settlements on the north-west coast of America, where it is in great demand for curing fish, &c.

The facility which many parts of the coast afford for this purpose, and the length of the dry season, are favourable to the process; and, together with the ready market which the natives find for it, will probably induce them, as they advance in civilization, to manufacture it in much greater abundance.

In the afternoon, Mr. Goodrich returned from Kairua, and informed us that the pilot-boat was at Keauhou, and would sail for Oahu in a fortnight.

BUILDING A CHURCH AT KAILUA

He also brought the more pleasing intelligence, that the governor was engaged in building a chapel for the public worship of God at Kairua, having at the same time enjoined on his people the observance of the Sabbath as a day of rest from labour and amusement, to be employed, moreover, in religious exercises. This welcome news rendered it desirable that one of us should repair to Kairua, in order to preach there on the coming Sabbath, and encourage them to persevere in the work they had so happily begun.

It was thought best that I should remove to Kairua, while Mr. Thurston remained at Towaihae, with the intention of visiting that part of Kohala which we had passed in the canoe on Wednesday evening, and also the most populous places in the vicinity. This arrangement, however, prevented our again uniting till we arrived at Oahu.

THURSTON VISITS KOHALA

On the 23d Mr. Thurston left Towaihae, and walked along the shore towards the north point. About noon he reached a small village, called Kipi, where he preached to the people; and as there was only one village between Kipi and the place where I had preached on Wednesday evening, he retraced his steps to Tawaihae. He preached at four other villages on his return, where the congregations, though not numerous, were attentive. The heat of the sun was oppressive, and the labours of the day fatiguing, yet it may be hoped that some good was effected. The coast was barren; the rocks volcanic; the men were all employed in fishing; and Mr. Thurston was informed that the inhabitants of the plantations, about seven miles in the interior, were far more numerous than on the shore. In the evening he reached Towaihae, and found that Mr. Goodrich had departed from Waimea, intending, after the Sabbath, to ascend Mouna-Kea.

The 24th was, probably, the first Christian Sabbath ever enjoyed by the people of Towaihae. which is a village containing 100 houses.

In the afternoon of the 25th, the brig Nio arrived from Oahu, intending to remain five or six days, and then return.

288

About five p.m. Mr. Thurston set out on a visit to the inland district of Waimea, having been furnished with a guide by Mr. Young. It was dark when he reached Ouli, a place belonging to the latter, where he put up for the night.

After worship with the people, on the morning of the 26th, Mr. Thurston walked on to Kalaloa, the residence of the chief of Waimea, Kumuokapiki, (Stump of Cabbage). Leaving Kalaloa, he walked on to Waiakea, from thence to Waikaloa, Pukalani, and Puukapu, which is sixteen or eighteen miles from the sea-shore, and is the last village in the district of Waimea. At these places he addressed the people.

The soil over which he had travelled was fertile, well watered, and capable of sustaining many thousand inhabitants. In his walks he had numbered 220 houses, and the present population is probably between eleven and twelve hundred.

Mr. Thurston preached twice to the people.

CHARACTER OF LAND IN HAMAKUA, KOHALA AND WAIMEA

The surface of the country is gently undulated, tolerably free from rocks, and easy of cultivation. In this district, and throughout the divisions of Hamakua and Kohala, together with the greater part of Hiro, the plough might be introduced with advantage, and the productions of intertropical climates raised in great abundance and excellent quality, as the sugar-cane and other indigenous plants, grown at Waimea, are unusually large.

From Puukapu he directed his steps towards the sea-shore, and in the twilight of the evening reached Puako, a considerable village, four or five miles to the southward of Towaihae, where he took up his lodging for the night. After addressing the people on the morning of the 27th, Mr. Thurston returned to Towaihae, where he arrived at 10 a.m.

MR. GOODRICH MAKES TRIP TO MAUNA KEA

About noon the same day, Mr. Goodrich returned from his journey to Mouna-Kea. Leaving Towaihae on the 23d, he had walked to Waimea, on the skirts of which he encamped with Mr. Parker, who was employed in shooting wild cattle. With him he spent the Sabbath, which was rainy and unpleasant.

Early on Monday the 25th, he commenced his journey up the mountain. The path lay along the side of a deep ravine; the soil was formed of decomposed lava and ashes.

At noon he dismissed his native companion, and, taking his great coat and blanket, began to ascend the more steep and rugged parts. The

289

way was difficult, on account of the rugged volcanic rocks and stunted shrubs that covered the sides of the mountain. In his way, he found numbers of red and white raspberry bushes loaded with delicious fruit.

CAMPING CONDITIONS AND EXPERIENCES

At 5 p.m. having reached the upper boundary of the trees and bushes that surround the mountain, he erected a temporary hut, kindled a small fire, and prepared for his night's repose. The thermometer shortly after sun-set stood at 43°; and the magnet, though it pointed north when held in the hand, was drawn between two and three degrees to the eastward, when placed on the blocks of lava, owing probably to the quantity of iron in the mountain.

After a few hours' rest, Mr. Goodrich arose at eleven o'clock at night, and the moon shining brightly, he resumed his journey towards the summit. At midnight he saw the snow about three miles distant, proceeded towards the place, and reached it about one o'clock on the morning of the 26th. The snow was frozen over, and the thermometer stood at 27°.

CONDITIONS AT SUMMIT

He now directed his steps towards a neighbouring peak, which appeared one of the highest; but when he had ascended it, he saw several others still higher. He proceeded towards one, which looked higher than the rest, and bore N. E. from the place where he was. On reaching the summit of this second peak, he discovered a heap of stones, probably erected by some former visitor. From this peak Mouna-Roa bore south by west, Mouna-Huararai west by south, and the island of Maui N. W.

The several hills or peaks on the summit of Mouna-Kea seemed composed entirely of volcanic matter, principally cinders, pumice, and sand. Mr. Goodrich did not discover apertures or craters on either of the summits he visited; probably there is a large crater somewhere adjacent, from which the scoria, sand, and pumice, have been thrown out. The whole of the summit was not covered with snow, there were only frequent patches, apparently several miles in extent, over which the snow was about eight inches or a foot in thickness. The ocean to the east and west was visible; but the high land on the north and south prevented its being seen in those directions.

Mr. Goodrich commenced descent about three o'clock, and after travelling over large beds of sand and cinders, into which he sunk more than ankle deep at every step, he reached about sun-rise the place where he had slept the preceding evening. The descent in several places, especially over the snow, was steep and difficult, and rendered the utmost caution necessary. After taking some refreshment at this place, Mr.

Goodrich continued his descent, and between four and five in the afternoon reached the encampment of Mr. Parker.

WILD CATTLE ON MAUNA KEA

In his way down, he saw at a distance several herds of wild cattle, which are very numerous in the mountains and inland parts of the island, and are the produce of those taken there, and presented to the king, by Captain Vancouver. They were, at his request, tabued for ten years, during which time they resorted to the mountains, and became so wild and ferocious, that the natives are afraid to go near them.

Although there are immense herds of them, they do not attempt to tame any; and the only advantage they derive is by employing persons, principally foreigners, to shoot them, salt the meat in the mountains, and bring it down to the shore for the purpose of provisioning the native vessels. But this is attended with great labour and expense. They first carry all the salt to the mountains. When they have killed the animals, the flesh is cut off their bones, salted immediately, and afterwards put into small barrels, which are brought on men's shoulders ten or fifteen miles to the sea-shore.

Early on the morning of the 27th, Mr. Goodrich left Mr. Parker, and returned through the fertile district of Waimea to Towaihae.

OTHER TRIPS TO MAUNA KEA

Nearly six months afterwards, Dr. Blatchely and Mr. Ruggles ascended Mouna-Kea, from Waiakea bay. After travelling six days, they reached the summit of the mountain, where, within the circumference of six miles, they found seven mountains or peaks, apparently 800 or 1000 feet high; their sides were steep, and covered with snow about a foot thick. The summit of the mountain appeared to be formed of decomposed lava, of a reddish brown colour. The peak in the centre, and that on the western side, are the highest.

The following observations respecting a subsequent visit to this mountain from Waiakea, contained in a letter from Mr. Goodrich to Professor Silliman, of New Haven, are copied from the Philosophical Magazine for September, 1826.

DESCRIPTION OF HILO SLOPE OF MAUNA KEA

"There appear to be three or four different regions in passing from the sea-shore to the summit. The first occupies five or six miles, where cultivation is carried on in a degree, and might be to almost any extent; but, as yet, not one-twentieth part is cultivated.

"The next is a sandy region, that is impassable, except in a few footpaths. Brakes, a species of tall fern, here grow to the size of trees; the bodies of some of them are eighteen inches in diameter.

"The woody region extends between ten and twenty miles in width.

"The region higher up produces grass, principally of the bent kind. Strawberries, raspberries, and whortleberries flourish is this region, and herds of wild cattle are seen grazing. It is entirely broken up by hills and valleys, composed of lava with a very shallow soil. The upper region is composed of lava in almost every form, from huge rocks to volcanic sand of the coarser kind. Some of the peaks are composed of coarse sand, and others of loose stones and pebbles. I found a few specimens, that I should not hesitate to pronounce fragments of granite. I also found fragments of lava, bearing a near resemblance to a geode, filled with green crystals, which I suppose to be augite.

WILD SHEEP, DOGS AND GOATS

"Very near to the summit, upon one of the peaks, I found eight or ten dead sheep; they probably fled up there to seek a refuge from the wild dogs; I have heard that there are many wild dogs, sheep, and goats. Dogs and goats I have never seen. I was upon the summit about 2 o'clock p.m., the wind S. W., much resembling the cold blustering winds of March, the air being so rare produced a severe pain in my head, that left me as I descended."

LEGENDS OF MAUNA KEA

In the native language, the word kea, though seldom used now, formerly meant, white. Some white men, who are said to have resided inland, and to have come down to the sea shore frequently in the evening, and to have frightened the people, were called na kea, (the whites).

The snow on the summit of the mountain, in all probability, induced the natives to call it Mouna-Kea, (mountain white), or, as we should say, white mountain. They have numerous fabulous tales relative to its being the abode of the gods, and none ever approach its summit— as, they say, some who have gone there have been turned to stone. We do not know that any have ever been frozen to death; but neither Mr. Goodrich, nor Dr. Blatchely and his companion, could persuade the natives, whom they engaged as guides up the side of the mountain, to go near its summit.

We could not but regret that we had no barometer, or other means of estimating the actual elevation of this mountain, either here or at Waiakea.

GOVERNOR KUAKINI BUILDS A CHURCH

Mr. Bishop, who, in company with Mr. Goodrich, had left Towaihae in a canoe belonging to Mr. Young, on the evening of the 19th, was obliged to put on shore about midnight, on account of the rough sea, which rendered it dangerous to proceed. Having slept in the open air till daylight, they resumed their voyage on the 20th, and reached Kairua about noon, after an absence of four weeks and five days.

The governor welcomed their return, and they were agreeably surprised to find him engaged in erecting a building for the worship of the true God. They learned that he had during the preceding week collected his people at Kairua, and addressed them on the duty of observing the Sabbath according to the laws of Jehovah. He also told them it was his desire that they should cease from work or amusement on that day, and attend divine service at his house.

The people assented to his proposal, and when the Sabbath arrived, such numbers assembled, that hundreds were obliged to stand outside. Numbers also repaired to the house of Thomas Hopu, to be instructed in what they denominate the new religion.

The next day the governor directed the people of Kairua to commence building a house, in which they might all meet to worship God; and in the morning on which Messrs. Bishop and Goodrich arrived, they had commenced their work.

HEIAU FURNISHES MATERIAL FOR CHURCH BUILDING

In the afternoon they walked to the place where the men were at work. Upwards of fifty persons were employed in carrying stones from an old heiau, which they were pulling down, to raise the ground, and lay the foundation of the place of worship. It was a pleasing sight to view the ruins of an idol's temple devoted to such a purpose; and they could not but hope that the spirit of Christianity would soon triumph over the superstition, prejudice, and wickedness of idolatry.

The place of worship is sixty feet long and thirty broad, erected in the native manner, and thatched with the leaves of the pandanus. The walls are ten feet high, with doors at each end, and four windows on each side. It was impossible to behold the work without contemplating it as an intimation of most benevolent designs, on the part of the Lord of missions, towards the benighted tribes around, or without praying that the time might soon arrive when houses for the worship of the living God shall be erected in every district in the islands.

Recent intelligence conveys the pleasing information, that five or six places of worship and a number of schools have already been erected in Hawaii, and a proportionate number in other islands of the group.

VICISSITUDES OF INTER-ISLAND TRAVEL

On the 22d, after the return of Mr. Goodrich to Towaihae, a small boat arrived, which had left Oahu some days before for Maui, but had been blown so far to the southward, that they had with difficulty made the south point of Hawaii. They stopped at Kairua a short time in order to procure water, for the want of which they had suffered severely. As they intended proceeding to Oahu, Mr. Bishop wrote to the mission family there, informing them that the tour of the island had been accomplished, and that the missionaries were waiting an opportunity to return.

On the 23d he visited the well, and found that the men had not made much progress. The rocks of lava, though hard, are cellular, so that powder has very little effect, and therefore they proceeded but slowly by blasting it.

NATIVES OBSERVE THE SABBATH

The morning of the 24th was the Sabbath, and was unusually still; not a canoe was seen in the bay, and the natives seemed to have left their customary labours and amusements, to spend the day as directed by the governor. Mr. Bishop spent half an hour with him this morning, explaining in English the 21st and 22nd chapters of Revelation.

I joined them at breakfast, having arrived at Kairua about an hour before daylight. I had left Towaihae on the preceding day at six in the morning, in a canoe kindly furnished by Mr. Young.

VISITING VILLAGES BETWEEN KAWAIHAE AND KAILUA

About nine a.m. I stopped at Kaparaoa, a small village on the beach, containing twenty-two houses, where I found the people preparing their food for the ensuing day, on which they said the governor had sent word for them to do no work, neither cook any food. When the people were collected, I addressed them, and after answering a number of inquiries respecting the manner in which they should keep the Sabbath-day, again embarked on board my canoe, and sailed to Wainanarii, where I landed, repaired to the house of Waipo, the chief, who, as soon as the object of my visit was known, directed the people to assemble at his house.

At Kaparaoa I saw a number of curiously carved wooden idols, which formerly belonged to an adjacent temple. I asked the natives if they would part with any? They said, Yes; and I should have purchased one, but had no means of conveying it away, for it was an unwieldy log of heavy wood, twelve or fourteen feet long, curiously carved, in rude and frightful imitation of the human figure.

After remaining there till two p.m. I left them making preparation to keep the Sabbath-day, according to the orders they had received from the governor.

KAMEHAMEHA'S FISH-POND AT KIHOLO

About four in the afternoon I landed at Kihoro, a straggling village, inhabited principally by fishermen. A number of people collected, to whom I addressed a short discourse, from 1 John i. 7.

294

W. Ellis del.

T. Dixon. sc.

A Missionary Preaching to the Natives, under a Screen of platted Cocoa-nut leaves at Kairua.

This village exhibits another monument of the genius of Tame-hameha. A small bay, perhaps half a mile across, runs inland a considerable distance. From one side to the other of this bay, Tamehameha built a strong stone wall, six feet high in some places, and twenty feet wide, by which he had an excellent fish-pond, not less than two miles in circumference.

There were several arches in the wall, which were guarded by strong stakes driven into the ground so far apart as to admit the water of the sea; yet sufficiently close to prevent the fish from escaping. It was well stocked with fish, and water-fowl were seen swimming on its surface.

DISCUSSIONS WITH THE PEOPLE OF KIHOLO

The people of this village, as well as the others through which I had passed, were preparing to keep the Sabbath, and the conversation naturally turned on the orders recently issued by the governor.

They said it was a bad thing to commit murder, infanticide, and theft, which had also been forbidden; that it would be well to abstain from these crimes; but, they said, they did not know of what advantage the palapala (instruction, &c.) would be.

I remained some time with them, and told them I hoped missionaries would soon come to reside permanently at Kairua, whither I advised them to repair as frequently as possible, that they might participate in the advantages of instruction—be made better acquainted with the character of the true God, and the means of seeking his favour.

FROM KIHOLO TO KAILUA

Just before sun-set, I left Kihora. The men paddled the canoe past Laemano, (Shark's-point), a point of land formed by the last eruption of the great crater on Mouna-Huararai, which took place twenty years ago.

Between seven and eight in the evening, we reached Kaupulehu, where the men drew the canoe on the beach, and, as the inhabitants were all buried in sleep, laid down to repose on the sand till the moon should rise. About eleven p.m. I awoke my companions; and the moon having risen, they launched the canoe, and, after paddling hard several hours, reached Kairua at the time above mentioned.

At breakfast the governor seemed interested in the narrative of the tour, particularly of the interview we had with the priestess of Pele at Waiakea.

SUNDAY SERVICES TO 800 AT KAILUA

At half-past ten, the bell rung for public worship, and about 800 people, decently dressed, some in foreign, others in native clothing, assembled under a large ranai (a place sheltered from the sun) formed by two large canvas awnings, and a number of platted cocoanut leaves, spread over the place from posts fixed in the fence which enclosed the court yard around the house of the governor's wife.

The governor and his attendants sat on chairs; the rest of the congregation reclined on their mats, or sat on the ground.

After singing and prayer, I preached from Acts xvi. 30, 31. The history of the Philippian jailor appeared to interest them, and, after the conclusion of the service, the governor in particular made many inquiries.

FONDNESS OF NATIVES FOR DOGS

We have often had occasion to notice the fondness of the natives for their dogs. The pets are usually of a small size; and though the females generally evince the greatest regard for them, frequently bringing them in their arms or on their backs, when they come to our public meetings, yet the men are occasionally seen attended by their favourite dog. This has been particularly the case at Kairua.

AFTERNOON AND EVENING SERVICES AT KAILUA

At half-past four in the afternoon the bell rung again, and the people collected in the place where the services had been held in the forenoon, and in equal numbers seated themselves very quietly. The exercises commenced in the usual manner, and I preached on the occasion from Acts v. 14. They were attentive, and appeared much affected with the account of the awful end of Ananias and Sapphira.

After the public exercises were finished, Mr. Bishop visited Thomas Hopu's house, where a small congregation was assembled for conversation and prayer. Mr. Bishop gave them a short exhortation; and many of the people remained after the service, to hear more from Thomas about Jesus Christ.

The Sabbath was spent in a manner truly gratifying. No athletic sports were seen on the beach; no noise of playful children, shouting as they gamboled in the surf, nor distant sound of the cloth-beating mallet, was heard through the day; no persons were seen carrying burdens in or out of the village, nor any canoes passing across the calm surface of the bay. It could not but be viewed as the dawn of a bright sabbatic day for the dark shores of Hawaii.

In the evening, family worship was conducted at the governor's house in the native language; his companions and domestics attended, and expressed themselves pleased with the singing.

On the 27th it was proposed to the governor to have a public meeting, and a sermon, as was the practice at Oahu; but he objected, saying that the people would not attend, and it was too soon yet to have preaching among them during the week.

Having heard of the arrival of the brig Nio at Towaihae, Mr. Bishop left Kairua in the evening, to return to Oahu; while I remained, in order to preach to the governor and his people on the next Sabbath, expecting then to reach Towaihae in season to proceed to Oahu by the Nio.

ISLAND SHIPPING IN 1823

The natives possess no inconsiderable share of maritime and commercial enterprise. The king and chiefs own fifteen or sixteen vessels, several of which, like the Nio, are brigs of ninety or a hundred tons burden. The greater part of them, however, are schooners of a smaller size.

The larger ones on a long voyage are commanded by a foreigner; but among the islands, they are manned and navigated by the natives themselves. A native captain and supercargo is appointed to each; the former navigates the vessel, while the latter attends to the cargo.

The natives in general make good sailors; and although their vessels have greatly multiplied within the last few years, they find constant employ for them, particularly the small craft, which are continually plying from one island to another, while their larger ones are either chartered to foreign merchants, or make distant voyages on their own account.

VOYAGES TO FOREIGN COUNTRIES

They have once sent a vessel to Canton loaded with sandal wood, under the care of an English captain and mate, but manned by natives. They have also traded to Kamtschatka and other parts of the Pacific, and have within the last few years made one or two successful voyages for the purpose of procuring seal skins, which they have disposed of to advantage.

ORIGIN OF HAWAIIAN FLAG

The national flag of the islands, which is an English jack, with eight or nine horizontal stripes, of white, red, and blue, was given them by the British government many years ago, accompanied by an assurance that it would be respected wherever the British flag was acknowledged.

SUPPLIES SOLD TO SHIPS

Although they are so expert in the manufacture of their canoes, they have made but little progress in building and repairing their ships, or in any of the mechanic arts. They seem much more fond of the pursuits of commerce, and are tolerable adepts in bartering. In exchange for foreign articles, they not only give sandal wood and salt, but furnish supplies to the numerous vessels which visit the islands for the purpose of refitting or procuring refreshments.

In the months of March and April, and of September and October, many vessels, principally whalers, resort to the Sandwich Islands for fresh provisions, &c. — we have seen upwards of thirty lying at anchor off Oahu at one time. The farmers in many places dispose of the produce of their land to these ships; but in Oahu and some other harbours, this trade is almost entirely monopolized by the king and chiefs.

OPPRESSIVE TAXATION BY CHIEFS—COMMERCE WITH SHIPS

There is indeed a public market, in which the natives dispose of their stock; but the price is regulated by the chiefs, and two-thirds of the proceeds of whatever the natives sell is required by them.

The Hawaiian Flag.
Said by Ellis to have been Designed by the
British Government.

This is not only unpleasant to those who trade with them, but very oppressive, and retards in no small degree the industry, comfort, and civilization of the people.

In return for most of the supplies which they furnish to the shipping, they receive Spanish dollars; but the sandal wood, &c., they usually exchange for articles of European or Chinese fabrication: the silks, crepes, umbrellas, furniture, and trunks of the latter, are most in demand; while those of the former are hardware, earthenware, linens, broadcloth, slops, hats, shoes, canvas, cordage, &c.

The season was approaching when the whalers, fishing on the coast of Japan, usually put in to some of the harbours of these islands. Hence Karaimoku had sent the Nio for a cargo of hogs, to meet the demand for these animals, which he expected would follow their arrival.

BISHOP AND GOODRICH RETURN TO HONOLULU

About noon on the 28th, Mr. Bishop reached Towaihae; and in the evening of the 30th, they received the unexpected information that the brig would sail that evening: Messrs. Bishop and Goodrich therefore went on board, leaving Mr. Thurston at Towaihae to preach to the people there on the next day, which was the Sabbath, and afterwards join the vessel at the north point of the island, where they were going to take in hogs for Karaimoku, to whom the division of Kohala belonged, though the island in general was under the jurisdiction of Kuakini the governor.

THE HAWAIIAN SYSTEM OF GOVERNMENT

Their system of government is rather complex; and having occasionally mentioned several of its leading members, some further account of it will perhaps be acceptable.

The government of the Sandwich Islands is an absolute monarchy. The supreme authority is hereditary.

The rank of the principal and inferior chiefs, the offices of the priests, and other situations of honour, influence, and emolument, descend from father to son, and often continue through many generations in the same family, though the power of nomination to every situation of dignity and trust is vested in the king; and persons by merit, or royal favour, frequently rise from comparatively humble rank to the highest station in the islands, as in the instance of Karaimoku, sometimes called by foreigners, William Pitt. This individual, from being a chief of the third or fourth rank, has long been prime minister, in rank second only to the king, and having, in fact, the actual government of the whole of the Sandwich Islands.

BASIS OF RANK IN HAWAIIAN SOCIETY

Hereditary rank and authority are not confined to the male sex, but are inherited also by the females; and, according to tradition, several of the islands have been once or twice under the government of a queen.

Four distinct classes or ranks in society appear to exist among them. The highest rank includes the king, queens, and all the branches of the reigning family. It also includes the chief counsellor or minister of the king, who, though inferior by birth, is by office and authority superior to the queens and other members of the royal family.

SECOND RANK IN SOCIETY

The second rank includes the governors of the different islands, and also the chiefs of several large divisions or districts of land. Many of these are the descendants of the ancient families of Taraiopu, Kehekii, Teporiorani, and Taeo, who were the kings of Hawaii, Maui, Oahu, and Tauai, when the islands were visited by Captain Cook; they retained their power until subdued by Tamehameha. Several of them were either the favourite and warlike companions of that prince, or are descended from those who were; among whom may be classed Kuakini

300

the governor, Kaahumanu, Piia, Boki, Wahinepio, Kaikeova, and others.

The third rank is composed of those who hold districts or villages, and pay a regular rent for the land, cultivating it either by their own dependants and domestics, or letting it out in small allotments to tenants. This class is by far the most numerous body of chiefs in the island.

Among the principal may be ranked Kamakau at Kaavaroa, Maaro at Waiakea, Haa at Waipio, Auae at Wairuku, and Kahanaumaitai at Waititi. They are generally called Haku aina, proprietors of land. This rank would also include most of the priests under the former dispensation.

In the fourth rank may be included the small farmers who rent from ten to twenty or thirty acres of land, the mechanics, viz. canoe and house builders, fishermen, musicians, and dancers; indeed, all the labouring classes, those who attach themselves to some chief or farmer, and labour on his land for their food and clothing, as well as those who cultivate small portions of land for their own advantage.

Though the chiefs did not receive that abject and humiliating homage which is frequently paid to superiors in barbarous nations, where the government is arbitrary, yet the common people always manifested a degree of respect to the chiefs, according to their rank or office. This, toward the sacred chiefs, amounted almost to adoration, as they were on no occasion allowed to touch their persons, but prostrated themselves before them, and could not enter their houses without first receiving permission.

The behaviour among the chiefs was courteous, and manifested a desire to render themselves agreeable to each other; while all observed a degree of etiquette in their direct intercourse with the king. He is usually attended by a number of courtiers or favourites, called Punahele, who join in his amusements and occupations, except in affairs of government, with which they seem to have no concern.

When in a state of inebriation, all marks of distinction were lost, but at other times even these favourites conducted themselves towards their sovereign with great respect.

I have often seen Kapihe and Kekuanaoa, the two who accompanied Rihoriho to England, come into his presence, and wait without speaking, whatever their business might be, till he should address them, and then continue standing until requested by him to sit down.

In some respects the government resembles the ancient feudal system of the northern nations. During many periods of their history, not only the separate islands, but the larger divisions of some of them, have been under the government of independent kings or chiefs; and it does not appear that until the reign of Rihoriho, the late king, they were ever united under one sovereign.

The king is acknowledged in every island as the lord and proprietor of the soil by hereditary right, or the laws of conquest.

When Tamehameha had subdued the greater part of the islands, he distributed them among his favourite chiefs and warriors, on condition of their rendering him, not only military service, but a certain proportion of the produce of their lands.

This also appears to have been their ancient practice on similar occasions, as the hoopahora or papahora, division of land among the ranakira or victors, invariably followed the conquest of a district or island.

DIVISION OF AUTHORITY BY ISLANDS AND DISTRICTS

Every island is given by the king to some high chief, who is supreme governor in it, but is subject to the king, whose orders he is obliged to see executed, and to whom he pays a regular rent or tax, according to the size of the island, or the advantages it may possess.

Each island is separated into a number of permanent divisions, sometimes fifty or sixty miles in extent. In Hawaii there are six, Kohala, Kona, &c.

Each of the large divisions is governed by one or two chiefs, appointed by the king or by the governor, and approved by the former. These large divisions are divided into districts and villages, which sometimes extend five or six miles along the coast; at others, not more than half a mile.

A head man, nominated by the governor, usually presides over these villages, which are again subdivided into a number of small farms or plantations.

The names of these are generally significant; as Towahai, the waters broken, from a stream which runs through the district, and is divided near the sea; Kairua, two seas, from the waters of the bay being separated by a point of land, &c.

Although this is the usual manner in which the land is distributed, yet the king holds personally a number of districts in most of the islands, and several of the principal chiefs receive districts directly from the king and independent of the governor of the island in which they are situated.

PAYMENT OF RENT AND TAXES

The governor of the island pays over to the king annually, or half yearly, the rents or taxes required by the latter. These he receives from the chiefs under him, who generally pay in the produce of the soil. Sometimes the king requires a certain sum in Spanish dollars, at other times in sandal wood.

This, however, is only a modern regulation, introduced since they have become acquainted with the use of money, and the value of sandal wood.

The rent was originally paid in canoes, native cloth, mats, fishing-nets, hogs, dogs, and the produce of the soil, for the use of the king, and the numerous train of favourite chiefs and dependents by which he was surrounded, and who were daily fed from the provisions of his house.

For this tax the governor is responsible, and it is his business to see it conveyed to the king, or disposed of according to his order.

A second tax is laid on the districts by the governor, for himself.

The inhabitants of those portions of the island, however, which belong to other chiefs, although they furnish their share towards the king's revenue, are not called upon to support the governor of the island, but are expected to send a part of the produce of the land to their own chiefs.

After this has been paid, additional requisitions are made upon the poor people cultivating the land, by the petty chiefs of the districts and villages; these, however, are but trifling.

NO FIXED TAX

There is no standing rule for the amount of rents or taxes, but they are regulated entirely by the caprice or necessities of their rulers. Sometimes the poor people take a piece of land, on condition of cultivating a given portion for the chief, and the remainder for themselves, making a fresh agreement after every crop.

In addition to the above demands, the common people are in general obliged to labour, if required, part of two days out of seven, in cultivating farms, building houses, &c., for their landlord.

A time is usually appointed for receiving the rent, when the people repair to the governor's with what they have to pay. If the required amount is furnished they return, and, as they express it, (komo hou) enter again on their land. But if unable to pay the required sum, and their landlords are dissatisfied with the presents they have received, or think the tenants have neglected their farm, they are forbidden to return, and the land is offered to another. When, however, the produce brought is nearly equal to the required rent, and the chiefs think the occupants have exerted themselves to procure it, they remit the deficiency, and allow them to return.

Besides the stipulated rent, the people are expected to make a number of presents to their chiefs, usually the first fish in season, from their artificial ponds, or from the sea, if the land they occupy be near the coast, together with the first fruits of the trees and plantations.

CERTAIN LANDS FREE OF TAX

Though these are the usual conditions on which land is held, there are a number of districts, called aina ku pono, (land standing erect), held free from all rent and taxes, except a few presents, the value and frequency of which are entirely optional with the occupier.

These privileges of exemption from the established usage, were probably granted originally in reward for eminent services rendered the king, and they continue permanent, for should the king, on account of any crime, banish an individual holding one of these districts, the next occupant would enjoy all the privileges of his predecessor.

PEOPLE PASS WITH THE LAND

The common people are generally considered as attached to the soil, and are transferred with the land from one chief to another.

In recently conquered districts, they were formerly obliged to abide on the land which they cultivated, as slaves to the victors; at present, though they frequently remain through life the dependents or tenants of the same chief, such continuance appears on their part to be voluntary.

No chief can demand any service or supplies from those who occupy the land of another without his direction.

The king occasionally changes the tenants of a farm, without taking the proprietorship from the chief who may hold it more immediately from himself; and when the rents are insufficient to meet his wants, if any of the neighbouring farmers have potatoes and taro in their fields, he, or any high chief, will send their men, and hao (seize) the greater part of them, without making any remuneration to the injured parties.

HARBOR DUES BELONG TO KING

Besides the sums which the king receives from the land, and the monopoly of the trade in live stock and other supplies furnished to the shipping at several ports in the islands, the revenue is augmented by the harbour dues at Oahu.

Every vessel anchoring in the outer harbour pays sixty dollars, and eighty for entering the basin, or inner harbour.

Till within two or three years, it was only forty for one, and sixty for the other.

ORIGIN OF HARBOR DUES

The demand for these dues originated in their unprofitable voyage to Canton in 1816. The cargo of sandal wood was sold, but instead

304

of a return in cloths, silks, &c., the vessel came back nearly empty, and in debt. The king inquired the reason; when the captain, a very incompetent person for such a business, told him, that some of the money had been stolen; that so much was demanded for pilotage, coming to anchor, &c., as to leave nothing for the purpose of fitting the vessel for sea, which had occasioned the debt. "If," replied the king, "that be the case, we will have a pilot here, and every vessel that enters the harbour shall pay me for anchorage."

The pilotage, which is a dollar per foot for every vessel, both on entering and leaving the harbour, is divided between the government and the pilot.

OTHER FORMS OF TAXATION

Another singular method of taxing the people, is by building a new house for the king or some principal chief.

On the first day the king or chief enters it, the chiefs and the people of the neighbourhood repair thither, to pay their respects, and present their gifts.

Custom obliges every chief to appear on such occasions, or expose himself to the imputation of being disaffected; and no one is allowed to enter without a present of money. The amount is proportioned to their rank or the land they hold. Some chiefs, on such occasions, give sixty dollars, others ten or five, and some only one.

A short time before his embarkation for England, a large native house was built for Rihoriho, at Honoruru, in the Island of Oahu. During three days after the king went into it, the people came with their gifts. No individual, not even the queens, entered the house without presenting the king a sum of money; several gave upwards of fifty dollars; and we saw more than two thousand dollars received in one day. A similar tax was also levied by Kuakini, the governor at Kairua, when he first entered a handsome framed house, recently erected there.

TRADITIONAL CODE OF LAW

Until the establishment of a Christian mission among them, the Sandwich Islanders had no records, and consequently no written laws.

There is, however, a kind of traditionary code, a number of regulations which have been either promulgated by former kings, or followed by general consent, respecting the tenure of lands, right of property, personal security, and exchange or barter, which are well understood, and usually acted upon.

The portion of personal labour due from a tenant to his chief is fixed by custom, and a chief would be justified in banishing the person who should refuse it when required; on the other hand, were a chief to banish a man who had rendered it, and paid the stipulated rent, his

305

conduct would be contrary to their opinions of right, and if the man complained to the governor or the king, and no other charge was brought against him, he would most likely be reinstated.

The irrigation of their plantations is of great importance in most parts, and there is a law that the water shall be conducted over every plantation twice a week in general, and once a week during the dry season.

REVERSION OF LAND UPON DEATH OF OWNER

On the death of a chief, his lands revert to the king or the governor of the island. He may nominate his son, his wife, or any other person, to succeed to his districts, &c., but the appointment must be confirmed by the king or governor, before the individual can take possession.

This regulation, next to the tabu, is the most effectual mode of preserving the authority and influence of the king and chiefs.

PENALTY FOR MURDER AND THEFT

In cases of assault or murder, except when committed by their own chief, the family and friends of the injured party are, by common consent, justified in retaliating. When they are too weak to attack the offender, they seek the aid of their neighbours, appeal to the chief of the district, or the king, who seldom inflicts a heavier punishment than banishment even for murder, which, however, is a crime very rarely committed by the natives.

Theft among themselves is severely punished. Formerly, when a garden or house had been robbed, and the robbers were discovered, those whose goods had been stolen repaired to the house or plantation of the offenders, and hao (seized) whatever they could find. This regulation was so well established, that though the guilty party should be strongest, they would not dare to resist the retaliation; for in the event of their making any opposition, the people of a whole district would support those who were thus punishing the individuals by whom theft had been committed.

PENALTY FOR ROBBERY AND ADULTERY

When robbery had been committed on the property of a high chief, or to any great amount, the thief, in some of the islands, was frequently bound hand and foot, placed in an old decayed canoe, towed out to sea, and turned adrift. The canoe speedily filled, and the culprit, being bound, soon sunk beneath the waves.

Adultery among the highest ranks has been punished with death by decapitation.

LAW RELATING TO BARTER

In the transactions of barter among themselves, there are several regulations which they punctually observe. No bargain was considered binding till the articles were actually exchanged, and the respective owners expressed themselves satisfied. Afterwards there was no withdrawing, however injurious the bargain might be to either party.

There is, in the Sandwich Islands, no class of men, either peasants or mechanics, who are regularly employed as day-labourers, or who receive for their work a stipulated payment, excepting those employed by foreigners.

In hiring workmen to dig stone, burn lime, build a house or canoe, &c. it is a common practice among the natives themselves to make the bargain with a petty chief, who requires the labour of all his dependants in its fulfilment. They usually pay beforehand; and those who have received such remuneration are bound, when called upon, to perform their work, or have their property seized, and their plantations plundered.

These, and several similar regulations, are generally well received, and govern the conduct of the people. The king can dispense with any of them; but such conduct would be contrary to the established usage, and is seldom done.

WILL OF KING AND CHIEFS IS SUPREME

The will of the king, however, being the supreme law, the government is more or less arbitrary as his disposition is humane or vindictive and cruel.

His power extends, not only over the property, but over the liberty and lives of the people.

This power is delegated by him to the governors of the different islands, and by them again to the chiefs of the districts.

A chief takes the life of one of his own people for any offence he may commit, and no one thinks he has a right to interfere. But though the power of the chiefs is so absolute over their own people, it extends no further. A chief dare not for any offence punish a man belonging to another, but must complain to the chief on whose land the offender resides.

CONSTITUTION OF COURTS

The king is chief magistrate over the whole islands. The governors sustain the same office in the islands under their jurisdiction, and the chiefs of the districts are the arbitrators in all quarrels among their own people.

A man dissatisfied with the decisions of his chief, may appeal to the governor, and finally to the king.

They have no regular police, but the king has generally a number of chiefs in attendance, who, with the assistance of their own dependents, execute his orders. The governors and high chiefs have the same, and employ them in a similar manner when occasion requires.

307

The house or front yard of the king or governor is the usual court of justice, and it is sometimes quite a court of equity. Judgment is seldom given till both parties are heard face to face.

They have several ordeals for trying those accused of different crimes. One of the most singular is the wai haruru, shaking water. A large calabash or wooden dish of water is placed in the midst of a circle, on one side of which the accused party is seated. A prayer is offered by the priest; and the suspected individuals are required, one by one, to hold both hands, with the fingers spread out, over the dish, while the priest or the chief looks steadfastly at the face of the water; and it is said, that when the person, who has committed the crime, spreads his hands over the vessel, the water trembles. Probably conscious guilt, and superstitious dread, may make the hands of the culprit shake, and occasion the tremulous appearance of the water in which they are reflected.

No unnecessary delays take place in the redress of grievances, or the administration of justice.

I was once sitting with Karaimoku, when a poor woman came to complain of the chief of her district, who, she said, had kept the water running through his own plantation for several days, while the potatoes and taro in her garden were parched up with drought.

After making a few inquiries, he called Kaiakoiri, one of his favourite chiefs, and said, "Go with this woman; and, if the chief has kept back the water, open the channels, and let it flow over her field immediately." The chief girded up his maro, and, followed by the woman, set off for the district in which she resided.

No lawyers are employed to conduct their public trials; every man advocates his own cause, usually sitting cross-legged before the judge; and I have often been pleased with the address the different parties have displayed in exhibiting or enforcing their respective claims.

There is no national council, neither have the people any voice in the proceedings of government. But the king, though accountable to no one for the measures he adopts, seldom acts, in any affair of importance, without the advice of his confidential chiefs. These counsellors are in no degree responsible for the advice they give, nor liable to suffer from any conduct the king may pursue. He, however, always pays a deference to their opinion, and seldom acts in opposition to their wishes.

In all matters of importance, it is customary to summon the governors and principal chiefs of the several islands to a national council, when the subject is freely discussed. Their deliberations are generally conducted with great privacy, and seldom known among the people till finally arranged, when they are promulgated throughout the island by the king's heralds or messengers.

The king sends his orders directly to the governor of the island, or principal chief of the district. Formerly a courier bore a verbal message; now he carries a written despatch.

The office of messenger, as well as that of herald, is hereditary, and considered honourable, as those who sustain it must necessarily have possessed the confidence of the king and chiefs.

PUBLIC ASSEMBLIES ON NATIONAL AFFAIRS

Occasionally they hold public meetings for discussing national affairs. These are interesting assemblies, particularly when hostile chiefs, or the agents of opposite parties, meet; national orators, and counsellors, whose office is also hereditary, are then employed. In general, however, these meetings are convened only for the purpose of promulgating what has been previously arranged between the king and chiefs.

STATUS OF HAWAIIAN SYSTEM OF GOVERNMENT

The Hawaiian system of government—whether derived from the country whence the first settlers emigrated, or established by warlike chieftains in a subsequent period of their history, as an expedient to secure conquests, to command the services of their tenants on occasions of war, and to perpetuate the influence which military prowess or success in the first instance had given them, exhibits, in its decided monarchical character, the hereditary descent of rank and office, and other distinguishing features, considerable advancement from a state of barbarism, and warrants the conclusion that they have been an organized community for many generations.

But whatever antiquity their system may possess, they have made but little progress in the art of good government.

PEOPLE CONSIDERED AS PROPERTY OF CHIEFS

The well-being of the subject seems to have been but rarely regarded by the rulers, who appear to have considered the lower orders in general as a kind of property, to be employed only in promoting the interests of their superiors; and the ardent love of wealth, which an acquaintance with the productions of foreign countries has excited in most of the chiefs, has not improved the condition of the people.

PEOPLE ABJECTLY SUBJECT TO CHIEFS

Industry receives no encouragement; and even those whom natural energy of character would induce to cultivate a larger portion of land

309

than was absolutely necessary for their bare subsistence, are deterred from the attempt by the apprehension of thereby exposing themselves to the rapacity òf avaricious or necessitous chiefs.

Nothing can be more detrimental to the true interest of the chiefs, and the civilization and happiness of the people, than the abject dependence of the latter, the uncertain tenure of lands, the insecurity of personal property, the exactions of the chiefs, and the restrictions on trade with the shipping, which they impose.

As the nation in general becomes enlightened, it is to be presumed that the policy of the rulers will be more liberal, and the general prosperity of the islands proportionably advanced.

RETURN OF THURSTON AND OTHERS TO HONOLULU

On the 31st, Mr. Thurston preached twice at Towaihae to attentive congregations, and with the labours of the day, closed a month of toil and interest greater than any he had before spent in the Sandwich Islands. In the retrospect, he could not but hope some good would result to the people.

Early on the 1st of September, Mr. Thurston left Towaihae in a canoe furnished by Mr. Young, and at eight in the forenoon reached the place where the Nio was lying at anchor, on board of which he joined Messrs. Goodrich and Bishop. Soon after four in the afternoon they weighed anchor and made sail. When they left Hawaii, the master intended touching at Maui; but contrary winds obliged them to shape their course towards Oahu, where they safely arrived late in the evening of the 3d, and had the satisfaction of finding the mission family in the enjoyment of comfortable health.

The time which I spent at Kairua was chiefly occupied in conversation with the governor on the history and traditions of the island; the advantages of instruction; and the blessings which the general adoption of Christianity would confer on the people. On this latter subject, the governor uniformly expressed his conviction of its utility; and said, he had therefore sent a messenger round among the people, requesting them to renounce their former evil practices, and keep the Sabbath according to the direction of the word of God.

310

CHAPTER XV

HEIAU OF AHUENA CONVERTED INTO A FORT

Adjacent to the governor's house stand the ruins of Ahuena, an ancient heiau, where the war-god was often kept, and human sacrifices offered. Since the abolition of idolatry, the governor has converted it into a fort, has widened the stone wall next the sea, and placed upon it a number of cannon.

The idols are all destroyed, excepting three, which are planted on the wall, one at each end, and the other in the centre, where they stand like sentinels amidst the guns, as if designed by their frightful appearance to terrify an enemy.

DESCRIPTION OF HAWAIIAN IDOLS

On the 29th, I visited the ruins, and took a sketch of one of the idols, which stood sixteen feet above the wall, was upwards of three feet in breadth, and had been carved out of a single tree.

The above may be considered as a tolerable specimen of the greater part of Hawaiian idols. The head has generally a most horrid appearance, the mouth being large and usually extended wide, exhibiting a row of large teeth, resembling in no small degree the cogs in the wheel of an engine, and adapted to excite terror rather than inspire confidence in the beholder. Some of their idols were of stone, and many were constructed with a kind of wicker-work covered with red feathers.

NATIVE TRADITIONS OF ORIGIN OF HAWAIIANS

In the evening our conversation at the governor's turned on the origin of the people of Hawaii, and the other islands of the Pacific, a topic which often engaged our attention, and respecting which, in the various inquiries we made, we often had occasion to regret that the traditions of the natives furnished such scanty information, on a subject so interesting and important. This portion, however, though small, and surrounded by an incredible mass of fiction, is still worth preserving.

The general opinions entertained by the natives themselves, relative to their origin, are, either that the first inhabitants were created on the islands, descended from the gods, by whom they were first inhabited; or, that they came from a country which they called Tahiti.

Many, as was the case with the chiefs at Maui, and also the governor

311

at this place suppose that, according to the accounts of the priests of Tane, Tanaroa, and other gods, the first man was made by Haumea, a female deity. We have not, however, met with any who pretend to know of what material he was formed.

Others, again, suppose the chiefs to have descended from Akea, who appears to have been the connecting link between the gods and the men; but this supposes the chiefs and the common people to have been derived from different sources.

The accounts they have of their ancestors having arrived in a canoe from Tahiti, are far more general and popular among the people.

When some of our party were at Towaihae, the subject was discussed. Mr. Young said, among the many traditionary accounts of the origin of the island and its inhabitants, one was, that in former times, when there was nothing but sea, an immense bird settled on the water, and laid an egg, which soon bursting produced the island of Hawaii. Shortly after this, a man and woman, with a hog, a dog, and a pair of fowls, arrived in a canoe from the Society Islands, took up their abode on the eastern shores, and were the progenitors of the present inhabitants.

Another account prevalent among the natives of Oahu, states, that a number of persons arrived in a canoe from Tahiti, and perceiving the Sandwich Islands were fertile, and inhabited only by gods or spirits, took up their abode on one of them, having asked permission of the gods, and presented an offering, which rendered them propitious to their settlement.

HAWAIIANS PROBABLY CAME FROM TAHITI

Though these accounts do not prove that the Sandwich Islanders came originally from the Georgian Islands, they afford a strong presumption in favour of such an opinion.

Tahiti is the name of the principal island in the group, called by Captain Cook the Georgian Islands. It is the Otaheite of Cook; the Taiti of Bougainville; and the Taheitee, or Tahitee, of Forster.

In the language of the Georgian and Society Islands, the word tahiti also signifies to pull up or take out of the ground, as herbs or trees are taken up with a view to transplantation, and to select or extract passages from a book or language, to be translated into another. Hence a book of scripture extracts is called, words tahitihea.

HAWAIIAN MEANING OF "TAHITI"

In the language of the Sandwich Islands, we do not know that the word is ever used in the latter sense, and very rarely in the former. It is generally employed to denote any foreign country, and seems equivalent to the English word abroad, as applied to parts beyond the sea. But though this is the signification of the word among the Sandwich Islanders at the present time, it is probable that it was primarily used to designate the whole of the southern group, or the principal island among them; and it may lead us to infer, either that Tahiti, and

An Idol on the Wall of a Heiau at Kailua, which
was Converted into a Fort by Governor Kuakini.

the Georgian and Society Islands, were all the foreign countries the Hawaiians were acquainted with, or that they considered the Marquesan Islands contiguous, and politically connected with them, and that these being the only foreign countries originally known to them, they have applied the term to every other part with which they have subsequently become acquainted.

DIFFERENCES BETWEEN INHABITANTS OF ISLANDS OF PACIFIC

It is an opinion generally received, that the various tribes inhabiting the islands of the Pacific, have an Asiatic, and probably a Malayan

313

origin. Applied to a great part of them, this opinion is supported by a variety of facts; but with respect to those groups with which we are acquainted, additional evidence appears necessary to confirm such a conclusion.

The natives of the eastern part of New Holland, and the inter-tropical islands within thirty degrees east, including New Caledonia, the New Hebrides, and the Fijis, appear to be one nation, and in all probability came originally from the Asiatic islands, to the northward, as their skin is black, and their hair woolly or crisped, like the inhabitants of the mountainous parts of several of the Asiatic islands.

But the inhabitants of all the islands to the east of the Fijis, including the Friendly Islands and New Zealand, though they have many characteristics in common with these, have a number essentially distinct.

The natives of Chatham Island and New Zealand, in the south; the Sandwich Islands, in the north; the Friendly Islands, in the west; and all the intermediate islands, as far as Easter Island, in the east, are one people. Their mythology, traditions, manners and customs, language, and physical appearance, in their main features, are, so far as we have had an opportunity of becoming acquainted with them, identically the same, yet differing in many respects from those on the islands to the westward of Tongatabu.

The dress of the Fijians, &c, is not the same as that of the natives of New Zealand, Tahiti, and the other islands; they do not appear to wear the cloak or the tiputa.

In war they throw long spears to a considerable distance, and use the bow and arrow, which the others only employ in their amusements.

The difference in their physical character is greater; the dark complexion, woolly hair, and slender make, indicate them to be a different people.

RESEMBLANCE OF PACIFIC ISLANDERS TO AMERICAN INDIANS

Various points of resemblance might be shewn between the aborigines of America and the natives of the eastern islands of the Pacific, in their modes of war, instruments, gymnastic games, rafts or canoes, treatment of their children, dressing their hair, feather head-dresses of the chiefs, girdles, and particularly the tiputa of the latter, which, in shape and use, exactly resembles the poncho of the Peruvians, but it would lead too far at this time.

LONG VOYAGES IN CANOES

We have every reason to believe the canoes of the natives were larger formerly than they are now, and yet we have known them make several long voyages, being sometimes a fortnight or three weeks at sea.

314

In the year 1821, a large canoe arrived at Maurua from Rurutu, and as it passed to the north of Huahine, must have sailed 500 miles, even supposing it had made a direct course.

Since that time, a boat from Tahiti reached one of the islands near Mangea, almost 600 miles, in a direct course, but probably not half the distance actually sailed by the natives in the boat.

Canoes are frequently arriving at Tahiti from some of the eastern islands. Two came recently from Hao, an island of which the Tahitians were before entirely ignorant.

INFLUENCE OF TRADE WINDS ON EMIGRATION

Several canoes passing among the islands, have been blown out to sea, and have never returned; and the native teachers sent from the Society Islands to the various islands lying between them and the Friendly Islands, have met among them several of their countrymen. These voyages have always been in a westerly direction. We have never heard of one to the eastward.

The trade-winds blowing within the tropics from the eastward more than three-fourths of the year, and their canoes not being adapted to sail close to the wind, render it difficult for the natives of the leeward islands to pass to windward. They never attempt it, except when the wind is somewhat westerly, which is but seldom, while it often blows steadily from the east for weeks together.

These circumstances seem to favour the conjecture that the inhabitants of the islands west of Tongatabu have an Asiatic origin entirely; but that the natives of the eastern islands may be a mixed race, who have emigrated from the American continent, and from the Asiatic islands; that the proximity of the Friendly and Fiji islands may have given both a variety of words and usages in common, while the people to which the former belong have remained in many respects distinct.

The nation inhabiting the eastern part of the Pacific has spread itself over an immense tract of ocean, extending upwards of seventy degrees north and south from New Zealand and Chatham Island to the Sandwich group, and between sixty and seventy degrees east and west from Tongatabu to Easter Island. This last is not farther from the islands adjacent to the continent than some of these groups are from any other inhabited island.

The Sandwich Islands are above twenty degrees from the Marquesas, and thirty-six from Tahiti, yet inhabited by the same race of people.

ADVANCE OF WRITING AMONG HAWAIIANS

The day after the conversation took place which led to the above remarks, the pilot-boat arrived at Kairua, on her way to Maui. On first

315

coming to anchor, Kahiori, the master, said he should sail in the evening; but when I told him I would go with him if he would wait till the Sabbath was over, he cheerfully agreed to do so. By him the governor received a note on business, written by Kamakau, the interesting chief of Kaavaroa, which, after he had read it, he shewed me, saying, he admired the diligence and perseverance of Kamakau, who, with but little instruction, had learned to write very well. "This letter writing," added the governor, "is a very good thing."

It also appears to them a most surprising art, which, till they saw what had been acquired by the natives of the southern islands, they imagined could never be attained by persons in their circumstances.

Supposing it beyond the powers of man to invent the plan of communicating words by marks on paper, they have sometimes asked us, if, in the first instance, the knowledge of it were not communicated to mankind by God himself.

HAWAIIAN MARRIAGE CUSTOMS

In the governor's family is an interesting girl, who is called his daughter, and has been spoken of as the future consort of the young prince Kauikeouli, instead of Nahienaena his sister.

Marriage contracts in the Sandwich Islands are usually concluded by the parents or relations of both parties, or by the man and the parents or friends of the woman.

We are not aware that the parents of the woman receive any thing from the husband, or give any dowry with the wife. Their ceremonies on the occasion are very few, and chiefly consist in the bridegroom's casting a piece of tapa or native cloth over the bride, in the presence of her parents or relations. Feasting is general, and the friends of both parties contribute towards furnishing the entertainment.

The marriage tie is loose, and the husband can dismiss his wife on any occasion.

MORE MALES THAN FEMALES DUE TO INFANTICIDE

The number of males is much greater than that of females in all the islands, in consequence of the girls being more frequently destroyed in infancy, as less useful than the males for purposes of war, fishing, &c. We do not know the exact proportion here; but in the Society Islands, in all our early schools, the proportion of girls to boys was as three to four, or four to five, though since the abolition of infanticide the numbers are equal.

Polygamy is allowed among all ranks, but practised only by the chiefs, whose means enable them to maintain a plurality of wives.

Among the higher ranks, marriage seems to be conducted on prin-

316

ciples of political expediency, with a view to strengthen alliances and family influence; and among the reigning family, brothers and sisters marry.

INTER-MARRIAGE OF RELATIVES

This custom, so revolting to every idea of moral propriety, that the mind is shocked at the thought of its existence, appears to have been long in use; and very recently a marriage was proposed at Maui, between the young prince and princess, both children of the same parents; a council of chiefs was held on the subject, and all were favourable.

The opinion of the missionaries there was asked. The chiefs assigned as a reason, that being the highest chiefs in the islands, they could not marry any others who were their equals, and ought not to form alliances with inferiors, as it was desirable that the supreme rank they held should descend to their posterity.

They were told that such marriages were forbidden in the word of God, were held in abhorence by all civilized and Christian nations, and had seldom been known to leave any descendants to wear the honour or sustain the rank the contracting parties desired thus to perpetuate.

MARRIAGE OF RELATIVES CHILDLESS

Several of the chiefs present made no profession of Christianity, and consequently were uninfluenced by some of the remarks, but the concluding observation appeared of importance to them all.

They said they thought there was some truth in it; that the late king Tamehameha, father of Rihoriho, had several wives, who were his near relations, and even his daughter-in-law, yet left no children, except those of whom Keopuolani was the mother, and who, though a sacred chief of higher rank than her husband, was the granddaughter of a princess of another island, and distantly connected with his family, and that the same was the case with Rihoriho.

The marriage was postponed; and it appears the opinion of the chiefs in general, that it ought not to take place.

The individuals themselves are entirely passive in the affair; and we view it as a happy circumstance, subversive of an evil custom, and tending to produce moral feelings highly advantageous, and illustrative of the collateral advantages arising from the influence of Christian missionaries.

FOREIGNERS IN HAWAII PRIOR TO CAPTAIN COOK

An interesting conversation took place this evening, relative to the first visits the islanders received from foreigners.

The possession of pieces of iron, particularly one supposed to be the point of a broad sword, by the natives of Tauai (Atooi), when discov-

317

ered by Captain Cook, induced some of his companions to think they were not the first European visitors to the islands. We have endeavoured to ascertain, by inquiring of the most intelligent of the natives, whether or no this was the fact.

They have three accounts of foreigners arriving at Hawaii prior to Captain Cook. The first was the priest, Paao, who landed at Kohala, and to whom the priests of that neighbourhood traced their genealogy until very recently. Of this priest some account is given in a preceding chapter.

WHITE MEN ON HAWAII

The second account states, that during the lifetime of Opiri, the son of Paao, a number of foreigners (white men) arrived at Hawaii, landed somewhere in the south-west part of the island, and repaired to the mountains, where they took up their abode. The natives regarded them with a superstitious curiosity and dread, and knew not whether to consider them as gods or men.

Opiri was sent for by the king of that part of the island where they were residing, and consulted as to the conduct to be observed towards them.

According to his advice, a large present of provisions was cooked and carried to them. Opiri led the procession, accompanied by several men, each carrying a bamboo cane, with a piece of white native cloth tied to the end of it.

When the strangers saw them approaching their retreat, they came out to meet them. The natives placed the baked pigs and potatoes, &c. on the grass, fixed their white banners in the ground, and then retreated a few paces. The foreigners approached. Opiri addressed them. They answered, received the presents, and afterwards conversed with the people through the medium of Opiri. The facility with which they could communicate their thoughts by means of Opiri, the governor said, was attributed to the supposed influence of Opiri with his gods.

The foreigners they imagined were supernatural beings, and as such were treated with every possible mark of respect.

After remaining some time on the island, they returned to their own country.

No account is preserved of the kind of vessel in which they arrived or departed.

The name of the principal person among them was Manahini; and it is a singular fact, that in the Marquesan, Society, and Sandwich Islands, the term manahini is still employed to designate a stranger, visitor, or guest.

318

The third account is much more recent and precise, though the period at which it took place is uncertain.

It states that a number of years after the departure of Manahini-ma (Manahini and his party), in the reign of Kahoukapu, king at Kaavaroa, seven foreigners arrived at Kearake'kua bay, the spot were Captain Cook subsequently landed. They came in a painted boat, with an awning or canopy over the stern, but without mast or sails. They were all dressed; the colour of their clothes was white or yellow, and one of them wore a pahi, long knife, the name by which they still call a sword, at his side, and had a feather in his hat. The natives received them kindly. They married native women, were made chiefs, proved themselves warriors, and ultimately became very powerful in the island of Hawaii, which, it is said, was for some time governed by them.

"EHUS," SUPPOSED DESCENDANTS OF FOREIGNERS

There are in the Sandwich Islands a number of persons distinguished by a lighter colour in their skin, and corresponding brown curly hair, called ehu, who are, by all the natives of the islands, considered as the descendants of these foreigners, who acknowledge themselves to be such, and esteem their origin by no means dishonourable.

OTHER TRADITIONS OF FOREIGN ARRIVALS

Another party is said to have afterwards arrived at the same place, but the accounts the natives give of their landing are not very distinct; and we feel undecided whether there were two distinct parties, or only two different accounts of the same event.

In addition to these, they have a tradition of some white men, called Kea, who lived wild in the mountains, occasionally coming down to the streams, or towards the sea-shore, in an evening, much to the terror of the natives, particularly the females.

We have heard from one of the chiefs of Hawaii, that there is a tradition of a ship having touched at the island of Maui prior to the arrival of Captain Cook; but, with the exception of this chief, all the natives we have conversed with on the subject, and we have conversed with many, declare that they had no idea of a ship before Captain Cook was seen off Tauai. The ship they called motu, an island, probably supposing it was an island, with all its inhabitants.

Marvellous reports respecting the ships and people were circulated through the islands, between the first discovery of Tauai and the return of the vessels from the N. W. coast of America. Aa mo (skin of lizard's egg), a native of Tauai, who was on board one of the ships, procured

319

a piece of canvas, about a yard and a half long, which Tiha, king of Tauai, sent as a present to Poriorani, king of Oahu. He gave it to his queen Opuhani, by whom it was worn on the most conspicuous part of her dress in a public procession, and attracted more attention than any thing else. The piece of cloth was called Aa mo, after the man who had the honour of bringing it from the ships.

The most unaccountable circumstance connected with the priest Paao, is his arriving alone, though he might be the only survivor of his party. If such a person ever did arrive, we should think he was a Roman Catholic priest, and that reported gods were an image and a crucifix.

The different parties that subsequently arrived were probably, if any inference may be drawn from the accounts of the natives, survivors of the crew of some Spanish ship wrecked in the neighbourhood, perhaps on the numerous reefs to the north-west; or they might have been culprits committed by their countrymen to the mercy of the waves.

The circumstance of the first party leaving the island in the same boat in which they arrived, would lead us to suppose they had been wrecked, and had escaped in their boat, or had constructed a bark out of the wreck of their ship, as has subsequently been the case with two vessels wrecked in the vicinity of these islands.

It is possible that one or other of the islands might have been seen by some Spanish ship passing between Acapulco and Manila; but it is not probable that they were ever visited by any of these ships.

An event so interesting to the people would not have been left out of their traditions, which contain many things much less important; and, had the Spaniards discovered them, however jealous they might be of such a discovery becoming known to other nations, that jealousy would not have prevented their availing themselves of the facilities which the islands afforded for refitting or recruiting their vessels, which must frequently have been most desirable during the period their ships were accustomed to traverse these seas.

These accounts, but particularly the latter, are generally known, and have been related by different persons at distant places. All agree respecting the boat, clothing, sword, &c. of the party who arrived at Kearake'kua.

Among others, the late king Rihoriho gave us a detailed account of their landing, &c. only a short time before he embarked for England. We feel but little doubt of the fact; but the country whence they came, the place whither they were bound, the occasion of their visit, and a variety of interesting particulars connected therewith, will probably remain undiscovered.

320

The 31st was the Sabbath. The stillness of every thing around, the decent apparel of those who were seen passing and repassing, together with the numbers of canoes all drawn up on the beach, under the shade of the cocoa-nut or kou trees, combined to mark the return of the la tabu, or sacred day.

An unusual number attended family prayers at the governor's house in the morning; and at half-past ten the bell was rung for public worship. About 800 people assembled under the ranai, and I preached to them from Heb. xi. 7. And after a succinct account of the deluge, I endeavoured to exhibit the advantages of faith, and the consequences of wickedness and unbelief, as illustrated in the salvation of Noah, and the destruction of the rest of mankind.

HAWAIIAN TRADITION OF THE FLOOD

After the conclusion of the service, several persons present requested me to remain till they had made some inquiries respecting the deluge, Noah, &c.

They said they were informed by their fathers, that all the land had once been overflowed by the sea, except a small peak on the top of Mouna-Kea, where two human beings were preserved from the destruction that overtook the rest, but they said they had never before heard of a ship, or of Noah, having always been accustomed to call it the kai a Kahinarii (sea of Kahinarii). After conversing with them some time, I returned to the governor's.

DISCUSSION WITH GOVERNOR CONCERNING THE FLOOD

The afternoon was principally employed in conversation with him on the flood, and the repeopling of the earth by the descendants of Noah.

The governor seemed to doubt whether it were possible that the Hawaiians could be the descendants of Noah; but said, he thought their progenitors must have been created on the islands.

I told him the account in the bible had every evidence that could be wished to support it; referred him to his own traditions, not only of Hawaii's having been peopled by persons who came in canoes from a foreign country, but of their having in their turn visited other islands, and planted colonies, as in the days of Kamapiikai; the superiority of their war canoes in former days; the resemblance in manners, customs, traditions, and language, between themselves and other islanders in the Pacific, many thousand miles distant.

The longevity of mankind in the days of Noah, also surprised him. Comparing it with the period of human life at the present time, he said, "By and by men will not live more than forty years."

321

At half-past four in the afternoon the bell rang again, and the people collected in numbers about equal to those who attended in the morning. I preached to them from the words, "Be not weary in well-doing, for in due season ye shall reap, if ye faint not." Their attention was encouraging.

Numbers thronged the governor's house at evening worship. The conversation afterwards turned upon the identity of the body at the resurrection, and the reward of the righteous in heaven. The governor asked if people would know each other in heaven; and when answered in the affirmative, said, he thought Christian relations would be very happy when they met there.

Some who were present asked, "If there is no eating and drinking, or wearing of clothes, in heaven, wherein does its goodness consist?" This was a natural question for a Hawaiian to ask, who never had an idea of happiness except in the gratification of his natural appetites and feelings.

In answer to the question, they were, however, informed, that the joys of heaven were intellectual and spiritual, and would infinitely exceed, both in their nature and duration, every earthly enjoyment.

At a late hour I took leave of the governor and his family, thanking him, at the same time, for the hospitable entertainment we had received, and the great facilities he had afforded for accomplishing the objects of our visit.

TRIP FROM KAILUA TO KAWAIHAE AND LAHAINA

About three o'clock in the morning, being awoke by the shouts of the men who were heaving up the anchor of the pilot-boat, I repaired on board, and immediately afterwards we sailed with a gentle breeze blowing from the land. The wind was light and baffling, and it was noon before we reached Towaihae, where I learned with disappointment that the Nio had sailed to Oahu. On landing, I was welcomed by Mr. Young, with whom I remained till the pilot-boat was ready to sail for Lahaina.

Late in the evening of the 2nd of September, after preaching to the people of the place at Mr. Young's house, I went again on board the pilot-boat, but found her so full of sandal wood, that there was not room for any person below, while the decks were crowded with natives. The weather was unfavourable for getting under way till nearly daylight; and every person on board was completely drenched by the heavy rain that fell during the night.

During the forenoon of the 3d, we drifted slowly to the northward, and about noon took in 800 dried fish, after which we made sail for Maui. The weather was warm, the wind light; and all on board being obliged to keep on deck, without any screen or shade from the scorching rays of a vertical sun, the situation was very uncomfortable. At three p. m. we took the channel breeze, which soon wafted us across to the S. E. part of Maui.

As the shores of Hawaii receded from my view, a variety of reflections insensibly arose in my mind. The tour which, in the society of my companions, I had made, had been replete with interest. The varied and sublime phenomena of nature had elevated our conceptions of "nature's God"; the manners and customs of the inhabitants had increased our interest in their welfare; while their superstition, moral degradation, ignorance, and vice, had called forth our sincerest commiseration.

We had made known the nature and consequences of sin; spoken of the love of God; and had exhibited the Lord Jesus Christ as the only Saviour to the multitudes who had never before heard his name, or been directed to worship the holy and living God, and who would probably never hear these truths again. We cherish the hope, that, under the divine blessing, lasting good will result, even from this transient visit.

Many of the individuals we have met on these occasions, we shall in all probability meet no more till the morning of the resurrection. May we meet them then on the right hand of the Son of God!

NATIVES SWIM ASHORE AT LAHAINA

At sun-set we arrived off Molokai, but were shortly after becalmed. The current, however, was in our favour through the night, and at daylight on the 4th we found ourselves off the east end of the district of Lahaina, and about a mile distant from the shore.

Many of the natives jumped into the sea, and swam to the beach, holding their clothes above their heads with one hand, and swimming with the other.

About ten a. m. a canoe came alongside, in which I went on shore, where I was welcomed by the mission family, and by Mr. Bingham, who was there on a visit. Soon after I had landed, Karaimoku arrived from Oahu, by whom I learned that Mrs. Ellis, though very ill, was better than she had been at some periods since my departure.

CHIEFS PRAY FOR RECOVERY OF KEOPUOLANI

I waited on Keopuolani, the king's mother, whom I found ill; Karaimoku, Kaahumanu, Kalakua, and several other chiefs, were reclining around her, weeping. After some time, Karaimoku proposed that they should unitedly pray for her recovery, and his proposal was acceded to.

323

At four p. m. a corpse was brought to the place of worship, and, previously to its being interred, I gave an exhortation to a multitude of people.

Towards evening, I visited the governor of the island, and also the king, who was then at Maui. The subsequent voyage of the latter to Great Britain, accompanied by his queen, and the melancholy event which terminated their lives while in London, excited considerable interest, and will probably be considered sufficient apology for a short account of them, although the event took place after my visit to Maui at this time.

BIOGRAPHY OF KAMEHAMEHA II

The late king of the Sandwich Islands was the son of Tamehameha, former king, and Keopuolani, daughter of Kauikeouli and Kakuiapoiwa. He was born in the eastern part of Hawaii, in the year 1795 or 1796.

The name by which he was generally known was Rihoriho, which was only a contraction of Kalaninuirihoriho, literally, the heaven's great black—from Ka lani, the heavens, nui, great, and rihoriho, applied to any thing burnt to blackness.

On public occasions, he was sometimes called Tamehameha, after his father, though names are not always hereditary. Besides these, he had a variety of other names, the most common of which was Iolani. The word lani, heaven or sky, formed a component part in the name of most chiefs of distinction. The following is a facsimile of the official signature of the late king.

SIGNATURE OF KAMEHAMEHA II.

The early habits of Rihoriho did not warrant any great expectations. His natural disposition was frank, and humane. The natives always spoke of him as good-natured, except when he was under the influence of ardent spirits; his manners were perfectly free, at the same time dignified, and always agreeable to those who were about him.

His mind was naturally inquisitive. The questions he usually presented to foreigners were by no means trifling; and his memory was retentive.

KAMEHAMEHA II A WELL-INFORMED MAN

His general knowledge of the world was much greater than could have been expected. I have heard him entertain a party of chiefs for

324

hours together, with accounts of different parts of the earth, describing the extensive lakes, the mountains, and mines of North and South America; the elephants and inhabitants of India; the houses, manufactures, &c. of England, with no small accuracy, considering he had never seen them.

He had a great thirst for knowledge, and was diligent in his studies. I recollect his remarking one day, when he opened his writing desk, that he expected more advantage from that desk than from a fine brig belonging to him, lying at anchor opposite the house in which we were sitting.

KAMEHAMEHA II A STUDIOUS MAN

Mr. Bingham and myself were his daily teachers, and have often been surprised at his unwearied perseverance. I have sat beside him at his desk sometimes from nine or ten o'clock in the morning, till nearly sun-set, during which period his pen or his book has not been out of his hand more than three-quarters of an hour, while he was at dinner.

We do not know that Christianity exerted any decisive influence on his heart. He was willing to receive the missionaries on their first arrival—availed himself of their knowledge to increase his own—and, during the latter years of his life, was decidedly favourable to their object; declared his conviction of the truth of Christianity; attended public worship himself on the Sabbath, and recommended the same to his people.

ANALYSIS OF CHARACTER OF KAMEHAMEHA II

His moral character was not marked by that cruelty, rapacity, and insensibility to the sufferings of the people, which frequently distinguish the arbitrary chiefs of uncivilized nations.

He appears in general to have been kind; and, in several places on our tour, the mothers shewed us their children, and told us, that when Rihoriho passed that way, he had kissed them—a condescension they seemed to think much of, and which they will probably remember to the end of their days.

But though generous in his disposition, and humane in his conduct toward his subjects, he was addicted to intoxication; whether from natural inclination, or the influence and example of others, is not now to be determined; frequently, to my own knowledge, it has been entirely from the latter.

MOTIVES FOR VISITING ENGLAND

Had he in early life been privileged to associate with individuals whose conduct and principles were favourable to virtue and religion, there is every reason to suppose his moral character, with respect at

325

least to this vice, would have been as irreproachable as his mental habits were commendable. But, alas for him! it was quite the reverse.

Though not distinguished by the ardour and strength of character so conspicuous in his father, he possessed both decision and enterprise: the abolition of the national idolatry was a striking instance of the former; and his voyage to England, of the latter.

The motives by which he was induced to undertake a voyage so long and hazardous were highly commendable. They were—a desire to see, for himself, countries of which he had heard such various and interesting accounts—a wish to have a personal interview with his majesty, the king of Great Britain, or the chief members of the British government, for the purpose of confirming the cession of the Sandwich Islands, and placing himself and his dominions under British protection.

It was also his intention to make himself acquainted with the tenor and forms of administering justice in the courts of law—the principles of commerce—and other subjects, important to the welfare of the islands.

The melancholy death of the king and queen, which took place shortly after their arrival in England, not only prevented the full accomplishment of these desirable objects, but awakened very generally a degree of apprehension that the people of the islands, unacquainted with the true circumstances of their death, would be led to suppose they had been neglected, unkindly treated, or even poisoned in revenge of the death of Captain Cook, and that the feelings of friendship with which they had been accustomed to regard the people of England, might be followed by enmity or distrust.

TREATMENT OF KAMEHAMEHA II IN ENGLAND

The fears of those who felt interested in the welfare of the Hawaiians, though natural, were groundless. The British government had entertained the young ruler of the Sandwich Islands, his consort and attendants, with its accustomed hospitality; and when they were attacked by diseases incident to a northern climate, but unknown in their native islands, every attention that humanity could suggest, and every alleviation that the first medical skill in London could afford, was most promptly rendered.

After their decease, the highest respect was paid to their remains, and, in honourable regard to the feelings of the nation who had suffered this painful bereavement, a British frigate, under the command of Captain Lord Byron, was appointed to convey to the Sandwich Islands the bodies of the king and queen, that their sorrowing people might have the mournful satisfaction of depositing their ashes among the tombs of their ancestors.

326

By the return of a highly esteemed missionary friend, Rev. C. S. Stewart, I have learned that the Blonde reached the islands in the month of May, 1825 : the natives were in some degree prepared for the arrival, by the intelligence of the death of their king and queen, which they had received about two months before from Valparaiso.

RETURN TO HAWAII OF BODIES OF KING AND QUEEN

Shortly after the vessel having the remains of the king and queen on board had anchored off Oahu, Boki, the principal chief, who had accompanied the king to England, attended by those of his countrymen who had also returned, proceeded on shore: on landing, he was met by his elder brother Kairaimoku, and other distinguished chiefs, and after the first emotions of joy at meeting again, and sorrow on account of the loss all had sustained, were somewhat abated, the survivors and their friends walked in solemn and mournful procession to the place of worship, where thanksgivings were presented to God, for the merciful preservation of those who were thus privileged to meet again, and supplications were made that the afflicting dispensation, which all so deeply felt, might exert a salutary influence in the minds of the surviving chiefs, and the sorrowing nation at large.

Karaimoku, the late prime minister, and present regent of the islands, then arose, and said, "We have lost our king and queen, they have died in a foreign land; we shall see them no more; it is right that we should weep, but let us not entertain hard thoughts of God. God has not done wrong. The evil is with us, let us bow under his hand; let all amusement cease; let our daily avocations be suspended; and let the nation, by prayer, and a cessation from ordinary pursuits, humble itself before God fourteen days."

REPORT BY BOKI OF INTERVIEW WITH BRITISH KING

Before the assembly separated, Boki stood up, and, in a brief outline of the voyage, narrated the most prominent events that had transpired since his departure from the islands, calling their attention in particular to the suitable and important advice he had received from his majesty the king of Great Britain, in an audience with which he was graciously favoured: viz. To return to his native country, attend to general and religious instruction himself, and endeavour to enlighten and reform the people.

The peculiar circumstances of the people at this time, the increased satisfaction they had for some time felt in attending every means of instruction within their reach, and the pleasing change in favour of religion, which many had experienced, rendered this recommendation, so congenial to their feelings, from a source so distinguished, unusually acceptable.

327

A deep and favourable impression was produced on all present, a new impulse was given to the means already employed for the instruction and improvement of the people, from which most advantageous results have already appeared.

They were also made acquainted by Boki and his companions with the kind reception, generous treatment, and marked attentions, which the late king and queen and their suite had received while in England. This intelligence, communicated by those whose testimony would be received with the most entire credence, would at once confirm the attachment and confidence they have so long felt towards England.

No disturbance of the general tranquillity, nor change in the government of the islands, has resulted from this event.

SUCCESSION TO THRONE BY KAMEHAMEHA III

Rihoriho left a younger brother, Kauikeouli, about ten years of age, who is acknowledged by the chiefs as his successor. A regency will govern during his minority, and the executive authority will probably continue to be exercised by Karaimoku, and the other chiefs with whom Rihoriho left it when he embarked for England.

ANALYSIS OF CHARACTER OF KAMEHAMARU, RIHORIHO'S QUEEN

The queen, who accompanied him, and who died at the same time, has left a fond mother and an affectionate people to lament her loss: she was the daughter of Tamehameha and Kalakua, and was born about the year 1797 or 1798, being two years younger than Rihoriho, and about twenty-six years of age when she left the islands.

Like all the persons of distinction, she had many names, but that by which she was generally known, was Kamehamaru, (shade of Kameha), from kameha, a contraction of her father's name, and maru, shade. She was distinguished for good-nature, and was much beloved by all her subjects.

The poor people, when unable to pay their rent, or under the displeasure of the king and chiefs, or embarrassed on any other account, frequently repaired to her, and found a friend whose aid was never refused.

She was also kind to those foreigners who might be distressed in the islands; and though she never harboured any, or countenanced their absconding from their ships, she has often fed them when hungry, and given them native tapa for clothing.

Kamehamaru was at all times lively and agreeable in company; and though her application to her book and her pen was equal to that of the king, her improvement in learning was more gradual, and her general knowledge less extensive.

She excelled, however, in the management of his domestic affairs, which were conducted by her with great judgment and address; and though formerly accustomed to use ardent spirits, from the time she put herself under Christian instruction, she entirely discontinued that, and every other practice inconsistent with her profession of Christianity. Her attendance on the duties of religion was maintained with commendable regularity.

Her influence contributed very materially to the pleasing change that has recently taken place, in connexion with the labours of the missionaries in the islands. For the instruction and moral improvement of the people, she manifested no ordinary concern.

Long before many of the leading chiefs were favourable to the instruction of the people, or their reception of Christianity, Kamehamaru on every suitable occasion recommended her own servants to serve Jehovah the living God, and attend to every means of improvement within their reach.

It was truly pleasing to observe, so soon after she had embraced Christianity herself, an anxiety to induce her people to follow her example.

ESTABLISHED A SCHOOL IN HONOLULU

At Honoruru she erected a school in which upwards of forty children and young persons, principally connected with her establishment, were daily taught to read and write, and instructed in the first principles of religion, by a native teacher whom she almost entirely supported.

In this school she took a lively interest, and marked the progress of the scholars with evident satisfaction; in order to encourage the pupils, she frequently visited the school during the hours of instruction, accompanied by a number of chief women. She also attended the public examinations, and noticed those who on these occasions excelled, frequently presenting a favourite scholar with a slate, a copy-book, pencil, pen, or some other token of her approbation.

In her death the missionaries have lost a sincere friend, and her subjects a queen, who always delighted to alleviate their distresses and promote their interests.

Her disposition was affectionate. I have seen her and the king sitting beside the couch of Keopuolani, her mother-in-law, day after day, when the latter has been ill; and on these occasions, though there might be several servants in constant attendance, she would allow no individual but her husband or herself to hand to the patient any thing she might want, or even fan the flies from her person.

The circumstances attending her departure from the islands were peculiarly affecting. The king had gone on board the L'Aigle; the boat was waiting to convey her to the ship. She arose from the mat on which she had been reclining, embraced her mother and other relations most affectionately, and passed through the crowd towards the boat. The people fell down on their knees as she walked along pressing and saluting her feet, frequently bathing them with tears of unfeigned sorrow, and making loud wailings, in which they were joined by the thousands who thronged the shore.

On reaching the water side, she turned, and beckoned to the people to cease their cries. As soon as they were silent, she said, "I am going to a distant land, and perhaps we shall not meet again. Let us pray to Jehovah, that he may preserve us on the water, and you on the shore."

She then called Auna, a native teacher from the Society Islands, and requested him to pray. He did so; at the conclusion, she waved her hand to the people, and said, "Aroha nui oukou:" (Attachment great to you) : she then stepped into the boat, evidently much affected.

The multitude followed her, not only to the beach, but into the sea, where many, wading into the water, stood waving their hands, exhibiting every attitude of sorrow, and uttering their loud u—e! u—e! (alas! alas) ! till the boat had pulled far out to sea.

INCIDENTS IN ENGLAND

The death of the king and queen, so soon after their arrival in England, was an event in many respects deeply to be deplored.

The officers of the London Missionary Society were unable to gain access to them until they should have been introduced to his majesty; and one of them, I believe the king, died on the very day on which that introduction was to have taken place.

The same circumstance also prevented many Christian friends, who felt interested in their welfare, from that intercourse with them which, under the blessing of God, might have been expected to have strengthened the religious impressions they had received from the instructions of the missionaries.

In their visit to England they were accompanied by a suite, which, though much less numerous than that which invariably attended their movements in their native islands, included nevertheless several individuals of rank and influence.

THE KING'S SUITE ON VISIT TO ENGLAND

Among the principal of these was Boki, the governor of the island of Oahu, and Liliha his wife; Kauruheimarama, a distant relation of the king's; Kakuanaoa and Kapihe, two of his favourite companions; the latter of whom was a man of an amiable disposition, and, considering the circumstances under which he had been brought up, possessed general intelligence. He had made a voyage to Canton, in China, for the purpose of acquiring mercantile information; and from the circumstance of his commanding the finest vessel belonging to the king, a brig of about ninety tons burden, called the Haaheo Hawaii, (Pride of Hawaii), he was sometimes called the Admiral, although that is an office to which there is nothing analogous in the present maritime system of the Hawaiians.

With this individual, who died at Valparaiso on his return to the islands, and the others who survived the death of the king, particularly with Boki, the officers of the London Missionary Society had several interviews, and received the strongest assurances of their continued patronage and support of the Christian mission established in the Sandwich Islands. Many benevolent individuals had also an opportunity of testifying the deep interest they felt in the civil, moral, and religious improvement of their countrymen.

While they were at Portsmouth, the late venerable Dr. Bogue, tutor of the Missionary Seminary at Gosport, accompanied by several Christian friends, visited Boki and his companions—expressed his hopes that no unfavourable results would follow their visit to Great Britain, and offered up his prayers that God would preserve them, and bless their return to their native islands.

BOKI'S ATTITUDE TOWARD CHRISTIANITY

Boki, together with his elder brother Karaimoku, had invariably manifested his friendship towards the missionaries, by countenancing every effort to enlighten the people; and, before he left the islands to accompany his sovereign, we had reason to hope that his own mind had received favourable impressions of that system of religion which it had been our object to unfold; but we were not without serious apprehensions that his visit to England might considerably weaken, if not altogether obliterate, those religious impressions, and originate others of a character totally different.

In this respect, however, we have been most agreeably disappointed. The death of the king and queen appears to have produced a salutary effect on his mind; and, by letters recently received from the islands, I have been gratified to learn, that, since his return, he has taken a most decided stand in favour of Christianity, and has given evidence of its influence on his heart so uniform and satisfactory, that he has been admitted a member of the Christian church in Oahu, and in the general tenor of his conduct exhibits to his countrymen an example worthy

331

of their imitation, materially contributing to the advancement of civilization, education, and Christianity, throughout the islands.

ATTITUDE OF CHIEFS TOWARD CHRISTIANITY

It is a pleasing fact, in connexion with the present circumstances of the nation, that not only Boki and his brother, the present regent, but almost every chief of rank and influence in the Sandwich Islands, are favourably disposed towards the instruction of the natives, and the promulgation of the gospel.

A deep sense of the kindness of the late Dr. Bogue and his friends, by whom they were visited at Portsmouth, appears to have remained on the minds of the Hawaiian chiefs long after their return to their native land; for when the Rev. C. S. Stewart, an American missionary, was about to leave the Sandwich Islands for Great Britain, Boki gave him a special charge to present his grateful regards to the Bishop of Portsmouth. Mr. S. told him he was not aware that there was such a dignitary; but Boki said, Yes, there was, for he visited him, with some of his friends, when they were on the point of sailing from England. Those who were acquainted with the venerable form and apostolic address of the late Dr. Bogue, will not be surprised at the mistake of the Sandwich chief, in his supposing he must be the Bishop of Portsmouth.

A LETTER FROM BOKI

Among the letters I was favoured to receive from the islands by the return of his majesty's ship Blonde, those from Boki and Liliha, or, as she was frequently called while in England, Madam Boki, were of a character so interesting, that I think I shall be pardoned for inserting one of them. It is from Boki, the chief who was with the king in London. I shall translate it very literally.

"Oahu. The first of the Twins is the month (answering to our October), 1825.

"Affection for you, Mr. Ellis, and sympathy with you, Mrs. Ellis, in your illness. This is my entreaty: Return you hither, and we shall be right. Grief was ours on your returning. Heard before this have you of the death of the king: but all things here are correct. We are serving God: we are making ourselves strong in His word. Turned have the chiefs to instruction: their desire is towards God. I speak unto them, and encourage them concerning the word of God, that it may be well with our land.

"Attachment to you two, attachment to the Ministers, and the Missionaries all.

"CAPTAIN BOKI."

At ten o'clock in the forenoon of the 9th, I took leave of my kind friends at Lahaina, and, in company with Messrs. Bingham and Richards, went on board the Tamahorolani, bound to Oahu. It was, however, four o'clock in the afternoon before the vessel hove up her anchor. We were becalmed till nine in the evening, when a fresh breeze sprung up; we passed down the channel between Morokai and Ranai; and between nine and ten in the forenoon of the 10th, arrived off the harbour of Honoruru.

On landing, I was grateful to meet my family in health and comfort, except Mrs. Ellis, who was confined by severe indisposition. I united with Messrs. Thurston, Bishop, and Goodrich, who had previously arrived, in grateful acknowledgments to God for the unremitted care and distinguishing goodness which we had enjoyed in accomplishing the interesting tour, from which, under circumstances of no small mercy, we had now returned.

APPENDIX

REMARKS ON THE HAWAIIAN LANGUAGE

HAWAIIAN ROCK CARVINGS

In the course of our tour around Hawaii, we met with a few specimens of what may perhaps be termed the first efforts of an uncivilized people towards the construction of a language of symbols.

Along the southern coast, both on the east and west sides, we frequently saw a number of straight lines, semicircles, or concentric rings, with some rude imitations of the human figure, cut or carved in the compact rocks of lava. They did not appear to have been cut with an iron instrument, but with a stone hatchet, or a stone less frangible than the rock on which they were portrayed.

On inquiry, we found that they had been made by former travellers, from a motive similar to that which induces a person to carve his initials on a stone or tree, or a traveller to record his name in an album, to inform his successors that he has been there.

When there were a number of concentric circles with a dot or mark in the centre, the dot signified a man, and the number of rings denoted the number in the party who had circumambulated the island.

When there was a ring, and a number of marks, it denoted the same; the number of marks shewing of how many the party consisted; and the ring, that they had travelled completely round the island; but when there was only a semicircle, it denoted that they had returned after reaching the place where it was made.

In some of the islands we have seen the outline of a fish portrayed in the same manner, to denote that one of that species or size had been taken near the spot; sometimes the dimensions of an exceedingly large fruit, &c. are marked in the same way.

NO WRITTEN LANGUAGE IN HAWAII

With this slight exception, if such it can be called, the natives of the Sandwich and other islands had no signs for sounds or ideas, nor any pictorial representation of events. Theirs was entirely an oral language; and, whatever view we take of it, presents the most interesting phenomenon connected with the inhabitants of the Pacific.

A grammatical analysis would exceed my present limits; a few brief remarks, however, will convey some idea of its peculiarities; and a copious grammar, prepared by my respected colleagues, the American missionaries in those islands, and myself, may perhaps be published at no distant period.

THE POLYNESIAN LANGUAGE

The language of the Hawaiians is a dialect of what the missionaries in the South Seas have called the Polynesian language, spoken in all the islands which lie to the east of the Friendly Islands, including New Zealand and Chatham Island.

The extent to which it prevails, the degree of perfection it has attained, the slight analogy between it and any one known language, the insulated situation and the uncivilized character of the people by whom it is spoken, prove that, notwithstanding the rude state of their society, they have bestowed no small attention to its cultivation, and lead to the inference, that it has been for many ages a distinct language; while the obscurity that veils its origin, as well as that of the people by whom it is used, prevents our forming any satisfactory conclusion as to the source whence it was derived.

COMPARISON BETWEEN HAWAIIAN AND MALAYAN

The numerals are similar to those of the Malays; and it has many words in common with that language, yet the construction of the words and the rules of syntax appear different.

In the specimen of languages spoken in Sumatra, given by Mr. Marsden in his history of that island, some words appear in each, common in the South Seas; and it is difficult to determine in which they preponderate.

In looking over the Malayan grammar and dictionary by the same gentleman, many words appear similar in sound and signification; but there are a number of radical words common to all the Polynesian languages, as kanaka, man, ao, light, pouri, darkness, po, night, ra or la, sun, marama, moon, maitai, good, ino, bad, ai, to eat, and moe, to sleep, though very nearly the same in all the South Sea languages, appear to have no affinity with orang, trang, klam, malam, mataari, and shems, bulan, baik, buruk, makan, and tidor, words of the same meaning in Malayan; notwithstanding this, there is a striking resemblance in others, and a great part of the language was doubtless derived from the same source.

COMPARISON WITH LANGUAGE OF MADAGASCAR

Since my return to England, I have had an opportunity of conversing with the Madagasse youth now in this country for the purposes of education, and from them, as well as a vocabulary which I have seen, I was surprised to learn, that in several points the aboriginal languages of Madagascar and the South Sea Islands are strikingly analogous, if not identical, though the islands are about 10,000 geographical miles distant from each other.

With the aboriginal languages of South America we have had no opportunity of comparing it; some of the words of that country, in their simplicity of construction and vowel terminations, as Peru, Quito, pronounced kito, Parana, Oronoko, &c. appear like Polynesian words.

COMPARISON WITH HEBREW

In the Sandwich Islands, as well as the Tahitian language, there are a number of words that appear true Hebrew roots, and in the conjugation of the verbs there is a striking similarity; the causative active and the causative passive being formed by a prefix and suffix to the verb.

In many respects it is unique, and in some defective, but not in that degree which might be expected from the limited knowledge of the people.

The simple construction of the words, the predominancy of vowels, and the uniform terminations, are its great peculiarities.

The syllables are in general composed of two letters, and never more than three.

There are no sibilants in the language, nor any double consonants.

HAWAIIAN SYSTEM OF PRONUNCIATION

Every word and syllable terminates with a vowel; and the natives cannot pronounce two consonants without an intervening vowel; nor a word terminating with a consonant, without either dropping the final letter, or adding a vowel; hence they pronounce Britain, Beritania, boat, boti; while there are many words, and even sentences, without a consonant, as e i ai oe ia ia ae e ao ia, literally, "speak now to him by the side that he learn."

The frequent use of the k renders their speech more masculine than that of the Tahitians, in which the t predominates.

The sound of their language is peculiarly soft and harmonious; great attention is also paid to euphony, on account of which the article is often varied; the same is the case in the Tahitian, in which the word tavovovovo, signifies the rolling of thunder.

A LANGUAGE ADAPTED TO POETRY

Each of the dialects appears adapted for poetry, and none more so then the Hawaiian, in which the l frequently occurs. Whether the smoothness of their language induced the natives to cultivate metrical composition, or their fondness for the latter has occasioned the multiplicity of vowels, and soft flowing arrangement of the sentences, which distinguish their language, it is difficult to conjecture.

In native poetry, rhyming terminations are neglected, and the chief art appears to consist in the compilation of short metrical sentences, agreeing in accent and cadence at the conclusion of each, or at the end of a certain number of sentences.

Rude as their native poetry is, they are passionately fond of it. When they first began to learn to read and spell, it was impossible for them to repeat a column of spelling, or recite a lesson, without chanting or singing it.

They had one tune for the monosyllables, another for the dissyllables, &c. and we have heard three or four members of a family sitting for an hour together in an evening, and reciting their school lessons in perfect concord.

HISTORY PRESERVED IN SONGS

Most of the traditions of remarkable events in their history are preserved in songs committed to memory, by persons attached to the king or chiefs; or strolling musicians who travel through the islands, and recite them on occasions of public festivity.

The late king had one of these bards attached from infancy to his household, who, like some of the ancient bards, was blind, and who, when required, would recite a hura (song) on any particular event relating to the family of his sovereign.

The office was hereditary; the songs transmitted from father to son; and whatever defects might attach to their performances, considered as works of art, they were not wanting in effect; being highly figurative, and delivered in strains of plaintive sadness, or wild enthusiasm, they produced great excitement of feeling.

Sometimes their interest was local, and respected some particular family, but the most popular were the national songs.

When I first visited the Sandwich Islands, one on the defeat of Kekuaokalani, the rival of Rihoriho, who was slain in the battle of Tuamoo, was in the mouth of almost every native we met; another, nearly as popular, was a panegyric on the late king, composed on his accession to the government; and soon after his departure for England, several bards were employed in celebrating that event.

HOW SONGS WERE FORMULATED

In my voyage from Hawaii, three or four females, fellow-passengers, were thus employed during the greater part of the passage, which afforded me an opportunity of observing the process. They first agreed on two or three ideas, arranged them in a kind of metrical sentence, with great attention to the accent of the concluding word, and then

337

repeated it in concert. If it sounded discordantly, they altered it; if not, they repeated it several times, and then proceeded to form a new sentence.

THE USE OF "T" AND "K"

The k in most of the islands is generally used in common intercourse, but it is never admitted into their poetical compositions, in which the t is universally and invariably employed.

The following Verses, extracted from a collection of Hymns in the native language, containing 60 pages, are a translation of lines on the "Sandwich Mission," by W. B. Tappan, on the embarkation of the missionaries from New Haven, (America), in 1822. The k is employed, though contrary to the practice of the natives. The original commences with—

"Wake, isles of the south, your redemption is near,
No longer repose in the borders of gloom."

HAWAIIAN

I na moku i paa i ka pouri mau,
Uhia 'ka naau po wale rakou,
Ano nei e puka no maila ke ao,
Hoku Bet'lehema, ka Hoku ao mau.

Huia ka rere a pau me ka kii,
E hooreia ka taumaha a pau;
I k'alana maitai rakou e ora'i,
Tabu ka heiau na ke Akua mau.

E ake rakou i nana wave ae,
Ka wehea mai'ka araura maitai,
A o ka kukuna 'ka Mesia mau,
"A kali na moku kona kanawai."

ORIGINAL

On the islands that sit in the regions of night,
The lands of despair, to oblivion a prey,
The morning will open with healing and light,
And the young star of Bethlehem will ripen today.

The altar and idol, in dust overthrown,
The incense forbade that was hallow'd with blood;
The priest of Melchisedec there shall atone,
And the shrines of Hawaii be sacred to God.

The heathen will hasten to welcome the time,
The day-spring the prophet in vision foresaw,
When the beams of Messiah will 'lumine each clime,
And the isles of the ocean shall wait for his law.

A COPIOUS LANGUAGE

Notwithstanding its defects, the Hawaiian has its excellencies. Ideas are frequently conveyed with great force and precision; verbs not only

338

express the action, but the manner of it, distinctly; hence, to send a message would be orero, to send a messenger, kono, to send a parcel, houna, to break a stick, haki, to break a string, moku, to break a cup, naha, to break a law, hoomaloka, &c.

Considering it is a language that has received no additions from the intercourse of the natives with other countries, and is devoid of all technical terms of art and science, it is, as well as the other dialects, exceedingly copious. Some idea of this may be formed from the circumstance of there being in the Tahitian upwards of 1400 words commencing with the letter a.

The greatest imperfections we have discovered occur in the degrees of the adjectives, and the deficiency of the auxiliary verb to be, which is implied, but not expressed.

The natives cannot say, I am, or it is, yet they can say a thing remains, as, ke waiho maira ka waa i raira, (the canoe remains there); and their verbs are used in the participial form, by simply adding the termination ana, equivalent to ing, in English.

Hence in asking a native, What he is doing? the question would be, "He aha-ana oe?" (What-ing you)? The answer would be, He ai ana wau. Eating (am) I. The He denoting the present tense preceding the question, the answer corresponds; but if he wished to say, what he was eating, the noun would be placed between the verb, and its participial termination, as He ai poe ana wau, literally, Eat poe-ing I.

In every other respect their language appears to possess all the parts of speech, and some in greater variety and perfection than any language we are acquainted with.

HOW WRITTEN LANGUAGE WAS FORMULATED

In reducing the language to a written form, the American missionaries adopted the Roman character, as the English missionaries had done before in the southern dialects.

The English alphabet possesses a redundancy of consonants, and though rather deficient in vowels, answers tolerably well to express all the native sounds.

The Hawaiian alphabet consists of seventeen letters: five vowels, a, e, i, o, u, and twelve consonants, b, d, h, k, l, m, n, p, r, t, v, w, to which f, g, s, and z, have been added, for the purpose of preserving the identity of foreign words.

The consonants are sounded as in English, though we have been obliged to give them different names, for the natives could not say el or em, but invariably pronounced ela and ema; it being therefore necessary to retain the final vowel, that was thought sufficient, and the other was rejected.

339

The vowels are sounded more after the manner of the continental languages than the English; A, as in ah, and sometimes as a in far, but never as a in fate; E, as a in gale, ape, and mate; I, as ee in green; e in me, or i in machine.

The short sound of i in bit, seldom occurs, and the long sound of i in wine is expressed by the diphthong ai; O, as o in no and mote; U, as u in rude, or oo in moon.

Several of the consonants are interchangeable, particularly the l and r, the b and p, t and k. There are no silent letters. I have known a native, acquainted with the power of the letters, spell a word, when it has been correctly pronounced, though he had never seen it written; for in pronouncing a word, it is necessary to pronounce every letter of which it is composed.

THE PARTS OF SPEECH

Articles.—They have two articles, definite (he) and indefinite (ke or ka), answering to the English the and a or an. The articles precede the nouns to which they belong.

Nouns.—The nouns undergo no inflection, or change of termination, the number, case, and gender, being denoted by distinct words or particles prefixed or added. Hence o, which is only the sign of the nominative, has been usually placed before Tahiti and Hawaii, making Otaheiti and Owhyhee, though the o is no part of the word any more than no the sign of the possessive, as no Hawaii, of Hawaii, and i the sign of the objective, as i Hawaii, to Hawaii.

Pronouns.—The scheme of pronouns is copious and precise, having not only a singular, dual, and plural number, but a double dual and plural; the first including the speaker and spoken to, as thou and I, and ye and I; the second, the speaker and party spoken of, as he and I, and they and I. Each of these combinations is clearly expressed by a distinct pronoun.

Adjectives.—The adjective follows the noun to which it belongs. There are several degrees of comparison, though the form of the adjective undergoes no change; the degrees are expressed by distinct words. There is, properly speaking, no superlative; it is, however, expressed by prefixing the definite article, as k kiekie, ke nui, (the high, the great.)

Verbs.—The verbs are active, passive, and neuter. The regular active verb in the Hawaiian dialect admits of four conjugations, as rohe, to hear, hoo-rohe, to cause to hear, rohe-ia, heard, and hoo-rohe-ia, to cause to be heard. Some of the verbs admit the second and fourth, but reject the third, as noho, to sit, hoo-noho, to cause to sit, and hoo-noho-ia, to cause to be seated. Others again allow the third and fourth, but not

340

the second, as pepehi, to beat, pepehi-ia, beaten, and hoopepehi-ia, to cause to be beaten. The verbs usually precede the nouns and pronouns, as here au, go I, and e noho marie oe, sit still you, instead of, I go, and you sit still.

The adverbs, prepositions, conjunctions, and interjections, are numerous; but a description of them, and their relative situation in the construction of their sentences, would take up too much room.

NUMERALS RESEMBLE MALAYAN

Their numerals resemble the Malayan more than any other part of their language.

Eleven would be either umi-kumu-ma-kahi, ten the root and one, or umi-akahi-keu, ten one over; this would be continued by adding the units to the ten till twenty, which they call iva-karua, forty they call kanahaa, or seventy-six they would say forty twenty ten and six, and continue counting by forties till 400, which they call a rau, then they add till 4000, which they call a mano, 40,000 they call lehu, and 400,000 a kini; beyond this we do not know that they carry their calculations: the above words are sometimes doubled, as manomano kinikini; they are, however, only used thus to express a large but indefinite number. Their selection of the number four in calculations is singular; thus, 864,895 would be, according to their method of reckoning, two kini, or 400,000s, one lehu, or 40,000, six mano or 4000s, two rau, or 400s, two kanaha, or 40s one umi or ten and five. They calculate time by the moon; allow twelve to a year; have a distinct name for every moon, and every night of the moon, and reckon the parts of a month by the number of nights, as po akoru ainei, nights three ago, instead of three days ago.

The following specimen of native composition will convey some idea of their idiom. The translation is servile; and with this I shall close these remarks on their language. It is a letter written by the late king in answer to one I sent, acquainting him with my second arrival in the islands, on the 4th of Feb. 1823.

"Mr. Ellis, eo.

Mr. Ellis, attend.

Aroha ino oe, me ko wahine, me na keiki a pau a

Attachment great (to) you, and your wife, with children all of ye orua. I ola oukou ia Jehova ia laua o Iesu Kraist, two. Preserved (have) you (been) by Jehovah they two Jesus Christ. Eia kau wahi olero ia oe, Mr. Ellis, apopo a kela la ku a ahiahi, This (is) my word to you, Mr. Ellis, to-morrow or the day after when a ku hoi mai. I ka tabu a leila ua ite kaua. A i evening, then I return. On the Sabbath

341

then (shall) meet we. But if makemake oe e here mai ianei maitai no
hoi. Ike ware oe i na'rii desire you to come here, well also. Seen indeed
(have) you o Tahiti. Aroha ware na'rii o Bolabola.
the chiefs of Tahiti. Attachment only to the chiefs of Borabora.*
    I ola oe ia Jehova ia Jesu Kraist.
    Save (may) you (be) by Jehovah by Jesus Christ.

IOLANI"

*The term for the Society Islands.

(Several pages of Hawaiian words and their English equivalents and of
declensions of Hawaiian pronouns are omitted.)

Many of the entries in this index are listed under their modern spellings rather than the spellings that appear in the text. The older spellings, however, usually appear in brackets after the main entries. Special Hawaiian words are not set in italics, nor are hamzas and macrons used to indicate glottal stops and long vowels. Readers should refer to a modern Hawaiian dictionary for further guidance.

awa [ava] (kawa—an intoxicating drink), 275
ax, 53, 227. *See also* adze; hatchet; tools

baby kissing, 325
bamboo: cane of, 248, 318; knife of, 247, 248; tapa printer of, 69
banana, 32, 42, 133, 143, 206, 239, 250, 251, 256
banishment, 305, 306
barb of spear, 102
barometer, 292
barter, 298, 305, 306. *See also* trade
basalt, 179, 227
basket, 247, 248; of ie root, 213; of wicker, 87, 228
bathing: tabu on, 280; in warm springs, 287
battle. *See* sham battle
battlefield. *See* Keei; war
bayonet (welau [verau]), 101
beads, as a present to children, 148
beans, 17
beard: of Makoa, 72; tabu on trimming of, 280
beer of ti root, 184
beheading, 306
Bennet, George, xvii
Bingham, Mr., 323, 325, 333
birds, 17, 157; in creation story, 312; as food, 148; ii, 25. *See also* duck; fowl; geese; owl
Bishop, Artemas, xvi, 28, 30, 32, 33, 35, 58, 71, 76, 89, 92, 93, 124, 125, 128, 154, 158, 167, 168, 169, 196, 201, 202, 205, 211, 219, 223, 242, 253, 286, 292, 293, 294, 297, 298, 299, 310, 333
Bishop of Portsmouth, 332
blasting powder, 277, 294
Blatchely, Dr., 176, 213, 291, 292
Blonde, H.M.S., xviii, 239, 327, 332
bluff, at Kahuku, 130
Bogue, Dr., 331, 332
Boki (governor of Oahu), 301, 327, 328, 330, 331; letter from, 332
bones: of Kamehameha, 258; pres- ervation of, 110, 112, 257; setting of, by kahuna, 237, 238; thrown into sea, 259; thrown into volcano, 259. *See also* burial; cave; Cook; heiau
bonito, 190

Bora Bora, 54, 342. *See also* Society Islands; Tahiti
Boston, xvi, 20
Bougainville, Captain, 312
boundaries, marking of, 250. *See also* land apportionment; stone wall
bow and arrow, 314
bowls. *See* calabash; fingerbowl; gourd
boxing, 86
bracelet, 60, 64. *See also* personal adorn- ment
brake, 291
breadfruit (ulu [uru], *Artocarpus incisis*), 17, 31, 42, 99, 109, 206, 239
breastplate, 103
British, 19, 22, 23, 149. *See also* cession; England; London
broadcloth, 299
brushwood, 132
buhenehene. *See* games
Bukohola. *See* Pukohola
buoa. *See* puoa
Bu-o-Kahawali. *See* Kahawali
burial: alive, 231, 233; in caves, 92, 258; position of body, 258, 259; of priest, 82, 258; at sea, 259; secrecy of, 257, 259. *See also* bones; cairn; Cook; funerals; grave; heiau; mourning; war
buskin (dance anklets), 60, 64, 208
Butler, Mr., 43
butterfly, 262
Buukea. *See* Puukea
Byron, Lord, xviii, 239, 326
Byron's Bay, 238, 239

cabbage, 17
cactus, 109
cairn, 79, 95, 106; on Mauna Kea, 290
calabash: as canteen, 99, 125, 154; as catch basin, 158, 189; as coffin, 233; decoration of, 268, 269; drum, 65; at Hale-o-Keawe, 112; how made, 268; trial by, 308
Calcutta, 18
California, 18
candicans, 285
candlenut. *See* kukui
cane of bamboo, 248, 318
cannibalism: in Society Islands, 108; in Marquesas Group, 232, 240
canoe: building of, 75, 147, 180; dec-

crepe, 299
crest, on helmet, 102
crime. *See* court of law; justice
criminals, disposition of, 259
Crook, Mr., 241
crystals, 129, 178, 292. *See also* lava
cucumber, 17
cultivation, 17, 32; by Kamehameha, 277. *See also names of plants.*
customs, 314; at homecoming, 191, 193; of Society Islanders, 247. *See also* courtesy; eating; hospitality; law; mourning; women
cuttlefish, 6

dagger, 54; described, 94. *See also* pahoa
dancers, 208, 301. *See also* hula
dancing, at end of war, 107. *See also* hula
dart (pahe). *See* games
Davis, Isaac, 18
death: of chief, 118–23; reversion of lands after, 306. *See also* burial; mourning
death penalty: for breaking tabu, 97, 259, 281; for robbery, adultery, 306
de Borda, Chevalier, 181
deluge. *See* flood
desert, 158
Diamond Head (Diamond Hill), 8
dimity, compared with tapa, 68
diving, 266
divining, relative to war, 97, 103. *See also* poi kilo
divorce, 316
Dixon, Captain, 18, 144
dogs, 16; barking of, 280; in creation myth, 312; farms for, 249; as fee of kahuna, 238; as food, 29, 148, 247, 248, 249; as pets, 29, 149, 297; skin of, as ornament, 45; teeth of, as ornament, 60, 103; as tribute or sacrifice, 179, 202, 203, 250; vanquished in war left to, 106; wild, 292
dollar, 304, 305. *See also* money, Spanish
Douglas, Captain, 18
dowry, 316
Dracaena terminalis (ti plant), 184
dream, Kamehameha's appearance in, 263
dress. *See* clothing
drum, 242, 245; of calabash, 58, 65; decoration of, 269; knee, 64; wooden,

62
duck, 17, 240, 273; muscovy, 148
Duff (ship), 19
Dutton, Meiric K., xv
dye: from earth, herbs, 268, 269; from kukui, 269; from leaves, bark, berries, roots, 69; vegetable, 15, 68

Eappo (deliverer of Cook's bones to Captain Clarke), 86, 87
ear: mutilation of, 120; perforation of, 121; of pig, perforated to indicate tabu, 281
Earl of Sandwich, 1
earring. *See* hair
earthenware, 299
earthquake, at Kaimu, 195, 196. *See also* Kilauea; volcano
Easter Island, 314, 315
eating: methods of, 228; tabus on, 278. *See also* ai noa; feast; food; meals
education, 107. *See also* schools
egg, Island of Hawaii hatched from, 312
ehu (supposed descendants of pre-Cook foreigners), 319
Eimeo, 3
Eleanor (ship), 18
elehua [erehua] (first victim in war), 104
elephant, 325
Ellis, Mrs., 28, 323, 332, 333
Ellis, William, xv, xvi
eloquence. *See* orators
Ely, Mr., 176, 213
emigration, 315. *See also* voyage
England, xvi, 1, 49, 122, 258, 305, 320, 325, 326, 327, 328, 330, 331, 332, 335, 337. *See also* British; Great Britain; London
entrails, examination of, by diviners or kahuna, 97, 203
eruption, warriors destroyed by, 143. *See also* Hualalai; Kaimu; Kilauea; volcano
erythrina (tree, type of wood), 199, 266
etiquette. *See* authority; courtesy; customs; hospitality; monarch; social class
Eugenia malaccensis (tree). *See* ohia
European, 1, 267. *See also* clothing; foreigners; trade
evil places, 258. *See also* spirits

346

351

Kani (music), 171
Kanona (wife of King Kalaniopuu), 83
kao [tao] (traditions), 205
Kaoleioku [Kaoreioku] (chief), 144, 145
Kaonohiokala (god), 93
Kapaau (village), 283
Kapalaoa [Kaparaoa] (village), 294
Kapapa (chief of Pueo), 229, 242
Kapapahanaumoku (Hades-like place), 262
Kapapala (district and village), 141, 142, 148, 149, 153, 155, 158, 165, 180, 185, 193, 194; overrun in eruption, 187
Kapauku (village), 136, 197
Kapihe [Kapihi] (priest to the god Kuahailo), 93, 191
Kapihe (retainer to Liholiho), 301, 331
Kapiolani (chiefess, wife of Naihe), xxi, 88, 231; Pele defied by, 187
Kapohaikahiola [Tapohaitahiora] (volcano god), 172
Kapoho (village), 205; lake at, 206, 207
kapu. See tabu
Kapua (village), 124, 125, 127
Kapuahi [Tapuahi] (head man of Kapapala), 149
Kapuahi (place name), 155
Kapulena (village), 253, 254
kapu loa [tabu roa] (strict prohibition), 112
Kau (district), 62, 126, 131, 143, 153, 180, 230
kaua. See kakou
Kaua [Taua] (Tahitian preacher), 43, 47
Kauaea (village), 201
Kauai [Tauai] (also called Atooi, Atowai), xvi, xvii, xxi, 13, 15, 24, 26, 267, 284, 300, 317, 319; civil war on, 107; population of, 12
Kauikeouli (Kamehameha III; brother of Liholiho), 13, 147, 316, 328,
Kauikeouli (son of Kalaiopu, brother of Keoua; also called Kiwalaao), 90, 93, 143, 324; defeat and death of, 94, 95
kauila [kauira] (hard, red wood), 102
kaukau (to eat), 279
Kaula [Taura] (island), 15
Kaula [Kaura] (valley), 250
Kaulanamauna (village), 126

Kauleonanahoa [Taureonanahoa] (pillars of lava off Kona coast), 124
Kaulu [Kauru] (village), 131, 132
Kauluheimalama [Kauruheimarama] (retainer to Liholiho), 330
Kaumualii [Taumuarii] (king of Kauai), xvii, 28, 247, 267; Kauai ceded by, 13
Kaupulehu (village), 296
kawa [ava] (an intoxicating drink; also spelled "kava"), 275
Kawaihae [Towaihae] (district, village), xxi, xxii, 19, 57, 58, 61, 126, 144, 253, 261, 275, 286, 288, 289, 291, 292, 293, 294, 298, 299, 310, 321, 322; heiau at, 55
Kawelohea [Kaverohea] (legendary rock), 137
kea (white; white man), 292, 319
Keaau [Kaau] (village), 211, 212, 213, 240
Keahialaka (village), 201
Keakealani (ancient queen), 74
Kealaala [Kearaara] (village), 187, 194. See also Kaalaala
Kealakaha [Kearakaha] (village), 252
Kealakekua [Kearakekua] (bay, district, village), xxi, 1, 25, 32, 35, 71, 89, 90, 92, 116, 126, 319, 320
Kealakomo [Kearakomo] (village), 154, 183, 187, 188, 190, 194
Kealiikukii [Keariikukii] (ancient king), 208
Keanaee (pathway behind lava cascade), 117
Keanakakoi (crater), 182
Keapuana (large cavern used for shelter), 155
Keauhou (village), 76, 77, 253, 288; graves at, 258
Keawaiki [Keavaiti] (canoe landing), 127, 128
Keawe [Keave] (ancient king), 110, 113, 114
Keaweaheulu [Keaveaheuru] (chief, father of Naihe), 144, 145
Keawemauhili [Teavemauhiri] (king), 200
Keeaumoku (governor of Maui, brother of Kuakini), 121
Keeaumoku (principal general for Kamehameha I; father of Kaa-

353

Luapua [Ruapua] (place name), 73
lukulua [rukurua] (both beaten), 105
lunapai [runapai] (messengers of war), 99

Maalo [Maaro] (chief of Waiakea), 48, 212, 213, 214, 215, 216, 218, 220, 221, 222, 223, 229, 230, 236, 242, 301
Madagascar, 335
magnet, 158
mahioli [mahiori] (chief's helmet), 102
mahogany, 102
Mahuka (place name), 194
maia. *See* plantain
maili [mairi] (plant): anklet of, 44; wreath of, as sign of peace, 107
makaainana (the common people), 61, 67
Makaaka (village), 146
Makanau (village), 144
Makanuiailono [Makanuiairono] (ancient physician), 238
maka-wai (category of slain enemies), 105
Makena (village), 196
Makoa (Hawaiian guide), 115, 128, 130, 132, 141, 154, 158, 193, 198, 200, 211, 212, 217, 219, 229, 245, 246, 249, 254; described, 71, 72; on foreign medicine, 257; portrait of, 72; as theologian, 252
Makolewawahiwaa [Makorewawahiwaa] (volcano god), 172
Malama (district), 201
Malama (hill), 205
Malanahae (place name), 253
malanai [maranai] (east wind), 242
Malay, Malayan, 16, 313, 335, 341
Maliu [Mariu] (hill), 205
malo [maro] (loincloth), 69, 102, 132, 308
malu [maru] (protection by king), 106
Maluae [Maruae] (chief at Kaalaala), 148, 154
mamake (tapa), 190
Mamakua (village), 190
Manahini (man's name; origin of word "Manahini [Malihini]"), 319; as term for "stranger," 318
Mangea (place name), 315
Manienie (place name), 252
Manila, 18, 320
Manona (wife of Kekuaokalani), 78, 79

manslaughter (pepehi kanaka), 113, 235
marae [morai] (heiau, temple), 35, 75
Marian Islands (Marianas Group), 18
markets: at Hilo, 229; public, 299
Marquesas, Marquesans, xv, xvii, xviii, 20, 22, 23, 138, 232, 241, 246, 284, 285, 313, 315, 318; cannibalism of, 240
marriage: ceremony of, 316; between relatives, 317
Marsden, Mr., 335
Massachusetts, xvii
mats, 228; as burial shroud, 258; as kahuna's fee, 238; of Niihau, described, 13, 15; as payment of toll, 229; weaving of, 118, 155, 206
Mauae [Maua] (man of Kaimu), 128, 129, 138, 154, 183, 188, 198; homecoming reception for, 191, 193
Maui (island), xviii, xxi, xxii, 6, 12, 18, 24, 26, 28, 34, 42, 51, 55, 73, 120, 121, 186, 210, 290, 293, 300, 310, 311, 315, 317, 319, 323, 324; population of, 5
Maukaleoleo [Maukareoreo] (mythical giant), 74
Maulua [Maurua] (place name), 315
Mauna Kea [Mouna-kea], 3, 4, 181, 212, 239, 245, 249, 251, 253, 288; exploration of, 289–92; as refuge during flood, 321
Mauna Loa [Mouna Roa], 3, 4, 61, 128, 131, 153, 155, 290; description of, 180, 181
meals: customs of chief for, 29, 247, 248; in European style, 249. *See also* eating; feast; food
Meares, Captain, 144
mechanic, 301, 307
medicine: foreign, 45, 109, 238, 257; of kahuna, 236, 237, 238. *See also* herbs; kahuna
medusae (jellyfish), 6
melon, 32, 239
mercy. *See* clemency
Mermaid (ship), 22
messages. *See* spirits; war
messengers, 309. *See also* herald; war
Metcalf, Captain, and son, 18
Mexico, 3, 18. *See also* Acapulco
military service, 99; required of chiefs,

355

276, 302. *See also* war
Milu [Miru] (ancient king; ruler of the hereafter), 262, 263
Milu [Miru, Meru] (Hades), 93, 264
minstrel, 65. *See also* musicians
Miomioi (chief of Halaua), 274, 275, 276, 277, 278, 281, 283
mirror. *See* looking-glass
Moanalua (district in Honolulu), 12
moho (steam, vapor), 172
moku (motu) (island; ship), 262, 319
Mokuohai (battle site), 93
Molokai [Morokai, Morotai] (island), 7, 26, 28, 41, 51, 55, 210, 323, 333; sacred grove of Kaluakoi on, 53
Molokini [Morokini] (island), 6
monarch, monarchy, 21, 300. *See also* authority
money, 305; Spanish, 299, 303. *See also* dollar; trade
Mooalii [Mooarii] (shark god, king of lizards or alligators), 51
moon, as unit of time, 194, 341
morai. *See* marae
Morinda citrifolia. See noni
Morus papyrifera (tree used in bark-cloth manufacture), 67
mother-of-pearl used as eyes in god image, 103
mourning, 44, 45, 256, 260; cutting of hair for, 118; for Liholiho, 327; self-mutilation for, 119, 120, 121, 122, 123, 124; song for, 121
mouse, 16
mullet, 142, 240
murder, 198, 276, 306
muscovy. *See* duck
music, 246; composition of, 337. *See also* chant; hula
musical instruments. *See* drum
musicians, 208, 301; strolling, 337
mussel, 240
mutilation. *See* mourning
mythology, 311, 312, 314. *See also* creation; flood; volcano

Nahienaena (sister of Kauikeouli), 6, 316
Nahoaalii [Nahoaarii] (volcano god), 130, 141
Naihe (chief of Kaawaloa), xxi, 33, 34, 88, 136, 137, 144, 187

nail, 85
Nalimaelua [Narimaerua] (attendant to Kamehameha), 94
Napopo (village), 256
necklace, of human hair, 58, 94. *See also* personal adornment
Negro, 240
Nero, 262
net. *See* fishnet
New Caledonia, 314
New Haven, 176, 291, 338
New Hebrides, 166, 314
New Holland, 314
New South Wales, 22
New Zealand, 22, 138, 243, 285, 314, 315, 335
Niihau [Nihau] (island), 11; mats from, 13, 15
Ninole (village), 145. *See also* Koloa
Nio (ship), 288, 298, 299, 310, 322
niu. *See* coconut
noa (ordinary, common), 278
Noah, 321
noni (tree), 277
nose-touching, 191
Nukuhiva [Nuuhiva] (island), 284
numerals. *See* Hawaiian language
Nuuanu [Anuanu] (valley and pali), 8, 9; battle of, 11; gods of, 10

Oahu (island), xvi, xvii, xxi, 7, 8, 11, 12, 13, 18, 23, 24, 26, 28, 41, 48, 55, 61, 85, 134, 136, 137, 138, 173, 176, 210, 215, 222, 227, 242, 244, 253, 284, 286, 288, 293, 294, 297, 298, 299, 300, 304, 305, 310, 312, 320, 322, 323, 327, 330, 331, 332, 333; population of, 12. *See also* Honolulu
Oani (priestess of Pele), 216–18
obelisk, 56
obsidian, 158
oculist. *See* kahuna
offerings, 112; at eruptions, 31; to gods, 191, 312. *See also names of individual gods and animals and* animals; gods; heiau; human sacrifice; priests
ohelo (shrub, berry), 141, 167, 168, 174, 180, 182, 185, 213, 214, 278; described, 162; as offering, tribute to Pele, 163
ohia (tree, type of wood), 4, 17, 206; described, 31, 32

356

Ohiaokelani [Ohiaotelani] (place at Kilauea), 216
Olaa [Ora] (village), 177, 190, 213
olivine [olivin], 125, 129, 148, 158, 179
Olonopuha [Oronopuha] (ancient physician), 238
ona i ka ruma (intoxicated with rum), 216
onion, 17
o-o (digging tool), 25, 135; described, 132
opelu [operu] (fish), 73
Opihikao (village), 200
Opili [Opiri] (son of Paao), 283, 318
Opuhani (queen of Oahu), 320
oracle, 56, 97
orange, 17
orators, 104; eloquence of, 98
origin of Hawaiians, 54, 311–15, 321. See also creation
Otaha (island of Tahaa), 25
Otaheite (Captain Cook's name for Tahiti), 25, 312, 340
Ouli (place name), 289
oven. See imu
Owawalua [Owawarua] (village), 285
Owhyhee (Captain Cook's name for Hawaii), 25, 28, 340
owl, 17

Paao (foreign priest), 283, 284, 318, 320
Pacific peoples, 311–15
paddle. See canoe
pahe (dart). See games
pahi (knife), 319
pahoa (dagger), 54, 94, 102, 145: used to stab Captain Cook, 84
pahoehoe (type of lava), 173
Pahoehoe (village), 75
pahu kapu [pahu tapu] (sacred enclosure), 82, 105, 112, 113, 261
Pai (head man of Waiohinu), 133
paint, 69, 243, 268. See also dye
painting, 270; of calabashes, canoes, drums, idols, surfboards, 243, 268, 269; of tapa, 69
Pakalana [Pakarana] (city of refuge at Waipio), 260
pa-kaua (fortress), 100
Pakini [Patini] (village), 128
Palaoa [Paraoa] (village), 144
palaoa [paraoa] (whale-tooth orna-

ment), 58, 94, 103
palapala (books, reading), 49, 198
pali [pari] (a high fortress), 100, 105
pali [pari] (precipice) : battle of the, 11; gods of, 10; of Nuuanu, 8, 9
Paliser's Islands, 107
palo [paro] (prayer), 52
pandanus (*Pandanus odorotissime*, a tree), 211, 212, 293; nuts of, used in lei, 191; seeds of, used for perfume, 68; used in house building, 224, 225; used in kukui torch, 269
papa (sled), 207, 208
papa he nalu [naru] (wave-sliding board). See surfboard
papahola [papahora] (division of land), 302
Papapohaku (district), 132
paper mulberry, 32, 149. See also tapa; wauke
Parker, Mr. (rancher), 274, 289, 291
Parkinson, Mr., 285
paroquet (bird), 17, 102
pau (lady's garment), 68, 69, 132
Pauahi (wife of Liholiho), 145
Pauepu (district), 283
Paumoto. See Paliser's Islands
pawpaw-apple, 17
peace: plantain and ti as symbols of, 185; terms of, 107; truce, 185
pearl, 103, 112
Pearl River, 7, 11, 12
Pele (goddess of volcanoes), xxi, 117, 130, 141, 150, 155, 162, 166, 168, 171, 172, 185, 194, 196; appearances of, 175; bones of dead offered to, 259; controversy with priestess of, 215–19; defied by Kapiolani, 187; favor of Kamehameha over Keoua, 174; fight with Kamapuaa, 173, 174, 183, 194; hair of, 177, 178; holua contest with Kahawali, 207–10; offerings to temples of, 179, 250; priest of, 272; priestess of, repudiated by Kaahumanu and chiefs, 186
pepehi kanaka. See manslaughter
pepper, 275
perforation of ears. See mourning
periwinkle, 42
permission to enter house, 301
personal adornment, 44, 64, 132. See also bracelet; hair; necklace; palaoa

357

Peruvians, 314, 336. *See also* America
petroglyphs, 334
pets. *See* dogs; hogs
Philippine Islands, 18. *See also* Manila
Philosophical Magazine, 176, 291
Phormium tenax (flax plant of New Zealand), 285
Pickering, John, xvii
Pico de Teyde, 181
pig. *See* hogs
Piia (chief), 94, 301
pikaninny (small), 279
pillow, of wood, 228
pineapple, 17
pipe, 193; as adornment, 132; passed around, 254
Piper methysticum (pepper plant), 275
Pitt, William (name for Kalaimoku), 300
plantain (banana), 17, 42, 67, 143, 148, 198, 239, 251, 253; as symbol of truce, 106, 185; used in house construction, 225
playing cards, 221, 230
Pluto, 263
Po (place of night, underworld), 262
poetry, 336, 337
pohiwi [pohivi] (shoulder or flank of an army), 101
poi [poe]: as child's food, 221; described, 29; sour, 125; as staple, 190. *See also* ai paa
poi kilo [poe kiro] (diviners, priests), 97
poison, 202; Kalaipahoa, god of, 52; tree of, 53, 54
pola [pora] (platform of double canoe), 242, 243
police, 279, 307
Poliolani [Poriorani] (king of Oahu), 320
Pololu (place name), landslide at, 273
pololu. *See* spear
polygamy, 316
Pomare (royal family of Tahiti), xvii, 23, 80, 108; proposed alliance with, by marriage of Kamehameha's daughter, 54
Ponahawai (village), 219
Ponahoahoa, Ponahohoa (place name), 150, 153, 159, 187
poncho. *See* kihei
population, proportion of males to

females, 316. *See also names of individual islands and places.*
Port Jackson, 22
Portlock, Captain, 18
Portsmouth, 331; Bishop of, 332
pot. *See* cooking
potato, 42, 73, 93, 131, 143, 147, 148, 185, 188, 189, 196, 200, 212, 246, 250, 277, 304, 308; as gift or offering, 138. *See also* sweet potato
power of the king, 307
prickly pear, 109
priestess, harangue of, against foreigners, 186. *See also* Oani
priests, xx, 237, 260, 263, 264; advantage of, during tabu, 281; as denunciators of abolition of idolatry, 218; authority of, during tabu, 279; discussions with, 205, 261; of Kaili, 278; of Kane and Kanaloa, 312; of Pele, 172, 218, 250, 272; as physicians, 236; role of, in war, 105; Roman Catholic, 320; succession to priesthood, 300; as trial officials, 308. *See also* authority; heiau; kahuna; Paao
printing, xvii, 22
property, 310; individual, 274; rental of, 301; rights of, 305; tabu as drain on, 136. *See also* land apportionment
prophet, inspired by shark, 34
proprietorship: king's, 302; of land, 301; of people by chiefs, 309. *See also* property; slavery
prostration before alii, 280, 301
protection, by king's malu, 106. *See also* pahu kapu; refuge; war
Puako (village), 289
Puakokoki (place name), 144
Pualaa (village), 201, 205
public meetings, 309
Pueo, Pueho (village), 229, 242
puhenehene [buhenehene]. *See* games
puhonua (place of refuge), 95, 105, 112, 113
Pukalani (village), 289
Puka [buka] makani (wind hole; window), 226
Pukohola [Bukohola] (heiau at Kawaihae), 55
Pulana (place name), 190
pule, pule kulana [kurana] (prayers),

360

361